Physical Education Methods for Elementary Teachers

Second Edition

Katherine T. Thomas, PhD

Iowa State University

Amelia M. Lee, PhD

Louisiana State University

Jerry R. Thomas, EdD

Iowa State University

Human Kinetics

Library of Congress Cataloging-in-Publication Data

Thomas, Katherine T., 1948-
  Physical education methods for elementary teachers / Katherine T.
Thomas, Amelia M. Lee, Jerry R. Thomas.
      p. cm.
Includes bibliographical references and index.
  ISBN 0-7360-4106-0 (Soft Cover)
  1. Physical education for children—Study and teaching (Elementary)
2. Physical education for children—Curricula. I. Lee, Amelia M.,
1938- II. Thomas, Jerry R. III. Title.
  GV443.T495 2003
  372.86—dc21

                                        2002155846

ISBN: 0-7360-4106-0

The Web addresses cited in this text were current as of January 2003, unless otherwise noted.

Lesson plans on pp. 21-28, 51-54, 76-83, 102-112, 128-142, 156-159, 161-165, 180-186, 215-230, 250-263, 278-289, 322-335, 358-373, and 395-401 are adapted, by permission, from K.T. Thomas, A.M. Lee, and J.R. Thomas, 2000, *Physical Education for Children: Daily Lesson Plans for Elementary School,* 2nd edition, (Champaign, IL: Human Kinetics).

Lesson plans on pp. 29-30 and 231-235 are adapted, by permission, from A.M. Lee, K.T. Thomas, and J.R. Thomas, 2000, *Physical Education for Children: Daily Lesson Plans for Middle School,* 2nd edition, (Champaign, IL: Human Kinetics).

Acquisitions Editor: Bonnie Pettifor
Developmental Editor: Myles Schrag
Assistant Editors: Jennifer L. Davis, Kathleen D. Bernard
Copyeditor: NOVA Graphic Services
Proofreader: Jan Feeney
Indexer: Betty Frizzéll
Permission Manager: Dalene Reeder
Graphic Designer: Fred Starbird
Graphic Artist: Angela K. Snyder
Photo Manager: Leslie A. Woodrum
Cover Designer: Jack W. Davis
Photographer (cover): Leslie A. Woodrum
Photographer (interior): Photos courtesy of authors,
    except where noted
Art Manager: Kelly Hendren
Illustrator: Argosy
Chapter- and Part-Opening Drawings: Students at South Side Elementary School, Champaign, Illinois
Printer: Versa Press

Printed in the United States of America 10 9 8 7 6 5 4 3 2 1

Human Kinetics
Web site: www.HumanKinetics.com

United States: Human Kinetics
P.O. Box 5076
Champaign, IL 61825-5076
800-747-4457
e-mail: humank@hkusa.com

Canada: Human Kinetics
475 Devonshire Road Unit 100
Windsor, ON N8Y 2L5
800-465-7301 (in Canada only)
e-mail: orders@hkcanada.com

Europe: Human Kinetics
107 Bradford Road
Stanningley
Leeds LS28 6AT, United Kingdom
+44 (0) 113 255 5665
e-mail: hk@hkeurope.com

Australia: Human Kinetics
57A Price Avenue
Lower Mitcham, South Australia 5062
08 8277 1555
e-mail: liahka@senet.com.au

New Zealand: Human Kinetics
P.O. Box 105-231, Auckland Central
09-523-3462
e-mail: hkp@ihug.co.nz

To our children and grandchildren, who have taught us so much.
Every day they demonstrate the joy of movement, reinforce that teaching
is a noble profession, and show us why physical education is important.
—*Jerry R. Thomas and Katherine T. Thomas*

To Jo, Annie, Joseph, Roxanne, Buddy, and Co, for their support and friendship.
—*Amelia M. Lee*

Contents

My Favorite thing to do in p.e. is Roller blade.

Eriana

I Love music

Preface

●●●

"**W**e don't have PE anymore since the student teacher left."

So spoke Deani, our (Kathi and Jerry's) then-six-year-old daughter. Thus began our quest to provide practical information to elementary classroom teachers and physical education teachers who are challenged with teaching physical education or supporting the work of a physical education specialist. We joined forces with Amelia Lee, a professor of physical education and veteran colleague of ours. Together, we wrote *Physical Education for Children: Concepts Into Practice*, published in 1988.

ABOUT THIS EDITION

Deani has since graduated from college as an elementary classroom teacher and is now finishing a master's degree in special education. Meanwhile, we (Mom, Dad, and Amelia) have continued to strive to bring the best pedagogical practices to classroom teachers and physical education specialists alike.

To this end, *Physical Education Methods for Elementary Teachers, Second Edition*, is an exciting culmination of many years of teaching and researching as well as of two very popular textbooks: our 1988 book and *Physical Education Methods for Classroom Teachers, First Edition* (Human Kinetics 1999). Both were written specially for the needs of the elementary teacher of physical education. From the 1988 book comes a firm footing in child development and why and how knowing this information will make you a better teacher. The 1999 book inspired discussions of organizational, management, and safety issues for today's schools, teachers, and students. Now in this one hybrid edition, you get the best of both—revised and updated.

A WELL-ROUNDED APPROACH

In this edition, you will find

- ▶ a sound foundation in the prerequisite content knowledge needed to teach physical education effectively;
- ▶ insights into how you can become the most effective physical education instructor;
- ▶ trouble-shooting advice for your particular challenges;
- ▶ practical information on how to enhance the elementary school mission through physical education while enhancing your students' health, development, and well-being;
- ▶ down-to-earth suggestions for effective class management; and
- ▶ ready-to-use, proven lesson plans to help guide you as you develop and hone your teaching skills in this content area.

Indeed, all are brought together in this exciting new edition.

Whether you are a preservice or inservice teacher, *Physical Education Methods for Elementary Teachers, Second Edition*, will provide you with a wealth of practical, researched, and field-tested information and application ideas for your situation.

WHY TEACH PHYSICAL EDUCATION

While there are many reasons we would prefer to have specialists teach all physical education, the reality is that most districts do not have the resources to accomplish this, and most states do not require it. Each state, and often each district, outlines the physical education minimums and who is licensed to teach physical education. States are responsible for deciding licensure requirements; universities are charged with preparing teachers based on those requirements. We believe physical education is important for elementary students. Therefore, we believe schools and teachers should meet at least the minimum requirements in their state or district. In some schools this will mean classroom teachers will be teaching 30 minutes of physical education to their class daily; in other schools specialists will teach daily physical education to children in grades 3–6. The point is that children need physical education from caring, trained teachers, regardless of whether they are specialists or classroom teachers. Your decision to become a teacher shows that you care. This book will help you learn why and how to teach physical education.

We understand that many classroom teachers are faced with a number of demands on their time and energy. You may be thinking right now that physical education is unimportant. We beg to differ!

Research shows that some children who have physical education and other opportunities for physical activity during the school day perform better academically (Sallis et al. 1999). Moreover, national interest in physical activity has grown. Why? Children's health is becoming more and more of a concern in regard to our sense of national well-being, especially in our quest to reduce obesity and overweight. While sport has always been important in our culture, and exercise has been popular with a particular segment of the population, never before has physical activity loomed so large on the national agenda. Physical activity is recognized for improving physical and mental health. The benefits of a developmentally appropriate program based on best practices are lifelong. But first, children need to develop skill, gain self-confidence, and experience the enjoyment of physical activity through a systematic, educational program. Such an opportunity should be embedded into every childhood.

Unfortunately, even with the emphasis on physical activity as a public health issue during the '90s and into the 21st century, physical education requirements have not increased. On the one hand, this is frustrating. On the other hand, the fact that many programs have not been downsized or eliminated as a result of increasing academic requirements and decreasing budgets is a positive.

The public outcry of parents and students is often at the heart of physical education's survival. Children and their parents know physical education is important, as do epidemiologists, pediatricians, public health professionals, and governmental agencies (e.g., NIH, CDC, USDA). Our observation is that elementary physical education programs are of higher quality and are more developmentally appropriate than in the past. So, while elementary physical education has not increased in quantity there are qualitative improvements whether the subject is taught by classroom teachers or physical education specialists. Among the factors supporting improvement are national standards, guidelines for developmentally appropriate programs, better-informed teachers, and practice based on sound research.

As a classroom teacher, you may teach all or part of the physical education curriculum to your students. This book will support your preparation to accept this responsibility and encourage you to teach physical education with the same dedication you give to other subjects. If you teach part of the curriculum, it is likely you will work closely with a physical education specialist. Understanding motor development, physical education curriculum, and instruction will allow communication and collaboration that will benefit your students.

GUIDING PRINCIPLES

In a nutshell, the purpose of this book is twofold:

▶ First, to prepare teachers to do their best teaching

▶ Second, to encourage quality physical activity programs—emphasizing physical education—for elementary school children

You need to be an informed advocate for children and physical activity. The information in this book will help you do this as well as help parents and other concerned people who want to advocate for your students.

Several specific principles guided our selection of the information and activities in this book:

▶ Children are naturally active; therefore, we are fostering a normal behavior by teaching physical education.

▶ Each child is unique. Differences in motor skill within and between children are normal. This means that a child may find some skills easier than other skills. This will vary from child to child.

▶ Boys and girls are more alike than different when doing physical activities.

▶ Motor skills develop as a result of practice.

▶ Children are naturally motivated in that they participate in sport and physical activity to have fun, learn skills, and be with their friends.

▶ Improvement, appropriate levels of challenge, being with friends, and having fun are important in physical education. Competition is not an essential ingredient. Remember, this is physical *education*, through which *all* children should be able to grow in competence in a supportive environment.

This leads us to the question: What is elementary physical education? Two major themes provide the answer:

▶ Elementary physical education is firmly placed on a foundation of motor development.

▶ Physical activity and skill development are the goals of elementary physical education.

A program that implements these two themes through effective teaching within an enjoyable, non-threatening context will encourage children to be

▶ more physically active outside of school,

▶ physically active across the lifespan, and

▶ more healthy overall.

SPECIAL FEATURES OF THIS EDITION

▶ **Lesson plans** with many activities for all grade levels are included at the end of most chapters to demonstrate the concepts in the chapter. The breadth and depth of these lessons provide both guidance for the student teacher and a starter set of lessons for the practicing teacher.

▶ A **lesson plan finder** makes it easy to refer to the lesson plans now and throughout your career. See pages viii-xii.

▶ **Mastery activities** at the end of each chapter provide activities that will help you better grasp main points and put that knowledge to use when you teach.

▶ **Sidebars** throughout the book provide teachable moments, tips on putting concepts discussed in the book into practice, and at-a-glance facts that provide you with opportunities to see how points made in the book play out in the real teaching environment.

▶ **Updated resources** synthesize current thought regarding the major issues you must deal with.

▶ Updated and expanded **electronic ancillaries** offer support materials for the instructor of this course:

  ▶ A graphics package of key points, including one PowerPoint presentation per chapter

  ▶ A comprehensive test bank, including several questions per chapter

  ▶ An instructor guide with learning activities and a sample syllabus

ORGANIZATION

The book is organized into four main parts to guide you toward implementing effective, developmentally appropriate physical education. It also includes a glossary at the back that provides a useful reference for teachers. These terms are easily found in lists that begin each chapter as well as in boldface type within the chapters as the reader first comes across them. The four main parts are as follows:

Part I: Introduction to Physical Education

Chapters 1 and 2 set the stage as you begin to understand why physical education is an important part of child development and health. With increased pressure to recognize a variety of learning styles and talents, there is also pressure to recognize psychomotor contributions.

You will see how health and child development are part of the mission of elementary school education.

Part II: Addressing the Child's Needs

Chapters 3–8 provide a foundation that describes growth and development, giving you a basis for understanding typical development as well as individual differences. You will learn about physical growth and maturation (3); motor performance during childhood (4); learning, practice, and cognition (5); physical activity and fitness (6); psychosocial factors (7); and individual differences (8).

Part III: Preparing to Teach Physical Education

Chapters 9–13 help prepare you to teach. You will learn about planning a curriculum (9); organizing for teaching (10); managing students (11); teacher's rights, responsibilities, and best practices (12); and equipment and facilities (13).

Part IV: Teaching Physical Education

Chapters 14–16 offer you specific information on how to provide effective instruction (14), conduct appropriate assessments (15), and grow as a teacher (16). We hope that not only will this book provide you with the basic knowledge and practice you need to succeed in the physical education setting but also arm you with additional strategies and experiences to teach across the curriculum.

Most of these chapters include lesson plans related to the concepts in the chapter. Most of the lesson plans are from *Physical Education for Children: Daily Lesson Plans for Elementary School, Second Edition* (Thomas, Lee, and Thomas 2000), and *Physical Education for Children: Daily Lesson Plans for Middle School, Second Edition* (Lee, Thomas, and Thomas 2000). The information in these chapters will guide teachers through the four components of effective developmentally appropriate physical education programs (objectives, planning, instruction, and evaluation). The activities are divided by grade and the type of activity so that a teacher can select activities for his objective (or standard) that are appropriate for the students. The lesson plan finder at the front of the book provides the teacher with an organized means of finding appropriate activities at a glance too.

Throughout this book, we challenge you to provide the best possible physical education experience for your students. At the same time, we offer concrete information and reality-based advice to make that possible, no matter your background or teaching experience. Through your efforts you can make a difference in the health and school performance of your students—now and throughout your career.

REFERENCE

Sallis, J.F., T.L. McKenzie, B. Kolody, M. Lewis, S. Marchall, and P. Rosengard. 1999. Effects of health-related physical education on academic achievement: Project SPARK. *Research Quarterly for Exercise and Sport* 70: 127–134.

Lesson Plan Finder

Use this resource to find at a glance the type of activity you want to plan for the grade level you are teaching.

Grades	#	Content	Warm-up	Skill development	Concluding activities	Ch/Page
K-1	2.1	Games and Sports	Run and Touch	Movement challenges (body parts)	Over and Under	2/24
K-1	3.1	Gymnastics	Stretching	Stations	Obstacle course	3/45
K-1	4.1	Games and Sports	Throw and Fetch	Movement challenges, Tossing a Beanbag, Beanbag Rope Toss, Beanbag Hoop Toss	Teacher Ball or Circle Toss Ball	4/76
K-1	5.1	Rhythmic Activities	Move and Freeze	Baa, Baa, Black Sheep; Mulberry Bush	Baa, Baa, Black Sheep; Mulberry Bush	5/102
K-1	5.2	Rhythmic Activities	Traffic Lights	Jump rope activities	Rope tasks	5/104
K-1	6.1	Fitness	Crunches, push-ups	Reveille, Sneaky Tag, fitness relay	Fitness concept: muscular endurance	6/128
K-1	6.2	Fitness	Pyramid	Circuit (jumping jacks, airplane circles, sit-ups, crab walk, push-ups, rope jump)	Fitness concept: physical activity makes us healthy	6/131
K-1	7.1	Games and Sports	Len's Ball Mix-Up	Laundry Basket Express	Towel Toss	7/154
K-1	8.1	Gymnastics	Warm-up routine	Partner Walk, Leapfrog, Wring the Dishrag, Back-to-Back Get-Up	Simon Says	8/180
K-1	9.1	Gymnastics	I See	Movement challenges, Identify the Body Part	Hokey Pokey	9/215
K-1	9.2	Gymnastics	Point and Run	Movement challenges, sliding, galloping	Partner Follow the Leader	9/217
K-1	9.3	Fitness	Pyramid	Circuit (big swings, big steppers, big curls, big jumps, big apples, big circles)	Physical fitness concept, alternative learning activities	9/219

Grades	#	Content	Warm-up	Skill development	Concluding activities	Ch/Page
K-1	9.4	Health		Discussion		9/222
K-1	10.1	Fitness	Stretching	Leader Ball, Pair Tag, Delivery Relay	Fitness concept: physical fitness	10/250
K-1	10.2	Games and Sports	Tortoise and Hare	Tasks for hoops	Jumping in patterns	10/252
K-1	11.1	Organization	Islands in the Ocean	Rules, boundaries	Rules	11/278
K-1	11.2	Organization	Wild One	Rules consensus, circle and line boundaries	Circle boundaries game	11/280
K-1	13.1	Gymnastics	Warm-up routine	Stations for large equipment (balance beams, jumping cubes, climbing rope, shapes or tunnel, vaulting cubes, ladder)	Equipment setup and storage	13/322
K-1	13.2	Gymnastics	Warm-up routine	Obstacle course (large equipment)	Equipment setup and storage	13/325
K-1	13.3	Games and Sports	Slap Tag	Stations (throw, bounce, roll, kick, strike)		13/327
K-1	14.1	Gymnastics	Warm-up routine	Bear walk, puppy run, Animal Walk Game, Rocker, one-leg balance, log roll, forehead touch, tightrope, forward roll		14/358
K-1	14.2	Rhythmic Activities	Fitness Circle	Keeping time to a beat	Movement to a beat	14/361
K-1	15.1	Gymnastics	Warm-up routine	Skills checklist, extension activities		15/395
2-3	2.2	Games and Sports	Sneaky Tag	Hopping skills, Follow the Leader, Name That Skill	Hopscotch	2/26
2-3	3.2	Gymnastics	Stretching	Stations	Obstacle course	3/47
2-3	4.2	Games and Sports	Delivery Relay	Throwing and catching tasks, dribbling	Circle Stride Ball, Keep Away	4/79
2-3	5.3	Rhythmic Activities	High, Low, Medium	Rope skills; Hot Pepper; High Water; Mabel, Mabel; Fourth of July	High Water, Hot Pepper	5/106
2-3	5.4	Rhythmic Activities	Animal Chase	Step-Close, Kinderpolka	Kinderpolka	5/108

(continued)

Grades	#	Content	Warm-up	Skill development	Concluding activities	Ch/Page
2-3	6.3	Fitness	Stretching circuit	Crows and Cranes	Fitness concept: muscular endurance	6/134
2-3	6.4	Fitness	Loose Caboose	Hoop challenges, hoop relay	Fitness concept: heart rate	6/136
2-3	7.2	Games and Sports		Len's Scooter Ball		7/155
2-3	7.3	Gymnastics	Warm-up routine	Partner stunts	Wave	7/156
2-3	8.2	Games and Sports	Delivery Relay	Dribbling in hoops, Movement tasks	Dribble-and-Throw Relay	8/183
2-3	9.5	Rhythmic Activities	Magic Movements	Locomotor tasks: gallop, slide, skip	Parachute	9/223
2-3	9.6	Fitness	Fitness circuit	Three-on-Three	Fitness concept: heart rate	9/225
2-3	10.3	Rhythmic Activities	High, Low, Medium	Rope jumping: 2-foot single, double, backward jump, helicopter, single-side taps, double-side taps, extension activities	Don't Miss	10/254
2-3	10.4	Gymnastics	Follow the Leader	Around the World, walking in place, heel click, double-jointed walk, knee touch, scoot-through	Simon Says	10/256
2-3	11.3	Organization	Formations review	Station rotation, giving out equipment	Nose Tag	11/282
2-3	11.4	Organization	Near–far concepts	Consequences, stations	Movement patterns	11/284
2-3	13.4	Games and Sports	Reveille	Locomotor obstacle course	Crows and Cranes	13/331
2-3	13.5	Games and Sports	Sneaky Tag	Parachute activities	Parachute games	13/333
2-3	14.3	Gymnastics	Listen and Move, warm-up routine	Forehead touch, forward roll, donkey kick	Pretumbling skills	14/363
2-3	14.4	Gymnastics	Warm-up routine	2 knee balance, V-sit, 360° turn	Movement challenges	14/367
2-3	14.5	Rhythmic Activities	Magic Movements	Levels and collapse, movement challenges	Create rhythmic sequence	14/369

Grades	#	Content	Warm-up	Skill development	Concluding activities	Ch/Page
2-3	15.2	Health		Fitness concept: crossword		15/399
4-5	2.3	Organization	Forming groups	Feelings about physical education: journal writing	Discussion	2/28
4-5	3.3	Gymnastics	Stretching	Planet "School Name"	Planet "School Name" Challenge	3/49
4-5	3.4	Gymnastics	Warm-up routine	Forward roll, straddle forward roll, backward roll, straddle backward roll, heel slap, run and take-off, needle scale	Splits, discussion	3/51
4-5	4.3	Games and Sports	Walk/jog	Throwing and catching tasks	Cooperative Ring Toss	4/81
4-5	4.4	Rhythmic Activities	Movement to sounds	Movement combinations, partner copy activity	Skill cards	4/82
4-5	5.5	Rhythmic Activities	Parachute steps	Elvira, grapevine steps	Grapevine line	5/109
4-5	5.6	Rhythmic Activities	Follow the Leader	Rope jumping: 2-foot double forward and backward, rock step, ski twist, straddle cross jump, jump to music	Jump rope routine	5/111
4-5	6.5	Fitness	Running and dodging games	Wand challenges, Partner Jump, Jump Over the Wand, Wand Follow the Leader, Pass the Wand	Fitness concept and quiz: what physical activity and fitness can and can't do	6/138
4-5	6.6	Fitness	Stretching routine	Crunches and push-ups, Line-Up, parachute exchange positions	Fitness concept: fitness is the opposite of sickness	6/140
4-5	7.4	Games and Sports		Sharon's Shoot Around		7/160
4-5	7.5	Games and Sports	Balance Challenge, Hoop Circle, Circle Untangle	Raging River	Discussion	7/161
4-5	7.6	Gymnastics	Warm-up routine	Partner stunts	Discussion	7/163

(continued)

Grades	#	Content	Warm-up	Skill development	Concluding activities	Ch/Page
4-5	8.3	Games and Sports	Circle conditioning	Softball: catching low balls	Throw and catch game	8/185
4-5	9.7	Rhythmic Activities	Movement to sounds	Movement combinations, partner copy activity	Movement sequences	9/227
4-5	9.8	Fitness	Jumping through long ropes	Jumping long ropes	Fitness concept: strength	9/229
4-5	10.5	Games and Sports	Rope jumping	Instep kicking	Kickover	10/259
4-5	10.6	Fitness		Learning about fitness plans	Contract	10/262
4-5	11.5	Organization	Single File	Rules, changing directions, task cards, station formation, partner relay, moving diagonally	Moving within an area	11/286
4-5	11.6	Organization	Boundaries	Formation, rules, cooperative groups	Formations, single file	11/288
4-5	13.6	Fitness		One-mile run and sit-ups		13/335
4-5	13.7	Games and Sports	Walk/jog	Juggling	Continuous juggling	13/336
4-5	14.6	Gymnastics	Warm-up routine	Skipping backward and sideways, change of directions, run and jump, leap, run and leap, jump from knees, donkey kick, skill practice	Challenges of combinations, splits	14/370
4-5	14.7	Rhythmic Activities	Schottische	Schottische and step-hop sequence	Routines	14/373
4-5	15.3	Fitness	Individual stretching exercises	Mile run test		15/401
6-8	2.4	Rhythmic Activities	Rhythmic patterns with ropes	Basic tinikling step	Basic tinikling step	2/29
6-8	9.9	Organization	Moving to visual signs	Form two teams, Touch Down, moving within a rectangle	Rules, cooperative discussion groups	9/231
6-8	9.10	Organization	Forming groups	Task cards, partner relay	Feelings about physical education	9/233
6-8	9.11	Organization	Forming groups	Cooperative learning groups	Cooperative discussion groups	9/235

Introduction to Physical Education

My favorite thing to do in p.e. is Roller blade.

Because most of us attended school, we have firsthand experience of how schools work. Part of that experience concerns physical education. In the time since you were in elementary school, many changes have taken place, and these changes will affect what you do as a teacher. Perhaps more important, your role will change dramatically as you move from being a student to being a teacher. Therefore, because you have accumulated a great deal of knowledge and experience with education, your perspective will change. Instead of seeing only from the student's point of view, you will now also see things as the teacher sees them. The first two chapters in this book are designed to help you make the transition from student to teacher. These chapters will set the stage in two ways: First, you will learn why physical education is important. As a result, you will understand why being a competent physical education teacher is also important. Teaching competency is defined in part by standards for teachers, which are introduced in chapter 1. This book covers material inherent in the 10 standards. Second, you will see that physical education is integral to the mission of the school. Therefore, in physical education, what you teach and how you teach it are important to the success of the students and of the school.

Health and Developmental Benefits of Physical Education

My favorite thing to do in p.e. is Roller blade.

Anna, age 9

Most children attend school, so schools are the best place to reach children. Schools nurture all aspects of development. Schools today are charged with delivering a message about the importance of physical activity as well as helping children learn motor skills that will allow them to remain active throughout their lives. Physical activity is the single most important controllable health risk factor, and teachers play a major role in helping children achieve physically active lifestyles:

School and community programs that promote regular physical activity among young people could be the most effective strategy for reducing the public health burden of chronic diseases associated with sedentary lifestyles. Programs that provide students with the knowledge, attitudes, motor skills, behavioral skills, and confidence to participate in physical activity may establish active lifestyles among young people that continue into and throughout their adult lives. (CDC 1997, page 22)

Learner Outcomes

The teacher will do the following:

- Demonstrate the value of physical activity by describing its importance.
- Provide examples of effective developmentally appropriate physical education programs.

- Document personal achievement of the Interstate New Teacher Assessment and Support Consortium (INTASC) standards.

Glossary Terms

physical activity
developmentally appropriate
physical education

INTASC standards
skill

Stand outside any elementary school and watch as the doors burst open for recess. You'll see children running, children excited, and children engaged. The same images are replayed at playgrounds and parks with younger children every day. The joy of movement is evident as we observe children at play. If we followed those children to quality physical education classes, we would see that same energy and joy as they are challenged to master new skills. Continuing to watch those children after school, we could see them engaged in play that might include riding their bikes or more formal sport experiences like soccer or T-ball. **Physical activity,** in the forms of sport, exercise, physical education, and play, makes an important contribution to child development. And, what is more, it is a joyful time for children.

One of the most enjoyable aspects of physical education is the sheer joy of movement that children have.

Everywhere we look, we see examples of exercise, sport, and physical activity in our culture. For example, an entire section of the daily newspaper is devoted to sports. The same is true of the evening television news: Entire television networks are devoted to sports and some to specific sports! In nearly every community, you can see people walking, jogging, or riding their bicycles for exercise. Entire industries, from those selling athletic shoes to those offering aerobics classes, serve people seeking health through exercise. Clearly, we don't have to look very far to see that exercise is popular. Being physically active includes lifestyle activity (gardening, walking, and cycling) and vigorous activity (jumping rope, running, and cross-country skiing). Because physical activity includes sport, exercise, and more general movements that expend energy, we can see that physical activity is also important in our culture.

WHY IS PHYSICAL ACTIVITY VALUED?

One reason we value physical activity is the health benefit associated with a physically active lifestyle. Other reasons are the developmental need to explore and master our environment, to express ourselves through movement, and to feel satisfaction resulting from successful movement. Physical activity also provides an opportunity for affiliation. Being part of a group—as a fan, a team member, or a walking partner—meets an important human need. Physical activity and sport al-

low people to test their skill, fitness, and determination. We derive pleasure from the effort and accomplishments found in physical activity. Physical activity is often fun—one other reason we value it. So, whether we are an elderly person or an infant reaffirming its independence by mastering its environment, a fan identifying with her team, a child expressing his joy through movement, a middle-aged adult exercising for health, or an adolescent working hard to learn a new skill and succeeding, physical activity is important to us as individuals and as a culture.

Standards

Three sets of standards (Content Standards in Physical Education, Interstate New Teacher Assessment and Support Consortium [INTASC], and Developmentally Appropriate Physical Education) set the framework for this book and guide elementary physical education instruction. The National Association for Sport and Physical Education (NASPE) defines a physically educated person (NASPE 1995) with seven statements of behavior (figure 1.1). These content standards provide a model for all educators: for physical education programs and for our behaviors as physical educators. Of course, this model also applies to classroom teachers who provide physical education for children in the classroom and in the gymnasium.

A physically educated person:

1. Demonstrates competency in many movement forms and proficiency in a few movement forms.

2. Applies movement concepts and principles to the learning and development of motor skills.

3. Exhibits a physically active lifestyle.

4. Achieves and maintains a health-enhancing level of physical fitness.

5. Demonstrates responsible personal and social behavior in physical activity settings.

6. Demonstrates understanding and respect for differences among people in physical activity settings.

7. Understands that physical activity provides opportunities for enjoyment, challenge, self-expression, and social interaction.

Figure 1.1 Content standards in physical education.

Ten learning outcomes for teachers were developed by the INTASC to guide teacher education programs. These suggest the content of teacher education programs and provide guidance for teachers to demonstrate their level of preparation (table 1.1). The INTASC standards apply to all teachers: elementary classroom, secondary classroom, and special subject (e.g., art, physical education, and music). To help students become physically educated, teachers need to have and apply knowledge about how children grow, move, and learn. Further, teachers need to know about teaching to be able to communicate effectively and to evaluate themselves and their students. Finally, teachers need to have subject matter knowledge. Subject matter knowledge in physical education includes how the body responds to exercise, how the body moves efficiently, how we learn motor skills, and knowledge of the actual activities (e.g., in dance, gymnastics, games, and sport). Compare this with secondary education, where content knowledge is relatively narrow and specific, such as in teaching chemistry. The elementary classroom teacher must have content knowledge of each subject area (e.g., mathematics, reading, and social studies), and the physical education teacher must understand and be able to apply the science of movement (e.g., physiology, biomechanics, and motor learning) and the forms of movement (e.g., activities) to meet this standard. Clearly, teaching elementary children is a challenge for physical education teachers and a double challenge for elementary classroom teachers! NASPE developed the initial physical education teacher preparation guidelines for the National Council for the Accreditation of Teacher Education (NCATE). NASPE (1999) used the INTASC standards as a model; therefore, the standards are similar (see table 1.1).

Perhaps the most important standards are those describing **developmentally appropriate** physical education. Developmentally appropriate programs meet the needs of children according to their age, maturation, and interests. Quality physical education programs are developmentally appropriate. More information on developmentally appropriate physical education is provided in chapter 9, "Planning Your Curriculum." The information in this book is guided by a developmental perspective, which recognizes that development is qualitative, sequential, directional, cumulative, multifaceted, and individual

(NASPE). Qualitative change focuses on process—the way a skill or behavior looks rather than the product or outcome. Development is orderly or sequential; therefore, predictions can be made about performance and used to plan programs. This means that children of different ages will be doing different activities. Development is a building process; it is cumulative. Early experience and competence are a foundation for later skill learning. Motor development is based on the concept of improvement; that is, as we get older, we get better. The developmentally appropriate curriculum recognizes this by using increasingly difficult benchmarks with lessons to help students achieve the standard. Development is a composite of the cognitive, social, affective, and psychomotor domains, which means development is multifaceted. Each child is a unique individual; therefore, instruction and programs must be sensitive to the individual learner. Children of the same age will learn at different rates and in different ways, but children of the same age are more alike than different.

Current Practices in Physical Education

Since the Surgeon General's Report on Health Promotion and Disease Prevention (1979), physical activity has been on the national health agenda. In 1990 (HHS), the Surgeon General's Report, Healthy People 2000, included specific goals for the nation:

▶ Increase to at least 50 percent the proportion of children and adolescents in 1st through 12th grade who participate in daily physical education.

▶ Increase to at least 50 percent the proportion of physical education class time that students spend being physically active, preferably engaged in lifetime physical activities.

In 1997, Guidelines for School and Community Programs to Promote Lifelong Physical Activity Among Young People from the Centers for Disease Control (CDC) further defined these objectives as follows:

▶ Implement daily physical education programs for all children in kindergarten through 12th grade.

Table 1.1   Standards for Teacher Preparation

INTASC	NASPE/NCATE
1. Subject matter: The teacher understands the central concepts, tools of inquiry, and structures of the discipline(s) he teaches and can create learning experiences that make these aspects of subject matter meaningful for students.	1. Content knowledge: A physical education teacher understands physical education content, disciplinary concepts, and tools of inquiry related to the development of a physically educated person.
2. Student learning: The teacher understands how children and youth learn and develop and can provide learning opportunities that support their intellectual, social, and personal development.	2. Growth and development: A physical education teacher understands how individuals learn and develop and can provide opportunities that support their physical, cognitive, social, and emotional development.
3. Diverse learners: The teacher understands how learners differ in their approaches to learning and creates instructional opportunities that are adapted to learners from diverse cultural backgrounds and with exceptionalities.	3. Diverse learners: A physical education teacher understands how individuals differ in their approaches to learning and creates appropriate instruction adapted to these differences.
4. Instructional strategies: The teacher understands and uses a variety of instructional strategies to encourage the students' development of critical thinking, problem solving, and performance skills.	4. Management and motivation: A physical education teacher uses an understanding of individual and group motivation and behavior to create a safe learning environment that encourages social interaction, active engagement in learning, and self-motivation.
5. Learning environment: The teacher uses an understanding of individual and group motivation and behavior to create a learning environment that encourages positive social interaction, active engagement in learning, and self-motivation.	5. Communication: A physical education teacher uses knowledge of effective verbal, nonverbal, and media communication techniques to foster inquiry, collaboration, and engagement in physical activity settings.
6. Communication: The teacher uses knowledge of effective verbal, nonverbal, and media communication techniques to foster active inquiry, collaboration, and supportive interaction in the classroom.	6. Planning and instruction: A physical education teacher plans and implements a variety of developmentally appropriate instructional strategies to develop physically educated individuals.
7. Planning instruction: The teacher plans and manages instruction based on knowledge of subject matter, students, the community, and curriculum goals.	7. Learner assessment: A physical education teacher understands and uses formal and informal assessment strategies to foster physical, cognitive, social, and emotional development of learners in physical activity.
8. Assessment: The teacher understands and uses formal and informal assessment strategies to evaluate and ensure the continuous intellectual, social, and physical development of her learners.	8. Reflection: A physical education teacher is a reflective practitioner who evaluates the effects of her actions on others (e.g., learners, parents and guardians, and professionals in the learning community) and seeks opportunities to grow professionally.
9. Reflection and professional development: The teacher is a reflective practitioner who continually evaluates the effects of his choices and actions on others (students, parents, and other professionals in the learning community) and who actively seeks out opportunities to grow professionally.	9. Collaboration: The teacher fosters relationships with colleagues, parents and guardians, and community agencies to support learners' growth and well-being.
10. Collaboration, ethics, and relationships: A teacher communicates and interacts with parents and guardians, families, school colleagues, and the community to support the students' learning and well-being.	

Data from NASPE 1995; INTASC 1992.

► Eliminate or sharply reduce the practice of granting exemptions for physical education classes.

► Increase the amount of time students are active in physical education classes.

Unfortunately, few states or schools have responded to the U.S. Surgeon General, the CDC Guidelines for Physical Activity, U.S. Congress Resolution 97 (which encourages daily physical education grades for grades K through 12)(NASPE 1997), or Healthy People 2000. While 47 states require physical education, only Illinois has a requirement for daily physical education for students in grades K through 12 (NASPE 1997). Three states have no mandate of any kind for physical education (Colorado, Mississippi, and South Dakota). The other states give various requirements: Many mandate physical education in elementary school but neither specify the amount of time required nor indicate who should teach the classes. For example, certified physical education teachers are required in seven states (Delaware, Idaho, Illinois, Michigan, Missouri, Nevada, and South Dakota), but classroom teachers are stipulated to teach physical education in four states (California, Hawaii, Oklahoma, and Washington). The remaining 39 states allow for instruction by either classroom teachers or specialists in the elementary schools. Middle school physical education tends to be taught by specialists; however, in many states classroom teachers teach these classes.

Although states have not responded to the increasing concern by the CDC, Surgeon General, and U.S. Congress, these agencies and many others continue to support physical activity and physical education programs for children and adolescents. The United States Department of Agriculture (with Team Nutrition), U.S. Congress (Physical Education for Progress grants), and the American Alliance for Health, Physical Education, Recreation and Dance (AAHPERD) have programs or funding to provide physical education and activity for children and adolescents. Parents support physical education and recognize the contribution that physical activity makes to the reduction and control of obesity. The focus of initiatives has changed slightly since 1990 as scientists have come to recognize the importance of skill development, fun, and confidence building to lifelong activity. Previously, early programs for young children focused more on physical fitness and less on skill. Now programs balance physical activity, fun, and the learning of lifelong motor skills (e.g., lifetime sports). Because physical activity drops dramatically during adolescence, especially among girls, the focus of programs has shifted to middle school and high school. As you will see from the Surgeon General's most recent Goals for the Nation 2010 (Healthy People 2010), however, physical activity is still important.

Certified physical education teachers are required in only seven states. Thirty-nine states allow for instruction by either classroom teachers or specialists in the elementary schools.

The physical activity goal for the U.S. Department of Health and Human Services Healthy People 2010 is this: "Improve health, fitness, and quality of life through daily physical activity." The impact of physical activity on health is outlined in Healthy People 2010. The objectives for 2010 include the following:

- ▶ Increase the proportion of adolescents who engage in at least 30 minutes of moderate physical activity on five or more of the previous seven days from 20 to 30 percent.

- ▶ Increase the proportion of adolescents who engage in vigorous physical activity that promotes the development and maintenance of cardiorespiratory fitness, on three or more days per week for 20 or more minutes per session, from 64 to 85 percent.

- ▶ Increase the proportion of the nation's private and public schools that require daily physical education for all students from 17 to 25 percent in middle school and from 2 to 25 percent in high school.

- ▶ Increase the proportion of adolescents who participate in daily school physical education from 27 to 50 percent.

- ▶ Increase the proportion of adolescents who spend at least 50 percent of school physical education class time being physically active from 32 to 50 percent.

- ▶ Increase the proportion of children and adolescents who view television two or fewer hours per day from 60 to 75 percent.

Clearly, the first objectives do not apply directly to elementary school children. However, a healthy base of physical education for children in elementary school may increase the chances of meeting those objectives as the children become adolescents and adults. Further, those first objectives do apply to teachers and college students! The objectives target adolescents, who are in the upper elementary grades, middle school, and high school. The final objective targets all elementary school students.

Consider the student who sits in school from 8:30 A.M. to 3:30 P.M., rides the school bus home, does homework or plays video games from 4:00 P.M. to 5:00 P.M., eats dinner (5:00 P.M. to 5:30 P.M.), watches television for two hours (5:30 P.M. to 7:30 P.M.), bathes, and goes to bed (8:00 P.M.). Where are the time and opportunity for physical activity? The three most frequently cited barriers to being physically active are time, access to convenient facilities, and access to a safe environment in which to be active. Clearly, these barriers affect children. Schools have not only the opportunity but also the responsibility to provide for students to be physically active every day. Physical activity experiences for children should include structured and unstructured movement—physical education, sport, exercise, play, and recess.

Young children are naturally active as they explore their environments and master skills such as walking and running. As children enter school, activity levels drop, partially because the children are required to sit throughout the school day. Children who are the least active—those who sit still and are quiet—are often rewarded the most by classroom teachers. During preschool and elementary school, children should have two movement opportunities: structured and unstructured. Structured experiences include physical education, sport, and exercise. Children learn motor skills, knowledge, behavioral skills, and confidence during these structured experiences. Unstructured experiences in which children engage in physical activity, learn behavioral and motor skills, and gain confidence include play and recess. Both unstructured and structured experiences are important because each provides unique learning experiences for children. Elementary school provides both types of experiences, in which teachers are involved as supervisors, facilitators, and instructors. This text focuses on structured experiences. Classroom teachers and physical educators are responsible for providing time for physical activity in a safe and nurturing environment and for helping children learn important motor skills.

Many organizations believe that physical activity is an important part of the school day. The National Association of State Boards of Education (NASBE) extends the role of schools in encouraging physical activity to providing after-school programs. NASBE policy includes recommendations for daily physical education for grades pre-K through 12, recess, and voluntary before- and after-school activity programs such as intramural clubs, joint school and community recreation programs, and programs involving the students' families. The Centers for Disease Control and Prevention (CDC) has developed the Coordinated School Health Program with the following eight components: health education, physical education, health services, nutrition services, staff health promotion, counseling and psychological services, healthy school environment, and parent/community involvement. **Physical education** is defined as "a planned sequential K–12 curriculum that provides cognitive content and learning experiences in a variety of activity areas such as basic movement skills; physical fitness; rhythms and dance; games; team, dual, and individual sports; tumbling and gymnastics; and aquatics." The message is clear and consistent: Physical education for children is important!

National Association of State Boards of Education Policy to Encourage Physical Activity

Every student shall be physically active—that is, shall develop the knowledge and skills necessary to perform a variety of physical activities, maintain physical fitness, regularly participate in physical activity, understand the short- and long-term benefits of physical activity, and value and enjoy physical activity as an ongoing part of a healthful lifestyle. In addition, staff are encouraged to participate in and model physical activity as a valuable part of daily life.

Perspective

The material in this book is designed to prepare teachers to meet the **INTASC** (and NASPE/NCATE) **standards** and provide children with developmentally appropriate physical education programs. Performing sport skills and other physical activities successfully requires practice to acquire skill and success to develop confidence. **Skill** (competence) and confidence are associated with physically active lifestyles in adults. The information in this book is grounded in motor development; we take a developmental perspective and apply it to developmentally appropriate physical education for children. Although this may seem overwhelming—especially to those who do not see themselves as athletic—it is not. Several things will help you: First, your desire to be a teacher is likely driven by concern and caring for children. All teaching tasks are easier when the students know you like them, care about their welfare, and believe they can learn. Second, you have time to learn and practice teaching physical education. Finally, you can work through the material in this book with your peers under the guidance of a knowledgeable and caring instructor.

MODEL FOR THIS BOOK

A single conceptual model guides this book—that is, the relationship among developmentally appropriate objectives, planning, instruction, and evaluation (figure 1.2) The NASPE physical education standards ("a physically educated person") are the overall goal of physical education. These are translated into curricular objectives, then unit objectives, and finally lesson objectives. Teachers should select units, lessons, and activities that help children and adolescents meet the standards. A variety of units and activities help children explore sport and physical activity. Note that children ages 6 through 12 years are in the "sampling" stage of sport; they try a variety of different activities and do not and should not specialize in one sport (Soberlek and Côté in press). Specializing too early may lead a child to drop out of a sport (Côté, Baker, and Abernethy 2001) or to become less active as an adult (Robertson-Wilson, Baker, Derbinshyre, and Côté in review). Each recommendation for physical activity for children stresses variety, skill development, and fun as important factors in developing physically active lifestyles, and teachers should test progress using age-appropriate benchmarks. Instruction that includes demonstration, directions, cues, practice, and feedback is designed to help students achieve the objectives of the lesson, so evaluation of the teaching and learning is focused on achievement of the objectives. Effective physical education programs translate the standards into developmentally appropriate activities and evaluations: Each age, grade, or skill level will participate in different activities to master the same standard in a developmentally appropriate program.

One way to assess the effectiveness of the translation of the standards is to assess how obvious the relationship is among the four components in figure 1.2. For example, if you watch instruction, can you determine the objective, or by looking at the evaluation can you identify the lesson plan? Another way to assess the effectiveness of the translation is to observe for differences among age, grade, and skill levels in the objectives, lesson plan, instruction, and evaluation. Developmentally appropriate programs are planned based on three principles:

1. The goal is to help all students become physically educated by achieving the content standards.

2. Plans are based on typical performance for the age, grade, and skill level of the students.

3. Planning and instruction accommodate individual differences.

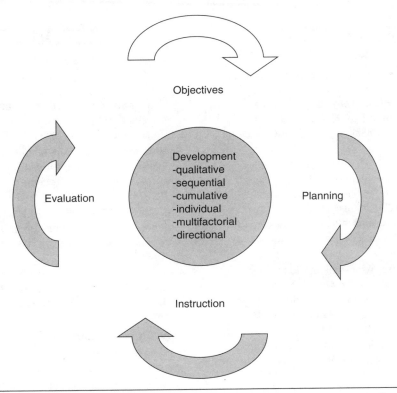

Figure 1.2 The relationship among objectives, planning, instruction, evaluation, and developmentally appropriate practice.

SUMMARY

Teaching is demanding. Helping elementary school children learn to be physically active is a challenge for both specialists and classroom teachers. The benefits to individual health and well-being, as well as the benefits to the public health, make this an important part of the elementary school curriculum. The long-term goal of elementary physical education is twofold: nurturing an important part of child development (the psychomotor domain) and ensuring physically active lifestyles. Developmentally appropriate physical education programs, which recognize the similarities and differences among children while considering progression and age issues, address these two important goals. Teachers who meet the standards for new teachers (either NCATE or INTASC) are ready to assume the challenge. Well-prepared teachers know what, how, and why to teach to maximize student learning. Children are naturally active and generally enjoy physical activity; this facilitates teaching physical education. Motor skills and the physical development associated with being active are important parts of child development and therefore essential ingredients in the elementary school curriculum. This concept will be explored further in the next chapter.

MASTERY LEARNING ACTIVITIES

1. Find the licensing requirements for physical education in your state. Could you find this on the Department of Education Web site?

2. Find the state mandates for physical education in your state. Could you find this on the Department of Education Web site?

3. Select a school district. How many sessions per week and minutes per session of elementary physical education are taught? Who provides elementary instruction in this district?

4. Go to one of the Web sites listed under "Resources" at the end of this chapter. Find a "new fact," that is, something you did not know before going to the site.

5. Find one physical education or physical activity Web site not listed under "Resources." What information does this site provide and how could you use the information?

REFERENCES

Centers for Disease Control and Prevention (CDC). 1997. *Guidelines for school and community programs to promote lifelong physical activity among young people.* [Online.] www.cdc.gov/mmwr/preview/mmwrhtml/00046823.htm [September 25, 2002].

Côté, J., J. Baker, and B. Abernethy. 2001. Stages of sport participation of expert decision-makers in team ball sports. In *Proceedings of the 10th World Congress of Sport Psychology.* Vol 3. Edited by A. Papaioannou, M. Goudas, and Y. Theodorakis, 150–52. Skiathos Island, Greece: International Society for Sport Psychology.

Interstate New Teacher Assessment and Support Consortium (INTASC). 1992. *Model standards for beginning teacher licensing and development: A resource for state dialogue.* Washington, D.C.: Council of Chief State School Officers.

National Association of Sport and Physical Education (NASPE). 1995. *Moving into the future: National standards for physical education.* Boston: WCB/McGraw-Hill.

NASPE. 1997. *Shape of the nation report.* Reston, Va.: NASPE Publications.

NASPE. 1999. *Guidelines for teacher preparation in physical education NASPE/NCATE guideline.* 4th ed. Reston, Va.: NASPE Publications.

NASPE. 1994. *Looking at physical education from a developmental perspective: A guide to teaching.* Reston, Va.: NASPE Publications.

National Association of State Boards of Education (NASBE). Fit, healthy, and ready to learn: A school health policy guide. [Online.] Available: http://nasbe.org/Educational_Issues/Reports/fithealthy.html#phyed [September 25, 2002].

Robertson-Wilson, J., J. Baker, E. Derbinshyre, and J. Côté. Forthcoming. Childhood sport involvement in active and inactive female adults. *AVANTE.* Canadian Association for Health, Physical Education, Recreation and Dance.

Soberlak, P., and J. Côté. Forthcoming. The developmental activities of elite hockey players. *Journal of Applied Sport Psychology.*

U.S. Department of Health and Human Services. 1979. Surgeon General's Report on Health Promotion and Disease Prevention. Washington, D.C.: Government Printing Office.

U.S. Department of Health and Human Services. 1990. *Healthy people 2000: Surgeon general's report.* Washington, D.C.: Government Printing Office.

U.S. Department of Health and Human Services. 2000. *Healthy people 2010: Conference edition.* Washington, D.C.: Government Printing Office.

RESOURCES

Byers, T., M. Nestle, A. McTiernan, C. Doyle, A. Currie-Williams, T. Gansler, and M. Thun. 2002. American Cancer Society guidelines on nutrition and physical activity for cancer prevention. *Calif. Cancer Journal Clin.* 52:92–119.

Centers for Disease Control and Prevention (CDC). 2000. *Chronic disease notes and reports, National Centers for Disease Prevention and Health Promotion* 14(1) (winter):7.

Lee, A.M., K.T. Thomas, and J.R. Thomas. 2000. *Physical education for children: Daily lesson plans for middle school.* 2d ed. Champaign, Ill.: Human Kinetics.

Thomas, K.T., A.M. Lee, and J.R. Thomas. 2000. *Physical education for children: Daily lesson plans for elementary school.* 2d ed. Champaign, Ill.: Human Kinetics.

www.cdc.gov/mmrwr/preview/mmwrhtml/00046823.htm

www.health.gov/healthypeople/

www.pbs.org/teachersource/health.htm

www.aahperd.org

www.cdc.gov

www.cdc.gov/nccdphp/cdwin2001.pdf

www.fns.usda.gov/tn/

chapter 2

Meeting the Mission of the Elementary School

Kristen, age 7

Elementary schools help children learn important skills that are an essential part of child development. Mastering skills allows children to become productive members of our society. Thus, the mission of the elementary school is to facilitate the transition from childhood to being a productive member of society. Physical education is generally acknowledged to be a contributor to child development: The psychomotor domain is one of the recognized domains of development. Further, physical education can make an important contribution to individual and, thus, public health.

Learner Outcomes

The teacher will do the following:

- State the goal of education.
- Describe why physical education is an essential part of the elementary school curriculum.
- List several ways physical activity and physical education contribute to the elementary school mission.
- Define an integrated physical education curriculum from three perspectives.
- Provide examples of integration.

Glossary Terms

mission
best practice
learning

educational outcomes
allocated time
academic learning time

What is the elementary school **mission?** Elementary schools help children become contributing members of society. The schools serve children, their parents, and the broader community. In their mission statements, schools generally recognize individual differences and the need for a variety of approaches to meet the needs of all students. The long-term outcome of education is independence for the student. Specifically, at the end of their school careers, students should be financially self-supporting, understand how to continue to learn, have reached their potential in all three domains (affective, cognitive, and psychomotor), and understand their rights and responsibilities as citizens. Elementary school establishes a foundation for students as they move toward independence. Each subject in the elementary school curriculum is meant to help all children, although some subjects may become the focus for certain children. For example, some children will dedicate their lives to music. Others develop mathematical skills into a vocation, and still others use language skills to enjoy reading and employment as a writer.

Citizens can either be negative or positive members of a society. For example, a person who lives a healthy lifestyle, works to meet a societal need, and finds personal satisfaction with life contributes to the community. That person has value and is valued—by self and others. It is important that each person feel valued for his contributions and be valued by himself and others. Each person contributes in his own unique way. During childhood we learn about the importance of contributing and we begin to identify and develop the skills necessary to make contributions. Poor health, unlawful behavior, and lack of skills are several factors that drain societal resources. These same factors may contribute to feelings of low self-worth in children. Therefore, elementary schools, and more specifically the teachers therein, make critical contributions to the well-being of society as they influence children.

Most elementary schools have mission statements. Each may be different in wording and emphasis, but common characteristics are emphasized. Among these are

- respect,
- individual differences,
- learning, and
- citizenship.

Respect includes the child's behavior toward the school and teachers, and the teacher's behavior toward the child. Related to this is the notion that everyone is different. Children will represent a variety of cultures, ethnicities, religions, and value sets and they will enter school with a variety of abilities and potentials. Schools and teachers are expected to embrace these differences. In fact, the **best practice** is to use the differences among children to enhance learning by all children. **Learning** is a broad term that focuses on acquisition of new skills or information retained over long time periods or used under new circumstances. Often, learning is viewed as specific to content—for example, subjects such as mathematics, reading, or physical education. Learning in those content areas is often defined in **educational outcomes** or learning outcomes. However, elementary schools facilitate other learning as well. As part of learning citizenship, children learn how to be members of a group, the importance of following rules, and how to be a leader.

At this point your choice to be a teacher may seem overwhelming! You are going to teach content to children, help them to become citizens, and identify the value in each child. Yes, it is a challenge—but one that comes with great rewards. The mission of the school is met because each teacher contributes to it. One lesson, one classroom, one child at a time, teachers help children to become productive members of society. Your decision to become a teacher shows your compassion, caring, and dedication to that goal. The rewards will be harvested in terms of student learning, attainment of goals, and the value your students will have in their communities. You will enjoy two more rewards as a teacher: being a member of a community of professional educators and having the opportunity to share in the joy of your student's achievements. Teachers share values and goals; therefore, teachers find a special collegiality in their schools. Further, teachers experience the personal joy of teaching, of their other accomplishments, and of the accomplishments of their students. Teaching is not a job; it is a career and a profession. What a wonderful profession!

Elementary schools are increasingly adopting programs that are cross-curricular and address specific needs. Often, these programs are not related to academic content. Character education programs are examples and are very popular. Whether or not your school has a school-wide program to address important, but nonacademic, learning, as a teacher you will have an impact on your students' beliefs and values. Your goal is to be a positive influence, helping the children become independent and contributing members of society. Children admire and model their teachers; they are important figures in a child's life. And the children—your students—are always watching.

Schools demonstrate what is valued in many ways; one way is in their mission statement. Many states now require schools to produce a school report card demonstrating the effectiveness of the school in educating students. Other schools use annual goals with benchmarks of performance. All teachers in the school are expected to make positive contributions to these school-wide efforts.

Successful schools often have three characteristics:

1. A shared mission—all teachers, staff, and often students and their parents working toward the same goals
2. Recognition of individual differences—a clear understanding of and plan to accommodate the strengths and weaknesses of everyone in the school
3. Developmentally appropriate curricula, with breadth, depth, and progression—a plan that respects the essential contributions of each subject area to the development of the whole child

In chapter 16, we will examine collaboration and professional development as we revisit the school mission. Chapter 8 focuses on individual needs, including special needs children, gender, and other diversity issues. Although chapter 9 covers curriculum development in physical education, we will cover the school-wide curriculum issues in the rest of this chapter. A critical point is the balance between meeting general school goals and covering specific content. Everyone—teachers, administrators, and students—feels the pressure of time. Allocating time to one initiative means taking time from another. Childhood is a time for considerable learning—all of which is important. Therefore, it is difficult to prioritize, especially when adding something to the curriculum may mean deleting something else. Schools and teachers face challenging decisions about the overall curriculum and what happens in each classroom. One method used to address this problem is integration, or the idea of teaching two things at once. For example, reading a book about science reinforces the reading curriculum while simultaneously teaching about science. There are other ways of integrating, as we shall see.

Physical activity can be integrated in the curriculum from four perspectives. The first is an integrated approach as presented in chapter 9, where the three domains (cognitive, psychomotor, and affective) are targeted as objectives in each unit and lesson. The second is integration with class units of instruction. For example, third graders might include playing a traditional Native American game as part of a social studies unit on Native American culture. Third, physical activity can be integrated into a school-wide event, such as National Reading Week. A fourth interpretation of integration is to make physical activity and the health benefits of a physically active lifestyle central to the mission of the school, as discussed in chapter 1.

Physical activity and physical education make important and independent contributions to child development and to the school curriculum. Children need physical activity to enhance the cardiovascular and muscular systems, to grow strong bones, to develop skills that allow them to be physically active and thereby healthier as adults, and to participate in important social activities during childhood. Motor skills and fitness are taught in physical education and not in other academic areas. Therefore, physical education programs should not need to be justified by suggesting that physical education contributes to the learning of academic content. However, physical education programs must be consistent with the mission of the school

and should contribute through integration as appropriate to academic learning.

Teachers need to understand integration for several reasons:

▶ To maximize student learning
▶ So all subject areas will work together
▶ To address the needs of the whole child

INTEGRATING THE DOMAINS

In chapter 9, the three domains are targeted as objectives in each lesson. The cognitive domain objectives focus on knowledge of motor skills, fitness, and physical activities—concepts taught in the lesson. The cognitive objectives do not focus on concepts taught in other subject areas. Integration by addressing the three domains is important because knowing precedes doing or develops in concert with doing. The general cognitive skills, such as recall and decision making, can be practiced on any content—from algebra and aquatics to zoology and the zone defense. Learning in physical education is as dependent on cognition as is learning in mathematics or reading, which means cognitive objectives are appropriate and important in physical education. In many physical activities, teamwork, arousal, and moral behavior become important factors for success; therefore, cooperative or affective objectives are appropriate for physical education. Integration of the three domains is critical for success in many physical activities. Regardless of who teaches physical education—a specialist or a classroom teacher—physical education helps children practice important skills from the cognitive, affective, and psychomotor domains. In addition, physical education is likely to be the only place you will see your students learn and demonstrate skills from the psychomotor domain.

Sample Cognitive Objectives

The student will

▶ name three locomotor skills;
▶ correctly identify skip, hop, and gallop;
▶ list two benefits of physical fitness; and
▶ state when a runner is "out" in baseball.

Classroom teachers may recognize success—and value—in some students when observing motor skills. A physical education specialist may find that a child with less motor skill contributes as a leader during class. In either case, two underlying beliefs are essential: First, each domain and objective of the elementary school is important and makes a contribution. Second, children must be allowed to maximize their individual potential within each domain and must be recognized and valued for success in any domain. Thus, physical education specialists must seek value in those children who are not as fit or skilled, and classroom teachers must recognize the value of physical education and children who find success in the psychomotor domain. Accepting and acting on these beliefs will help all teachers meet the mission of the school. Consequently, physical education becomes a core value of the school as it contributes to health and child development.

Integration With School-Wide Initiatives

Two factors make the integration of physical education with school-wide initiatives essential. First, physical education is uniquely qualified to demonstrate and foster being a team player. School-wide initiatives, such as National Reading Week or a character education program, will succeed only when everyone has bought into the program. Teachers in every subject area need to engage themselves in the program activities, support the program, and work toward the success of the program for it to be successful. Second, because the physical education specialist is often isolated, sometimes because the school does not convey information on school-wide initiatives to the physical education teacher and at other times because the teacher chooses not to actively participate in school-wide events. Thus school-wide initiatives provide an excellent opportunity for physical education specialists to be more of an integral part of the school and to further promote their curriculum to their students. Often this means being proactive, however, and finding ways, on their own, to contribute.

So, how could a physical education teacher contribute to National Reading Week? How could a classroom teacher use physical activity to contribute to a National Reading Week initiative? Here are some ideas:

- ▶ Identify books about physical activity in the school library and suggest that your students read them.
- ▶ Select a theme from a book and develop physical education class activities related to that book.
- ▶ Assign a reading activity related to physical education.
- ▶ As a physical education teacher, volunteer to read to one or more classes.
- ▶ As a classroom teacher, lead the class in the physical activity from the selected book.

Ideas for integrating physical education into school-wide programs are presented in table 2.1 and figure 2.1; these use a reading campaign and Team Nutrition (a USDA nutrition and physical activity program) as the targets of the integration. Sources for award-winning books are available on the American Library Association Web site (www.ala.org). For example, *The Story of Jumping Mouse: A Native American Legend,* retold and illustrated by John Steptoe (Lothrop; Caldecott Honor Book in 1985), and *Casey at the Bat: A Ballad of the Republic Sung in the Year 1888,* illustrated by Christopher Bing, written by Ernest Lawrence Thayer (Handprint Books; Caldecott Honor book in 2000), both can be integrated into a physical education lesson or unit.

Integration With Subject Matter

There are two approaches to integrating physical education with subject matter (e.g., social studies or mathematics). One approach is to work with the teacher and plan a systematic integration. When the classroom teacher teaches physical education, the communication is simple, but the process still requires planning and thought. As with everything, finding time to plan can be a barrier to integration; classroom teachers have many subjects to plan and may feel less comfortable or knowledgeable about integrating physical activity. One solution, especially in the upper grades, is to have your students help with integration! In social studies, the students can research games or dances from another culture; in other subject areas, teams of students can create games or activities that meet criteria you establish. For example, to integrate with math, the game must be

Table 2.1   Mrs. Braden's Reading Project

Overview of project	The book *Flat Stanley* is about a boy who becomes flat like a piece of paper. He has many adventures, as we will learn from reading the book. This project will create an adventure for each second grader: A paper image of each child will be mailed to a different school with a cover letter and return envelope. The school's second grade will be asked to take a photo of the little visitor participating in the class' favorite physical activity. The class will write a description of that activity and return everything (the photo, the visitor, and the description). Our class will post the photos with the "flat second graders" and then play the games during physical education.
Timeline	Who, what, when, where
Month 1	Contact second grade classroom teachers about project.
Month 2	Contact librarian and make arrangements to check out book *Flat Stanley*. Make a list of schools and address labels. Write letter explaining project.
Month 3	Art teacher assists making "flat second graders." Mail "flat second graders" to schools with letters explaining project.
Months 4–5	Wait.
Month 6	Open mail, post "flat second graders," and play games.

TEAM NUTRITION 🏃 IOWA™

Hop, Jump and Dance Like Betsy

No equipment.

☺

x x x x x

Arrange the children in a long line facing you.

Betsy is a frog in the book "Hop, Jump" (by Ellen S. Walsh, 1993, Harcourt, Brace & Co). This activity copies Betsy's movements, and allows the children to create movements of their own. Betsy watches the other frogs hop and jump, but she wants to try other movements. At first the other frogs say "no room for dancing", but after watching her they try dancing and like it. Then they say "no room for hopping and jumping", but Betsy tells us there is room for everyone.

Begin by jumping forward (jumping is with both feet at the same time). Try short quick jumps, long jumps and jumps up into the air.
Next try hopping (jumping on one foot at a time, several hops at a time). Repeat on the other foot.
Betsy leaped (long running step) and did twisting and turning. Show the children leaping, have them try. Repeat with several turns.
Betsy and the frogs began to dance combining jumps, hops, turns, leaps and other movements. Expand by having everyone hop-jump while one person dances, reverse.

Figure 2.1   Team Nutrition Iowa from Physical Activities and Healthy Snacks for Young Children.

Team Nutrition Iowa from Physical Activities and Healthy Snacks for Young Children Iowa Department of Education, Bureau of Food and Nutrition, (2001) by L. Sands (snacks) and K.T. Thomas (physical activity). Reprinted by permission.

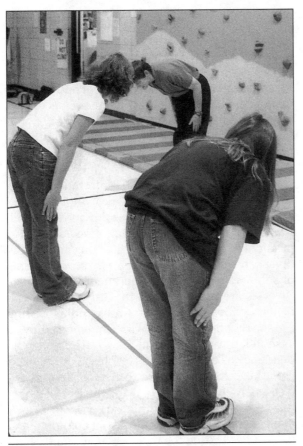

Children bow and count in Korean to integrate physical education with a unit on Asia.

The physical education specialist may be able to infer from what the children say or what she can learn from the curriculum how to use classroom skills in the gym. Classroom teachers can help physical education specialists by sharing information; we will elaborate on such collaborations in chapter 16. Regardless of who teaches physical education, one example of integration is to use numbers in scoring that will challenge the math skills of the students. For example, rather than using one point for each score, use 7 or 9 points, then for penalties you can divide the score by .25 and really challenge the students! If the students are studying Native Americans in social studies class, playing games or performing dances from that culture would be an excellent integration. This requires some research but is worth the effort. Two important things should guide your decisions about this type of integration, whether you are a classroom teacher or a physical education specialist: First, make sure your content information is accurate—do the research! Second, do not sacrifice physical education content to reinforce subject area knowledge. Physical education is important, and the content stands alone. However, when integration is possible and practical, all areas of education can benefit.

scored using numbers divisible by 7, or for a reading unit the game must use characters or sayings from a book or story the class read recently. Although it is helpful to collaborate with colleagues or physical education specialists on ideas, this is not always possible or practical. Do not be discouraged: Take the risk and try integration.

Concepts Into Practice

As part of its summer enrichment program, a local elementary school selected the Philippines as their project. The school adopted a recently immigrated family, read books about the country, tasted ethnic foods, and made traditional costumes. The physical education teacher taught Tinikling—a Filipino dance using bamboo poles. The summer unit culminated with a program for parents in which the students wore the clothes, served snacks, and performed the dance of the Filipino culture.

Concepts Into Practice

In physical education in the primary grades, the teacher challenges his students to think of a new word learned in each physical education class. He writes these words on poster paper and tapes them high on the gym wall. After a few weeks, he asks the children to read and think creatively to meet the challenge of identifying the new words!

A Final Note or Two About Integration

Although integration is a sound and generally accepted educational approach, the idea of integration has been confused with and confounded by two other educational issues. One is the feeling that more time is needed for academics and therefore time should not be allocated to physical education. This has led physical educators to the second issue: They tend to justify their programs based on the programs' contributions to academic performance rather than to performance in physical education. There is little evidence that either of these approaches works in successfully promoting physical education (Kavale and Matson 1983). Trying to improve reading or math skills by performing certain skills in physical education (e.g., balancing or bouncing a ball), teaching academic skills while doing movements (e.g., tossing a ball into a target exhibiting the answers to math problems) have not improved academic skills and have often interfered with the learning of motor skills, an undesirable outcome.

Several studies have looked at time spent in physical education. The results show that more time in physical education does not lower standardized test scores (Sallis, MacKenzie, Kolody, Lewis, Marshall, and Rosengard 1999). Further, more time in school or academic class does not necessarily enhance test scores or grades (Berliner 1990). In fact, there is evidence that **allocated time** (the time spent in school for instruction and practice) does not predict student learning for most students (Berliner1990). Increased **academic learning time** is associated with improved outcomes for some sectors of the population (e.g., students from socioeconomically low, at-risk homes). Learning is probably enhanced to a greater degree by the quality rather than the quantity of time. There is some evidence that both physical education and recess may enhance academic performance and classroom behavior in some children (e.g., in girls and special-needs children; Keays 1995, Sallis et al. 1999, Shepard 1983). The point is that there is no evidence that the 25 to 50 minutes of physical activity during each school day negatively affects academic performance. There is a great deal of evidence, however, that physical activity is an important part of child development and has a long-term positive impact on health.

Integration does not mean replacing physical education, and the learning of motor skills, with practice time for academic skills. Integration does mean supporting all areas of the curriculum and teaching the whole child. The goal for all physical education programs is to develop positive lifestyles and skills in students, to make physical activity central to the mission of the school, to work toward the school mission (including schoolwide programs), and to integrate physical activity into academic subjects as appropriate.

TEACHING THE WHOLE CHILD

Many theories of child development and learning have influenced elementary education as educators and psychologists develop curriculum and instruction based on a theory or a blend of theories. Two currently popular theories are Gardner's multiple intelligences (MI; Gardner 1983) and constructivism (Perkins 1992). Unfortunately, educators often view theories as methodologies and as mutually exclusive. Theories provide a testable framework to explain observations and to make predictions. Testing and predications are usually done in research studies, often with several teams of scholars conducting experiments. Sometimes theories are adopted as truth with very little empirical evidence (e.g., research studies testing the theory) or dispensed with when one study or case failed to support the theory. Thus, our dependence as practitioners (teachers) on theories must be carefully thought through. Theories are often perceived as mutually exclusive, meaning that the theories have nothing in common. In fact, most theories have a great deal in common, and the studies testing the theories have similar findings. Think about what might cause the theories to be similar. The fact that the theories are focusing on how children learn and often on how teachers facilitate that learning means that the theories will have many similarities. For example, information processing theory and Piaget's theory identify the same ages for critical changes in how children solve problems (Thomas, Gallagher, and Thomas 2000). The two theories explain the changes differently and have used different methods, but both have been tested extensively by many scholars around the world.

A practical approach is to examine the theories and follow those that reflect commonalities and themes that run through several dominant theories. Those themes are likely to be the most important for teachers to use as they plan curriculum and instruction.

Gardner's Theory of Multiple Intelligences

Gardner challenged the traditional view of intelligence (Brualdi 1996; Gardner 1983, 1991). Intelligence has been viewed as a singular dimension, representing a person's ability to solve problems. The traditional view of intelligence is that you are born with it, that it cannot be changed, and that it can be measured. Traditional views hold intelligence to be an innate ability that represents potential for learning and cognitive performance. Tests of intelligence were designed to help schools identify areas in which students might need assistance. Those tests typically focus on numeric skills and literacy (e.g., the Scholastic Aptitude Test and the Stanford–Binet IQ Test). Gardner has suggested that these tests do not accurately represent a person's ability because the test is limited in focus. Thus, he suggests seven intelligences: musical, logical-mathematical, linguistic, spatial, interpersonal, intrapersonal, and bodily kinesthetic intelligence (Gardner 1983). Recently he has added naturalistic as an eighth intelligence and suggests that there may be additional intelligences (Checkley 1997).

The impact of traditional intelligence testing on education has been its focus on literacy and numeracy as primary values and therefore curricular areas. Students who did not excel in one or both of those areas were often left out of the educational plan. Thus, Gardner suggests that tests, teachers, and schools use a broader array of markers and widen the focus of the curriculum to include all seven intelligences and others as well. The critical feature of this theory is to find value in each child and to find a path to success for each student. Further, educators need to use multiple and creative sources of information to assess children's abilities. Clearly, Gardner advocates away from multiple-choice tests and toward more authentic assessments of a broad range of content.

MI theory is controversial, especially bodily kinesthetic intelligence (Checkley 1997). One reason for dispute is that intelligence has traditionally been viewed as stable and innate; this definition is more consistent with the traditional definition of performance, which is unstable and influenced by both innate and learned factors. Gardner has used examples of athletes to demonstrate bodily kinesthetic intelligence. Movement is controlled in the brain, is important across cultures, and varies among individuals; thus it meets Gardner's criteria for inclusion as an intelligence. Three criticisms of MI are that (1) Gardner does not deal with the issue of practice, (2) considerable research indicates that only a small portion of athletic performance is biological (or inherited), and (3) sport experts are often experts because of their cognitive decision making.

Gardner states that MI is best implemented in schools because "a teacher takes individual differences among children very seriously" (Checkley 1997). Teachers often confuse MI with learning styles, according to Gardner. For example, a visual learner is not the same as a person with high bodily kinesthetic intelligence. The descriptions Gardner uses for the seven or eight intelligences are similar to descriptions of talent. Gardner indicates that this is a fair description. Gardner does not suggest that an appropriate use of MI theory is to teach math or reading by having children who are high in bodily kinesthetic intelligence use movement to learn that content. Clearly, he does encourage teachers and schools to respect and nurture a variety of ways for students to contribute.

Constructivism

Constructivism is another theory that has been used to guide educational practice. Constructivist theory advocates for students to create their own understanding through active involvement in the learning process. The theory has evolved from information processing theory (Anderson, Reder, and Simon 1998) and Piaget's theory. Bruner (1973) noted the benefits of active versus passive learning during his information processing research; thus, he was a pioneer in constructivist theory. Social and cognitive constructivism have further defined the theory. Cognitive constructivism is the basis for some language, math, and science practice, so educators often refer to this as constructivist theory. Cognitive constructivism has two dimensions. One is presentation of information with the two perspectives being BIG, which means taking the activity beyond the information given by the teacher, and WIG, which means without information given by the teacher (Perkins 1992). In the former case, constructivists would have students create learning to extend what was presented. In the latter case, students would create all information. The other dimension concerns how far the theory has moved away from information processing. Radical constructivists do not believe in practice, assessment, or instruction and would be more likely to follow WIG. Conservative constructivists tend to rely on the empirical evidence from information processing and extend that to classroom practice with a focus on active learning and contextual accuracy. A weakness of constructivism is the lack of empirical evidence supporting the theory—especially radical constructivism (Anderson, Reder, and Simon 1998). However, as we shall see in chapter 5, there is considerable empirical evidence supporting information processing theory. Conservative constructivism, then, is grounded in theory that has empirical support and the major premise of the theory—active learning—is well respected.

The idea is that understanding, learning, and memory are enhanced when the student is actively involved in the process. For example, rather than explain in a lecture that there are several ways to solve a math problem, the teacher might challenge students to create as many ways as possible to arrive at the correct answer. Many physical education lessons use this approach; in one example, the teacher says, "How many ways can you move your body without moving your feet?" The student would then be challenged to demonstrate many nonlocomotor tasks, such as swaying, bending, twisting, stretching, and wiggling. Motor learning theory has demonstrated the benefit to active rather than passive practice for many years (Schmidt and Lee 1999).

Regardless of the educational philosophy or theory to which you and your school subscribe, two things are important to understand: First, the information in this book is likely to help you support the mission of your school. Second, physical activity and physical education do not operate in a vacuum. The psychomotor domain is an important component of child development; it makes unique contributions and is mastered in ways similar to other domains. Consequently, physical education activities directly and indirectly support the mission of the school.

SUMMARY

Each teacher in an elementary school should help her school accomplish its mission. Likewise, each subject area makes a contribution to the development of the child and to the mission of the school. Teachers and students have different strengths

and thus contribute differently. The fact that each person is unique creates a richer learning environment and supports accomplishing the mission of the school. Integration of content is an efficient and effective way to address the multifaceted mission of the school and to help children develop across all domains. Teachers make decisions about curriculum and instruction based on theory, practical issues, knowledge about child development, and the school mission.

The following principles might guide your decisions as a teacher:

1. Active participation enhances learning.
2. Each child is different and valuable.
3. Using a variety of approaches is desirable.
4. Each domain is important.
5. All teachers contribute to the school mission and influence a student's development in each domain.

The next section of the book provides information about child development, specifically motor development. This information helps the teacher understand the science of children's physical activity—in other words, the "why" of the teaching and learning process.

MASTERY LEARNING ACTIVITIES

1. Find an elementary school Web site that gives the school's mission statement. Identify three ways that physical education helps support the school's mission statement.
2. Read Kavale and Matson, and in 75 words or fewer discuss what is wrong with perceptual motor programs.
3. Read about two theories of education, and identify two differences and two similarities between the theories.
4. Make two lists, one for classroom teachers and one for physical education specialists. One list should identify five different ways classroom teachers can support physical education goals (e.g., facilitating physically active lifestyles and skill development) in the classroom. The other should identify at least five different ways the physical education teacher can support classroom learning.

REFERENCES

Anderson, J.R., L.M. Reder, and H.A. Simon. 1998. Radical constructivism and cognitive psychology. In *Brookings papers on education policy: 1998*, edited by D. Ravitch, 227–55. Washington, D.C.: Brookings Institution.

Berliner, D. 1990. What is all the fuss about instructional time? In *The nature of time in schools: Theoretical concepts, practitioner perceptions*, edited by M. Ben-Peretz and R. Bromme, 3–35. New York: Teachers College Press.

Brualdi, A.C. 1996. Multiple intelligences: Gardner's theory. [Online.] *ERIC Digest* (ED410226). Available: http://ericir.syr.edu/ [September 8, 2002]. Washington, D.C.

Bruner, J. 1973. *Going beyond the information given.* New York: Norton.

Checkley, K. 1997. The first seven...and the eighth: A conversation with Howard Gardner. *Educational Leadership* 55 (September):1–7.

Edelman, M.W. 1999. *Lanterns: A memoir of mentors.* Boston: Beacon Press.

Gardner, H. 1983. *Frames of mind.* New York: Basic Books.

Gardner, H. 1991. *The unschooled mind: How children think and how schools should teach.* New York: Basic Books.

Kavale, K., and P.D. Matson. 1983. One jumped off the balance beam: A meta analysis of perceptual motor training programs. *Journal of Learning Disabilities* 16:165–73.

Keays, J.J. 1995. The effects of regular moderate-to-vigorous physical activity on student outcomes: A review. *Canadian Journal of Public Health* 86:62–65.

Perkins, D.N. (1992). Technology meets constructivism: Do they make a marriage? In *Constructivism and the technology of instruction: A conversation*, edited by T.M. Duffy and D.H. Jonassen. Hillsdale, N.J.: Erlbaum.

Sallis, J.F., T.L. McKenzie, B. Kolody, M. Lewis, S. Marshall, and P. Rosengard. 1999. Effects of health-related physical education on academic achievement: Project SPARK. *Research Quarterly for Exercise and Sport* 70:127–136.

Schmidt, R.A., and T.D. Lee. 1999. *Motor control and learning: A behavioral approach.* 3d ed. Champaign, Ill.: Human Kinetics.

Shepard, R.J. 1983. Physical activity and the healthy mind. *Canadian Medical Association Journal* 128:525–30.

Thomas, K.T., J.D. Gallagher, and J.R. Thomas. 2000. Motor development and skill acquisition during childhood and adolescence. In *Handbook of Sport Psychology*, 2d ed., edited by R.N. Singer, H.A. Hausenblas, and C. Janelle, 20–52. New York: Wiley.

RESOURCES

Sources for children's books:
U.S. Department of Education: www.ed.gov
American Library Association: www.ala.org

LESSON PLANS

The organization lesson plan for grades 4 and 5 uses journal writing to stimulate thinking about physical education. Practice at writing supports language arts and is one way of integrating subjects to meet the school mission. Journal writing does not detract from physical education content; instead, the journals help teachers understand student learning and beliefs. The rhythmic lesson for grades 6 through 8 presents Tinikling, which was used as an example of integration with social studies earlier in this chapter. Cognitive concepts important in physical education and in the classroom are presented in lessons. The concepts for grades K and 1 are body parts and relationships (over and under), and the concepts for grades 2 and 3 are directions.

Games and Sports

GRADES K-1

LESSON 2.1

Body Parts

Student Objectives

- Demonstrate various relationships between beanbags and their bodies (high, behind, on knees).
- Balance the beanbag on various body parts when moving.
- Participate in a simple game using beanbags.
- Cooperate when playing Over and Under.

Equipment and Materials

- 1 beanbag per child, minimum
- Signal

Safety Tips

- For the warm-up game, stress touching body parts gently, not bumping, banging, or hitting.

- Remind the children to respect other children's personal space (space they can be in without touching anyone else).

Warm-Up Activities (5 minutes)

Run and Touch

Arrange the children in a widespread scatter formation.

1. Explain the activity:

    I will call a body part, and each of you must run to another child and touch those body parts together. For example, when I call "knees," you run and touch your knees to a partner's knees.

    On each call, you must find a new partner, never repeating partners.

2. Have the children play Run and Touch.

Skill-Development Activities (15 minutes)

Movement Challenges

Arrange the children in scatter formation, each with a beanbag.

1. Tell the students:

    Put your beanbag up high. (Child's name)'s beanbag is really high (low)!

2. Ask the students:

    How low can you hold your beanbag? Can you hold it in front of you (behind you, under you, beside you, between high and low)? Tell the students: *Touch your foot (head, neck, knee, ankle, shoulder, elbow, calf, chest, shin, forearm, wrists, hip, tummy, back, chin) with your beanbag.*

3. Discuss any body parts that the children have trouble recognizing, such as shin, chin, or forearm.

4. Tell the students:

    Balance your beanbag on your forearm (head, elbow, knee, shoulder, wrist, ankle, chest, foot). Balance your beanbag on your hand (arm, thigh, head, shoulder, chest) and walk slowly.

24

Concluding Activities (10 minutes)

Over and Under

Arrange the children in a circle facing counter-clockwise. Give a beanbag to each of three to six children spaced around the circle so that approximately the same number of children are between each beanbag.

1. Describe and demonstrate the game:

   On the start signal, you will pass the beanbags alternately over one child's head and between (or under) the next child's legs.

   Do not drop any beanbags, never go over or under two children in a row, and try to move as many beanbags as quickly as possible around the circle.

   I will gradually increase the number of beanbags and the speed. When you make mistakes (drops or two overs or unders), I will stop the game and slow down the speed or take away one or more of the beanbags.

   I am looking for you to really cooperate with each other.

2. Have the children play Over and Under.

From *Physical Education Methods for Elementary Teachers, Second Edition,* by Katherine T. Thomas, Amelia M. Lee, and Jerry R. Thomas, 2003, Champaign, IL: Human Kinetics. Adapted from *Physical Education for Children: Daily Lesson Plans for Elementary School, Second Edition,* by Katherine T. Thomas, Amelia M. Lee, and Jerry R. Thomas, 2000, Champaign, IL: Human Kinetics.

LESSON  **2.2**

Hopping

Student Objectives

- Move through space using various combinations of hopping steps.
- Work cooperatively when playing Follow the Leader.
- Identify hopping (as opposed to jumping).

Equipment and Materials

- Paint, chalk, flour, or tape to mark 1 hopscotch area per group
- Signal

Warm-Up Activities (5 minutes)

Sneaky Tag

Arrange the children into two groups, one group on a start line and the other group on Xs (see figure on this page). (You can make the lines and Xs on a hard surface with tape and on grass or dirt with paint or flour.) The children on the start line are the "Sneakers," and the children on the Xs are the "Taggers."

1. Describe and demonstrate the game:

    On the signal, the Sneakers move through the Taggers trying to get to the endline without being tagged. Sneakers must stay within the boundaries, and Taggers must keep at least one toe touching their X.

    If you are tagged, you run around the outside trackway and back to the start line during the next round (from finish line to start line).

    After several rounds, we will switch Taggers and Sneakers.

    Sneakers use this strategy: When a Tagger is trying to reach you on one side, run by on the other side.

2. Have the children play Sneaky Tag.

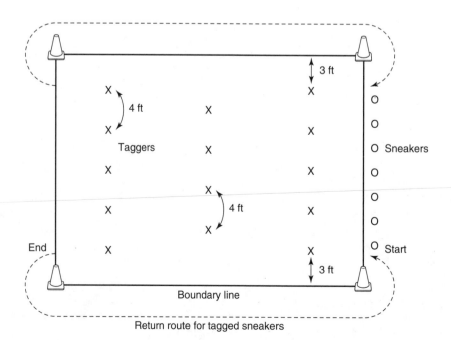

Skill-Development Activities (15 minutes)

Hopping Skills

Arrange the children in scatter formation.

1. Challenge the children with the following tasks:

   Hop forward and backward (then side to side).

   Hop and change direction (speed, pathway) on the signal.

   Hop a figure eight.

   Hop as far as you can.

   Hop and land facing another direction.

2. Have them repeat the challenges on the other foot.

Follow the Leader

Divide the children into groups of four to six.

1. Describe the game:

   Choose one child to lead, and the rest of you follow, imitating the leader's actions.

   The leader must use a hopping pattern (changing combinations of right- and left-footed hopping).

   Change the leader when you hear the signal.

2. Have the children play Follow the Leader, signaling groups to change leaders every 60 seconds.

Name That Skill

1. Ask a child to demonstrate hopping, then jumping.
2. Demonstrate jumping and ask a different child to name the skill.
3. Repeat with hopping.

Concluding Activities (10 minutes)

Hopscotch

Arrange the children in groups of four to six, and place each group at a hopscotch area.

1. Describe the activity:

   Hop through the diagrams first on your right foot and then on your left.

   Repeat, going backward.

   If you step on a line or lose your balance, you must start again.

2. Have the children play Hopscotch.

From *Physical Education Methods for Elementary Teachers, Second Edition,* by Katherine T. Thomas, Amelia M. Lee, and Jerry R. Thomas, 2003, Champaign, IL: Human Kinetics. Adapted from *Physical Education for Children: Daily Lesson Plans for Elementary School, Second Edition,* by Katherine T. Thomas, Amelia M. Lee, and Jerry R. Thomas, 2000, Champaign, IL: Human Kinetics.

Organization

LESSON

Forming Groups, Journal Writing

Student Objectives

- Form groups of different sizes quickly and quietly.
- Share their feelings about physical education in writing.

Equipment and Materials

- 1 notebook and pencil per child
- 1 color-shape-number card per child

Warm-Up Activities (10 minutes)

Forming Groups

Continue to work on forming groups with the following adaptation.

1. You can make cards before class and distribute them to the children as they enter the gym.
2. Cards should be four different colors (red, blue, yellow, green). Stamp them with different shapes (circle, triangle, rectangle, square).
3. Number the cards from 1 to the number of children in the class.
4. Present the following tasks:
   Find a partner who has the same color.

   Find a partner who has the same shape.
5. Form two groups: Red and blue make one group and yellow and green make the second group.
6. Continue with other combinations:
   Form two groups: Group 1 = first half of numbers; Group 2 = second half of numbers.
   Form four groups: Group 1 = circles; Group 2 = squares; Group 3 = rectangles; Group 4 = triangles.
7. Continue using color and shape combinations to form groups.

Skill-Development Activities (15 minutes)

Feelings About Physical Education

Arrange children in scatter formation, each child with a notebook and pencil.

1. Ask the children: *What were your feelings when you were in physical education last year?*
2. Stimulate children's thinking by asking some of the following open-ended questions:
   I feel good in physical education when I . . .
   The activity I enjoyed most was . . .
   It was my favorite activity because . . .

   The times I feel uncomfortable in physical education are when . . .
   I believe physical education is (or is not) important for children because . . .
3. Insist that this be a serious activity, and you should keep children's responses private, not discus them in class.
4. Read the journals to get ideas about what children think and feel about their experiences in physical education.

Concluding Activities (5 minutes)

Discussion

Arrange children in an advanced information formation. Continue the discussion of the importance of rules:
Why is it important to stop and listen quickly on the teacher's signal?

What might happen if some children do not use the equipment in the way it is intended?
Describe what a good physical education class would look like to a stranger.

From *Physical Education Methods for Elementary Teachers, Second Edition,* by Katherine T. Thomas, Amelia M. Lee, and Jerry R. Thomas, 2003, Champaign, IL: Human Kinetics. Adapted from *Physical Education for Children: Daily Lesson Plans for Elementary School, Second Edition,* by Katherine T. Thomas, Amelia M. Lee, and Jerry R. Thomas, 2000, Champaign, IL: Human Kinetics.

LESSON

Tinikling

Student Objectives

- Perform the Basic Tinikling Step.

Equipment

- One short jump rope for each child
- Record: "Tinikling," Kimbo (KEA 8095, 9015)
- Six to eight sets of bamboo poles (8 to 12 feet)

Warm-Up Activities (5 minutes)

Rhythmic Patterns With Ropes

Arrange the children in scatter formation with their jump ropes in circles on the ground.

1. The children jump in and out of the circles in a 3/4 rhythm. For example, two jumps in and one jump out.

2. The children continue jumping rhythmically to a drumbeat. Have them try one jump in and two jumps out.

Skill-Development Activities (20 minutes)

Basic Tinikling Step

Arrange the children in groups of four in scatter formation. Each group has a set of Tinikling poles.

1. Have the children listen to Tinikling music, clapping and counting the 3/4 time.
2. The children in each group begin by standing with right sides to the poles.
3. Describe and demonstrate counts 1 to 3.

Count 1: Step in place with the left foot (the foot away from the pole).

Count 2: Step with the right foot between the poles.

Count 3: Step with the left foot between the poles (lift up right foot).

Arrange the sticks on the floor and practice with the sticks stationary. In each group all students practice at the same time.

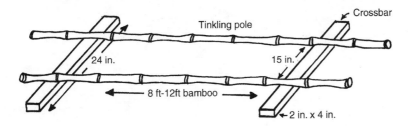

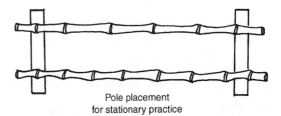

Pole placement
for stationary practice

5. Have the children practice counts 1 to 3. Say to the children: *Step left, right between, left between.*

6. Describe and demonstrate counts 4 to 6.

   Count 4: Step with the right foot out to the right of the poles.

   Count 5: Step with the left foot between the poles.

   Count 6: Step with the right foot between the poles (lift up left foot).

   Count 7: Step with the left foot to the left side of the poles. (Count 7 becomes count 1 for the second step.)

7. Have the children practice all the counts. Say to the children: *Step left, right between, left between, right out, left between, right between, left out.*

8. Have the children repeat the basic Tinikling steps, counts 1 to 6.

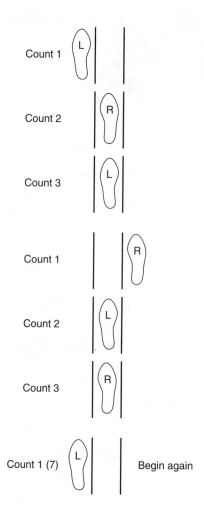

Concluding Activities (5 minutes)

Basic Tinikling Step

The students perform the Basic Tinikling Step, one child in each group at a time, to music; on the seventh count, the second child enters while the first child exits. Repeat until each child in each group has had several turns.

From *Physical Education Methods for Elementary Teachers, Second Edition,* by Katherine T. Thomas, Amelia M. Lee, and Jerry R. Thomas, 2003, Champaign, IL: Human Kinetics. Adapted from *Physical Education for Children: Daily Lesson Plans for Middle School, Second Edition,* Amelia M. Lee, Katherine T. Thomas, and Jerry R. Thomas, 2000, Champaign, IL: Human Kinetics.

part II

Addressing the Child's Needs

C hildren are not miniature adults—if they were, teaching would be easier and parenting would be less of a mystery! The chapters in this section describe six aspects of development that have an impact on physical activity and physical education. As you will see in chapter 3, the increases in students' height and weight that we readily observe are accompanied by equally important—but less observable—changes in other physical parameters. Growth interacts with practice to improve performance of many skills, such as running, jumping, and kicking. These improvements are presented in chapter 4. Most of us can recall an anecdote that is enjoyable because a child has used information differently than an adult might. For example, when asked to count "higher," a kindergartner we know climbed high onto the back of the couch and once again counted to 10! Children have less experience and different perspectives on how and why to remember, learn, and try. Chapter 5 focuses on learning, memory, and practice, and chapter 7 explores motivation and other psychological variables. Chapter 6 presents information about children's responses to exercise and physical activity. Educational platitudes suggest to us that each child is unique and important, whereas teacher education focuses on what is typical. Thus, the final chapter in this section explores individual differences—those differences that create unique and interesting people.

chapter 3

Physical Growth and Maturation

Sachi, age 7

During childhood and adolescence, children grow larger and become mature. Proportions change because body parts and systems grow and mature at different rates. Age-related differences in body size, proportion, and composition influence motor performance. Boys and girls are comparable in these areas prior to puberty. Even after puberty, however, the differences should be small and have a relatively small impact on performance of motor skills.

Learner Outcomes

The teacher will do the following:

▶ Define growth and maturation.

▶ Describe the impact of puberty on growth for boys and girls.

▶ Relate growth to performance.

▶ Distinguish among growth factors that are genetic and environmental.

▶ Use knowledge of growth and maturation to select, plan, teach, and modify appropriate activities for children.

Glossary Terms

maturation
growth
development
experience

puberty
stature
body composition
physique

Every teacher should understand how children mature, grow, and develop. **Maturation** is the rate of progress toward an adult state, which is controlled genetically by the child's chronometer (biological time clock). This means the environment has little influence on maturation and that each child has a unique maturational calendar. Characteristics appear in the same order for all children but at different chronological ages among children. **Growth** is a change in body size that results from more and bigger body cells and more intercellular material. Growth and maturation are related; that is, growth patterns are influenced by and indicative of maturation. **Development** is the change in a child's level of functioning. Development is a combination of growth, maturation, and experience. **Experience** is external or environmental and includes factors such as nutrition, education, and home life. This chapter will focus on growth and maturation as components of development.

Teachers should understand growth, maturation, and development for three reasons:

1. Teachers should monitor growth, maturation, and development in their students. If unusual deviations occur, the principal, nurse, or parents should be advised so the child can be evaluated by appropriate professionals.

2. Teachers should select and teach activities based on their knowledge about growth, maturation, and development.

3. Teachers need to be able to answer questions children ask about their bodies and the process of development.

MATURATION

Maturation can be measured in many ways. Maturational age (MA) describes the age of a person based on her progress toward a mature state. MA and biological age (BA) are essentially the same. Chronological age (CA) is the amount of time since birth. An early-maturing person would have an MA that is greater than her CA, so she might be 12 years old but look 15 years old, whereas a late-maturing person could look 4 years old and actually be 7 years old. MA can be estimated using skeletal age, sexual maturation, dental age, and physical growth. Some measures of MA are used for specific periods of time (e.g., sexual maturation is used during puberty); others require expensive testing (skeletal maturation requires an x-ray), yet all reveal important and consistent information about an individual's MA. While all are estimates of maturation, the important point is that these provide valuable information about a child's development that may be the same as or more helpful than chronological age.

For example, many children replace baby teeth with permanent teeth during kindergarten and first grade (ages 5–7 years). So, when you see a boy who has lost a front tooth, you can guess he is in kindergarten or first grade. He may be a late-maturing child, however, and actually be 9 years of age. So his CA is 9, but his MA is 6. Since maturation is determined genetically, the little boy has no control over his slower rate of maturation. A teacher who understands that the boy is less mature than his classmates is likely to be more compassionate toward him. The teacher may help him to understand this as a natural variation among children and one he will outgrow. Remember, once people are mature—that is, once they are adults—early and late maturation will no longer matter because everyone will be an adult. Differences in maturation matter most during childhood and adolescence. Explaining this to your students—whether they are early or late maturing—may help them to accept and understand differences in maturation.

Maturation determines when a child will go through puberty. **Puberty** is when the genital organs mature, the secondary sex characteristics (facial and body hair and a deeper voice) develop, and we become sexually mature (able to reproduce). Pubescence (the beginning of puberty) begins for boys with growth of the testicles, followed by a growth spurt in height at about 9 or 10

years of age. For girls, a growth spurt signifies pubescence around 9 to 10 years of age, followed by development of the breasts. Menarche (the beginning of menstruation in girls) occurs on average at 13 years of age. Puberty ends when we are able to reproduce. Figure 3.1 demonstrates one of the changes associated with maturation and puberty—notice how the growth curve levels off for girls at about 13 years of age.

When girls begin to menstruate, their growth slows dramatically. The figure also shows that boys are maturing about two years later than girls. Growth and maturation are clearly related, so one predicts the other.

Skeletal maturation is another way to assess MA. X-rays of the hand and wrist are examined for replacement of cartilage with bone, shape and size becoming adult like, and closure of the growth plates (epiphyses). The skeleton continues to change throughout the life span. Consider the fingers of your grandmother or elderly aunt. Recall how the joints tend to be enlarged and the fingers bent. Compare that to your own hands. Toddlers have short fingers with relatively large palms. An x-ray would reveal more cartilage and less bone in the toddler's hand than in yours.

Physical growth can also be used to assess maturation. Take, for example, age at peak height velocity: Growth is steady from 3 to about 9 years of age (averaging about 2.3 inches, or 6 centimeters, per year), then the rate of growth for height

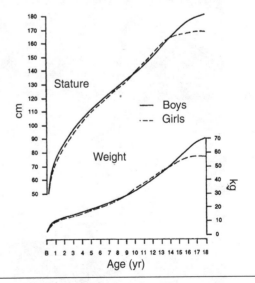

Figure 3.1 Average height and weight curves for American boys and girls.

Reprinted, by permission, from R.M. Malina, 1984, Physical growth and maturation. In *Motor development during childhood and adolescence*, edited by J. Thomas (Minneapolis, MN: Burgess), 7. Reprinted by permission of R.M. Malina.

increases rapidly. Peak height velocity is the point at which the rate is the highest. Usually, this rate is more than 4 inches (10 centimeters) per year and occurs at 11 to 12 years of age for girls and 14 to 15 years of age for boys.

Children who mature early or late compared to their classmates may feel odd and may not understand that the process of maturation is both normal and out of their control. Early-maturing children often experience a temporary advantage in performance during puberty, however. Several factors explain this advantage: First, the early-maturing child experiences her circumpubertal growth spurt earlier than other children, so she will be taller than her classmates. Second, other advantages of maturity are also likely to be present, such as greater muscle mass, which means she will be stronger, or earlier maturation of the nervous system, which means she will have greater control of her movements. This advantage is brief because the other girls will grow steadily for a longer time period then rapidly during the circumpubertal growth spurt. Generally, this means the early-maturing child will be a shorter adult than an individual who matures later. This is one of the factors contributing to the "relative age effect," which will be discussed in chapter 8.

Boys and girls are very similar in maturation until at least 9 or 10 years of age; for many characteristics, the genders remain similar even longer. This suggests that our expectations of maturity should be similar for boys and girls. We also need to consider variation among children. Some girls are more mature than other girls, and some boys are more mature than other boys. Variation is normal (figure 3.2). We have discussed height in relation to maturation; the next section will examine the growth factors that explain the increase in height during childhood and adolescence.

GROWTH

As children grow, their height and weight increase steadily (see figure 3.1); the average heights and weights for boys and girls are nearly the same during childhood. However, the average adult male is taller than the average adult female. Boys mature later; therefore they grow two or more years after the girls stop growing. The difference in average height between adult males and females is the growth that occurs in males during those years.

Figure 3.2   Notice the differences in height among these children that are the same age and in the same grade.
© Human Kinetics.

Recall that children gain about 4.3 inches (6 centimeters) in **stature,** or height, each year during childhood. By looking at figure 3.3, however, we can see that the changes are more complex than the child's body just getting larger. At birth, the head accounts for about 25 percent of the infant's length and is 2.3 times larger in circumference than your head when compared to body size. By school age, the head is approximately 20 percent of total stature and nearly two times larger than yours when compared to body size. During childhood, the proportional size of the head decreases until it is at about 12 percent—the proportional size of an adult's head! Think about trying to do motor tasks if your head was twice its current size. A forward roll or balancing on one foot, for example, would be more difficult with a larger head. Head size is just one of the challenges of movement during childhood.

The extremities (arms and legs) grow rapidly from birth to maturity, more rapidly than the head or torso. The torso grows more rapidly than the head, but not as rapidly as the extremities. This is why the legs increase from 30 to 50 percent of total stature from birth to maturity. Legs are the levers for many movements, so during childhood the levers that send the body up or out while running and jumping are relatively small. Clearly, part of the reason children do not run as fast or jump as far as adults is that their levers are shorter.

To summarize, we have made several observations:

▶ Children increase in stature steadily during childhood.
▶ Children increase rapidly in stature at the beginning of puberty.
▶ Children increase in stature because the legs grow faster than other body parts.
▶ Children increase in stature because the torso grows, but it does not grow as fast as the legs.
▶ Children improve in motor skills partly because the relative size of the head decreases.
▶ Boys and girls are similar in stature and pattern of stature during childhood.
▶ Stature, because of leg length, influences performance.
▶ Boys continue to grow after girls stop growing (because of differences in maturation); therefore, as adults, males are on average taller than females.

As the legs and arms grow longer, the bones also increase in diameter and circumference. A typical pattern of growth is length, then breadth and circumference, and finally the bones "fill in," becoming denser. Strong bones are wider, bigger around, and denser. Broader and denser bones are associated with more physical activity. Bones should be the heaviest tissue in the body. Dense bones are

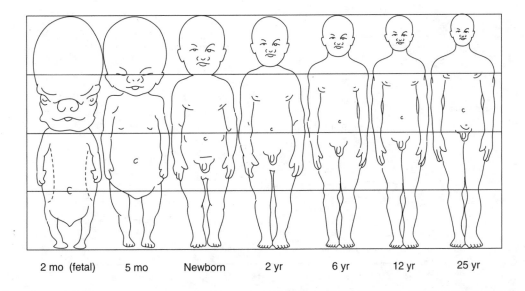

2 mo (fetal)   5 mo   Newborn   2 yr   6 yr   12 yr   25 yr

Figure 3.3   Changes in form and proportion of the human body during fetal and postnatal life.

From K.M. Newell, 1984, Physical constraints to the development of motor skills. In *Motor development during childhood and adolescence,* edited by J.R. Thomas (Minneapolis, MN: Burgess), 108. Reprinted by permission of Jerry Thomas.

Children of all shapes, sizes, and backgrounds enjoy physical activity; it is the teacher's job to nurture that natural interest.

important because as we age, we experience a gradual loss of calcium. Bones that have more density at the beginning of this loss will be stronger and therefore less likely to fracture as bone density decreases during old age.

As children grow taller, body breadths also increase. See, for example, the shoulders (biacromial breadth) and hips (bicristal breadth). The distance between the outsides of the hip bones and the shoulder bones is presented in figure 3.4a. Notice how the four lines are the same until puberty, when the males' shoulders grow more than the females' shoulders. Figure 3.4b shows this as a ratio. There are three important concepts demonstrated in these two figures. First, boys and girls are alike prior to puberty. Second, the differences after puberty are attributable to the boys' shoulders (and not the girls' hips) being relatively larger. So, after puberty boys have an advantage in some

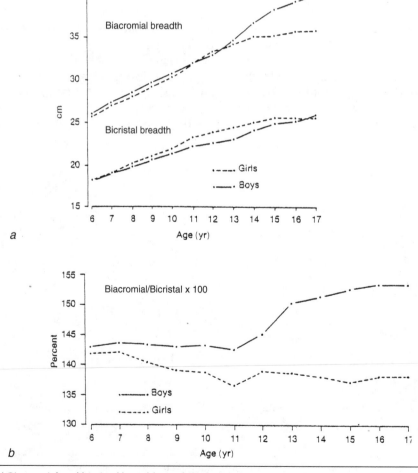

Figure 3.4   (*a*) Biacromial and bicristal breadths and (*b*) their ratios.

Reprinted, by permission, from R.M. Malina, 1984, Physical growth and maturation. In *Motor development during childhood and adolescence*, edited by J. Thomas (Minneapolis, MN: Burgess), 10. Reprinted by permission of R.M. Malina.

activities because of broader shoulders. Third, the larger hip circumferences observed in females is not a reflection of wider hip bones but is related to greater soft tissue (e.g., fat and muscle).

Using **body composition,** the body can be divided in two parts: lean tissues and fat. Lean body mass (lbm) is the weight of all lean tissues, including bone, muscle, and organs. Fat is all fat tissues, including subcutaneous (fat just under the skin), visceral (deep body fat found around organs), and other fats such as cholesterol. The changes during development in lbm and fat can be seen in figure 3.5. Boys and girls gain lean tissue as they grow; the increase is dramatic for boys at pubescence. Boys and girls also gain fat during growth. By dividing absolute fat by total body weight, we estimate relative fatness, or percent body fat. The

average percent of body fat for boys is relatively stable at less than 15 percent during childhood and adolescence. The percent for girls climbs steadily during this same time period, from 15 to 25 percent. Two factors influence the increase in body fat in girls: First, at puberty a minimum of 15 percent body fat is necessary for menstruation to begin. If the increase is caused only by the preparation for menstruation, we would expect the increase in fat to resemble the line for lean body mass in males, with a more abrupt change. The second factor is physical activity: Girls tend to be less active than boys. This idea will be discussed in greater detail in chapter 5. In short, girls gain body fat rapidly because of a combination of biological factors (e.g., menstruation) and cultural factors (e.g., less physical activity).

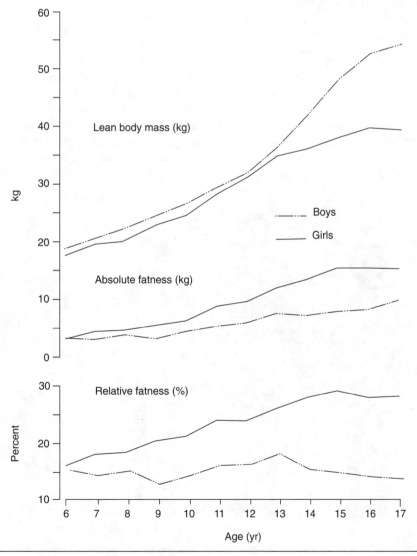

Figure 3.5   Median lean body mass, fat mass, and percent fat.

Reprinted, by permission, from R.M. Malina, 1984, Physical growth and maturation. In *Motor development during childhood and adolescence,* edited by J. Thomas (Minneapolis, MN: Burgess), 15. Reprinted by permission of R.M. Malina.

Physique

Somatotype rating is a specific way of assessing **physique,** so changes attributable to age, diet, exercise, or disease can be traced. Physique is the way a body looks. It includes three prototypes (figure 3.6):

1. Endomorphy is assessed using the sum of three skinfolds corrected for height and is typically seen as a soft, round, or pear-shaped body.

2. Mesomorphy is determined with humerus and femur breadths, and calf and biceps circumferences, all corrected for skinfolds, and height. This is a muscular body that may be relatively short and large boned.

3. Ectomorphy is based on ponderal index (mass corrected for height) and is the linear or tall lean body.

Most people are balanced in body type, which means they do not look exactly like any of the prototypes. Instead they are a combination of two. A relationship does exist between physique (or somatotype) and maturation. Late-maturing children tend to be ectomorphic. Early-maturing males tend to be mesomorphic, whereas early-maturing females tend to be endomorphic. These physiques

can be observed as early as preschool, in which as many as 50 percent of the girls (but only 25 percent of the boys) show a tendency toward endomorphy, whereas more than 50 percent of the boys (and only 16 percent of the girls) tend toward mesomorphy. Worldclass athletes have a high occurrence of ectomorphy, indicating a tall, lean, and probably late-maturing body. The soft tissues (fat and muscle) change over time because of exercise, diet, and disease, whereas height and bone breadths remain stable after maturity. Somatotype can change, however, and the changes are more subtle after growth stops.

Children, especially older children who are nearing puberty, are often concerned about their body type or physique. Physique is difficult to change at any age. Often, what society considers the ideal body type—for example, the Barbie doll body—is impossible to achieve. Most of us will look like one of our parents or a blend of our parents. What is important for children and adolescents to understand is that larger bones and a healthy amount of muscle are good. Physical activity can help our bodies by increasing muscle and bone growth and reducing extra fat. We may even grow a bit taller as a result of being active. There are parts of our shape we cannot change, however. A specific body type neither guarantees success in any area, including sports, nor necessarily prevents us from

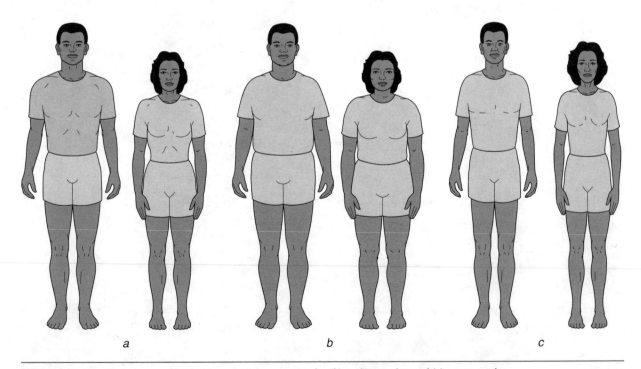

Figure 3.6   The three types of body types are (*a*) mesomorphs, (*b*) endomorphs, and (*c*) ectomorphs.

Reprinted, by permission, from the NSCA, 2000, *Essentials of Strength Training and Conditioning,* 2nd ed., edited by T.R. Baechle and R.W. Earle (Champaign, IL: Human Kinetics), 173.

attaining success. Understanding that bodies are different is important; understanding, too, that one body type is not better than another is essential. Having too much fat or being too thin both increase health risk. Therefore, it is important for children to understand their bodies, including physique. Teachers can help children by accepting as equally valuable each physique and encouraging healthy, active bodies. Further, teachers should never decide which sport or activity is best for a child based on the child's body type. As a teacher, you have the opportunity and the power to influence the way children think and feel about their bodies.

Inherited Compared With Environmental Factors

Height and maturational rate are inherited. Therefore, physical activity has little impact on sexual maturation or stature. One predictor of height is the average of the height of the parents. If both parents are tall and matured later, the child is likely to be tall. Conversely, a child who inherits early maturation from parents of average height is likely to be of average or below-average height. The location of fat on the body is inherited, as demonstrated earlier in the discussion of physique. Some aspects of bone density are inherited, as indicated by the mineral content of bones for different ethnic groups. This means you are less likely to have osteoporosis if you are African American and more likely to have it if you are Caucasian. Variables such as body weight and percent body fat are influenced by the environment. Physical activity does have a positive impact on the skeleton (mineralization and density, robustness), body weight and fat (less), and body composition (more muscle, less fat).

GROWTH AND MOTOR PERFORMANCE

Children age and grow simultaneously; during that time, motor skills change as well. It is difficult to pinpoint the factors influencing changes in motor skill because so many factors are changing at the same time. Is it additional practice, growth, or a combination that explains the improvement in skill? Why is performance of some skills worse in older children? Clearly performance improves—

older boys run faster than younger boys and a girl will jump farther at 10 years of age than she did when she was 6. Performance of motor skills improves with increased age during childhood. Often, performance improves only because the children have grown larger. This point is of particular importance when considering changes that children undergo during a school year: Are the changes attributable to a good physical education program or simply a result of growth? For boys, growth and maturation nearly always result in better motor performance—that is, running faster, jumping higher, and throwing farther. For girls, the picture is a bit different. Girls show steady improvement in motor performance of most skills during childhood, until adolescence. During adolescence, growth and maturation have a negative impact on some aspects of motor performance. For example, running speed, jumping distance, and aerobic capacity decrease after puberty. The decrease is caused largely by an increase in body fat. (Girls who remain lean tend to maintain their performance.) In addition, girls tend to become less active during adolescence. This inactivity can result in larger increases in body fat and a decrease in skill caused by a lack of training and practice; the situation becomes self-perpetuating. The gender differences should be smaller than what is observed because the biological contribution is small (about 10 percent).

Bigger children tend to be stronger than smaller children of the same age. This observation is similar to the improvements in skill noted in children as they grow taller, and heavier children have an advantage when throwing or kicking. However, those same larger children are at a disadvantage for running and jumping. Clearly, growth influences performance, but the impact can be either positive or negative, depending on the skill considered. That physical or biological factors are very important in predicting success in physical activity is a general misconception. The contributions of biology—growth, maturation, and other biological factors—are rather small. In worldclass athletes, the differences in physical factors may be as small as 10 to 20 percent, and biology explains very little of the differences among average people. Thus, we must be careful when interpreting changes in skill (either positive or negative) during growth. Further, we must be careful not to judge skill based on a physical characteristic. For example, allowing children to specialize in a sport or a position within a sport at an early age—especially when the decision is based

Teachers can better understand their wide variety of students when they comprehend some details about children's growth and maturity.

on body type or size—may have a negative impact on lifelong participation (Robertson-Wilson, et al. forthcoming). A child who seems big for his age is likely to be maturing early, which means that child may be smaller relative to others after maturity. There are three reasons why teachers should help children and their parents avoid early specialization: First, children who sample a variety of activities before adolescence are more likely to remain active and also to achieve greater expertise within a specific sport (Robertson-Wilson, et al. forthcoming). Second, there seems to be very little correlation between biological factors and performance in the typical adult (Ransdell and Wells 1999; Thomas and Thomas 1988 and 1999). Third, the success of predicting which children will excel and which activity a child is suited for is very low, and the advantage from early maturation and increase in size is very short in duration.

SUMMARY

Teachers need to understand growth and maturation so they can monitor their students' health and development. Further, understanding growth and maturation allows teachers to plan more effectively by selecting and modifying activities as necessary to accommodate individual needs. Teachers will also understand the problems children face when trying to learn new skills. The challenges that movement presents to children is different than the challenges facing adults, because children are not miniature adults. Information allows teachers to avoid stereotypes and to help children and adolescents understand the normal and natural processes of growth and maturation. Teachers and children need to know the difference between variables that can be changed (e.g., environment) and those that must be accommodated (e.g., genetics). Finally, understanding the processes of growth and maturation will allow teachers to make wise decisions when faced with gender issues. Generally, boys and girls are more alike during childhood than different in terms of growth and maturation.

MASTERY LEARNING ACTIVITIES

1. Develop a profile for grades K, 3, and 5 based on what you have learned about growth and maturation. What would the children in each grade look like? Would they have their front teeth? How tall would they be? What about leg length? Would there be secondary sex characteristics?

2. Observe a group of children. See if you can determine how old they are based on what you learned in this chapter.

3. Measure the weight, stature (standing height), and sitting height of several boys and girls at ages 5, 9, and 13. Average the data and graph the averages. Do your data look the way you expected?

4. Compare the three gymnastics lessons in this chapter. What accommodations are made for the different ages (and sizes) of the children?

5. Review the following concepts. Provide supporting information for each concept by using definitions, examples, and applications.

There are specific techniques for measuring maturation (MA) and growth (anthropometric techniques):

   a. MA and CA are not the same.

   b. MA is biological age and is controlled by genetics. CA is time since birth.

   c. Some techniques for estimating MA are valid for a brief period of time or are retroactive. Others are good for the life span.

   d. Usually MA is of concern at the younger end of CA but is also useful at other times of change (e.g., menopause and old age).

Body proportions change during growth:

   a. Extremities grow relatively fast.

   b. Lengths, breadths, then circumferences increase.

   c. Changes influence performance.

Body composition changes with age and after puberty differs for the genders:

   a. All children gain lbm during childhood.

   b. At puberty, males gain more lbm than females, and the gain in lbm in males is rapid.

   c. At puberty, females gain more fat than males.

Somatotype rating is a specific way of assessing physique so that changes caused by age, diet, exercise, or disease can be traced:

   a. Endomorphy is assessed using the sum of three skinfolds corrected for height.

   b. Mesomorphy is determined with humerus and femur breadths, calf and biceps circumference (corrected for skinfolds), and height.

   c. Ectomorphy is based on ponderal index (mass corrected for height).

   d. Soft tissue (fat and muscle) changes over time because of the effects of exercise, diet, disease, and growth.

   e. Early-maturing males are mesomorphs; early-maturing females are endomorphs.

   f. Late-maturing children are ectomorphs, and athletes are ectomorphs.

REFERENCES

Malina, R.M. 1984. Physical growth and maturation. In *Motor development during childhood and adolescence,* edited by J.R. Thomas, 2–26. Minneapolis, Minn.: Burgess.

Ransdell, L.B., and C.L. Wells. 1999. Sex differences in athletic performance. *Women in Sport and Physical Activity* 8: 55–81.

Thomas, J.R., and K.T. Thomas. 1988. Development of gender differences in physical activity. *Quest* 40: 219–229.

Thomas, K.T., and J.R. Thomas. 1999. What squirrels in the trees predict about expert athletes. *International Journal of Sport Psychology* 30: 221–234.

Robertson-Wilson, J., J. Baker, E. Derbinshyre, and J. Côté. Forthcoming. Childhood Sport Involvement in Active and Inactive Female Adults. *AVANTE.*

RESOURCES

Baxter-Jones, A., P. Helms, N. Maffull, J. Baines-Preece, and M. Preece. 1995. Growth and development of male gymnasts, swimmers, soccer and tennis players: A longitudinal study. *Annals of Human Biology* 22:381–94.

Broekoff, J. 1985. The effects of physical activity on physical growth and development. In *The Academy papers. Effects of physical activity on children,* no. 19, edited by G.A. Stull and H.M. Eckert, 75–87. Champaign, Ill.: Human Kinetics.

Carter, J.E.L. 1980. *The Heath-Carter somatotype method.* San Diego, Calif.: San Diego State University Syllabus Service.

Espenschade, A.S. 1963. Restudy of relationships between physical performances of school children and age, height, and weight. *Research Quarterly* 34:144–53.

Gallahue, D.L., and J.C. Ozmun. 1995. *Understanding motor development,* 3d ed. Madison, Wisc.: Brown & Benchmark.

Nelson, K.R., J.R. Thomas, and J.K. Nelson. 1991. Longitudinal changes in throwing performance. Gender differences. *Research Quarterly for Exercise and Sport* 62:105–108.

Payne, G.V., and L.D. Isaacs. 1998. Human motor development: A lifespan approach. Mountain View, Calif: Mayfield.

Rarick, G.L., and Smoll, F.1967. Stability of growth in strength and motor performance from childhood to adolescence. *Human Biology* 39:295–306.

Scammon, R.E. 1930. The measurement of the body in childhood. In *The Measurement of Man*, edited by J.A. Harris, C.M. Jackson, D.G. Jackson, and R.E. Scammon, 171–215. Minneapolis: University of Minnesota Press.

Tanner, J.M. 1978. *Foetus into man: Physical growth from conception to maturity.* Cambridge, Mass.: Harvard University Press.

Thomas, K.T., J.D. Gallagher, and J.R. Thomas. 2001. Motor development and skill acquisition during childhood and adolescence. In *Handbook of Sport Psychology*, 2d ed., edited by R.N. Singer, H.A. Hausenblas, and C. Janelle, 20–52. New York: Wiley.

LESSON PLANS

The three gymnastics (tumbling) lesson plans at the end of this chapter are designed to accommodate the differences in growth, especially proportion, by age. Gymnastics skills are challenging for younger children who have relatively larger heads and shorter legs and torsos than older children. Notice that the slanted triangle (wedge) mat is used to help younger children master forward rolls. Younger children benefit from practice with activities that are adapted to their smaller bodies. For example, the rope-climbing task allows younger children to practice the movement without having to support body weight while at the same time learning the movement. The wedge mat is used for the backward roll for children in grades 2 and 3; this allows gravity to do part of the work. Children at this age still have relatively short legs and little strength, so gravity makes the task easier. Once they master the mechanics of the backward roll, have them practice the backward roll on a flat mat. As children practice on the balance beam, looking at a stationary spot (not at their feet or the beam) makes balance easier in two ways: First, looking at the stationary spot allows ambient (peripheral) vision to make rapid corrections in balance. Second, keeping the head over the body, rather than in front of the body, maintains equilibrium (balance).

The lessons cover similar skills with adaptations that consider developmental differences in children. The skills allow for progression from level to level (e.g., from grades K and 1 to grades 2 and 3, then to grades 4 and 5). In addition, learning motor skills, children learn about independent practice in lessons using stations. Teachers can and must practice time management during station lessons. Gymnastics is a popular activity with children in elementary school. Gymnastics lessons allow children to learn skills; practice independently; and work on muscle strength, endurance, and flexibility.

LESSON **3.1**

Tumbling Using Triangle Mat

Equipment

- 6–8 mats
- 1 long thick rope (10+ feet long and 1" or more diameter)
- 1 24" high vaulting box (or stack of mats)
- 1 balance beam

- 1 poster or target
- Tape for the poster or target
- 1 wedge mat (or 1 regular mat placed at an angle on another stacked mat)

Warm-Up Activity (5 minutes)

Arrange the children in four groups facing you.

Stretching

Ask the children to do each of the following stretching challenges as you demonstrate and do the activity with the children:

1. *Reach for the sky with both hands, slowly bend at the waist and hips (keeping legs straight but do not lock knees)—and reach for the floor—sweep the dust bunnies with your hands. Repeat several times.*

2. *Place your right hand behind your right shoulder, reaching as far down and back as possible. Put you left hand on your right elbow and push gently. Repeat several times and reverse to stretch the left shoulder.*

3. *Standing with feet shoulder-width apart, rise to toes, slowly return to stand, then bend knees and lower yourself to a partial squat position so that your thighs are parallel to the ground. Return to stand and repeat several times.*

4. *With the arms straight and extended in front of your body, push palms together for the count of 5. Slowly move the arms sideward and then back trying to touch palms behind you. Hold the backmost position for 5 counts. Repeat several times.*

5. *Complete 5 vertical jumps in place.* Challenge the children to jump as high as possible. After you demonstrate and complete 5 jumps, walk around to groups of children asking them to jump and touch your hand—hold your hand at a challenging but reachable point above the child's head.

Skill Development Activities (20 minutes)

Arrange children in four groups, one group at each station.

Stations

Each group will practice at each station for approximately four minutes. Use two minutes to explain what happens at each station and approximately 30 seconds to rotate groups at the end of each four-minute practice time. Arrange the jump-

ing and tumbling stations near each other so that you can supervise both of these.

Rope

The rope is tied to a sturdy object (a door handle works well). The children lie on their backs with their feet in the air pointed toward the ceiling. The object is to pull yourself, head first, from the loose end of the rope toward the secure end of the rope, in a manner similar to climbing a rope. Hint: This works best on the smooth gym floor (i.e., no mat necessary). Cue words: *Reach and pull.*

Jumping

Place the jumping cube or a stack of mats at the joint of two mats placed together lengthwise. One at a time, children will run to the jumping cube and jump or climb to a standing position on top of the cube. Children will jump forward off the cube onto the mat.

Tumbling

Place two mats next to each other. Place the wedge mat on top of one. Children do the log roll on the flat mat and forward rolls on the wedge mat.

Log Roll   Lying on one side with your arms and legs together and stretched out (extended), roll onto your tummy and quickly over onto your other side, continuing rolling over until you reach the other end of the mat. Remind children to go straight and stay on the mat at all times! Cue words: *Stay straight.*

Forward Roll   Begin in a squat with your feet on the tall side of the wedge mat. Your hands are on the wedge mat shoulder-width apart, chin on chest, looking at your tummy. Bend your arms to bring your shoulders closer to the mat, overbalance, roll onto your shoulders, and continue to roll with your legs tucked. Keep your heels close to your bottom and your knees close to your chest, until your feet touch the ground and you are squatting again. The object is to roll down the slant of the wedge mat. Cue words: *Pushing hands.*

Balance Beam

The beam is placed on a mat (or more than one mat). Tape the target or poster to the wall at eye level for the children. Place the beam on a mat so that the target or poster is about 10 feet from one end of the beam. Children should walk, one at a time, the length of the beam while looking at the target or poster. Cue words: *Heads up.*

Concluding Activity (5 minutes)

Keep the children in their four groups at stations.

Obstacle Course

Individual children will rotate through all activities. State the order as Beam to Rope, Rope to Tumbling, Tumbling to Jumping, and so forth. Each child in the group will complete the activity for that station, then she will move to the next station and wait for a turn. This continues until all the children have been to all the stations or time is up.

From *Physical Education Methods for Elementary Teachers, Second Edition,* by Katherine T. Thomas, Amelia M. Lee, and Jerry R. Thomas, 2003, Champaign, IL: Human Kinetics.

LESSON

Stations

Equipment

- 6–8 mats
- 1 wedge mat (or 1 regular mat placed at an angle on another stacked mat)
- 1 long thick rope (10+ feet long and 1" or more diameter)

- 1 36" high vaulting box (or stack of mats)
- 1 balance beam

Warm-Up Activity (5 minutes)

Arrange the children in four groups.

Stretching

All children will count aloud as they do the repetitions for each exercise. Demonstrate each stretch, then have the children do the stretch:

1. *Reach for the sky with both hands, slowly bend at the waist and hips (keeping legs straight but do not lock knees), and reach for the floor—sweep the dust bunnies with your hands. Repeat 10 times.*

2. *Place your right hand behind your right shoulder, reaching as far down and back as possible. Put you left hand on your right elbow and push gently. Repeat five times and reverse to stretch five times for the left shoulder.*

3. *Standing with feet shoulder-width apart, rise to toes, slowly return to stand, then bend knees and lower yourself to a partial squat position so that your thighs are parallel to the ground. Return to stand and repeat 10 times.*

4. *With the arms straight and extended in front of your body, push palms together for the count of five, slowly move the arms sideward and then back trying to touch palms in behind you. Hold the back-most position for five counts. Repeat five times front and back.*

5. *Complete three sets of five vertical jumps in place (jump five times, rest a few seconds, and repeat). Challenge the children to jump as high as possible.*

Skill Development Activities (20 minutes)

Keep the children in four groups, one group at each station.

Stations

Each group will practice at each station for approximately four minutes. Use two minutes to explain what happens at each station and approximately 30 seconds to rotate groups at the end of each four-minute practice time. Arrange the jumping and tumbling stations near each other so that you can supervise both of these.

Rope

The rope is tied to a sturdy object (a door handle works well). The children lie on their backs with their feet in the air pointed toward the ceiling. The

object is to pull yourself, head first, from the loose end of the rope toward the secure end of the rope, in a manner similar to climbing a rope. Repeat going feet first. To make this more challenging, do this on a mat, which creates more resistance. Cue words: *Reach, Pull.*

Jumping

Place the jumping cube or a stack of mats at the joint of two mats placed together lengthwise. One at a time, children will run to the jumping cube and jump to a squat, then rise to standing position on top of the cube. Children will jump forward off the cube onto the mat. Cue words: *Heads up.*

Tumbling

Place two mats next to each other. Children do the forward roll on one mat and backward roll on the wedge mat.

Forward Roll Begin squatting with your hands on the mat shoulder-width apart, chin on chest, looking at your tummy. Bend your arms to bring your shoulders closer to the mat, overbalance, roll onto your shoulder blades, and continue to roll with your legs tucked. Keep your heels close to your bottom and your knees close to your chest until your feet touch the ground and you are squatting again. Cue words: *Shoulder blades.*

Backward Roll Squat (feet on the top end of the wedge mat) with your back to the down slant of the mat, Put your hands on your shoulders with your palms turned upward. Tuck your chin tightly to your chest, looking at your tummy. Lean backward slightly, overbalancing so that your bottom touches the mat. Keep rolling backward until your back touches the mat. Stay tightly tucked in a ball, with chin on chest and knees against chest. Continue rolling so your hands touch the mat (your hands are still on your shoulders). Now push with your hands, and begin to straighten your arms. As your body passes over your head so that your hands are pushing on the mat, you can let your chin leave your chest. Recover by landing on your feet. Young children will often land on their knees, but with practice should learn to land on their feet. Cue words: *Push-up.*

Balance Beam

The beam is placed on a mat (or more than one mat). Children should walk, one at a time, the length of the beam. Encourage children to look forward and not at the beam. Children should walk forward, backward, and forward bending to touch the beam on different turns. Cue words: *Look up.*

Concluding Activity (5 minutes)

Children remain in four groups at the stations.

Obstacle Course

Individual children will rotate through all activities. State the order as Beam to Rope, Rope to Tumbling, Tumbling to Jumping, and so forth. Each child in the group will complete the activity for that station, then he will move to the next station and wait for a turn. This continues until all the children have been to all the stations or time is up.

From *Physical Education Methods for Elementary Teachers, Second Edition*, by Katherine T. Thomas, Amelia M. Lee, and Jerry R. Thomas, 2003, Champaign, IL: Human Kinetics.

Gymnastics

LESSON  **3.3**

Planet "School Name"

Equipment

- 6–8 mats
- 1 climbing rope (or chin-up bar)
- 1 36" high vaulting box (or stack of mats)

- 1 balance beam
- Music

Warm-Up Activity (5 minutes)

Arrange the children in four groups facing you.

Stretching

Demonstrate the first stretch. Have one child in each group lead that stretch for their group. Repeat with the remaining stretches.

1. *Reach for the sky with both hands, slowly bend at the waist and hips (keeping legs straight but do not lock knees), and reach for the floor—sweep the dust bunnies with your hands. Repeat 10 times.*

2. *Place your right hand behind your right shoulder, reaching as far down and back as possible. Put you left hand on your right elbow and push gently. Repeat five times and reverse to stretch five times for the left shoulder.*

3. *Standing with feet shoulder-width apart, rise to toes, slowly return to stand, then bend knees and lower yourself to a partial squat position so that your thighs are parallel to the ground. Return to stand and repeat 10 times.*

4. *With the arms straight and extended in front of your body, push palms together for the count of five. Slowly move the arms sideward and then back trying to touch palms in behind you. Hold the back-most position for five counts. Repeat five times front and back.*

5. *Complete three sets of five vertical jumps in place (jump five times, rest a few seconds, and repeat). Challenge the children to jump as high as possible.*

Skill Development Activities (20 minutes)

Arrange children in four groups, one at each station on the planet.

Planet "School Name"

Each group will practice at each station for approximately four minutes. Use two minutes to explain what happens at each station and approximately 30 seconds to rotate groups at the end of each four-minute practice time. Arrange the jumping and rope-climbing stations near each other so that you can supervise both of these. Play appropriate but popular music; students will rotate when you stop the music.

Rope

Students will climb the vertical rope. Students will hold the bottom of the rope for group members. If you do not have a climbing rope do pull-ups on the pull-up bar, also with group members spotting each other.

Jumping

Place the jumping cube or a stack of mats at the joint of two mats placed together lengthwise. One at a time, children will run to the jumping cube and vault over the cube. The two vaults are the tuck vault and the side vault. For the tuck, place hands shoulder-width apart on the cube, bend legs bringing knees to the chest and between the arms.

For the side vault, place both hands near one end of the cube, jump swinging straight legs over the end of cube opposite from the hands. For both vaults land on the far side of the cube on your feet. Keep the head up by looking forward during the vault. Cue words: *Head up.*

Tumbling

Place two mats next to each other. Children do the forward and backward rolls on one mat and elbow–knee balances on the other mat.

Forward Roll

Begin squatting with your hands shoulder-width apart, chin on chest, looking at your tummy. Bend your arms to bring your shoulders closer to the mat, overbalance, roll onto your shoulders, and continue to roll with your legs tucked. Keep your heel close to your bottom and your knees close to your chest until your feet touch the ground and you are squatting again. Cue word: *Tuck.*

Backward Roll

Squat with your back to the length of the mat, put your hands on your shoulders with your palms turned upward. Tuck your chin tightly to your chest, looking at your tummy. Lean backward slightly, overbalancing so that your bottom touches the mat. Keep rolling backward until your back touches the mat. Stay tightly tucked in a ball, with chin on chest and knees against chest. Continue rolling so your hands touch the mat (your hands are still on your shoulders). Now push with your hands, and begin to straighten your arms. As your body passes over your head so that your hands are pushing on the mat, you can let your chin leave your chest. Recover by landing on your feet. Cue words: *Roll, push, stand.*

Elbow–Knee Balance

Squat; place your hands on the mat, arms inside your legs, and knees touching your elbows. Hold your head up; looking straight ahead helps. Shift your weight from your feet to your hands, and rest your knees on your elbows. The critical point is to maintain balance with only your hands supporting your body weight. Cue words: *Look up.*

Tripod

Begin in a squat with your hands and arms placed on the mat outside your knees and legs. Bend forward until your forehead (at the hairline) touches the mat. Your head will serve as a balance point but will support very little weight. Bend your arms and make your knees touch your elbows. Support most of your body weight with your arms. Stop moving when your knees are resting on your elbows, your head is resting on the mat, and your feet are off the mat. Remember, support most of your weight with your arms. Your head touches the mat but does not support much body weight. Cue words: *Head touching.*

Balance Beam

The beam is placed on a mat (or more than one mat). Beanbags are scattered around on the floor near the beam. Children should walk, one or more at a time, the length of the beam. Children are to pick up as many of the scattered beanbags as possible without falling. If one child falls, all beanbags are returned to the floor and the group starts again to pick up the beanbags.

Concluding Activity (5 minutes)

Join two groups together to form two large groups.

Planet "School Name" Challenge

One of the groups will go to the jumping cube, the other to the balance beam. The object is to get as many group members as possible successfully through the challenge. For the vaulting, all group members must go over the cube using either of the two vaults. For the balance beam, members will walk the beam picking up one beanbag each. Repeat until all beanbags are picked up. If someone steps off, the group starts again. When either group finishes the challenge successfully, the groups reverse stations (so the group on the beam moves to the cube and vice versa) and complete the other challenge.

From *Physical Education Methods for Elementary Teachers, Second Edition,* by Katherine T. Thomas, Amelia M. Lee, and Jerry R. Thomas, 2003, Champaign, IL: Human Kinetics.

LESSON **3.4**

Tumbling

Student Objectives

- Demonstrate the forward roll and the run and take-off.
- Attempt a straddle roll and a heel slap.
- State two important things to remember about the forward roll.
- Practice a variation of the forward roll.

Equipment and Materials

- 1 or more mats (4 ft × 8 ft) per group

Warm-Up Activities

Use grades 4–5 warm-up routine from lesson 7.6, page 163.

Skill-Development Activities (18 to 20 minutes)

Forward Roll

Create small groups, and assign each to a mat.

1. Describe and demonstrate the stunt:

   Bend over and place your hands on the mat shoulder-width apart and, looking at your belly and bending your arms, shift more and more body weight onto your hands as your legs provide less and less support.

As your center of gravity moves forward, your body will overbalance and roll forward, hitting the mat on your shoulder blades. Continue to roll in a curved position.

Bend your legs at the knees and accept weight on your legs as your shoulders leave the mat.

Return to standing with your arms extended overhead.

2. Have the children practice the forward roll.

Straddle Forward Roll

Arrange partners on the mats.

1. Describe and demonstrate the stunt:

   This is actually two consecutive rolls. You start by doing a forward roll then add the straddle part. Beginning in closed standing position with feet together and arms extended overhead, bend, placing your hands on the mat shoulder-width apart.

   Look at your belly, bend your arms, and accept more and more of your body weight onto your hands as your legs decrease support.

   As your center of gravity moves forward, your body will overbalance and roll forward, hitting the mat on the shoulder blades. Continue to roll in a curved position.

   Now this stunt begins to differ from a regular forward roll. Keep your legs straight and spread apart in the straddle position so you land on your legs for the first roll with your feet spread, body bent slightly forward, and arms extended forward.

   Begin the second roll immediately from the straddle position, with your head tucking under and your body moving forward to a shoulder-blade landing.

   Recover to standing with your feet closed, as in the regular forward roll.

   Work with your partner—one partner stands in front of the roller after the roll phase to help him recover. Roller, reach out to your partner and try to shake hands as you come up. This will get your arms and weight forward by moving your center of gravity forward.

2. Have the children practice the straddle forward roll.

Backward Roll

Continue with the same setup, except partners are not necessary.

1. Describe and demonstrate the stunt:

   Begin standing, arms extended overhead (palms up) and your back toward the length of the mat and your chin moving to your chest. Lower your body to a tuck position by bending the knees. Overbalance your body backward to begin the roll, and remain in tuck position as your shoulders and hands contact the mat.

   Push with your hands to lift your body (hips, legs, and torso) over your head. Your head and neck should not support your weight and you should touch the mat as little as possible.

   As your feet touch the mat, straighten your arms until your feet are supporting your weight. Rise to standing with your arms extended overhead.

2. Have the children practice the backward roll.

Straddle Backward Roll

Continue with the same setup.

1. Describe and demonstrate the stunt:

   Begin standing in a straddle balance position, with your back toward the length of the mat.

   Move your hands between your legs as your torso moves forward to lower your body, with your hips moving back and down, until your seat touches the mat.

   Move your hands to your shoulders as in the regular backward roll. Immediately roll your body backward, while your legs remain in the straddle position.

   Recover to the straddle balance position (as shown in figure below).

2. Have the children practice the straddle backward roll.

3. Have the children extend the skill by beginning in closed standing position and rolling to a straddle balance, then rolling again from the straddle balance to a closed standing position (two rolls).

Heel Slap

Continue with the same setup.

1. Describe and demonstrate the stunt:

   The object is to touch your heels with your hands just under your seat, then land on both feet.

   Jump up from both feet, lifting both feet toward your seat while reaching back with your arms.

2. Have the children practice the heel slap.

Run and Take-Off

Continue with the same setup.

1. Describe and demonstrate the stunt:

   Many sports use this movement (e.g., springboard diving).

   Begin with several quick (running) steps leading to a hurdle.

   To hurdle, raise one leg so that your thigh is parallel to (flat as) the ground and your lower leg is at a 90-degree angle to the thigh (like the corner of a square).

   Reach your arms high overhead as your body lifts off the ground. Both your raised arms and lifted thigh help your body gain momentum. Momentum helps you gain height in the hurdle.

   Land from the hurdle on both feet (spread about shoulder-width apart).

   Follow the landing immediately with a jump to full extension.

   This movement can come right before a tumbling stunt or end with a jump.

   Today, I want you to practice finishing with a jump and landing on two feet.

2. Have the children practice the run and take-off.

Needle Scale

Continue with the same setup, except match partners; one partner practices the needle scale while the other helps balance by gently holding the knee of the nonsupporting leg.

1. Describe and demonstrate the stunt:

   The object is to stand on one foot and grasp the ankle of your supporting leg, making your legs move as close to a split position as possible.

   Begin in a scale, balancing on one leg, with your arms to the sides and your other leg extended to the rear.

Bend your torso and grasp the ankle as you lift your nonsupporting leg as high as possible into the air, balance, then recover by reversing the movements.

2. Have the children practice the needle scale.

Concluding Activities (5 minutes)

Splits

Continue with the same setup.

1. Tell the children: *A split is any one of several positions in which the legs are fully extended away from each other.*

2. Describe and demonstrate the straddle split and the regular split.

Straddle Split

Begin in the straddle balance position and end with your legs extended as far apart as possible. If you are very flexible, recover into a regular split. Otherwise, lean forward, taking your weight on your arms and chest, then swinging both legs together to the rear to lie on your front.

Regular Split

Begin with your feet together in a "T" position, where one foot faces front and the other foot is perpendicular to and behind the front foot, with the feet meeting the heel of the front foot to the arch of the rear foot. Slowly slide one foot forward and the other backward, until your legs are fully extended.

   Note: A child may also do regular splits with only one leg moving while the other leg remains stationary. To recover, the child leans forward with the torso over the front leg and swings the back leg around to the side until it is touching the front leg.

Discussion

Arrange the children in a semicircle. Discuss what the children have learned today:

What should you remember about the forward roll? (Head tucked, weight on hands.)

How is the straddle forward roll different from the forward roll? (Legs apart.)

From *Physical Education Methods for Elementary Teachers, Second Edition,* by Katherine T. Thomas, Amelia M. Lee, and Jerry R. Thomas, 2003, Champaign, IL: Human Kinetics. Adapted from *Physical Education for Children: Daily Lesson Plans for Elementary School, Second Edition,* by Katherine T. Thomas, Amelia M. Lee, and Jerry R. Thomas, 2000, Champaign, IL: Human Kinetics.

chapter 4

Motor Performance During Childhood

Madison, age 7

Motor skills develop in an orderly and predictable way, and, with practice, children improve the efficiency and effectiveness of their performance. Teachers can facilitate skill development by adapting the environment so tasks are challenging to the student. At the same time, the student must be allowed to be successful at the task.

Learner Outcomes

The teacher will do the following:

► Define and describe locomotor, nonlocomotor, and manipulative skills.

► Track changes in fundamental skills during childhood.

► List the environmental factors that affect skill performance.

► Identify the skill level of a child on a task and adapt the environment so that the task is challenging and the child finds success.

Glossary Terms

fundamental movement patterns
phylogenetic skills
motor milestones
fundamental skills
locomotor skills
manipulative skills

proficiency barrier
ontogenetic skills
opposition
effect sizes
speed-accuracy trade-off
nonlocomotor skills

Developing the motor skills important within our culture is a complex process that involves both inherent abilities and practice during childhood and adolescence (Thomas 2000). We enter childhood with a variety of skills mastered during infancy; these motor milestones include sitting, standing, and walking. Infants master the skills of locomotion and manipulation so they can function in their environments. Then, general movement patterns, called **fundamental movement patterns,** such as throwing, catching, running, and jumping, are learned. Finally, specific sport skills are ac-

quired, such as throwing a baseball and striking a tennis ball. One must understand how movements develop in order to influence those skills. Further, one must understand the characteristics of the movements to know what aspects of the movement can be changed to increase the efficiency and effectiveness of the movement. Motor skill assessment can be used similarly to maturational age (MA) to estimate developmental age, which, like MA, is not always the same as chronological age (CA).

Children, and adults, are more likely to participate in sports, exercise, and physical activity when they are skilled (Thomas 2000). Enjoyment and success are closely linked and are related to higher skill levels. Therefore, motor skills and skilled movement should be viewed as a prerequisite to a physically active lifestyle. Fitness and skill are related as well. Adequate levels of physical fitness are necessary for successful participation in sport activities; otherwise, participants become fatigued before the activity is completed. At the same time, participation in vigorous sports promotes physical fitness as the person breathes hard and sweats. Finally, when a person has very low skill, the level of participation may be inadequate to result in health benefits.

Every teacher, regardless of grade or discipline that she teaches, should understand how motor skills develop and what is normal at each age. There are four reasons why teachers should acquire this knowledge:

1. Teachers should monitor motor skills; unusual deviations should be referred to the parents, principal, or nurse for further evaluation.

2. Teachers should base movement experiences for children on the normal sequential development of motor skills.

3. Teachers need to be able to differentiate between factors that are a result of practice and those that emerge without practice.

4. Motor skills, especially sport skills, are important in our culture. Thus, an understanding of motor skills is part of being an educated person.

REFLEXES AND REACTIONS

Reflexes and reactions are the earliest movements observed in humans; these movements do not disappear with age, however. Instead, more complex voluntary movements often replace the reflexes and reactions observed as the primary movements of infancy. The primitive reflexes of infancy are simple motor responses to a stimulus. These are followed by reactions that are responses to changes in the movement environment; for example, when we lose our balance, our arms move to "catch" us before we fall. Reflexes and reactions are observed most often during the first two years of life. As voluntary movements become more frequent, reflexes and reactions are less frequently observed. Sometimes reflexes and reactions can be observed to varying degrees in children and adults. Most of the time we see reflexes under a specific environmental circumstance; one example is the Moro (or startle) reflex, evident in most of us when something unexpected happens. When startled, the individual inhales and exhales (often making a loud sound, even yelling), opens and closes the hands (which may cause dropping of objects), and flails the arms in the Moro reflex. However, even when startled, adults often manage to override part of the reflex. If we could not do this, we would drop whatever we were holding in our hands every time we were startled because part of the reflex is the opening and closing of the hands. Thus, when we are startled and do not drop the cup of coffee in our hand, we have successfully suppressed the reflex. When we drop the cup of coffee, however, we have failed to suppress the reflex. When reflexes dominate movement and persist past the age at which the reflex should be suppressed, there is cause for concern. Often, this is a result of a neurological problem.

Reactions are movements that are neurologically linked to environmental stimuli. Generally, reactions help us to control our bodies without being aware of the reaction. For example, when we begin to lose our balance, reactions automatically make small, rapid corrections to maintain a stable body position. Reactions do not have to be learned or practiced. Reflexes and reactions are considered a base or building block for other skills for two reasons. First, reflexes and reactions appear first; second, these movements may prepare the muscles and nervous system for the voluntary movements that emerge later (figure 4.1).

Rudimentary Movements

Phylogenetic skills are movements that are observed in all individuals in a group. The rudimentary movements can be observed during the first year of life (infancy) and are sometimes called **motor milestones.** That is because these movements are important markers of child development, including sitting, standing, and walking. Children who do not demonstrate motor milestones during infancy are developmentally delayed. Long delays may be symptoms of serious developmental disorders. The typical ages for attaining the motor milestones are presented in figure 4.2.

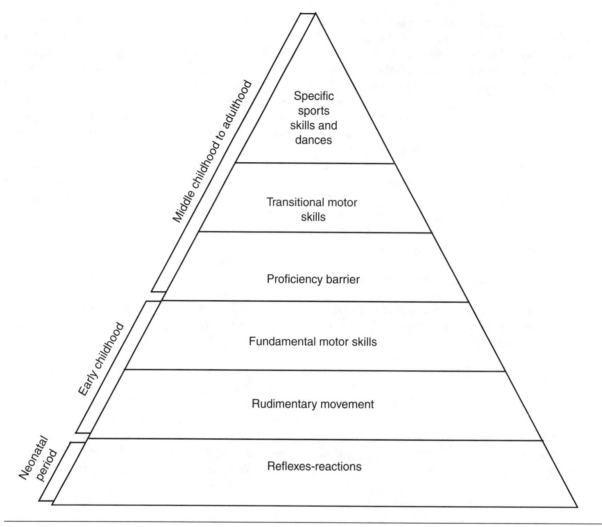

Specific sports skills and dances

Transitional motor skills

Proficiency barrier

Fundamental motor skills

Rudimentary movement

Reflexes-reactions

Middle childhood to adulthood

Early childhood

Neonatal period

Figure 4.1 Developmental motor skill acquisition.

From J.R. Thomas, 1984, *Motor development during childhood and adolescence* (Minneapolis, MN: Burgess). Reprinted by permission of Jerry Thomas.

Nature Versus Nurture

You have probably read about at least one of the three classic studies that examined nature and nurture in the development of motor skills. The studies were McGraw's study of Johnny and Jimmy (1935), Dennis' study of Del and Rey (1935), and Dennis and Dennis' study of the Hopi Indian babies (1940). Johnny and Jimmy, twins, were compared on skills such as roller-skating, tricycle riding, and climbing slanted boards. The purpose was to investigate the influence of early training on motor skill acquisition. One twin lived a "normal" life; the other was trained at an early age to perform the motor tasks that would normally be learned weeks or months later. The results showed the following:

1. There was a short-term benefit to the intervention—the trained twin did perform the skills earlier than the untrained twin or other children.

2. There were no long-term benefits to early training—the untrained twin and other children performed the skill as well as the trained twin did, and the untrained twin caught up at the time the other children naturally completed the skill.

3. Skill acquisition was easier and took fewer trials when it was learned at the typical age.

4. Infants and young children can learn and benefit from early training (McGraw 1935, Roberton 1984).

Figure 4.2 Motor milestones.

From Changing motor patterns during childhood, 1984. In *Motor development during childhood and adolescence,* edited by J.R. Thomas (Minneapolis, MN: Burgess), 54. Reprinted by permission of Jerry Thomas.

Was the cost of the early intervention worth the benefits? The trained twin often cried and was frustrated when practicing; however, he was able to perform the task at an earlier age. Because there were no long-term benefits, the answer comes down to one question: Is it important for a child to perform the skill a few weeks before the skill would normally be performed? Under normal circumstances, children demonstrate skills in the same order, gradually improving the quality of the performance and mastering increasingly difficult versions of the skill. It is possible, but difficult, to force children to do many skills earlier than their developmental readiness allows. Even when we can push earlier performance of skills, the benefits are often small and the costs great. It is more important for children to have the opportunity to practice age-appropriate skills.

Del and Rey, female twins, participated in a deprivation study focusing on reaching and grasping and sitting and standing (Dennis 1935). The opportunity and motivation to do the skills were removed by eliminating toys, visual models, and encouragement. As soon as the majority of a group of girls the same age performed the skill, Del and Rey were given the opportunity to try it. The twins were able to successfully complete each task very quickly. For example, one of the twins reached for and grasped a brass ring within the first few tries! The results of this study indicate that practice did not influence the onset of these skills; as soon as there was opportunity and incentive, the girls performed the skills.

The Hopi Indians have a tradition of keeping infants on a cradle board (Dennis and Dennis 1940). The babies stay on the board for most of their first year. The babies are bound to the board with cloth and removed for brief periods to change swaddling and for cleaning. At the time of this study (in the 1930s), some Hopi Indians lived in the traditional villages, whereas others lived in modern villages. The Hopi living in the modern villages did not use the cradle boards. The results indicated that both modern and traditional Hopi babies walked about three months later than White babies did, but there was no influence from the cradle board. In other words, environment had little impact on walking, but there are genetic influences on phylogenetic skills such as walking.

When these studies are considered together, we can learn several things:

1. Some skills are influenced by genetics—these are phylogenetic skills—and environment has little impact. This supports what we already learned about maturation in chapter 2.

2. Phylogenetic skills develop without practice and when given even modest opportunity.

3. Learned (ontogenetic) skills are susceptible to training at an earlier than normal age; however, the training is likely to produce short-term benefits and frustration for the child.

FUNDAMENTAL MOTOR SKILLS

Phylogenetic skills also include some of the fundamental skills, both locomotor and manipulative. **Fundamental skills** (Haubenstricker and Seefeldt 1986) are general patterns of these skills that emerge and are refined during early childhood. **Locomotor skills** are movements that take us from one place to another; these include running, jumping, and hopping. **Manipulative skills** are movements used to interact with an object, such as object projection (kicking, striking, throwing) and object interception (catching). The normal evolution of these skills is orderly and predictable, which helps teachers because once a teacher can identify a child's performance level, she will know what should happen next. The rubrics presented in tables 4.1 and 4.2 provide a summary of the changes in these skills. The optimal performance for children is shown in the column labeled "most effective." Children move from "rudimentary" to "most effective" with age and practice, and teachers can facilitate this journey by planning appropriate practice, goal setting, and corrective feedback.

The rubrics are based on intratask sequences, which describe each movement by component (e.g., body part) and level (e.g., increase in effectiveness). The manipulative and locomotor skills observed in children change with growth, practice, and development. The normal progression from an inefficient and ineffective skill to an efficient and effective skill charts a course for elementary physical education. We can observe a child, determine her present level of performance, and predict what should occur next in the skill. Instruction can increase consistency at the current level and guide the student to the next level of performance because the rubrics serve as maps for instruction, feedback, and evaluation. Another way to consider skill development is the intertask sequence. Rather than follow the same skill from ineffective to effective, the intertask sequence looks across skills. This approach is more familiar and is captured in the saying "You have to walk before you can run."

Intertask sequences, like intratask sequences, are an orderly and predictable progression. For example, locomotor skills develop in a predetermined order: A child learns to crawl (abdomen on the surface), creep (on all fours), walk, run, leap, jump, gallop, hop, and skip. Within each task, form changes considerably with practice and growth and as variations are added. For example, a child can gallop forward, then she learns to gallop sideward (which is actually sliding). When a child is asked to perform a skill that has not been learned, he will simply substitute a different skill that he has mastered. For example, when asked to skip, the child will substitute a gallop if she cannot skip. By observing, we can learn a great deal about the child's developmental level.

When children learn initial motor skills, it sets the framework for them to handle more complex skills as they grow older.

Table 4.1   Locomotor Skills Rubric

	Most effective	Improving	Needs Improvement	Rudimentary
Walking	• Arms swing in opposition, proportional to step size • Steps on the midline, heel strike • Trunk rotates with step • Head within 2" of same plane	• Hands and arms stationary, at side (or) • Arms extend with step on same side • Longer strides, narrower steps	• Hands and arms held waist high and stationary • Steps may be ataxic (too much knee flexion)	• Hands and arms held high and stationary • Short, wide steps, flat-footed • No trunk rotation
Running	• Foot contact on ball of foot or heel–toe, support leg at full extension, leg swings 180° • Humerus drives independent of spine, elbow at 90°, opposition	• Foot and knee cross midline on forward swing, leg swings 90° or less • Spine rotates arms	• Arms flailing, locked or bent	• Flat-footed, foot swings outside legs • Arms in at shoulder or waist and stationary
Jumping	**Take-off** • Symmetrical and full extension of legs and arms • Neck aligned **Flight and landing:** • Hips and knees flex separately • Arms lower and reach forward for landing	**Take-off** • Neck flexed • Arms not extended **Flight and landing:** • Hips and knees flex during flight, extending for landing • Trunk flexes 30° for flight, flexes more for landing • Arms shoulder high for flight, or windmill	**Take-off** • Symmetrical, but not extended • Trunk leans less than 30°, neck aligned • Shoulders retract, winging **Flight and landing:** • Asymmetrical legs and 1-foot landing • Trunk hyperextends and flexes for landing • Arms wing for flight and parachute for landing	**Take-off** • One-foot asymmetrical take-off • Trunk forward 30° and neck hyperextended • Arms in opposition or stationary **Flight and landing:** • Asymmetrical, one-foot landing • Trunk 30° • Arm opposition
Hopping	• Swing leg leads projection • Weight transferred smoothly from foot to ball for take-off • Arm opposition	• Swing leg pumps but is in front of body • Projected take-off for several steps • Arms assist from front of body position or • Arms in semi-opposition	• Swing leg inactive in front • Body leans forward • Arms reactive and winging	• Swing leg high in front or to side • Momentary flight from pulling motion for 1-2 steps • Arms stationary

Table 4.2 Manipulative Skills Rubric

	Most effective	Still Improving	Improving	Needs Improvement	Rudimentary
Throwing	Delayed forearm lag Hand going back while hips move forward Differentiated trunk rotation (hips and shoulder move separately) Step with opposition—half body length (vigorous)	Downward and circular back swing Forearm lags behind ball Step with opposite foot	Upward backspin to ear Elbow may point skyward Hand leads elbow and arm Blocked trunk rotation (hips and shoulders move together) Step with same foot as throw	Dartboard—anterior–posterior motion Body stationary or sways No step	Pushing motion—shot put Body stationary
Catching	Correct hand position depending on line of flight Moves to ball Absorbs shock	Can change position to catch ball not thrown directly to hands	Arms at side before catch Control with hands	Active—arms move before contact Attempt to catch but will trap	Passive—ball strikes hand or arm before movement begins Trapping—ball is captured against chest
Kicking	May take a step first Arms may lift body off ground at impact		Forward lean in preparation Arm and leg opposition Follow-through	Active—leg moves before ball hits (ball often rolls under leg)	Passive—ball strikes foot before movement begins Pushing—the leg and foot push ball No backspin
Striking	Spiral motion of body Wrists uncock at impact Body weight		Swing does not cross midline Body position perpendicular to line of flight	Active—moves hand, arm, or object before ball hits Anterior–posterior motion Stands facing line	Passive—ball strikes hand or arm before movement begins Pushing—the hand or arm pushes ball No backspin

Proficiency Barrier and Transitional Skills

Fundamental skills begin to develop in virtually all children (Haubenstricker and Seefeldt 1986); with experience, children master these skills. Mastery means that the child can execute the skill correctly without having to think about the movements. Practice and instruction (especially feedback) facilitate the mastery of these skills. The **proficiency barrier** is an explanation for children not mastering the fundamental skills. The barrier is usually a result of too little practice and ineffective instruction. Children who do not break through the barrier find it difficult or impossible to move on to transitional and sport skills. Transitional skills are those activities that help children make the leap from fundamental skills to sport, dance, gymnastics, and exercise applications. Transitional skills focus on combining the fundamental patterns in unique and demanding ways to create new movements, such as jumping rope.

Specific Sport Skills

Specific sport skills are learned and mastered with a great deal of practice (French and McPherson 1999). These are called **ontogenetic skills**—learned skills that vary by cultural and peer group. In-line skating and snow skiing are two examples of skills that some people do and others do not. Many dances are good examples of the peer influence observed in ontogenetic skills. For example, dances that were popular with your great-grandparents (the Lindy), grandparents (the jitterbug), and parents (the twist) seemed old-fashioned to each new generation, whereas dances popular with you and your friends are probably labeled passing fads by previous generations.

Reflexes, reactions, motor milestones, and fundamental motor skills are most frequently evaluated by the time of onset. These become markers of development based on the age at which a child completes the skill. Developmental age (similar to MA) is sometimes assessed using these motor skills. Fundamental motor skills are also assessed using process or qualitative instruments such as the rubrics. Skill efficiency is the measurement. Other ways to assess motor skills are by the outcome (or product measurements) such as time, distance, and accuracy and by observing the student using the skill in a real-world setting such as a game or dance.

Sport, dance, and gymnastics require that we combine skills, often in novel ways and often quickly. During middle childhood these skills become the focus of physical education (Thomas and Thomas 1999). The taxonomy of psychomotor and cognitive domains (table 4.3), which is similar to Bloom's taxonomy of cognitive performance, provides a way of thinking about how motor skill progresses from the most basic level of recognizing or naming a skill to the highest level of evaluating skill. Teachers are expected to evaluate motor skill and therefore must have mastered many aspects of the psychomotor domain.

Benjamin Bloom (1956) brought the notion of mastery learning to the United States. He also identified six levels of cognition that recognized the different demands and understanding of cognitive tasks. The simplest level is knowledge that represents definitions and memorization; the next level is comprehension that demonstrates understanding, such as actions and providing examples. Application is the next level; this takes place when information can be used, for example, in calculating an answer. The next two levels are analysis and synthesis—breaking apart knowledge and using it in a new way. The highest level is evaluation—making a judgment. Bloom suggests that mastering all levels of the taxonomy leads to wisdom. Bloom's taxonomy has been examined, refined, and criticized; yet it is still the basis for research and thinking. For example, cognitive assessment is based on the level of the question, using Bloom's taxonomy.

Locomotor Skills

As children grow and age, performance of motor skills improves. Part of the improvement is caused by increases in size; another part is attributable to increased efficiency of the movement. The rubrics summarize the changes in efficiency. This section will examine the locomotor skills in greater depth and will cover the changes in motor outcome (e.g., speed and distance).

Walking and Running

The major difference between walking and running is the nonsupport (flight) phase that defines running. In walking, the pattern is right foot, both feet, left foot, both feet, and right foot. At least one foot is always on the ground, and part of the time both feet are in contact. In a mature walk, the head remains in the same plane, deviating no more than two inches in any direction (up to down, front to back, side to side). The heel touches the ground first, followed by the ball of the foot; then the push-off from the ground for the next step is from the toes. The arms are relaxed at the sides of the body, moving in opposition to the legs. **Opposition** means that as the right arm goes forward, the left arm goes back. So, as the step is taken on the left foot, the right arm swings forward. The arm opposition should be proportional to the size of the step. One

final characteristic is that the step should touch the ground on an imaginary line that runs through the middle of the body from front to back.

In running, the pattern used is right foot, (air), left foot, (air), and right foot. Running speed increases during childhood because the stride length increases (figure 4.3). The stride increases as the legs grow longer and stronger and as the pattern becomes more efficient. As the child progresses, she takes longer steps or strides and stays in the air longer. When a young child is asked to run faster, he will generally take quicker steps—often in place. Rather than say, "Run faster," teach-

Table 4.3   Taxonomy of Psychomotor and Cognitive Domains

Psychomotor	Action descriptors	Cognitive	Action descriptors
Perceiving	Name, identify	Knowledge	Define, list, state
Patterning	Demonstrate	Comprehension	Give example, compare
Adapting	Modify	Application	Demonstrate, calculate
Refining	Transfer, use in game	Analysis	Distinguish, test, examine
Varying	Combine, create	Synthesis	Propose, design, construct
Valuing	Judge, correct	Evaluation	Judge, predict, choose

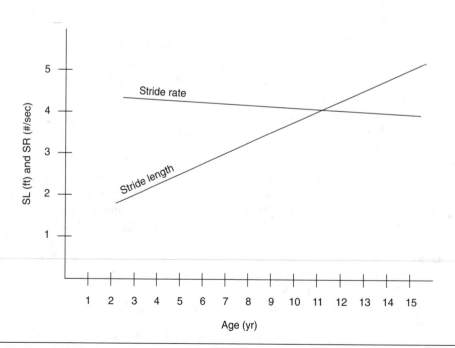

Figure 4.3   Stride rate and stride length during childhood.

From M.A. Roberton, 1984, Changing motor patterns during childhood. In *Motor development during childhood and adolescence,* edited by J.R. Thomas (Minneapolis, MN: Burgess), 62. Reprinted by permission of M.A. Roberton.

ers should say, "Take bigger steps." The fastest runners use their arms to pull them forward. The arms move in opposition, with the upper arm (humerus) driving forward forcefully. In young children, the arms may be stationary or may flail in no particular pattern. As skill increases, the arms begin to rotate in opposition, but this movement is generated by a twisting of the spine rather than by conscious movement of the humerus. Girls demonstrate the mature running form described in the rubric at a slightly earlier age than boys, with most children demonstrating a mature run by seven years of age. The following problems in running should be identified by teachers for remediation: arms swinging too much or too little, crossing the midline of the body, or flailing; feet toeing in or out or flat-footed steps; or trunk leaning too far forward and twisting.

The average running speed for boys and girls is nearly the same during elementary school (figure 4.4; Thomas and French 1985). At puberty, the boys continue to increase running speed, whereas girls' running speed tends to level off or decrease slightly. Another way to compare boys and girls is to examine effect sizes. **Effect sizes** are calculated by dividing the difference between

two means (e.g., boys' running speed minus girls' running speed) by the standard deviation of the means. If the answer is zero or close to zero, the effect size suggests that the two groups are not different. An effect size of .5 is moderate, and .8 is large. Looking at an effect size is advantageous because the results of many studies can be combined, providing a more accurate picture of the true differences. The effect sizes for the dash and shuttle run indicate that from 4 to 12 years of age the differences favoring boys are small to moderate (figure 4.5). At puberty, the differences increase substantially. The differences during the elementary years are attributed to different treatment of girls and boys (Thomas and French 1985; Nelson, Thomas, and Nelson 1991). For example, boys have greater opportunity, encouragement, and expectations for achievement in sports and physical education than do girls. Considering the factors that influence running speed (e.g., leg length), there is no reason to expect any differences during elementary school. Therefore, it is critical that teachers provide equal opportunity for, have similar expectations of, and encourage boys and girls equally.

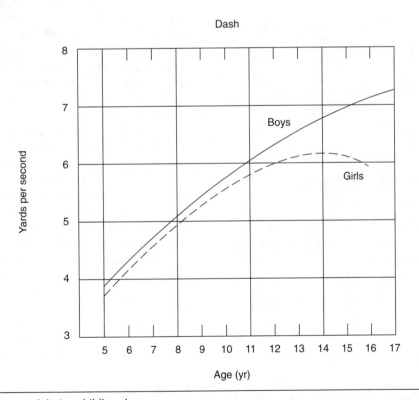

Figure 4.4 Running speed during childhood.

From Changing motor patterns during childhood, 1984. In *Motor development during childhood and adolescence,* edited by J.R. Thomas (Minneapolis, MN: Burgess), 61. Reprinted by permission of Jerry Thomas.

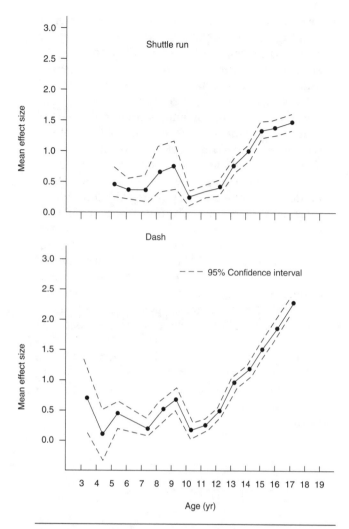

Figure 4.5   Effect sizes for dash and shuttle run.

Adapted, by permission, from J.R. Thomas and K.E. French, "Gender differences in motor performance: A meta analysis," *Psychological Bulletin* 98: 260-282. Copyright © 1985 by the American Psychological Association.

Jumping, Hopping, Galloping, Sliding, and Skipping

Jumping has several forms, each of which has intratask sequences of development. The intertask sequence for jumping begins with a step down and progresses as follows (Wickstrom 1983):

1. Jump down from one foot, landing on the other.
2. Jump up from two feet, landing on two feet.
3. Jump down from one foot, landing on two feet.
4. Jump down from two feet, landing on two feet.
5. Run and jump forward from on one foot; land on the other (leaping).
6. Jump forward from two feet; land on two feet (standing long jump).
7. Run and jump forward from one foot; land on two feet (running long jump).
8. Jump over an object from two feet; land on two feet.
9. Jump from one foot to same foot rhythmically (hopping).

As you can see, hopping and leaping are variations of jumping. By 10 years of age, approximately 60 percent of the boys and girls demonstrate a mature standing long jump pattern. Typical problems teachers should identify for the long jump include a poor initial crouch, failure to use the arms or to extend the body, and poor balance at landing. Boys and girls from 5 to 10 years of age jump forward on two feet (standing long jump) about as far as they are tall. The differences between boys and girls are similar to those observed for running.

Hopping is mastered between 7 and 8 years of age by 60 percent of the children (Haubenstricker and Seefeldt 1986). Early hopping is characterized by children jumping forward on both feet or loss of balance as they try to hop. Young children will hold the nonsupport leg to the front and actually look at the foot. They are probably making sure that the foot is off the ground. Several problems may persist, including flat-footed hopping; too much arm movement; failure to maintain balance; inability to hop equally well on both feet; and lack of a smooth, rhythmic movement. Girls often hop greater distances and on either foot at earlier ages than boys. However, by age 9 there are no longer gender differences.

Galloping is most easily cued in young children by saying "Move like a horse." Immediately, children will step forward on one foot, draw the other foot close, and continue this pattern with the same foot leading. Galloping evolves into sliding. Children generally master one foot leading before the other but should be able to do either foot effectively during early elementary school.

Skipping is a combination of hopping and walking; the pattern is step-hop, step-hop. Most children can skip proficiently by age seven; however, some children learn to skip during the preschool years. Gender and age differences are related to experience—and primarily to practice. Skipping should be a smooth, rhythmic movement.

Climbing

Climbing up is accomplished before climbing down. This is likely because going up, you are not

Concepts Into Practice

A teacher asks her students to skip across the gym floor. Most of the second graders can perform this skill, but one student is galloping. She sees the difference in the movement pattern because in galloping the same leg is always in the front, while in skipping legs alternate moving forward. What she does not know is why the student is galloping instead of skipping. Consider each of the following possible reasons the student is galloping:

- ►He cannot skip.
- ►He doesn't know the difference between skipping and galloping.
- ►He is trying to gain the teacher's attention by doing the wrong skill.
- ►He is testing to see if the teacher cares whether the skills are done correctly.

Regardless of the reason, the teacher must address this with the student. Why?

Manipulative skills are movements used to interact with an object, such as throwing.

aware of the height because you are focused on the goal at the top. Climbing down, we look at the goal, which makes us more aware of the height. This awareness of height also makes us aware of the possibility of falling! So children, like kittens who get stranded in trees, sometime have more difficulty climbing down than they did climbing up. They first climb up or down in a creeping (on all fours) position. This is followed by climbing in a standing position but while "marking time," which means children lead with the same foot for every step. Finally, children climb using alternate feet. Children will often mark time going up and creep back down or step alternately going up and mark time going down. The pattern a child uses gives insight into their confidence as well as their skill level.

Manipulative Skills

Most sports require interaction with objects. The pyramid of skills suggests that the fundamental skills of catching, kicking, striking, and throwing become more refined and specific as these are applied in various sports. During childhood, games require the use of these skills. Therefore, children who have poor skills often have less opportunity to interact with their peers. Manipulative skills are important during childhood and adolescence.

Catching

Catching requires prediction, anticipation, and coordination; however, most children master catching an 8.5-inch ball by the time they are in third grade. This means that the children demonstrate efficient form and catch the ball most of the time. The easiest catch is a ball thrown in an arc that approaches the child's chest at a 45-degree angle. In this scenario, the ball, ideally 8.5 inches in diameter, should be tossed from 10 to 15 feet away. By fifth grade, children are able to consistently catch a tennis ball under similar conditions. Boys and girls are similar in skill level when catching. Large differences are observed between children who have practiced and those who have not in catching balls thrown with force, line drives, and ground balls. These differences tend to be interpreted as gender differences because boys have traditionally had more practice.

Striking and Kicking

Striking and kicking are similar in their intratask sequences and performance curves (Roberton 1984). Boys demonstrate mature patterns at seven years, about a year and a half before girls. Boys kick farther and with 40 percent more velocity than girls during elementary school. Both patterns begin as passive reactions; that is, the ball touches the child before any attempt at movement occurs. Younger children also involve as few body parts as possible in kicking and striking; with age and practice, more body parts are incorporated into the pattern. This generates more force and greater velocity and distance.

Throwing

The overhand throwing motion is used in many sports (e.g., with the javelin, the tennis serve, the football pass, and baseball pitching). Other methods of projecting the ball include rolling and tossing; however, when the word throw is used, over-arm throwing is usually meant. Throwing is, perhaps, the most interesting skill because it is important and because the gender differences are larger and appear earlier than any other skills (figure 4.6). Most of you have heard the phrase "throws like a girl," and you know what this means. The throw is a slow, weak lower-arm motion accompanied by a short step on the same foot as the throwing hand (Yan, Payne, and Thomas 2000). The arm motion often looks like a dart throw. Contrast this to the typical throw for a boy, which is vigorous—the entire body coils backward; as a large step is

taken forward, the hips rotate forward, followed by the shoulder, then upper arm, and finally the lower arm and hand. The throw ends with the body leaning forward over the stepping leg.

Several explanations for the difference include evolution, sociocultural factors, and the emergence of gender-specific forms of throwing (Thomas and Marzke 1992). One theory suggests that although evolution favored males who could throw effectively, this trait did not influence the evolution of women. Another theory suggests that men develop one throwing pattern and women a different pattern, and they therefore develop different skills. Finally, a third theory suggests that the sociocultural importance of throwing well for males creates an atmosphere in which girls who throw poorly are allowed to continue throwing poorly and boys who throw poorly are trained until they throw well. The answer may well be a combination of the three theories. The fact is that sizable differences between males and females exist, and training reduces those differences but does not eliminate them (Thomas, Michael, and Gallagher 1994; Thomas 2000).

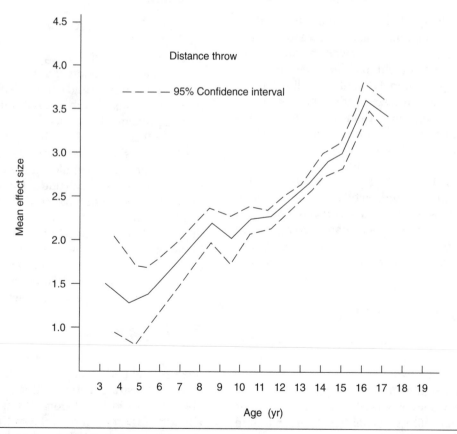

Figure 4.6   Effect size for overarm throwing.

Adapted, by permission, from J.R. Thomas and K.E. French, "Gender differences in motor performance: A meta analysis," *Psychological Bulletin* 98: 260-282. Copyright © 1985 by the American Psychological Association.

All children should be expected to throw with an efficient pattern. As children practice, encourage them to take a large step, throwing with force. Do not worry about accuracy until a mature pattern is well established—that is, the child consistently demonstrates a mature throwing pattern. For most boys this occurs at around five years of age; for most girls it occurs around age eight (Haubenstricker and Seefeldt 1986).

Using a batting tee is an example of modifying task demands of striking to fit the skill level of the participants.

© Human Kinetics.

Speed-Accuracy Trade-Off

One of the most robust phenomena in movement science is the **speed-accuracy trade-off.** This means that as the demand for accuracy increases, the speed of movement decreases. In tasks in which force (or distance) is important, such as throwing, demanding accuracy will increase movement time and therefore reduce force. Generally, it is better to practice forceful or fast movements first, then add accuracy gradually. For teachers, this means students should practice without a target. Children will switch from an overhand throw to tossing underhand when accuracy demands are increased. Practicing tossing will not develop overhand throwing skill.

The speed-accuracy trade-off applies to many skills (e.g., kicking and hitting); as the demand for speed increases, accuracy decreases because of

errors (Yan, Thomas, and Stelmach 2002). In skills that are dangerous (e.g., in climbing), reducing speed usually makes the skill safer because errors are reduced. Teachers will want to consider the speed-accuracy trade-off as they plan lessons and provide instruction.

Other Groups of Motor Skills

Numerous techniques for classifying motor skills have been used; thus far, we have covered phylogenetic and ontogenetic (e.g., classifying by inherent or learned skills) as well as locomotor and manipulative skills. Another group encompasses virtually all other skills—these are **nonlocomotor skills.** Balancing, stretching, and bending are nonlocomotor skills. In this chapter, manipulative skills were divided into object reception and object projection tasks. By adding body projection (locomotor) and body stability (nonlocomotor) categories, virtually all basic movements will have been included (table 4.4). Many terms mean the same thing. The purpose of using the terms is simply to be able to consider groups of skills in a logical way. As we develop curriculum, one technique is to cover all of the categories in a classification system to ensure that the curriculum is comprehensive.

MOTOR ABILITIES UNDERLYING PERFORMANCE

Some children will find it easier to acquire and perform certain skills than other children will. As with any other task (e.g., reading, mathematics, and language), inherited abilities that underlie performance vary from child to child. Abilities such as balance and speed will influence skill acquisition and sometimes performance. The amount of influence depends on the importance of the ability to the task (Thomas 2000). For example, in the 100-meter dash, speed is critical. However, in dancing the waltz, speed is not a critical component. In sports, where strategy is important (e.g., where there is an offense and defense), underlying abilities did not predict skill level. Reaction time is often cited as a critical component of the abilities of expert athletes, yet reaction time may not matter as much as other factors in most sport settings. For example, in a

Table 4.4   Classifying Skills

These skills represent the broad base of movements children should master in early elementary school that will allow them to perform more advanced sport, dance, and gymnastics skills.

Locomotor skills	Manipulative skills	Nonlocomotor skills
Walking	Throwing	Standing
Running	Catching	Bending
Jumping	Kicking	Stretching
Hoppping	Striking	Curling
Galloping		Wiggling
Sliding		Swaying
Skipping		

swimming race that lasts 60 seconds from start to finish, the difference between the fastest and slowest reaction time would account for less than one-fifth of a second! The majority of the time is spent on strokes, which are learned through practice. So, the advantage gained by having a fast reaction time in a swimming race is very small—so small that it probably makes no difference in the outcome to the typical person, even the typical athlete. However, this could make the difference between breaking a world record and not breaking it.

Some sports or events are more related to underlying abilities than others. For example, the balance beam logically demands good balance. Other important attributes for success on the beam include strength and flexibility. So, simply having good balance will not guarantee success. Underlying abilities are complicated to measure, usually requiring more than one test and often yielding surprising results. The average effect sizes for several tests of balance (figure 4.7) indicate that boys and girls have similar balance during childhood, but, at several ages, small differences favor the boys. At adolescence, the differences increase—still favoring the boys! This is contrary to popular opinion, which is that girls have better balance. Why? Girls may perform better on some balance tasks and girls were better at balance at ages three and four years; however, when balance is inverted (e.g., headstand, handstand), boys' strength and endurance are an advantage. (Thomas and French 1985). So, even on a task that

seems as simple as balance, the answer is complex. Remember two important things when considering gender differences in underlying abilities: First, underlying abilities in the normal range will probably not hinder performance and better-than-average abilities provide a very small advantage—and then primarily only during early skill learning or at the worldclass level. Second, stereotypes are often wrong and always limit someone's opportunities. In developing skilled movements, underlying abilities are not nearly as important as opportunity, encouragement, and practice.

MODIFYING TASK DEMANDS

Teachers can modify the same task in many ways to meet the individual needs of students. For example, adding a target or changing the size of a ball makes a task more or less difficult. Some motor skills are carried out when we decide to initiate the skill; for example, in golf the player swings at the ball when she is ready. Tennis is different than golf because once the ball is in play, the player must respond when the ball is hit. Golf is a self-paced task because the golfer establishes the timing; tennis volleying is an externally paced task because the player does not decide when to hit the ball. Certain tasks, such as bowling, change very little from time to time. In bowling, the lanes

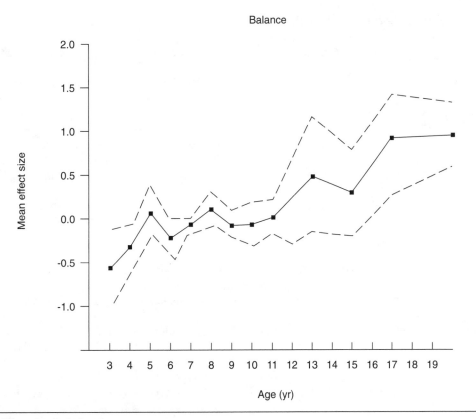

Figure 4.7 Effect size for balance.

Adapted, by permission, from J.R. Thomas and K.E. French, "Gender differences in motor performance: A meta analysis," *Psychological Bulletin* 98: 260-282. Copyright © 1985 by the American Psychological Association.

and other conditions remain constant, especially when compared with a sport like football. In football, the object is to change the conditions (e.g., the predictability of the offense or defense) as often as possible. In addition to the strategy of making the game unpredictable, players have to deal with environmental issues such as wind and field conditions. Applying the concepts of stability of the environment and pacing (figure 4.8) to more basic skills, teachers can regulate the difficulty of motor tasks. As students master tasks, teachers should increase the difficulty so the task remains challenging. Shifting a task from self-paced to externally paced or from stable to unstable accomplishes this goal. The organization of baseball in many communities applies this principle. The youngest players play T-ball (where they hit the ball off a tee); next, they play coaches pitch (where their own coach pitches); then, the opponent's pitcher pitches. This progression gradually makes the task less predictable because batting from the tee is very stable, whereas trying to hit a ball thrown by another 12-year-old is most often unpredictable!

Most motor tasks have many dimensions that influence the difficulty of the task. Locomotor

	Skill Initiation	
	Self-paced	Externally paced
Open	Golf Softball pitching Jogging	Tennis Softball batting Soccer
Closed	Bowling Balance beam T-ball batting	Speed swimming 100-meter dash Cotton-eyed Joe

(Movement Environment)

Figure 4.8 Matrix of task difficulty.

tasks can be modified by changing speed of the movement, direction of the movement, number of skills, level of the movement, and pacing of the movement (table 4.5).

Tables 4.6 through 4.8 present different ways to modify manipulative tasks, including using target

Table 4.5 Modifying Locomotor Skills

	Easiest	Moderate	Most difficult
Speed of movement	Slow	Medium	Fast
Direction of movement	In place	Forward	Backward
Number of skills	One	Two	Three or more
Level of movement	Medium	Low	High
Pacing	Self-paced		Externally paced

Table 4.6 Modifying Tasks That Use a Target (e.g., throwing, kicking, striking)

	Easiest	Easy	Challenging	Difficult
Target size	No target	Very large—an area (e.g., a wall)	Moderate size for distance (e.g., 4 × 4 from 10 ft [3 m])	Small (1 ft² [.09 m²] from 20 ft [6 m])
Target distance	No distance	5 ft (1.6 m)	10–20 ft (3–6 m)	Long distance
Target movement	None	Moderate speed and predictable	Fast	Fast and unpredictable

Table 4.7 Modifying Striking Implements

	Easiest	Challenging	Difficult
Handle length	None	Short	Long
Striking surface size	Large (oversized tennis racket)	Moderate (paddle)	Small (e.g., bat)

Table 4.8   Modifying Object Interception Tasks (e.g., striking, kicking)

	Easiest	Easy	Challenging	Difficult
Speed of the object	None	Moderate	Slow	Fast
Direction of the object	In front	From front	From side	From rear
Predictability of object	Stable			Unstable
Size of object	Large—13 in. (33 cm) diameter	Moderate—8.5 in. (21.5 cm) diameter	Small (tennis ball)	Very small (golf or Ping-Pong ball)
Object projection	None (object is waiting)	Directly to interceptor	Requires one step adjustment	Requires several steps or change of direction
Object trajectory	None	On ground	45° angle interception point at chest	Line drive

characteristics, implement characteristics, and object projection characteristics. This list is not all-inclusive, but provides samples of environmental variables that can be used to challenge children or accommodate lower skill levels.

SUMMARY

Teachers apply their knowledge of how motor skills develop to plan lessons and provide instruction. The notion of developmentally appropriate physical education is grounded in knowledge of skill development. Further, teachers have the opportunity to influence the sociocultural environment so that expectations and opportunities are optimal for both boys and girls. Some skills evolve naturally, whereas others require considerable practice and instruction. Children who practice are able to maximize their potential. Teachers need to understand the factors that influence task difficulty so that instruction can demonstrate progression (e.g., in assessing the speed-accuracy trade-off). Teachers who understand how skills develop will be able to deliver a developmentally appropriate physical education program that is challenging to children and allows children to be successful.

MASTERY LEARNING ACTIVITIES

1. Working with a partner, watch as your partner walks toward you on a line. Be sure your partner is looking at you. Look for the characteristics of a mature walk (head on same plane, arm opposed and proportional, step on midline, heel strike). Reverse roles and repeat. Alternatively, go to a public place and record the various deviations from a mature walk you observe in adults.

2. Using the information from this chapter and the previous chapter, consider the following concept and the statements explaining the concept. What evidence supports the concept and the statements?

Human behavior and performance are a result of both nature and nurture.

a. Early in development (birth to 2 years), most of what we see is attributable to genetics (nature).

b. During childhood (3 to 18 years), environment becomes increasingly important.

c. At puberty, genetics, maturation, and nature are very important.

d. Much of what is observed is caused by environmental influences.

e. Enrichment tends to have short-term benefits; deprivation has little influence on phylogenetic skills.

3. Motor skills can be classified in various categories, as follows:

   a. Phylogenetic and ontogenetic

   b. Locomotor, nonlocomotor, and manipulative

   c. Object projection, object interception, body projection, and stability

Define and give examples of each of these classifications. How can teachers use classifications such as these?

4. Make a checklist of problems that may persist for each locomotor skill and the age at which a teacher should expect the skill to be mastered.

5. Boys and girls perform most motor skills in a similar way during childhood, but one skill is performed differently by each gender. Name that skill, describe the differences between genders, and present at least two possible causes for the large gender differences in that skill.

6. Select a skill not covered in this chapter and describe the speed-accuracy trade-off for that skill.

7. Compare the activities in the lesson plans. What changes are made based on the age of the children? Are there opportunities in the lessons to accommodate varying skill? How would you achieve this balance?

REFERENCES

Bloom, B.S. 1956. *Taxonomy of educational objectives: Cognitive domain.* New York: McKay.

Dennis, W. 1935. The effect of restricted practice upon the reaching, sitting, and standing of two infants. *Journal of Genetic Psychology* 47:17–32.

Dennis, W., and M.G. Dennis. 1940. The effect of cradling practices upon the onset of walking in Hopi children. *Journal of Genetic Psychology* 56:77–86.

French, K.E., and S.L. McPherson. 1999. Adaptations in response selection processes used during sport competition with increasing age and expertise. *International Journal of Sport Psychology* 30:173–93.

Haubenstricker, J., and V. Seefeldt. 1986. Acquisition of motor skills during childhood. In *Physical activity and well-being*, edited by V. Seefeld, 41–102. Reston, Va.: American Alliance for Health, Physical Education, Recreation and Dance (AAHPERD).

McGraw, M.B. 1935. *Growth: A study of Johnny and Jimmy.* New York: Appleton-Century-Crofts.

Nelson, K.R., J.R. Thomas, and J.K. Nelson. 1991. Longitudinal changes in throwing performance: Gender differences. *Research Quarterly for Exercise and Sport* 62:105–108.

Roberton, M.A. 1984. Changing motor patterns during childhood. In *Motor development during childhood and adolescence*, ed. J.R. Thomas, 48–90. Minneapolis, Minn.: Burgess.

Thomas, J.R. 2000. C.H. McCloy Lecture: Children's control, learning and performance of motor skills. *Research Quarterly for Exercise and Sport* 71:1–9.

Thomas, J.R., and K.E. French. 1985. Gender differences across age in motor performance: A meta-analysis. *Psychological Bulletin* 98:260–82.

Thomas, J.R., and M. Marzke. 1992. The development of gender differences in throwing: Is human evolution a factor? In *The academy papers—Enhancing human performance in sport*, edited by R. Christina and H. Eckert, 60-76. Champaign, Ill.: Human Kinetics.

Thomas, J.R., D. Michael, and J.D. Gallagher. 1994. Effects of training on gender differences in overhead throwing: A brief quantitative literature analysis. *Research Quarterly for Exercise and Sport* 65:67–71.

Thomas, K.T., and J.R. Thomas. 1999. What squirrels in the trees predict about expert athletes. *International Journal of Sport Psychology* 30:221–34.

Wickstrom, R.L. 1983. *Fundamental motor patterns,* 3d ed. Philadelphia: Lea & Febiger.

Yan, J.H., V.G. Payne, and J.R. Thomas. 2000. Developmental kinematics of young girls' overarm throwing. *Research Quarterly for Exercise and Sport* 71:92–98.

Yan, J.H., J.R. Thomas, and G.E. Stelmach. 2002. How children and seniors differ from adults in controlling rapid aiming arm movements. In *Motor Development Research and Reviews*, edited by J.E. Clark and J. Humphrey. Vol. 2. Reston, Va.: NASPE.

RESOURCES

Fitts, P.M. 1954. The information capacity of the human motor system in controlling the amplitude of movements. *Journal of Experimental Psychology* 47:381–91.

Halverson, L., M.A. Roberton, and S. Langendorfer. 1982. Development of the overarm throw: Movement and ball velocity changes by seventh grade. *Research Quarterly for Exercise and Sport* 53:198–205.

Isaac, B. 1987. Throwing and human evolution. *The African Archaeological Review* 5:3–17.

Nelson, J.K., J.R. Thomas, K.R. Nelson, and P.C. Abraham. 1986. Gender differences in children's throwing performance: Biology and environment. *Research Quarterly for Exercise and Sport* 57:280–87.

Roberton, M.A., L.E. Halverson, S. Langendorfer, and K. Williams. 1979. Longitudinal changes in children's overarm throw ball velocities. *Research Quarterly for Exercise & Sport* 50:256–64.

Seefeldt, V., and J. Haubenstricker. 1982. Patterns, phases, or stages: An analytical model for the study of developmental movement. In *The development of movement control and co-ordination*, edited by J.A.S. Kelso and J.E. Clark, 309–18. New York: Wiley.

Thomas, K.T., J.D. Gallagher, and J.R. Thomas. 2001. Motor development and skill acquisition during childhood and adolescence. In *Handbook of sport psychology*, 2d ed., edited by R.N. Singer, H.A. Hausenblas, and C. Janelle, 20–52. New York: Wiley.

Wild, M.R. 1938. The behavior pattern of throwing and some observation concerning its course of development in children. *Research Quarterly* 9:20–24.

LESSON PLANS

The four lesson plans that follow demonstrate the progressive use of locomotor, nonlocomotor, and manipulative skills at three age levels (grades K–1, 2–3, and 4–5). The first three lessons trace the activity of catching from kindergarten through fifth grade and would be appropriate at the beginning of the year. Catching a tossed object is easier than catching a thrown object. Therefore, catching is combined with tossing in the early grades. In grades K and 1, beanbags are used because these are easier to grasp than balls and require less chasing when missed, whereas in grades 2 and 3 beanbags and balls are thrown. At the beginning of the school year, activities should include reviewing skills taught the previous year. In grades 2 and 3, a review of beanbag throwing and catching is followed by throwing a ball. In the early grades, students practice with self-tossed beanbags; this activity is followed by tossing and catching or using a beanie launcher. Teacher tossing is also a good way for beginners to practice. Partner work comes after children have mastered the basics and move under control.

LESSON  **4.1**

Throwing and Catching Beanbags

Student Objectives

- Toss a beanbag above their heads and catch it, toss a beanbag from hand to hand successfully, and toss and catch a beanbag with the same hand.
- Demonstrate a high and low toss and throw.
- Practice tossing into a hoop from varying distances (kindergarten children).
- Toss a beanbag into a hoop from 10 ft away (first grade children).
- Demonstrate cooperation when playing Beanbag Rope Toss.
- Correctly identify five body parts (wrist, elbow, arm, chest, head) by placing the beanbag on the part during Movement Challenges.

Equipment and Materials

- 1 beanbag per child, plus extra beanbags
- 1 hoop per group (30–36 in.)
- 1 rope (at least 20 ft long)
- 1 foam ball per group (1st grade)
- 2 standards and rope

Safety Tip

- Remind the children to respect each other's personal space.

Warm-Up Activities (5 minutes)

Throw and Fetch

Arrange the children in a line facing a long, open area, each child with a beanbag.

1. Describe the activity:

    Throw your beanbag as far as possible.

    Then on the signal, run to the beanbags, pick one up, and return to the line. It doesn't matter which beanbag you get.

    We will continue this several times as quickly as possible.

2. Have the children play Throw and Fetch.

Skill-Development Activities (20 minutes)

Movement Challenges

Arrange the children in scatter formation, each with a beanbag.

1. Ask the students: *Can you walk and balance the beanbag on your head?*
2. Have the students practice balancing the beanbag on their shoulder, wrist, arm, or chest.

Tossing a Beanbag

Keep the children in scatter formation, each with a beanbag.

1. Ask the students: *Can you toss the beanbag up and catch it, like this?*
2. Demonstrate. Cup a beanbag in both hands and toss it four to six in. high.

3. Tell the students: *Keep it low! Now try a little higher.* Look for tosses above the children's heads. They should still be tossing, using both hands. *This is harder. Try with one hand; start low! Put the other hand behind your back. Try throwing above your head with one hand.*

4. Stop the children. Demonstrate tossing from hand to hand. Tell the students: *You try! Can you make the beanbag arc up high?*

Beanbag Rope Toss

Arrange partners in two lines, facing each other 6 to 10 ft apart, with a rope suspended in the air midway between the lines at the children's eye level (use two standards to hold the rope). Give each pair a beanbag.

1. Describe the game: *Partners toss one beanbag back and forth over the rope for four or five minutes. Try to toss so it is possible to catch and try hard to catch.*

2. Have the children play Beanbag Rope Toss. If this is too easy, raise the rope or move the children farther from the rope (or move pairs who are successful farther apart or move the rope at one end higher to make it more challenging).

Beanbag Hoop Toss

Divide the children into groups of four or five, each group around a hoop laid on the ground.

1. Have the children practice tossing beanbags into the hoops for four or five minutes.

2. Ask the children: *How far can you toss and hit inside the hoop?*

Concluding Activities (5 minutes)

Play either Teacher Ball or Circle Toss Ball depending on the age group.

Teacher Ball (kindergarten)

Divide the children into small groups, arranged in circles. For each group, select a Teacher to stand in the middle with a beanbag.

1. Describe and demonstrate the activity:

   The Teacher tosses the beanbag to one of the other children, who in turn tosses it back to the Teacher.

   Continue until each child in your group has one turn.

   Then the Teacher chooses a new Teacher.

2. Have the children play Teacher Ball.

Circle Toss Ball (first grade)

Divide the children into groups of four to six, standing in a circle. Place one child in the middle with a foam ball. Scatter the circles. The first time you play this you will probably want to play as one large group. After the chidren have learned the game, divide into groups to play. Note: This is a good game for helping the children get to know each other's names at the beginning of the school year.

1. Describe and demonstrate the game:

   The child in the middle of the circle tosses the foam ball high (and straight up) into the air and calls the name of one of the other children.

   The child whose name is called tries to catch the ball before it hits the ground.

   The tosser joins the circle, and the catcher becomes the tosser.

   Note: If the children do not try to catch the ball, replace the tosser only when the ball is successfully caught.

2. Have the children play Circle Toss Ball.

From *Physical Education Methods for Elementary Teachers, Second Edition,* by Katherine T. Thomas, Amelia M. Lee, and Jerry R. Thomas, 2003, Champaign, IL: Human Kinetics. Adapted from *Physical Education for Children: Daily Lesson Plans for Elementary School, Second Edition,* by Katherine T. Thomas, Amelia M. Lee, and Jerry R. Thomas, 2000, Champaign, IL: Human Kinetics.

LESSON  **4.2**

Throwing, Catching, and Dribbling

Student Objectives

- Dribble while moving.
- Refine skills of throwing and catching with a partner.
- Contrast dribbling and bouncing.
- Work cooperatively in Circle Stride Ball or in small groups in Keep Away.

Equipment and Materials

- 1 playground ball (8+ in.) per child
- Chalk, flour, or tape to mark lines
- 1 playground ball (13 in.) per group
- Signal

Warm-Up Activities (5 minutes)

Delivery Relay

Arrange the children in groups of four divided between two lines marked about 60 ft apart. Give one child in each group a ball.

1. Describe and demonstrate the game:

   On the signal the child with the ball delivers (carries) the ball to a teammate at the other line.

That child returns the ball to a child at the first line, and so on, until each person in your group has carried the ball over the distance.

2. Have the children play Delivery Relay.

Skill-Development Activities (15 minutes)

Throwing and Catching Tasks

Arrange pairs in scatter formation, each pair 10 ft apart with one playground ball.

1. Challenge the children with the following tasks:

   Toss (throw underhand) and catch with your partner.

   Back up one step at a time until you can no longer catch and toss.

   Each of you should toss from each distance before moving.

Move the pairs back to 10 ft apart.

2. Have them throw (overhand) and catch, again backing up after each successful round, as in step 1.

After several trials, move them back to 10 ft apart.

3. Have them bounce and catch the ball, following the same procedure.

Dribbling

Arrange the children in scatter formation, each child with a ball.

1. Ask the children: *What is the difference between dribbling and bouncing a ball?* Demonstrate: *Dribbling is with one hand.*

2. Have the children practice dribbling.

3. Tell the children: *Dribble the ball rhythmically, keeping the ball below your waist and close to your body so your elbow stays bent when the ball is at its peak. Spread your fingers so your*

fingers and palm cover as much of the surface of the ball as possible.

4. Have the children perform some dribbling tasks: *Dribble with your left hand. Don't move your feet. Now try with your right hand.* Repeat several times.

Line up the children across one end of the play area.

5. Ask the children: *Can you dribble and walk to there?* Point out an endline or opposite side of the play area. Have the children go back and forth several times.

Arrange partners in scatter formation.

6. Have one partner dribble around the other, then have partners switch roles. Do this several times.

Concluding Activities (10 minutes)

Circle Stride Ball

Use this activity with second graders. See Keep Away (next activity) for third graders. Divide the children into groups of six to nine each. Have the children stand in a circle with their feet spread apart so that they touch the feet of each of their neighbors. Place one child in the center of each circle with a large ball.

1. Describe and demonstrate the game:

   The child in the center tries to roll the ball out of the circle between another child's legs.

   If the child in the center is successful, the two players exchange places; if not, play continues.

   Players may not move their feet and must stop the ball with their hands.

2. Have the children play Circle Stride Ball.

3. You can also have the children play this game with the circle facing outward and the children looking back through their legs.

Keep Away

Use this game with third graders. See Circle Stride Ball (previous activity) for second graders. Arrange groups of three in scatter formation.

1. Describe and demonstrate the game:

   Two of you in each group play catch (you may bounce, roll, toss, or throw the ball) while the third person tries to gain control of the ball.

   Anyone who loses control of the ball switches roles with the child who gains control of the ball.

   At set intervals (e.g., 30 to 60 seconds), I will signal that the child trying to gain control is allowed to switch places with one of the other children if they don't get to switch by gaining control of the ball.

2. Have the children play Keep Away.

From *Physical Education Methods for Elementary Teachers, Second Edition,* by Katherine T. Thomas, Amelia M. Lee, and Jerry R. Thomas, 2003, Champaign, IL: Human Kinetics. Adapted from *Physical Education for Children: Daily Lesson Plans for Elementary School, Second Edition,* by Katherine T. Thomas, Amelia M. Lee, and Jerry R. Thomas, 2000, Champaign, IL: Human Kinetics.

Throwing and Catching

Student Objectives

- Toss up a ring and catch it with right and left hands.
- Work cooperatively with a group to achieve a goal.

Equipment and Materials

- 1 ring (quoit) per child
- 1 hoop per group
- Chalk, flour, or tape for marking Cooperative Ring Toss areas
- Cones or other markers for marking jogging course

Warm-Up Activities (5 minutes)

Walk/Jog

Mark a jogging course and arrange the children on the starting line.

1. Start with a walk/jog for five minutes.

2. Increase to 10 to 12 minutes, encouraging the children to gradually increase the distance they cover.

Skill-Development Activities (15 minutes)

Throwing and Catching Tasks

Arrange the children in scatter formation, each child with a ring.

1. Challenge the children with the following tasks:

   Throw your ring up and catch it with the same hand.

   Practice until you can catch five times without a miss.

   Throw your ring up with one hand and catch it with the other.

From a low level throw your ring up and catch it.

Throw your ring up and jump high to catch it.

Jump high and then throw your ring and catch it.

2. Repeat all several times.

3. Challenge the children: *Throw your ring up and turn around (or touch the ground, clap three times, click your heels) before you catch it.*

4. Ask the children to think of other stunts to perform.

Concluding Activities (10 minutes)

Cooperative Ring Toss

Divide the children into groups of four to six, give each child a ring, and place each group at a game area. Mark each game area with lines 6, 12, and 24 ft from a hoop. Mark a square around the hoop about one in. larger than the hoop.

1. Describe and demonstrate the game:

   The goal of the game is for a group to achieve a combined score of 24 points.

   During each round each child must have a turn and the group must decide if the throw is from 6, 12, or 24 ft.

Team members can throw from different lines, but the team with a total score closer to 24 points wins.

A ring landing in the hoop scores four points from 6 ft, six points from 12 ft, and eight points from 24 ft. All rings landing in the square around the hoop score two points.

2. Have the children play Cooperative Ring Toss.

3. Repeat the game several times, encouraging the children to decide the best way for their team to score close to 24 points total.

From *Physical Education Methods for Elementary Teachers, Second Edition,* by Katherine T. Thomas, Amelia M. Lee, and Jerry R. Thomas, 2003, Champaign, IL: Human Kinetics. Adapted from *Physical Education for Children: Daily Lesson Plans for Elementary School, Second Edition,* by Katherine T. Thomas, Amelia M. Lee, and Jerry R. Thomas, 2000, Champaign, IL: Human Kinetics.

LESSON **4.4**

Locomotor and Nonlocomotor Combinations

Student Objectives

- Combine locomotor and nonlocomotor movements into a sequence.
- Create a movement sequence for a partner to copy.
- Work cooperatively with a group to achieve a goal.

Equipment and Materials

- 2 rhythm sticks
- 1 drum
- 1 tambourine
- Skill cards (listing locomotor and non-locomotor skills)

Warm-Up Activities (5 minutes)

Movement to Sounds

Arrange the children in scatter formation.

1. Explain the activity:

   The sound of the sticks hitting together is the signal to move forward.

   The sound of the drum is the signal to move backward.

   And the sound of the tambourine is the signal to move in place.

   Respond to the instrument in time with the beat and in the correct direction, running.

2. Have the children practice responding, repeating each sound several times.

Skill-Development Activities (20 minutes)

Movement Combinations

Make sure the children are still in scatter formation.

1. Have the children perform the following movement combinations:

   Leap forward (four counts), *leap backward* (four counts), *leap turning* (four counts), *jump in place* (four counts), *and collapse.*

   Hop right (four counts), *hop left* (four counts), *run forward* (four counts), *stretch* (two counts), *and curl* (two counts).

   Swing right leg, forward and back (eight counts), *swing left leg, forward and back* (eight counts).

   Hop in place (four counts), *hop forward* (four counts), *hop backward* (four counts), *hop in place* (four counts).

   Walk forward (eight counts), *jump in place* (eight counts), *walk backward* (eight counts), *jump in place* (eight counts).

   Slide right (eight counts), *slide left* (eight counts).

   Run (three counts), *leap* (one count). Repeat several times.

   Run (two counts), *leap* (two counts). Repeat several times.

2. Repeat challenges as time allows.

Partner Copy Activity

Arrange partners in scatter formation.

1. Select two or more locomotor or nonlocomotor skills you wish to target and a variety of counts (e.g., 4, 8, 12, 16, 24).

2. Explain the activity:

The goal of the activity is for the leader to use the skills in a sequence with the specified number of counts. For example, the task might be to use walk, hop, and jump for 16 counts. The sequence could be walk (eight counts), hop (four counts), and jump (four counts).

One of you creates the movement sequence and the partner watches.

The partner then repeats the sequence.

Then trade roles and repeat the activity using other skills and counts.

3. Present the following tasks for partners:

Walk, run, stretch, and twist for 12 counts.

Gallop forward, gallop backward, jump forward, jump backward for 24 counts.

Walk forward, walk backward, hop in a circle for 12 counts.

Skip and slide for 16 counts.

4. After several practice trials, have the children select their own movements and number of counts.

Concluding Activities (5 minutes)

Skill Cards

Divide the class into groups of four to six. Have prepared a number of cards listing different locomotor and nonlocomotor skills.

1. Describe the activity:

Each group selects four (or more) cards from the stack of cards.

The group has to prepare a sequence using the skills on the cards.

2. Allow the groups time to create and practice their sequences.

From *Physical Education Methods for Elementary Teachers, Second Edition,* by Katherine T. Thomas, Amelia M. Lee, and Jerry R. Thomas, 2003, Champaign, IL: Human Kinetics. Adapted from *Physical Education for Children: Daily Lesson Plans for Elementary School, Second Edition,* by Katherine T. Thomas, Amelia M. Lee, and Jerry R. Thomas, 2000, Champaign, IL: Human Kinetics.

chapter 5

Cognition, Learning, and Practice

Morgan, age 11

*C*hildren have less knowledge and fewer cognitive strategies than adults. A child's performance usually improves when she practices appropriately while using adult strategies.

Learner Outcomes

The teacher will do the following:

▸ Distinguish between learning and memory.

▸ Describe the age-related changes in information processing.

▸ Define three methods to organize practice and give the influence of each on learning.

▸ Organize practice appropriately, based on the learning objective and the learner.

▸ Design instruction to facilitate learning.

Glossary Terms

cognition
learning
memory
practice
attention
capacity
vigilance
overexclusive attention
overinclusive attention
selective attention
information processing
declarative knowledge

procedural knowledge
strategic knowledge
control processes
FIT principle
extrinsic feedback
intrinsic feedback
reinforcement and general encouragement
constant
variable practice
blocked practice
random practice

*T*eaching and learning are two sides of the same process; thus, a teacher must understand how children learn in order to teach effectively. In physical education, teachers must understand how children learn concepts, facts, and motor skills. This creates a unique challenge, because motor skills include typical errors of learning such as problems with memory and decision making. However, motor skill learning includes a unique source of error—motor execution, or skill, error. When a child makes an error on a story problem in math, not being able to write the number is not likely to be the source of error. However, in physical education the error could be decision making, memory, or execution. For example, the child is supposed to throw the ball to second base when the first batter hits the ball. The child throws the ball between first and second base. What type of error was this? Did he know where to throw it? Was he trying to throw it to first or second base? This could be a decision error (not knowing where to throw), a skill error (not throwing where he intended), or both!

Skill is an issue at all levels of sport. The very best professional baseball players know that the object of batting is to hit the ball safely into fair territory, but the best batters do this only about one-third of the time! Skill makes sport unique and challenging. The expert teacher understands how children learn, especially how they learn motor skills.

COGNITION, LEARNING, AND MEMORY

Learning, memory, and cognition are related but different. **Cognition** is thinking; it is the basis for learning and memory. **Learning** has four definitive characteristics: It results from practice, it is permanent, it is dependent on feedback, and it is demonstrated by retention and transfer. **Memory** comprises two parts: working (short-term) memory, which is limited in capacity; and long-term memory, which is unlimited and is where knowledge is stored. Learning depends on memory, and **practice** is repetition to facilitate memory and a critical ingredient in learning. Learning of motor skills has been described in three stages.

Learning Motor Skills: Stage 1

Stage 1 is "getting the idea" and is characterized by many different mistakes and large errors (Fitts and Posner 1967). This stage is primarily cognitive, as the learner tries to figure out how to do the task the first time, often without getting hurt and with as little embarrassment as possible. Teachers can help students in stage 1 by giving hints about and modeling how to make the first attempt at the skill and by identifying the relationship between practice and improvement.

Learning Motor Skills: Stage 2

Stage 2 starts when the performances become stable—there are still errors, but the learner tends to make the same mistake over and over (Fitts and Posner 1967). Sometimes a learner will stay in this stage indefinitely. Here, the learner can detect errors but cannot correct them. As you can see, feedback from a teacher is essential in stage 2. This feedback should focus on how to correct errors.

Students must go through stage 1 (trial by error) and stage 2 (fewer errors, more mastery) when learning a new skill.

Learning Motor Skills: Stage 3

Finally, the learner performs the movement consistently, with few errors—this is stage 3 (Fitts and Posner 1967). The learner is now able to detect and correct errors. The movement is automatic; that is, the learner does not have to think about the movement once it starts. During stage 3, instruction shifts from skill execution to the more strategic or conceptual aspects of performance. The goal of learning for all skills is to reach stage 3, which is called the autonomous stage—the learner is now independent.

Teachers need to understand cognition, learning, and practice for four reasons:

1. Teachers are responsible for monitoring cognition and learning; if unusual deviations are discovered, the teacher may need to refer the student for evaluation.

2. Teachers cannot assume that children will do anything to help themselves learn when compared to the many specific activities adults and older children do to learn. Certainly, children do not do the same things adults do to facilitate memory and learning; teachers must know the difference in order to help the students learn.

3. Teachers need to understand how the organization of practice influences learning so they can select practice regimes appropriate for students of various skill and maturational levels.

4. Teachers need to be able to explain to students how learning occurs so that students will eventually be responsible for their own learning.

ATTENTION

Attention has three usages: It means cognitive **capacity** or space; this is used interchangeably with short-term memory. Short-term memory and attention are limited. You may have heard of Miller's magical number seven, plus or minus two. This means that the typical person has the short-term memory capacity to deal with seven items at once (Thomas 2000). People with greater capacity may remember up to nine, whereas those with less capacity can deal with five items. In the simplest case, we can think of this as juggling seven single-digit numbers in short-term memory. Short-term memory is the component of cognition that makes decisions and deals with current events. Capacity or attention can be focused on external events (sensory information), on solving problems (decision making and control processes), or on searching long-term memory. This concept is demonstrated in figure 5.1. Attention can also be divided so that you are monitoring sensory information and searching long-term memory and solving a problem at the same time. For example, you are watching for your friend, trying to remember what ingredients are in a recipe, and deciding if you can actually make the recipe. Later in this chapter, we will see how our cognitive systems maximize efficiency, which allows more information to be dealt with simultaneously. In this case a person can juggle seven complex tasks or units in short-term memory.

A second usage of attention is **vigilance.** This refers to the length of time one can allocate attention to a particular task. A common misconception is that children have short attention spans. If you have read a favorite bedtime story to a three-year-old, you have evidence that children do not have short attention spans. When you try to skip a page or miss a word in that favorite story, what happens? The child usually notices! Frequently, very young children ask for the story to be read again. In fact, Teletubbies®, a popular television show for very young children, uses this idea and repeats the story segment during each episode. Children do not have short attention spans; however, they may not be interested in the things adults want them to "pay attention to." Therefore, adults conclude that children have short attention spans. Most of us can recall a parent or teacher saying, "Pay attention!" Often we were thinking, *Why? This is boring.*

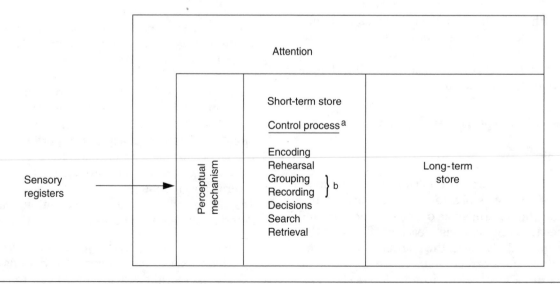

Figure 5.1   The information processing system.

The third use of attention refers to the focus or object of our attention—in other words, what we are paying attention to. Once again, children differ from adults. Three stages of attention are generally recognized: The first, from birth to about five years, is called **overexclusive attention.** The infant and young child focus on one thing and ignore all others. Attention can be focused inward on cognitive activities or outward on the environment. From 5 to about 12 years, the child is in the **overinclusive** stage of attention; this means the child tries to capture everything. The result is distraction and the inability to select the critical element to solve a task. Overinclusive children try to solve problems by considering every possible issue. They may seem picky or even petty. However, the process is likely to be important as they work toward strategies for quickly and accurately selecting important information. Sometime around the 12th birthday, children begin to use selective attention. **Selective attention** occurs when the appropriate information is used and all other information is ignored. Performance on tasks is enhanced as attention becomes focused (Ladewig and Gallagher 1994; Thomas, Gallagher, and Thomas 2000).

Expert teachers determine the critical aspects of a task and help their students by informing the children—that is, cuing them to consider the critical aspects—and thereby encouraging them to use selective attention to enhance performance. Further, teachers should not automatically assume that children will not stay on task because of short attention spans. If children are off task (not paying attention), examine the task and the instruction. Is the task too easy or difficult? Are the children improving? Is this fun? Does a child or group of children demonstrate more on-task behavior on self-selected tasks?

INFORMATION PROCESSING

Information processing is a specific part of cognition; it includes perception, working memory, and long-term memory. The same information processing system a student uses in the classroom enables her to think in the gymnasium. The difference is in the output. In the classroom, the output is usually a verbal or written response. In the gym, the response is most often a movement but can be verbal or written as well. Children have less experience and therefore less knowledge or information than adults (Thomas, Gallagher, and Thomas 2000). Because knowledge is critical to suc-

cessful performance, lack of it is problematic for children in several ways: First, children have less information or **declarative knowledge** (e.g., facts and rules) than adults. This is largely because it takes time to acquire information, and children have had less time than adults to gather information simply because they are younger. Second, **procedural knowledge** is information about how to do something and is a result of learning. Because children have learned less than adults during their shorter life spans, they have fewer procedures to help them solve problems. Finally, children do not use the strategies or control processes that adults use to help them solve problems and remember; this makes learning more difficult for them. These control processes are sometimes called **strategic knowledge. Control processes** are cognitive strategies such as rehearsal (figure 5.2). During elementary school, children master many of the control processes. Teachers can help children learn to use control processes and can make learning easier by designing instruction to accommodate the differences between children and adults in cognition, learning, and memory.

Adults understand that most of the time we have to do something—perform a deliberate act—to remember information or learn how to do a task (Helsen, Starkes, and Hodges 1998). However, children do not understand the deliberate part of memory and learning. Even experts have trouble organizing practice, so it is no wonder that children need a teacher's guidance (Deakin 2001). The first thing teachers can do to help children learn is to describe how to learn. Statements such as "When I want to remember something, I say it over and over quietly to myself" are very helpful. Unfortunately, children are often provided useless or vague information, such as "Try hard" or "Put on your thinking cap" (Gallagher and Thomas 1984, 1986; Ornstein and Naus 1985; Thomas, Thomas, Lee, Testerman, and Ashy 1983). An adult does not believe that putting on a thinking cap facilitates learning, so why would this statement be helpful to a child? Children cannot turn "Try hard" into action. Another misconception held by children is that people either can or cannot do something. Rarely do children understand the concept of practice as a factor in being able to do a task. Once children understand that practice is important, the feelings of being incompetent or abnormal are eliminated. Further, there is motivation for practice. The more specific the information is about learning and memory, the more help the information will be.

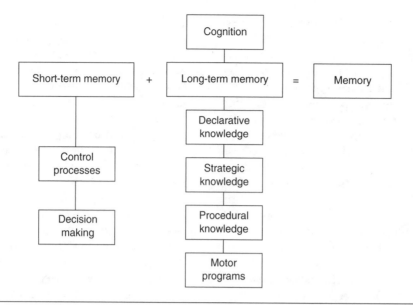

Figure 5.2   Storage and action components in memory and cognition.

Teachers can help children understand the role of practice by recounting personal stories of hard work to master tasks. Statements such as "Most of us have to practice a long time to learn how to . . . ." are helpful.

The object of learning is to put correct and important information into long-term memory—for that information to become knowledge. Part of this process is to make using information as automatic as possible. Both declarative and procedural knowledge can be automatic, such as an answer to a multiplication fact (e.g., 3 times 4 is 12) or typing words on a keyboard. As we consider a fact, idea, or problem, it is in short-term memory. If we do not move it to long-term memory, it will fade away. Control processes are deliberate actions that move information into long-term memory, sometimes as facts and sometimes as actions. The first control process to emerge, at about two years of age is labeling (Ornstein and Naus 1985; Gallagher and Thomas 1984, 1986). Early labels are names and typically involve physical characteristics. Labeling becomes more abstract and the labels are connected to other labels or concepts during childhood. Applying a name or label to an action or object makes it easier to remember and use. For example, if there was no label for the double play in baseball or parallel parking, think how difficult and time consuming these would be to describe. Some of the characteristics we must remember about movements are the end locations, distance or speed, force, amplitude, and acceleration or deceleration. Cues or words that label these characteristics help beginning students

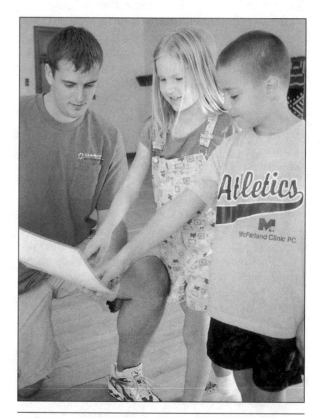

Teachers are helpful when they offer students specific instructions on how to perform a task.

to remember the important aspects of the movement. Describing the beginning and ending locations of the hands and feet (or other critical body parts), the speed or distance of the movement (e.g., by counting or moving quickly versus slowly), and whether the movement speeds or slows (acceleration or deceleration) give children labels they can use during practice to make correct attempts.

Rehearsal, another control process, is repetition and begins at about 7 years of age. Early rehearsal is rote repetition of a single piece of information; mixed rehearsal sets—where several items are repeated in random order—begins at about 11 years of age (Gallagher and Thomas 1984, 1986). Consider how difficult it would be for you to remember something if you could not say or write it over and over. Children enter school and spend two or three years there before they begin to repeat, yet they are asked to memorize information during that time. Teachers often force children to repeat, but rarely explain why or how this helps learning. Spelling is a perfect example of teachers using rehearsal strategies for memorization. Each day of the week a new task that requires repetition of the spelling words (e.g., Monday, write the word five times; Tuesday, write the word in a sentence; and Wednesday, take a self-test) is assigned. In physical education, repetition is used as part of instruction; however, to master many skills, a student often finds it necessary to practice outside of class. One of the most powerful messages teachers can send to children is the importance of practice (rehearsal) in skill acquisition. Teachers should encourage practice, provide time for repetition, and relate improvement to hard work (e.g., practice).

Typical Ages for Cognitive Processes Used by Children

▶ Labeling	2 years
▶ Rote rehearsal	7 years
▶ Mixed rehearsal	11 years
▶ Chunking and grouping	11 years

Grouping occurs when information is organized in a logical way so that discrete units are combined. Skipping combines two discrete skills—hopping and stepping. Another example of grouping is when we arrange things from simple to difficult or large to small. You may use this technique when you use a word to remember a sequence of events, so that the first letter in the word stands for the first event and so forth. The **FIT principle** is also an example of grouping. Three words—frequency, intensity, and time—and the

definitions and formulas for each are nested in the three-letter word FIT. Grouping begins in children around 11 years of age. Teachers can use metaphors, acronyms, or other grouping strategies to help children recall lots of information with a short cue. (This concept will be discussed in more detail in chapter 6.)

Search and retrieval occur when you think about something you know (which is in long-term memory) and you move it from long-term to short-term memory. This process develops with the others; that is, once something is placed in long-term memory, we must search to retrieve it. The more connections or pathways there are to a piece of information, the more likely it will be retrieved. Information also progresses from being understood as concrete (fact or definition) to being thought of in a more abstract way (e.g., application, concept, or theory). As information becomes better learned, it will be easier to retrieve; often this means the information is more conceptual. Have you ever taken an exam during which you remembered the location in the textbook of an answer to a question—the page and place on it—but you could not remember the answer itself? The search led to appropriate information, but the information stored was superficial, as was the recollection of the information. Bloom's taxonomy mentioned in chapter 4 has six levels that lead to wisdom: comprehension, knowledge, application, analysis, synthesis, and evaluation (Bloom 1956). Mastery was described in levels from knowledge to evaluation, which reflects the idea of shifting from concrete and superficial understanding to conceptual or abstract representations of information. As children practice, hints about how to remember information facilitate later recall. The more connections there are to a piece of information, the more likely the recall of that information.

Decision making is based on simple matching: Either the response matches the stimulus or it does not. Even complicated problems are broken down into parts that are eventually answered this simply. Procedural knowledge is a stored set of decisions that comprise situations called if-then-do statements. We are familiar with many of these. In math we learned how to "carry" and what to do with the remainder as we learned division; both carrying and dealing with remainders are examples of procedures. Sport and physical activity provide many of these as well. In youth baseball, when the ball is fielded after a hit, the ball is thrown to second base. There are several reasons to throw to second base. Running skill is better than throwing and catching skills in young children, so stopping a runner by throwing to second base has a higher probability of success than getting an out at first base. Also, second base is a shorter throw for many hits than first base. Another example comes from T-ball: With the 9th or 10th batter, everything (runners and ball) goes to home. In many activities, rapid and accurate decisions are critical to becoming an expert. Driving a car requires rapid and accurate decisions; so does teaching or playing ice hockey. Experts know many procedures and use them automatically. Physical education requires teachers to teach motor skills as well as how and when to use the skills (procedures). During game play, expert teachers explain the strengths and weaknesses of various decisions. Reaction time is a simple decision: Young children take longer to make decisions than older children and adults, as can be seen in figure 5.3. Generally, strategies are the focus of instruction for children in the third stage of learning motor skills. Students learning and using strategies in a game go through the same stages as they do when

learning motor skills. You can see from figure 5.4 how much error is reduced when children who would not ordinarily use a strategy are given a strategy to solve the specific task. In this case, the task was remembering a distance run, similar to remembering the distance in an offensive football play. The receiver runs a specific distance and turns to catch the ball; if the distance run is inaccurate—no matter how good the throw—the play will fail. The children were capable of counting and remembering but not of figuring out to count! Often, it is too difficult to try to teach the skill and the application at the same time.

Control processes demand attention or capacity. One goal of learning is for responses to become automatic, so the response demands less attention. This allows us to do more than one thing at once, which is usually desirable. Early in skill learning, all of our attention may be devoted to doing the motor skill, so we are unable to consider the context. As we gain skill, more capacity (attention) can be allocated to the context. The context could be the offense and defense of a sport or the music and expression of emotion in a dance. Early in

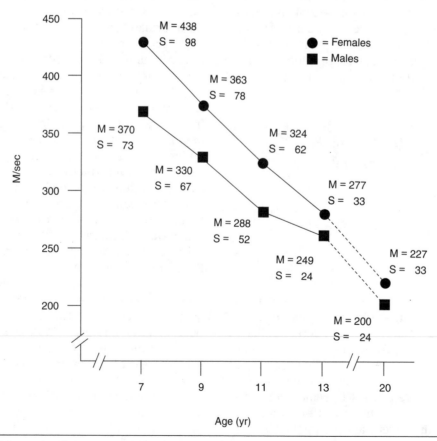

Figure 5.3   Simple reaction time across age.

Reprinted with permission from *Research Quarterly for Exercise and Sport*, 52: 359-367, Copyright 1981 by the American Alliance for Health, Physical Education, Recreation and Dance, 1900 Association Drive, Reston, VA 20191.

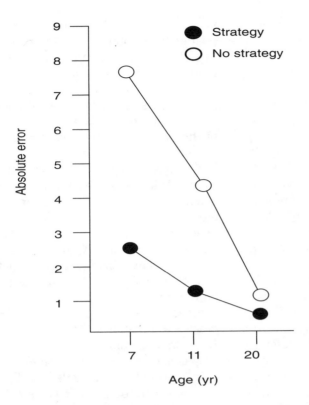

Figure 5.4 A comparison of errors made without strategy versus with a strategy.

learning a dance, the focus is on the steps; later, in practice, students can feel the joy of moving to music and can identify with people from other cultures who performed the dance. Teachers need to focus the content of learning appropriately, based on the stage of learning and the mastery of the three types of knowledge.

FEEDBACK

Feedback is information about performance. **Extrinsic feedback** is information about performance that cannot be obtained by the performer. **Intrinsic feedback** is information the performer receives that could be visual (I missed the target), proprioceptive (it didn't feel right), or auditory (everyone is cheering). The dominant source of sensory or intrinsic feedback is vision; we believe what we see and ignore everything else. This affects learning motor skills because the way something feels is often critical for improving or maintaining performance. Further, we often practice in situations where visual feedback is available but will not be available during the actual performance. For example, a student can practice in front of a mirror,

so when a teacher says, "Look at your hand," he can receive visual feedback (but during actual performance, looking at the hand will not work). Teachers should cue students to think about and remember how movements feel. **Reinforcement and general encouragement** (e.g., "good job" and "keep trying") are often confused with feedback. Although reinforcement and general encouragement are important, they do not serve the same purpose as feedback because they do not provide information to either correct or repeat the movement.

Feedback is reinforcing, motivating, and corrective. When a student makes an error that she cannot detect herself, the teacher should provide corrective feedback. Reinforcing feedback is given when a student does something correctly. The critical feature of either reinforcing or corrective feedback is that the learner must be given the information necessary to do the skill correctly on the next try. In overarm throwing, the feedback could include statements like "Great— you stepped on the correct foot that time; keep it up" or "I can see you are working hard; if you want to take this to the next level, try stepping on the opposite foot next time. I know you can do it!" In both examples, encouragement is coupled with specific extrinsic feedback. This is the sandwich technique—something positive, the corrective feedback, something positive.

How can feedback, especially corrective feedback, be motivating? There are three reasons corrective feedback is motivating. First, the message to the student from the teacher is "I am watching and I notice what you do." The second message is "I believe you can do this." The third message is "I care about you and this skill; I want you to learn this." Children have consistently reported preferring coaches who provide corrective feedback to those who provide general encouragement. Physical education teachers give very little corrective feedback, often only a few statements in a whole class (Thomas 2000). Children want to learn skills and need to see improvement. Feedback can also provide evidence of improvement.

Feedback can document progress during learning; general encouragement cannot document progress. For example, "Great job" repeated over and over shows no progress, whereas "Now I see you stepping on the opposite foot most of the time" does document progress. Since feedback must focus on information not otherwise available to the student, feedback generally must be about the process rather than the outcome. A student can see that the ball missed the target and can usually figure out that hitting 6 of 10 today is better than hitting 4 of 10 yesterday. This means that teacher's feedback should indicate knowledge of performance (KP) rather than knowledge of results (KR). The locomotor and manipulative skill rubrics in chapter 4 provide a good source of information for teacher feedback as well as lesson design and evaluation.

Four factors should be considered as teachers give feedback to students:

1. Postfeedback interval
2. Modality
3. Precision
4. Frequency

Younger children need more time to think about feedback than older children and adults (Thomas, Solmon, and Mitchell 1979). Once a child has feedback, there should be 10 or more seconds allowed for making a plan to correct the movement before the next try. Unfortunately, children left on their own take almost no time to consider the feedback. So, teachers need to allow the time and encourage children to use the time to make corrections.

Providing more time after the feedback (the postfeedback interval) can improve performance by reducing error, as can be seen in figure 5.5. The modality of feedback indicates whether the feedback is verbal, visual, or physical. The most familiar of these is verbal; however, teachers often may demonstrate the incorrect and correct versions of the task. Sometimes teachers guide students through the correct movement by moving the body parts through the correct pattern. The first two modalities of feedback are effective, especially when used together. The third modality, guided movement, can be helpful, but there is also evidence that guided feedback and practice are not always effective. Clearly, guided movement should not be used exclusively. Precision of feedback refers to the type of information from general ("Push harder") to specific ("Your elbow was bent two degrees too much"). For younger children, less precise information is better (Newell and Kennedy 1978). In fact, young children ignore information they consider too precise. Older children select only the part they can understand (e.g., "Your elbow was bent too much"). Feedback should provide information about the direction of the error (e.g., too much, too little, left, right, up, down) and how to correct the error. Frequency of feedback means how often feedback is given. Early in learning, more feedback is better; in fact, feedback on every try is great. With more practice, feedback should be given less often, perhaps half the time. Late in practice, feedback is given once in a while. If we averaged the amount of feedback across learning from early to late, the average would be that 50 percent of the tries would have feedback. The reason is that learners can become dependent upon extrinsic feedback, which means the student does not learn to detect and correct errors himself. To be an independent performer, we must learn to detect and correct our own errors. One of the major responsibilities of a teacher is to give feedback but at the same time to help students learn to detect and correct their own errors. Ironically, good teachers teach themselves out of a job! In a teaching situation, it is almost impossible to give feedback to every student on half of their trials, so a realistic goal is to give feedback as often as possible to as many students as possible.

A common misconception about feedback is that it must be immediate (Adams 1987). Feedback must occur before the next trial of a task but does not have to occur immediately. One study examined feedback that was given immediately, one day

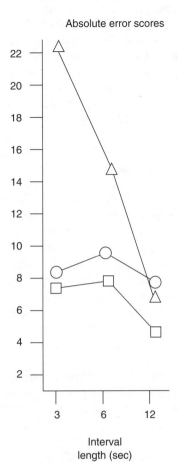

Absolute error scores

△ = 7-year-olds
○ = 11-year-olds
□ = Adults

Interval
length (sec)

Figure 5.5   Postfeedback interval.

Journal of Motor Behavior, "Effects of varying post-KR intervals upon children's performance." J.D. Gallagher and J.R. Thomas. 12: 41-46, 1980. Reprinted with permission of the Helen Dwight Reid Educational Foundation. Published by Heldref Publications, 1319 18th Street, NW, Washington, DC 20036-1802. Copyright © 1980.

and one week after the performance, and reported no differences in learning! Immediate feedback is not important to learning motor skills. So, if you cannot give feedback at the end of class today, do it before practice begins during the next class. This effect is so strong that feedback after several trials about the group of trials (averaged feedback) is just as good as immediate feedback about one trial at a time.

Teachers should give corrective feedback as often as possible. The feedback should be specific so the student can correct the next performance. Students, especially younger students, need time to make corrections before the next trial. Teachers might want to use the sandwich technique, with praise, feedback, and encouragement given together. Finally, feedback should be directly related to the objectives of the lesson and should target important characteristics of the skill or task.

Concepts Into Practice

Mr. Jones notices Sean making an error. Mr. Jones says, "Sean, I can see you are trying hard; you need to take a larger step if you want to improve. Keep working; I know you can do it!" Mr. Jones used the sandwich technique, providing reinforcement, specific corrective feedback, and encouragement. This is considerably more effective than saying, "Nice job."

MOTOR PROGRAMS

Motor programs are a way to conceptualize how movements are stored in memory. Four characteristics of motor programs are order, overall timing, relative timing, and relative force. Order is the sequence in which movement events occur (e.g., step, then hop in skipping). The overall timing is the speed of the movement. In this case, we can run either fast or slow, but running is still the same motor program. However, if we change the relative timing, it will no longer be the same motor program. For example, if the speed of one leg changes, but the other does not, we are likely to be galloping rather than running. This would be a different motor program. The same is true for force; the overall force can change, but the points in a movement with the most force must always have the most force. So, we can throw hard or soft (changing the overall force), but the greatest force must still be at ball release. Understanding this explains why practice in slow motion may not work. Movements that are rapid or forceful are best practiced in real time or with a normal amount of force. Teachers can provide cues or labels for the order of the movements, design practice so that relative force and timing are constant, and encourage students to recall the "feel" of the movement after each trial.

A motor program is selected as we make a decision to move. That program is retrieved from long-term memory (knowledge) and programmed in short-term memory. Once the movement is programmed, it can be executed with minimal attention (Yan, Thomas, Stelmach, and Thomas 2000). Usually, we monitor motor programs during movement but do not have to use much capacity to do so. That means we can use that capacity for other things. One of the outcomes of elementary physical education is developing a variety of motor programs. This leads to the question "How are motor programs learned?" The obvious answer is practice. Practice with intrinsic and extrinsic feedback helps motor programs become efficient and automatic. As we learn a new movement, most of the movement is controlled by sensory feedback. This means that we use vision and proprioception to guide the movement (Meyer, Abrams, Kornblum, Wright, and Smith 1988; Yan et al. 2000). The result is a slower movement and many corrections during the movement. For young children and beginners, only the start of the movement is controlled by a motor program. With practice, more of the movement is controlled in this way. With practice, motor programs become larger, controlling more of a movement. Motor programs tend to produce faster and more efficient movements than movements guided by feedback.

Scientists have used the speed-accuracy trade-off to examine motor programs (Plamondon and Alimi 1997; Kerr 1985; Salmoni and Pascoe 1979). The speed-accuracy trade-off was described in chapter 4. As we increase speed, accuracy decreases and vice versa. In order to study motor programs, children and adults were asked to make a series of movements as quickly as possible, with targets of varying difficulty. The movements were divided into primary and secondary phases. The primary phase is the programmed part; the secondary phase is the portion of the movement controlled by sensory feedback. What happens is this: The child moves quickly toward the target, then slows down and uses vision to guide the movement to the target. Young children (5-year-olds) and the elderly (70-year-olds) have very short primary phases; this means most of the movement is controlled by vision (Yan et al. 2000). Their movements include many small corrections. Older children (e.g., 11-year-olds) and adults have long primary phases and brief secondary phases; their movements are smoother and faster. Motor programs reduce reliance on sensory information and reduce corrections and errors.

Trying to change a motor program once it begins working usually creates large errors. So, once we begin to perform a well-learned movement, it is best to think about the movement as little as possible and then allow the motor program to select the appropriate sensory information. One example of this technique is how balance can be enhanced by vision. Focal vision is the type of vision you are using to read these words. Information from focal vision goes to short-term memory, is analyzed, and is then incorporated into the motor program and eventually sent to the muscles.

This process takes one reaction time (between one fifth and one third of a second). Information about body position from ambient vision, which is peripheral vision that you are not aware of, is sent almost directly to the muscles. Therefore, corrections are made more rapidly (one reaction time faster—in fact, the corrections are made automatically) (Thomas 2000; Yan et al. 2000). For a skill such as balance, telling a student, "Look at a spot on the wall, and just feel the movement as you walk the beam" uses this concept. Similarly, when students are batting or catching, teachers often say, "Watch the ball all the way to the bat or glove." In fact, information from ambient vision makes the last corrections faster and better than focal vision, which would be used to watch the ball all the way to the target. So, teachers should be saying, "Watch a spot through which the ball will pass; watch the thrower's hand, then feel yourself make contact with the ball." Ambient vision will capture the changes in ball position during the end of the ball's flight and allow the arms and hands to react automatically.

In physical education, children learn how to execute and control movements (i.e., motor programs), what movements to select (i.e., decision making or procedures), and why to move (i.e., physical activity is fun and healthy). Teachers can make learning easier and more efficient by understanding how motor programs develop and are used during physical activity.

DESIGNING PRACTICE

Two dimensions should be considered when designing practice. The first is the amount of the skill that can be practiced. Can the skill be divided logically into parts? If the answer is yes, then several options for part and progressive part practice are possible. If the answer is no, then whole practice is the only choice. Part practice means practicing the parts first, then joining the parts together for whole skill practice. Progressive part practice is similar; but in this system, one part is taught first, then another part is added. Once that is mastered, the next part is added, and so forth until the whole skill is mastered. You will see examples of the progressive part method in some of the rhythmical lessons at the end of this chapter. Jumping from a height and landing would be difficult to divide into parts, so the entire skill would be practiced at once. Jumping from a springboard could be divided into three parts: the running approach, the

Practice can help a child gain confidence and expertise in physical activities.

hurdle, and the take-off and landing. These could be practiced using the progressive part method, so students would first practice running to the springboard so that the last step was positioned for the hurdle. Then students could practice the hurdle, followed by the run and hurdle. Finally, the three parts could be practiced together.

The second dimension that should be considered when designing practice is how to organize trials. Four methods are

1. constant,
2. variable,
3. blocked, and
4. random practice.

Constant means doing one skill over and over. An example of constant practice would be repeatedly tossing beanbags at the same target. **Variable practice** is similar to constant, but one dimension

of the task changes (Yan, Thomas, and Thomas 1998). Extending the constant practice example to variable practice could be done by tossing the beanbags into the target from several positions, such as from 4 feet, 8 feet, and 13 feet. **Blocked practice** takes several skills, practices all of one, then moves on to the another skill, practicing all of that skill. An example of blocked practice is striking underhand 10 times, hitting 10 backhands, and then hitting 10 forehand drives. In **random practice,** the same skill cannot be practiced two times in a row. In the case of random practice, the student would complete one forehand drive, one underhand strike, and one backhand until each task had been repeated 10 times. Constant practice leads to rapid acquisition; that is, improvement is rapid and large. The down side is that retention is low (recall that retention is a measure of learning). So, while performance seems good, learning is not actually occurring because when the learner returns to the task after a period of no practice, the performance is similar to the first trials. Blocked practice is similar to constant practice because acquisition is rapid but retention is low. Random practice is the most difficult, with little progress early in practice. Retention is high, however. An interesting point is that children, especially younger children, benefit most from random practice (figure 5.6a; Yan, Thomas, and Thomas 1998). Practice is also best for tasks that are more difficult—those that are complex or rapid (figure 5.6b). Variable practice is a practice format related to random practice. It means practicing the same skill with varying demands (for example, tossing beanbags at a target from various distances). The skill is tossing; the variation is distance. Variable practice is usually better than constant or blocked, but not as good as random for learning. The differences between blocked and random practice can be seen in figure 5.6 as effect sizes. The larger the effect size is, the greater the benefits from random practice as compared to blocked practice.

There are several possible reasons that random practice produces greater learning than other types of practice. One reason is that random practice closely simulates the way skills will be used; that is, random practice provides a more similar context to sport, dance, and exercise. In most sports, players perform a series of tasks, often not knowing what the order will be; rarely do they do the same thing over and over. Sports in which the object is to do the same thing over and over are less complex, and random practice is less helpful for those skills. Another reason could be that with random practice the motor program is selected and programmed for each trial, whereas in blocked practice, the same program is run over and over. One benefit may be in practicing retrieving and programming the movement. Finally, random practice is the most difficult, so it is possible that this forces learners to concentrate or to pay attention to the practice more, which benefits learning.

Often a skill is so difficult that beginners must have some constant or blocked practice early in learning. In such a case, the teacher should switch practice to a random format as soon as possible, probably as soon as the skill becomes stable, and the student recognizes error and has the idea; in other words, this happens as soon as the learner reaches stage 2 of learning. At this stage, teachers can begin to encourage students to correct their own errors. This can be done by asking, "What are you doing wrong?" and "What should you do?" Of course, when students cannot identify the error, teachers must provide feedback. This serves three purposes. The student is made aware of his responsibility for learning and thinking about what he is doing. The student is guided to detect errors and to associate corrections with errors. Finally, the message to the student from the teacher is "I am confident you can learn this. I care about you and want you to learn."

Regardless of the type, design, and organization of practice, two criteria must be met for practice to be optimal: Every student should be involved and active as much of the time as possible so that the amount of practice is maximized. In the chapters on managing children (chapter 11) and organizing for teaching (chapter 10), we will cover techniques to assist you in planning these other aspects of a lesson so that practice is optimal.

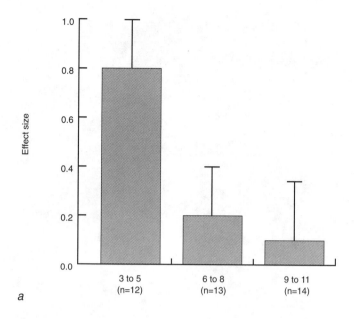

a

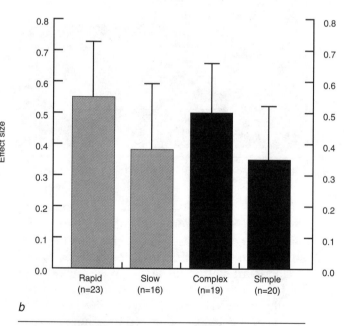

b

Figure 5.6   Effect sizes between blocked and random practice for age groups and types of task.

Reprinted with permission from *Research Quarterly for Exercise and Sport*, 69: 210-215, Copyright 1998 by the American Alliance for Health, Physical Education, Recreation and Dance, 1900 Association Drive, Reston, VA 20191.

SUMMARY

A teacher's goal is for students to learn. Because children have less experience and knowledge than adults and learn differently, teachers must understand how children learn so they can teach them effectively. The content of elementary physical education comprises developing skills (or motor programs) and procedures (decision making), learning facts (declarative knowledge), and becoming physically active (understanding why physical activity is important and incorporating it into their lives). Teachers need to

▶ provide as much appropriate practice as possible,

▶ help children understand why and how practice works,

▶ provide learning strategies like labeling and rehearsal,

▶ use appropriate cues that help children focus on important sensory information, and

▶ use the sandwich technique as often as possible to give corrective feedback.

Children, especially younger children, benefit from practice where control processes or specific strategies are used. Figure 5.4 demonstrates how error decreases for children of all ages when they use a specific strategy to remember movement characteristics. A similar pattern, with similar benefits, has been found for labeling, rehearsal, and grouping. As we get older, we get better—largely attributable to more efficient cognitive processing.

MASTERY LEARNING ACTIVITIES

1. Make a list of 20 different words of encouragement, praise, and reinforcement to use after a poor performance.

2. Select a task. Design practice (random versus blocked, constant versus variable) for the task with cues, adaptations for higher and lower skilled students, and notes about how you will know when to switch from early (constant or blocked) to advanced (random or variable) practice.

3. Select a motor skill. Identify the beginning and ending locations, distance or speed characteristics, and acceleration or deceleration cues. Provide cues for each of those characteristics.

4. Define and provide and examples of the following words: motor program, attention, memory, decision making, knowledge, practice, and control processes.

5. Identify specific things a teacher could do to improve student learning. Find at least one each for attention, information processing, feedback, motor programs, and practice.

6. Count out 12 seconds. Observe a teacher and count the length of the postfeedback interval and the number of feedback statements. Did the teacher use the sandwich technique? Were there at least two feedback statements during a class?

7. Fill in the following table with information from the text.

Type of practice	Definition	Acquisition performance	Retention performance
Constant			
Blocked			
Random			
Variable			

8. Review the following three concepts and provide supporting information for each one using definitions and applications:

  a. Learning is

- a result of practice,
- demonstrated with retention and transfer tests (e.g., permanent), and
- often confused with performance (and memory).

  b. Individuals process information in a predictable way, which changes with age and experience.

- Attention has three meanings: capacity, vigilance, and stage of development.
- The perceptual mechanism gives meaning to sensory information and is where stimulus identification occurs.
- Working, or short-term memory, is where decisions are made and all "cognitive activities" occur—it is limited by attention (capacity). Capacity is 7 ± 2 (Miller's magical number).
- Children can be forced to use control processes (working memory) to improve their performance; adult-like strategies almost always improve children's performance in cognitive tasks.
- Response selection occurs in working memory with either decision making or retrieval.
- Reaction time is a way of examining the simplest of decisions.
- Children begin to label at 2 years, use rote rehearsal at 7, and use mixed rehearsal at 11 years.
- Giving specific strategies to solve tasks helps children to perform better, but they are unlikely to use the strategy on their own—even in a similar situation.

  c. Feedback should be information the learner can't obtain for herself (it is not intrinsic).

- Two types of extrinsic feedback are knowledge of performance (KP) and knowledge of results (KR).
- Feedback reinforces, motivates, and provides information.
- Sensory modality, skill level, frequency, scheduling, and processing time should be considered when planning feedback.

REFERENCES

Adams, J.A. 1987. Historical review and appraisal of research on the learning, retention, and transfer of human motor skills. *Psychological Bulletin* 101:41–74.

Bloom, B.S. 1956. *Taxonomy of educational objectives: Cognitive domain.* New York: McKay.

Deakin, J. 2001. What they do versus what they say they do: An assessment of practice in figure skating. In *Proceedings of the 10th World Congress of Sport Psychology, Vol 3,* edited by A. Papaioannou, M. Goudas, and Y. Theodorakis, 153–55. Skiathos Island, Greece: International Society of Sport Psychology.

Fitts, P.M., and M.I. Posner. 1967. *Human performance.* Belmont, Ca.: Brooks/Cole.

Gallagher, J.D., and J.R. Thomas. 1984. Rehearsal strategy effects on developmental differences for recall of a movement series. *Research Quarterly for Exercise and Sport* 55:123–128.

Gallagher, J.D., and J.R. Thomas. 1986. Developmental effects of grouping and recoding on learning a movement series. *Research Quarterly for Exercise and Sport* 57:117–127.

Helsen, W.F., J.L. Starkes, and N.J. Hodges. 1998. Team sports and the theory of deliberate practice. *Journal of Sport and Exercise Psychology* 20:12–34.

Kerr, R. 1985. Fitts' law and motor control in children. In *Motor development: Current selected research,* edited by J. Clark and H.H. Humphrey, 45–53. Princeton, N.J.: Princeton Book Co.

Ladewig, I., and J. Gallagher. 1994. Cue use to enhance selective attention. *Research Quarterly for Exercise and Sport* 65:s64.

Meyer, D.E., R.A. Abrams, S. Kornblum, C.E. Wright, and J.E.K. Smith. 1988. Optimality in human motor performance: Ideal control of rapid aimed movements. *Psychological Review* 95:340–70.

Newell, K.M., and J.A. Kennedy. 1978. Knowledge of results and children's motor learning. *Developmental Psychology* 14:531–36.

Ornstein, P.A., and M.J. Naus. 1985. Effects of knowledge base on children's memory strategies. In *Advances in child development and behavior,* edited by H.W. Reese, 113–48. New York: Academic Press.

Plamondon, R., and A.M. Alimi. 1997. Speed/accuracy trade-offs in target-directed movements. *Behavioral and Brain Sciences* 20:279–303.

Salmoni, A.W., and C. Pascoe. 1979. Fitts reciprocal tapping task: A developmental study. In *Psychology of motor behavior and sport-1978,* edited by G.C. Roberts and K.M. Newell, 355–86. Champaign, Ill.: Human Kinetics.

Thomas, J.R. 2000. C.H. McCloy Lecture: Children's control, learning, and performance of motor skills. *Research Quarterly for Exercise and Sport* 71:1–9.

Thomas, K.T., J.D. Gallagher, and J.R. Thomas. 2000. Motor development and skill acquisition during childhood and adolescence. In *Handbook of Sport Psychology,* 2d ed, edited by R.N. Singer, H.A. Hausenblas, and C. Janelle, 20–52. New York: Wiley.

Thomas, J.R., M.A. Solmon, and B. Mitchell. 1979. Precision knowledge of results and motor performance: Relationship to age. *Research Quarterly for Exercise and Sport* 50:687–98.

Thomas, J.R., K.T. Thomas, A.M. Lee, E. Testerman, and M. Ashy. 1983. Age differences in use of strategy for recall of movement in a large scale environment. *Research Quarterly for Exercise and Sport* 54:264–72.

Yan, J.H., J.R. Thomas, G.E. Stelmach, and K.T. Thomas. 2000. Developmental features of rapid aiming movements across the lifespan. *Journal of Motor Behavior* 32:121–40.

Yan, J.H., J.R. Thomas, and K.T. Thomas. 1998. Children's age moderates the effect of practice variability: A quantitative review. *Research Quarterly for Exercise and Sport* 69:210–15.

RESOURCES

Gallagher, J.D., and J.R. Thomas. 1980. Effects of varying post-KR intervals upon children's motor performance. *Journal of Motor Behavior* 12:41–46.

Newell, K.M., and C.R. Barclay. 1982. Developing knowledge about action. In *The development of movement control and co-ordination,* edited by J.A.S. Kelso and J.E. Clark, 175–212. New York: Wiley.

LESSON PLANS

The lesson plans provided here demonstrate methods that appropriately help children learn motor skills, make decisions, and learn facts. For grades K and 1 (the Mulberry Bush and Baa, Baa Black Sheep), grades 2 and 3 (Kinderpolka and rope jumping), and grades 4 and 5 (country dance), lessons use progressive part instruction and repetition to help children remember the skills. The concluding activity is a retention test—doing both dances again after short periods without practice. Another grade K and 1 lesson using jump ropes incorporates cognitive concepts such as over, around, shapes, and letters into movement challenges. The rope jumping lesson for grades 4 and 5 uses blocked practice to introduce the skills; later lessons practice these skills again and move toward a random practice schedule in routines. In addition to these lessons, the cognitive concepts presented in the fitness lessons at the end of chapter 6 demonstrate the use of decision making, rehearsal, and other concepts to develop declarative and procedural knowledge.

Baa, Baa, Black Sheep and Mulberry Bush

Student Objectives

- Remember the words to the songs.
- Perform the movement sequences to the words of the songs.

Equipment and Materials

- 1 tambourine
- Music (optional): "Baa, Baa, Black Sheep" (Folkraft 1191, Victor E-83) and "Mulberry Bush" (Folkraft 1183, Victor 20806)

Warm-Up Activities (5 minutes)

Move and Freeze

Arrange the children in scatter formation.

1. Tell the children: *Walk freely around the area to a drumbeat and freeze when the drumbeat stops.*

2. *When the drum starts again, find another way to travel (backward; sideways; in a circle; with a jump, hop, leap, [or the like]).*

Skill-Development Activities (20 minutes)

Baa, Baa, Black Sheep

Arrange the children in a circle, facing center.

1. Describe and demonstrate the following steps, based on the lyrics:

   Baa, baa, black sheep (three claps),
   Have you any wool (three stamps)?
   Yes, sir, yes, sir (nod two times),
   Three bags full (hold up three fingers).
   One for my master (turn and bow right),
   One for my dame (turn and bow left),
   One for the little boy (turn in place once),
   Who lives down the lane (bow forward).
   Baa, baa, black sheep (three claps),
   Have you any wool (three stamps)?
   Yes, sir, yes, sir (nod two times),
   Three bags full (hold up three fingers).

2. Sing *"Baa, baa, black sheep"* (line 1).

3. Repeat as the children sing with you.

4. Continue with each line until you complete the song.

5. *Now we will sing the entire song.* (Sing the whole song with the children.) Have the children practice the movements: *When we sing "Baa, baa, black sheep," we will clap three times, like this.* Sing and clap each part of the song.

6. Tell the children: *Now let's do all the movements.*

Mulberry Bush

Keep the children in a circle, facing center.

1. Describe and demonstrate the following steps, based on the lyrics:

   Here we go 'round the mulberry bush (walk or skip to the right),
   The mulberry bush, the mulberry bush,
   Here we go 'round the mulberry bush,
   So early in the morning.

This is the way we wash our clothes (stop, drop hands, and turn in place once),

Wash our clothes, wash our clothes (pantomime washing clothes on a washboard),

This is the way we wash our clothes,

So early Monday morning.

2. Repeat, having the children use the following actions:

Iron our clothes (Tuesday)

Mend our clothes (Wednesday)

Sweep our floor (Thursday)

Make a cake (Friday)

Build a house (Saturday)

Bake our bread (Sunday)

3. Sing "Mulberry Bush," having the children practice each action with the song.

Concluding Activities (5 minutes)

Baa, Baa, Black Sheep or Mulberry Bush

Repeat, going through the words and movements several times.

From *Physical Education Methods for Elementary Teachers, Second Edition,* by Katherine T. Thomas, Amelia M. Lee, and Jerry R. Thomas, 2003, Champaign, IL: Human Kinetics. Adapted from *Physical Education for Children: Daily Lesson Plans for Elementary School, Second Edition,* by Katherine T. Thomas, Amelia M. Lee, and Jerry R. Thomas, 2000, Champaign, IL: Human Kinetics.

Rhythmic Activities

LESSON **5.2**

Rope Activities

Student Objectives

- Create letters and shapes with a rope.
- Jump rhythmically back and forth over a rope on the floor.

Equipment and Materials

- 1 small (6 ft) jump rope per child
- 1 drum
- Music: "Sunshine" from *Modern Tunes for Rhythm and Instruments,* Hap Palmer (AR 523)
- Color cards: 1 red, 1 green, and 1 yellow

Warm-Up Activities (5 minutes)

Traffic Lights

Arrange the children in scatter formation. A leader (you, at first) faces the class, holding movement cards.

1. Describe the warm-up:

   The leader chooses and calls out a locomotor skill.

   The leader holds up a red card indicating "freeze," a green card indicating "run," and a yellow card indicating "walk slowly." You perform the movements at the right speeds.

2. Have the children warm up.

3. Variation: You can select other movements for yellow and green, such as walking in place or walking backward and running sideways or leaping forward.

Repeat several times.

Skill-Development Activities (20 minutes)

Jump Rope Activities

Make sure the children are still in scatter formation, and give each a jump rope.

1. Challenge the children with the following tasks:

   Can you make a circle (square, triangle) with your rope?

   Can you walk (jump, hop) around your triangle?

   Can you make a letter with your rope?

   Can you jump (leap, hop) over your letter?

   Can you think of another way to move over your letter?

   Can you put your rope in a straight line? Now with your side to the rope, jump from side-to-side over the rope (facing the rope, jump over the rope and back).

2. Repeat the challenges several times.

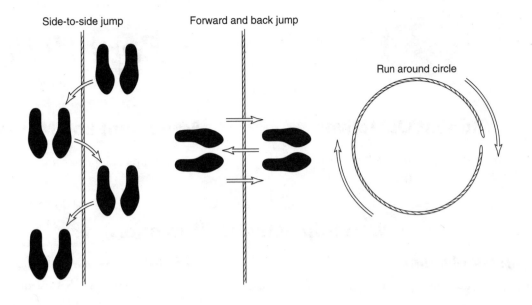

Side-to-side jump   Forward and back jump   Run around circle

Concluding Activities (5 minutes)

Rope Tasks

Have the children stand beside their ropes, which are laid out straight on the ground.

1. Tell the children: *Jump side to side (forward, backward) to a drumbeat (to music) over the rope.*

2. Repeat several times.

From *Physical Education Methods for Elementary Teachers, Second Edition,* by Katherine T. Thomas, Amelia M. Lee, and Jerry R. Thomas, 2003, Champaign, IL: Human Kinetics. Adapted from *Physical Education for Children: Daily Lesson Plans for Elementary School, Second Edition,* by Katherine T. Thomas, Amelia M. Lee, and Jerry R. Thomas, 2000, Champaign, IL: Human Kinetics.

LESSON

Rope Jumping

Student Objectives

- Jump hot pepper and high water with a long rope.

Equipment and Materials

- 1 long jump rope per group

Warm-Up Activities (5 minutes)

High, Low, Medium

Arrange the children in scatter formation.

1. Describe the activity:

   I will tell you "high," "low," or "medium."
   On "high," run high on tiptoe.
   On "low," run low with your body close to the ground.
   On "medium," run at an in-between level.
   I will change commands several times.

2. Have the children warm up.

3. Have the children skip or gallop rather than run.

Skill-Development Activities (20 minutes)

Rope Skills

Divide the children into groups of three or four, each group with a long jump rope.

   Have the children practice running in the front door and running out the back door, with two-footed single and double jumps (see lesson plan 10.3).

Hot Pepper

Keep the same formation.

1. Describe and demonstrate the skill: *Jumping hot pepper is jumping with the rope turning very fast.*

2. Have the children practice hot pepper, one child at a time in each rope. Rotate turners so everyone has a chance.

High Water

Keep the same formation.

1. Describe and demonstrate the skill: *Jumping high water is jumping with the rope turning so that it gradually gets higher and higher from the ground. Turners, be careful to move up gradually, instead of quickly, so the jumper will be safer.*

2. Have the children practice high water, one child at a time in each rope. Rotate turners so everyone has a chance.

Mabel, Mabel

Keep the same formation.

1. One by one, say and have the children practice each line of the rhyme:

   Mabel, Mabel, set the table,
   Don't forget the salt and pepper.
   (On "pepper," turn the rope faster and faster, and jumper jumps until he or she misses.)

2. Practice the entire rhyme.

Fourth of July

Keep the same formation.

1. One by one, say and have the children practice each line of the rhyme:

   I asked my mother for 15 cents,
   To see the elephant jump the fence.
   He jumped so high he reached the sky,
   And never came back 'til the Fourth of July.

(Use regular jumps for the first two lines. On the third line, the rope is gradually raised and the jumper must jump higher and higher until the end of the rhyme. Again, turners, be careful to raise the rope gradually.)

2. Practice the entire rhyme.

Concluding Activities (5 minutes)

High Water and Hot Pepper

Have the children practice high water and hot pepper again, using the rhymes Mabel, Mabel and Fourth of July.

From *Physical Education Methods for Elementary Teachers, Second Edition,* by Katherine T. Thomas, Amelia M. Lee, and Jerry R. Thomas, 2003, Champaign, IL: Human Kinetics. Adapted from *Physical Education for Children: Daily Lesson Plans for Elementary School, Second Edition,* by Katherine T. Thomas, Amelia M. Lee, and Jerry R. Thomas, 2000, Champaign, IL: Human Kinetics.

Rhythmic Activities

LESSON

Folk Dance

Student Objectives

- Combine a step-close and a stamp to perform the Kinderpolka.

Equipment and Materials

- Music: "Kinderpolka (Children's Polka)" (Folkraft 1187)

Warm-Up Activities (5 minutes)

Animal Chase

Mark two goals, 30 ft apart. Arrange the children along one goal line.

1. Use the following commands:

Animals run backward one time.
Animals run sideways two times.
Animals jump forward one time.

2. Repeat.

Skill-Development Activities (20 minutes)

Step-Close

Arrange the children in a single circle, with partners facing each other.

1. Describe and demonstrate the step-close: *To do the step-close, step to the side, then close with the opposite foot.*
2. Have the children practice the step-close.

Kinderpolka

Keep the children in a single circle, with partners facing each other.

1. Demonstrate and describe the movements:
   - Part 1:

   Two step-close steps to the center,
   Three stamps in place (performed slowly),
   Two step-close steps back to original position,
   Three stamps in place. (Cues: Step, close, step, close, stamp, stamp, stamp.)
   - Part 2:

   Repeat part 1.

- Part 3:

Clap own thighs one time,
Clap hands together one time,
And clap hands to partner's hands three times.
- Part 4:

Repeat part 3.
- Part 5:

Shake right index finger three times at partner.
Repeat with left index finger.
Turn around four steps in place,
And stamp three times.

2. Have the children practice the movements with cues.
3. Have them listen to the music.
4. Have them clap in rhythm to the music.
5. Say the cues to the music as the children perform.

Concluding Activities (5 minutes)

Kinderpolka

Have the children perform the entire sequence with the music. Repeat.

From *Physical Education Methods for Elementary Teachers, Second Edition,* by Katherine T. Thomas, Amelia M. Lee, and Jerry R. Thomas, 2003, Champaign, IL: Human Kinetics. Adapted from *Physical Education for Children: Daily Lesson Plans for Elementary School, Second Edition,* by Katherine T. Thomas, Amelia M. Lee, and Jerry R. Thomas, 2000, Champaign, IL: Human Kinetics.

LESSON **5.5**

Country Dance

Student Objectives

- Perform the grapevine step to music.

Equipment and Materials

- Music: "Elvira" by the Oak Ridge Boys, *Greatest Hits* (MCA 5496)
- 1 parachute
- Signal

Warm-Up Activities (5 minutes)

Parachute Steps

Arrange the children around the parachute and ask them to hold it with one or both hands.

1. Explain the warm-up:

   Moving clockwise, slide in a circle.
   On the signal, change directions.

2. Have the children warm up, repeating the instructions several times. You can also have them try jumping, hopping, and running in place.

Skill-Development Activities (20 minutes)

Elvira

Arrange the children in scatter formation.

1. Have the children listen to "Elvira" and clap to the beat.

2. Have them stand in place and step to the music.

Grapevine Steps

Keep the children in scatter formation.

1. Describe and demonstrate the skill, going to the right:

   Step to the right with your right foot.
   Bring your left foot behind and step on it.
   Step to the right again with your right foot.
   Bring your left foot in front, lifting your left knee across in front of your right knee while balancing on your right foot.

Summarize: *It takes four counts: step, back, step, cross (or lift).*

2. Have the children practice grapevine steps, going to the right. Cue the children: *Right, back, right, lift.*

3. Repeat, going left. Cue the children: *Left, back, left, lift.*

4. Have the children practice the grapevine step, going to the right and left (with a partner, in a line, in a circle).

5. Have the children practice the grapevine step to the music.

6. Have the children practice the grapevine step with a quarter turn (pivot) on the lift, after completing the right, back, right. Cue the children: *Right, back, right, lift, and pivot.*

Concluding Activities (5 minutes)

Grapevine Line

Arrange the children in a single-file line. Have the children perform the grapevine step right and left, in a line, to the music, making a quarter turn to the left at the end of each grapevine step to the left.

From *Physical Education Methods for Elementary Teachers, Second Edition,* by Katherine T. Thomas, Amelia M. Lee, and Jerry R. Thomas, 2003, Champaign, IL: Human Kinetics. Adapted from *Physical Education for Children: Daily Lesson Plans for Elementary School, Second Edition,* by Katherine T. Thomas, Amelia M. Lee, and Jerry R. Thomas, 2000, Champaign, IL: Human Kinetics.

Rhythmic Activities

LESSON **5.6**

Rope Jumping

Student Objectives

- Perform the rock step, ski twist, and straddle cross jump with a jump rope.
- Jump rope to music.

Equipment and Materials

- 1 short jump rope per child
- Music: *Aerobic Rope Skipping* (AR 43); *Jump Aerobics* (KIM 2095); *Jump to the Beat* (KIM 8097)

Warm-Up Activities (5 minutes)

Follow the Leader

Divide the children into groups of four, each group with four ropes. Arrange the groups in scatter formation.

1. Explain the warm-up:

   Each group creates rope obstacles by arranging its four ropes into a formation.

   Choose a leader, who leaps, jumps, or hops through the pattern with the rest of you following.

   Give everyone a chance to lead and create a pattern.

2. Have the children warm up.

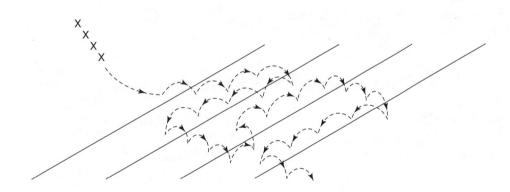

Skill-Development Activities (20 minutes)

Two-Foot Double Jump Forward

Arrange individuals in scatter formation, each with a jump rope.

1. Describe and demonstrate the skill: *Jump on both feet twice for each turn of the rope.*
2. Have the children practice the two-foot double jump forward.

Two-Foot Double Jump Backward

Keep the children in scatter formation, each with a jump rope.

1. Describe and demonstrate the skill: *Throwing the rope backward overhead, jump on both feet two times for each turn of the rope.*
2. Have the children practice the two-foot double jump backward.

Rock Step

Keep the children in scatter formation, each with a jump rope.

1. Describe and demonstrate the skill: *Using a double-jump rhythm, place one foot in front of the other; jump on the front foot, leaning slightly forward and with the same turn of the rope, and rebound on the back foot.*
2. Have the children practice the rock step with the left leg forward.

3. Have them practice the rock step with the right leg forward.

Ski Twist

Keep the children in scatter formation, each with a jump rope.

1. Describe and demonstrate the skill: *Using a double-jump rhythm, twist your knees and ankles in the same direction.*
2. Have the children practice the ski twist.

Straddle Cross Jump

Keep the children in scatter formation, each with a jump rope.

1. Describe and demonstrate the skill: *Using the double-jump rhythm, land first with your feet about shoulder-width apart; and then on the second jump, land with your feet crossed.*
2. Have the children practice the straddle cross jump.

Jump to Music

Keep the children in scatter formation, each with a jump rope. Using any of the steps learned, have the children jump rope to music.

Concluding Activities (5 minutes)

Jump Rope Routine

Keep the children in scatter formation, each with a jump rope. Direct the children to perform the following routine to music:

Eight two-foot double jumps,
Eight rock steps,
Eight ski twists, and
Eight straddle cross jumps.

From *Physical Education Methods for Elementary Teachers, Second Edition,* by Katherine T. Thomas, Amelia M. Lee, and Jerry R. Thomas, 2003, Champaign, IL: Human Kinetics. Adapted from *Physical Education for Children: Daily Lesson Plans for Elementary School, Second Edition,* by Katherine T. Thomas, Amelia M. Lee, and Jerry R. Thomas, 2000, Champaign, IL: Human Kinetics.

chapter 6

Physical Activity for Children

Sawyer, age 7

*P*hysical inactivity is a major independent health risk factor, meaning that even if you take away all other potential risk factors, physical inactivity still carries health risk. Thus, a physically active lifestyle will reduce a person's potential burden on public health, which begins during childhood. Children respond differently to training than adults do, however; so, programs that promote physical fitness for children must accommodate these differences.

Learner Outcomes

The teacher will do the following:

- Define and contrast physical activity and physical fitness.
- List and describe the benefits of a physically active lifestyle.
- Use the FIT principle.
- Define the components of physical fitness and describe how each is trained.

Glossary Terms

physical activity
sedentary
physically active
physical fitness
body composition
FIT principle
frequency
intensity
duration

aerobic training
muscle strength
muscle endurance
flexibility
systolic pressure
diastolic pressure
anaerobic threshold
norm-referenced tests
criterion-referenced tests

During the 1990s the focus of physical education and exercise shifted from physical fitness to a broader term, physical activity. **Physical activity** is a continuum from sedentary to physically fit (figure 6.1). **Sedentary** describes a person who is inactive (e.g., a person who sits at work and during leisure time). **Physically active** describes a person who engages in one hour per day of whole-body movement (e.g., walking), 30 minutes of which is moderate to vigorous (i.e., it makes them breathe hard and sweat). Lifestyle physical activities include cleaning house, gardening, and using the stairs instead of the elevator. Physically active people have reduced health risk. **Physical fitness** is taking a physically active lifestyle to a higher level and is defined by a specific regimen of training and testing.

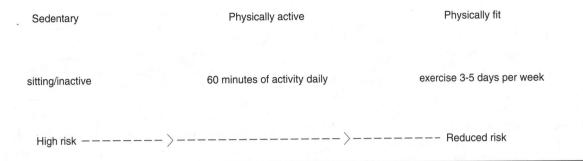

Figure 6.1 The physical activity continuum demonstrates the relationship among health risk; level of physical activity; and the terms fitness, sedentary, and physically active.

Teachers, parents, and coaches need to know about physical activity, physical fitness, and the physiological responses to exercise, as well as differences between children and adults regarding exercise, for several reasons:

▶ Because reducing health risk is a long-term benefit of a physically active lifestyle

▶ Because the roots of a physically active lifestyle are found in childhood

▶ To be able to plan appropriate activities to encourage being physically active

▶ To be able to provide safe environments for physical activity

▶ To be able to present knowledge so children will understand the benefits of being physically active

▶ To be able to assess physical activity and fitness appropriately

BENEFITS FROM BEING PHYSICALLY ACTIVE

The following are the 10 leading health indicators in *Healthy People 2010* (USDHHS 2000):

1. Physical activity
2. Overweight and obesity
3. Tobacco use
4. Substance abuse
5. Responsible sexual behavior
6. Mental health
7. Injury and violence
8. Environmental quality
9. Immunization
10. Access to health care

School initiatives to provide healthy environments and reduce disparities based on gender, ethnicity, income, and age include requiring immunizations, providing school nurses and physical education, and banning tobacco and illegal substances. Schools have provided health education and participated in co-curricular programs educating children and adolescents about gangs, substance abuse, tobacco use, sex, and mental health. Schools and teachers embrace improving the health of students as part of their mission (Simons-Morton, Parcel, Baranowski, Forthofer, and O'Hara 1991). Teachers and their schools have the opportunity to significantly influence what children do during school, after school, and throughout their lives. With so many other problems to deal with, though, why should physical activity be a priority for schools? The answer to that question is found in the statistics.

Adults who are physically active have several advantages over those who are not (USDHHS 2000):

▶ Lower death rates
▶ Lower rates of cardiovascular deaths
▶ Lower incidence of diabetes
▶ Lower risk for colon cancer
▶ Lower blood pressure
▶ Increases in muscle mass, muscle strength, and bone strength

A number of psychological benefits can be gained from regular activity:

▶ Reduced symptoms of depression
▶ Improved mood
▶ Reduced risk of developing depression
▶ Enhanced psychological well-being

Regular physical activity also has several other perks for adults:

► Weight control

► Weight loss

► Decreases in body fat

Children and adolescents need regular weight-bearing physical activity to ensure normal skeletal growth (Bailey 2001). Clearly, physical activity is related to lifelong health, and physically active lifestyles begin during childhood. In addition to enhancing physical and mental health, physical activity contributes to development and meets important social needs, which will be addressed in chapter 7.

> Longitudinal research indicates that physical activity and fitness are more important factors for reducing mortality than is obesity. Longitudinal research follows the same subjects (e.g., people) across time. Obese physically fit adults had lower death rates than sedentary adults of normal weight (Lee, Blair, and Jackson 1999).

Adults who are physically active report having learned sport skills as children and developing confidence as a result of those experiences (Welk 1999). Barriers to being active include lack of time, lack of access to facilities, and lack of access to safe environments. People with more education and more income are more active than people with less education and less income (CDC 1997). Women are less active than men, African Americans and Hispanics are less active than Whites, and the disabled are less active than the general population. People living in the north central and western states are more active than those living elsewhere in the United States.

Children face barriers similar to those faced by adults—time, access, and safety. Children are more likely to be active, however, when important adults (e.g., parents, teachers, and coaches) encourage them to be active. Children enjoy the social aspect of exercise, so planning family or group activities that include physical activity is a good way to encourage children to be active. Schools can reduce barriers to activity for children and provide social support so children are more likely to be active.

To summarize, a physically active lifestyle begins during childhood when there is opportunity, including time, place, and social support. Developing skill and confidence during childhood is important to maintaining a physically active lifestyle. Physical activity reduces health risk directly and in a secondary role as activity reduces overweight and obesity.

PHYSICAL FITNESS

In 1956, European children performed better on fitness tests than did U.S. children; as a result, youth fitness testing was established by President Eisenhower (Park 1988). At the same time, the Soviet Union was rapidly developing its space program, so the concern about physical fitness doubled as the United States started to train astronauts. Presidents Kennedy and Johnson continued to support the fitness movement, which eventually became the President's Council on Physical Fitness and Sport. Your parents may remember taking the President's Youth Fitness Test; some of you may have taken a more recent version called the Presidential Test. Early youth fitness tests did not require or even suggest how to train children to do well on the test. Often the test was given in the fall and spring and forgotten in between. Depending on the year, only the top 5 to 15 percent of the students could earn an award. This meant that many children who took the test had a failing experience. Further, the test included items that had nothing to do with fitness (e.g., throwing a softball).

Several other fitness tests have emerged to compete with the Presidential Test; among them were FITNESSGRAM and American Alliance for Health, Physical Education, Recreation and Dance (AAPHERD) Health Related Fitness Test. The Physical Best Program was developed by AAHPERD during the 1980s. This program has several levels of awards and suggested activities to train for fitness during the year. Recently, FITNESSGRAM has included a computer program to track physical activity. (FITNESSGRAM and ACTIVITYGRAM are available from Human Kinetics Publishers and the Cooper Institute of Aerobics Research.) The changes in fitness testing reflect a change in fitness philosophy during the 1990s. That is, physically active lifestyles are for everyone and provide the most benefit to health, whereas physical fitness is for some people and provides additional benefits with small additional risks.

The American College of Sports Medicine (ACSM 1995) describes three components of physical fitness: cardiovascular endurance, body composition, and musculoskeletal health (which includes flexibility, muscle strength, and endurance). The most documented benefit from fitness is that from cardiovascular fitness because it reduces the risk of cardiovascular disease. **Body composition**—specifically, maintaining a healthy body weight and healthy percentage of body fat—also contributes to reduced risk of cardiovascular disease, adult-onset diabetes, and cancer. Flexibility, muscle strength, and endurance reduce lower back pain and increase posture, functional capacity, and the ability to conduct daily activities.

The cardiovascular fitness, flexibility, muscle strength, and endurance components of fitness translate directly into fitness tests and training activities (table 6.1). Body composition does not have specific activities but is positively influenced by the activities training the other components.

Three terms are used to describe fitness training, which can be remembered using the acronym **FIT**:

▶ **Frequency**—the number of training sessions per week

▶ **Intensity**—the percent of maximum for the training

▶ **Time**—the amount training in minutes or repetitions, also called **duration**

To meet the minimum for **aerobic training** (cardiovascular fitness), you must exercise (swim, jog, cycle) three days per week, for 20 minutes at your training heart rate. This is calculated by subtracting your age from 220 and multiplying the result by .7. The most familiar training activities for muscle strength and endurance are sit-ups or crunches, push-ups, chin-ups, and pull-ups. Weight training also contributes to muscle strength and endurance. Muscle strength and endurance training also require a frequency of three days per week. **Muscle strength** is the maximum amount of force a muscle can produce at one time. To train strength, the intensity is usually high (close to the maximum) and the time (repetitions) is low. **Muscle endurance** activities are low intensity (50 to 70 percent of maximum) and high time (three sets of 10 repetitions or more). Some activities are considered muscle endurance for one person and muscle strength for another. For example, a person who can do 10 chin-ups is training muscle endurance, whereas the student who cannot quite do one chin-up is working on muscle strength. **Flexibility,** defined as the range of motion in a joint, is increased by low-intensity stretching with many repetitions, done three or more days per week. As you can see, one issue complicating physical fitness in elementary schools is that many programs do not allow enough time for physical education (e.g., days per week and time per day) to train fitness in children. Clearly, to do so, programs would need three days per week for approximately an hour each day to meet minimum fitness criteria.

One of the challenges facing teachers and schools is to help children develop the competence (e.g., skill and knowledge) and initiative to be responsible for their own fitness, beginning in childhood. The challenge results from two factors. First, time is needed to train for fitness. Typically, physical education—whether taught by a classroom teacher or by a specialist—is not offered daily. Although daily physical education might be ideal, it is not common. Even with daily physical education, the time demand of physical fitness training reduces the time available for skill acquisition. Second, the optimal situation is for children to assume responsibility for their own fitness. Adults must decide to train and to continue to train for fitness, and children can begin to learn this habit, with the goal of lifelong fitness becoming a self-responsibility. Some individuals will choose to be active rather than fit. Skill is a predictor of physically active lifestyles, though, so allocating physical education time to skill development is important. How do teachers decide how much time to allocate? This will be partially a personal choice; however, all children need to understand how to train for fitness and need to have a variety of exercises designed for them that will meet fitness goals. Further, all children need skill to participate in a variety of physical activities that can contribute to a physically active lifestyle. The relationship among activity level, health risk, and fitness compared with physically active is demonstrated in the physical activity continuum in figure 6.1.

Being physically active is a goal for everyone, whereas physical fitness is a goal for some. To provide safe and effective programs, teachers need to understand some of the differences in the ways in which children and adults experience exercise. Just as children grow, mature, and have skills that evolve with time and practice, their bodies change in other ways that cannot be directly observed.

Table 6.1   Fitness Components, Tests, Training Activities, Frequency and Duration

Component	Test	Training activities	Frequency and duration
Cardiovascular endurance	Mile run, step tests, PACER	Jogging, cycling, swimming, aerobic dance	20 min, 3 days per week at training heart rate
Muscular strength and endurance	Sit-ups, push-ups, pull-ups, chin-ups	Sit-ups or crunches, push-ups, weight training, chin-ups, or pull-ups	3 times per week with 3 sets of 10 repetitions
Flexibility	Sit and reach, back-saver	Stretching of most major muscle groups	3 times per week
Body composition	BMI, skin-folds		

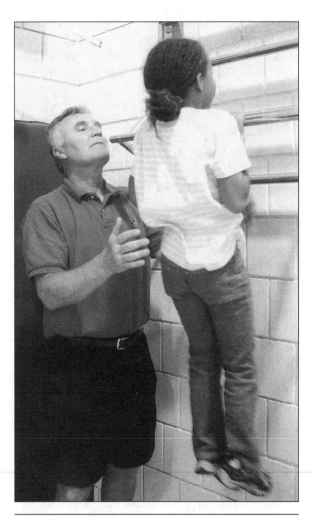

A child performs a muscle strength activity under the watchful eye of her teacher.

BIOLOGICAL AND PHYSIOLOGICAL DIFFERENCES IN CHILDREN

The discussion in chapter 3 on growth and maturation demonstrated that children are not smaller versions of adults. This concept translates into children exercising differently than adults do. The body makes two major adjustments during aerobic exercise (prolonged, rhythmic exercise like jogging, running, or cycling). First, muscles do their work during exercise by using fuel (food) and oxygen. The more intense the work, the more oxygen and fuel used. The oxygen is used very rapidly, so the blood must deliver more oxygen (and fuel, too, but this is not a major issue at most levels and durations of exercise) as work continues or increases. This means the lungs and heart must work harder. As a general rule, respiration and heart rate increase with the intensity of the exercise. At some point, the circulatory system can no longer keep up in delivering oxygen and removing waste. Fatigue sets in quickly at that point, and work must be stopped or substantially reduced.

The second effect of exercise is production of heat. The body dissipates some heat by breathing but most of it by sweating: The circulatory system increases blood flow to the skin, and the heat is lost by radiation and evaporation of sweat. Teachers need to be conscious of this process, particularly during hot and dry weather, when excessive sweating and evaporation may produce a loss in total body fluid. This can result in dehydration. Fluid lost should be replaced by regular water intake during heavy exercise in hot and dry weather. People of all ages are susceptible to dehydration. Children should always be permitted to drink as much water as they want to during and after exercise. Water is as good a fluid replacement as any of the advertised commercial products. The USDA warns that children do not drink enough water and should be encouraged to drink water regardless of whether they are exercising, so encouraging children to drink water meets the demands of exercise and a more general nutritional need.

Children and adults handle heat and oxygen production differently during exercise and physical activity. Children have higher resting heart rates than adults; this means that at rest children's hearts are working harder than adult's hearts. For example, a 6-year-old boy has a resting heart rate of 86 beats per minute (a girl's at the same age would be 88); by age 13, his resting heart rate would be 66 (hers would be 70). The maximum heart rate for a 6-year-old is 215, as compared with 201 for a 13-year-old. The easiest way to estimate heart rate is to gently touch your fingers to the carotid artery and count the beats for 10 seconds, then multiply by 6. The carotid artery can be located by placing the fingers next to the Adam's apple (figure 6.2).

Blood pressure increases steadily during childhood and adolescence. **Systolic pressure,** the maximum pressure immediately after a heart beat, increases from 108 to 115 millimeters Hg during childhood and adolescence in boys, and in girls from 101 to 111 millimeters Hg (Hg is the symbol for the element mercury as read on the gauge). **Diastolic pressure,** the minimum pressure just before a heart beat, goes from 72 to 82 millimeters Hg in boys and 65 to 75 millimeters Hg in girls.

Respiration volume increases directly in relation to the intensity of exercise, but only about 50 to 60 percent of maximum aerobic power or maximum oxygen uptake ($\dot{V}O_2$max). Maximum aerobic power, maximum oxygen uptake, and $\dot{V}O_2$max are terms used to describe the upper limit of the cardiorespiratory system in its ability to deliver oxygen to the body during exercise. At this point, respiration increases very rapidly. The change from steady to rapid increase in respiration has been called the anaerobic threshold. The **anaerobic threshold** is the point at which the body can no longer keep up with the oxygen demands or the waste build-up in the muscles. The muscles are working without adequate oxygen, and in this state fatigue sets in very rapidly. Respiration response is the same for girls and boys. As children exercise, respiration rate can provide information about level of fatigue. For example, a child who can talk easily while jogging is probably breathing steadily; when respiration interferes with talking, the child is moving toward fatigue.

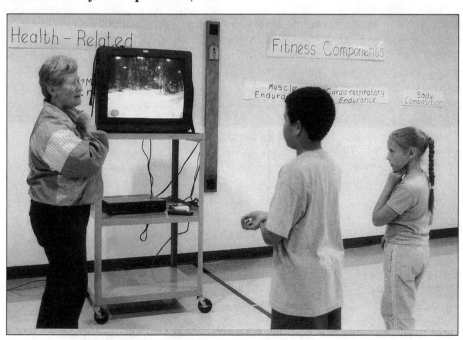

Figure 6.2   You can easily estimate your heart rate by gently touching your fingers to the carotid artery and counting the beats for 10 seconds, then multiplying by 6.

Anaerobic power, the ability to work without oxygen, is also lower in children than adults. This is because children have less of an important enzyme (phosophofructokinase or PFK) in their muscles; this enzyme allows the muscles to work without oxygen. Children will produce more PFK after puberty. Anaerobic power is important in activities such as sprinting.

Children also have a lower hemoglobin concentration in the blood than adults. Since hemoglobin is the part of blood that carries oxygen to the working muscles (e.g., in the heart and legs), children transport less oxygen per unit of blood than adults. This means that children can do less work than adults. Hemoglobin content in the blood increases at puberty; however, the increase is not as great in women as it is in men.

Children become more fit as a result of fitness training. The responses to training tend to be lower in children for several reasons:

▶ Children tend to be more fit at the onset, so training results in less improvement.

▶ Children have higher resting and maximum heart rates, which limits the intensity of training ($.7 \times$ maximum heart rate = training heart rate).

▶ Children have less hemoglobin, which limits maximal oxygen uptake.

Exercise training produces three benefits for children and adults. First, hearts become stronger as a result of training as stroke volume (the amount of blood the heart can pump in one beat) increases. Second, more capillaries develop as a result of training, which provides a better supply of blood to the heart and working muscles. Third, better extraction of oxygen from the blood leads to improved enzymatic reactions. Recall that in order to benefit from training, children must exercise 3 days per week for at least 20 minutes per day for 10 or more weeks at the training heart rate. Training or target heart rates for various age groups are presented in table 6.2.

The relationship between the type of cardiovascular (aerobic fitness exercise) used for training and the type of testing used is critical. A child who has trained regularly as a swimmer will have trained cardiovascular endurance, but if that child is tested using the mile run, the benefits may not show up in the test results. There are two reasons for this: First, the muscles used for swimming (arms) and running (legs) are different, so muscle endurance may be low in the legs and detract from the child's performance. Second, the knowledge of how to pace for the mile run is critical and learned through practice. Failure to pace carefully is one reason many children do poorly on the mile run test. You may remember a classmate running full speed for the first part of the mile run, then stopping or at least slowing considerably for the rest of the mile. The object of pacing in the mile run is to maintain a relatively constant speed with enough energy remaining to run faster at the end. Practice creates immediate improvements in test scores, which are not related to improved fitness.

Aerobic fitness tests fall into two categories: norm referenced and criterion referenced. **Norm-referenced tests** are based on the normal (bell-shaped) curve and compare one person to the group. **Criterion-referenced tests** use a standard and generally place people into two groups (pass and fail, or master and nonmaster). Early fitness tests were norm referenced and used the levels of the best 5 to 15 percent as criteria for an award. Recent tests tend to be criterion referenced, with

Table 6.2   Target Heart Rate Zones to Estimate the Intensity of Exercise

Age range in years	Target HR zone (beats per minute)
6–12	160–190
12–25	150–185
30–39	140–180
40–49	135–170
50–59	130–170
60–69	125–170

the criterion selected based on predicting health risk. The concept is that a student who is 10 years old and can run the mile in 9 minutes and 48 seconds or less will have less health risk than a student who runs the mile in 9 minutes and 49 seconds or more. Unfortunately, the various tests use different standards for passing (Morrow, Jackson, Disch, and Mood 2000). For example, a 9-year-old boy would have to run the mile at different speeds to pass the various tests: FITNESSGRAM (12 min), Physical Best (10:30 min), President's National (8:31 min), and Presidential Tests (<10 min), respectively. This is confusing and leads to controversy about the level of fitness of youth in our country (Blair 1992). Further, there are gender differences at each age for all tests, beginning at 6 years of age. The times for girls are 48 seconds or more greater (meaning that girls run more slowly and still pass) than boys at each age for each test (Wilkinson, Williamson, and Rozsdilsky 1996).

Careful consideration needs to be given to test selection, use, and interpretation. If we maintain separate, lower standards, the message we send to girls as young as 6 is this: Is girls' health less important than boys' health? Is there a biological reason to expect girls to perform more poorly when compared with boys? The answer to these questions is no. Prior to puberty, boys and girls are similar in ability, and their performance should be similar as should our expectations. The passing rates on the four tests are very different: FITNESSGRAM (84%), Physical Best (51 or 52%), President's National (63 or 65%), and Presidential Tests (21%), respectively (the passing percentage for boys is presented first; the passing percentage for girls is shown second, where there are differences). By selecting the test, a teacher can manipulate the passing rate for all children. If we want to demonstrate that most of our students are fit, we should use the FITNESSGRAM. However, if we want to demonstrate a need for fitness, we should use the Presidential Test. Interpreting test results for students, parents, and administration must be done in terms of the test characteristics and the purpose of testing. Often, it is best on any test to compare scores for a particular child rather than to compare scores between children or to test criteria alone. In this way, maintenance or improvement, rather than awards and comparisons to highly variable standards, will be the focus of the discussion.

We must take care in the use of fitness training and testing, since there is no evidence that being fit or training for fitness actually "carries over" to adult physical activity. Tracking is a term used to describe whether a behavior or characteristic remains constant across time. Unfortunately, no relationship has been demonstrated between physical fitness as a child and adult fitness or activity (Bouchard, Shepard, and Stephens 1994). Further, school programs that train for fitness in children have had little success in maintaining fitness (or activity) levels once the program ended. There is little carry-over from during-school programs to out-of-school activity. Clearly, there are many challenges when planning and implementing a fitness program. The fact that there are challenges does not suggest that fitness is not important or valuable. However, the role of fitness and fitness testing in physical education must be kept in perspective. The goal is maintaining good long-term health and providing a challenge for those students interested in taking physical activity to the next level.

MUSCULOSKELETAL FUNCTION

Girls and boys gain strength during childhood and adolescence. Part of this increase is caused by growth—bigger muscles and longer levers (limbs) generate more force, which translates to greater strength. As children grow, they become more efficient in the production of movements; this results in greater strength, as we learned in chapter 3. The nervous system recruits muscles more efficiently, which also increases strength. So, strength increases because of growth, maturation, and practice. At puberty, testosterone levels increase in boys, and as a result, muscle mass increases. So, at around 13, girls gain fat and reach maturity whereas boys gain muscle and continue to grow and mature (Thomas and French 1985). Consequently, muscle strength increases for boys and can be observed in tasks that require strength. Girls and boys are (and should be) similar in strength during childhood, although some tasks have large gender differences. Grip strength, sit-ups, and the vertical jump have small effect sizes until puberty (figure 6.3). Tasks that require upper-body strength, such as chin-ups and pull-ups, however, show large gender differences: Girls can do 0 to 1 chin-up and boys can do 1 to 10 chin-ups, on average, during elementary school, as you can see from figure 6.4. Practice is the most likely

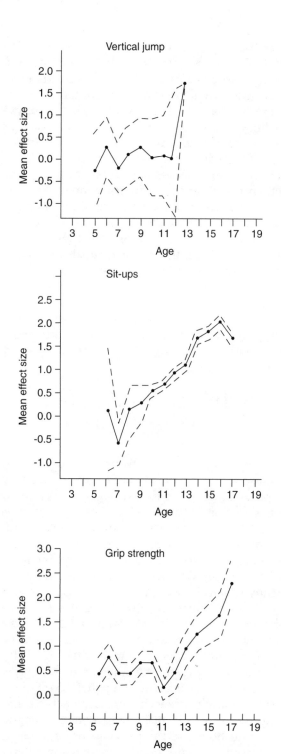

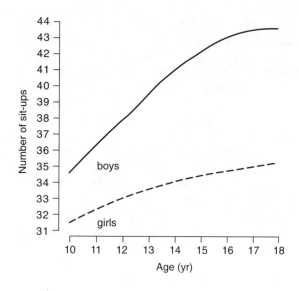

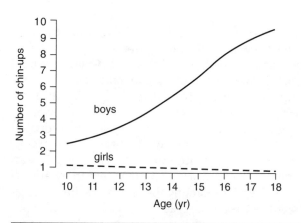

Figure 6.4 Performance curves for chin-ups and sit-ups.

Adapted from J.G. Ross et al., 1985, "Performance curves for chin-ups and sit-ups," *JOPERD 56* NCYFS-22.

Figure 6.3 Effect sizes for vertical jump, sit-ups, and grip strength.

Adapted, by permission, from J.R. Thomas and K.E. French, "Gender differences in motor performance: A meta analysis," *Psychological Bulletin* 98: 260-282. Copyright © 1985 by the American Psychological Association.

reason for the differences in these tasks; if girls were expected, encouraged, and practiced, their performance would be similar to that of boys. Consider young female gymnasts, who demonstrate upper-body strength; clearly, it is possible for girls to do chin-ups!

Weight training for children is a controversial topic. The two most important issues are cost–benefit trade-off and potential for injuries. Weight training takes a lot of time, and for prepubescent children, the gains are small (Faigenbaum, Westott, Loud, and Long 1999). Therefore, the time might be better spent doing something else, such as practicing skill (COPEC 1998). As children are growing, there is risk of injury; training regimens that are low intensity (low weight), however, can be safe (LePostellec 2002). Specific guidelines for prepubescent weight training are available (Kraemer and Fleck 1992). One critical component of weight training for children is involving a teacher or coach who is certified to coach young children (Kraemer and Fleck 1992). Generally, weight training is not a good use of physical education time during elementary school.

Most children do well on the sit-up tests, although practice and training are important. Scores often decrease from spring to fall, however, which suggests that practice during physical education improves performance. Girls are more flexible than boys in a comparison of test scores for the sit and reach. Again, practice is the most likely cause of these differences. Flexibility is the easiest component of fitness to train and the first to deteriorate when we are inactive. Most of us have experienced a time when movement was restricted and flexibility was significantly reduced.

Muscle strength, muscle endurance, and flexibility improve with training. While gender differences are observed in these components of fitness, no biological reason for the differences is evident before puberty. Therefore, teachers and parents should encourage and expect boys and girls to practice a variety of activities that will maintain or enhance skill performance, such as sit-ups, sit and reach, and pull-ups.

BODY COMPOSITION

Obesity and being overweight are independent health risk factors. Physical inactivity is related to obesity and being overweight. Parents are concerned about children who are overweight. The assumption is that excess weight is fat, so if you are overweight, you are too fat. People of all ages need some fat. Too much fat is unhealthy, however. The American College of Sports Medicine

Children with a large body type can be successful in physical activity.
© Human Kinetics.

recommends maximum body fat of 14 to 19 percent for males and 20 to 24 percent for females ages 20 to 60+ years. Body weight is made up of both fat and lean tissue. Remember that lean body mass is muscle, bone, organs, and all tissues other than fat. There is a second assumption about body weight and fat: that the bones are a constant density or mass. There are differences among races and across age in bone density, so this assumption can be a problem. People who have "light" bones, or osteoporosis, could be in the normal weight range and still be too fat. Someone who has dense bones might be overweight yet have a low amount of body fat. The same could be true of a person who is very muscular. Muscle is dense and, as a result, heavy. Therefore, very athletic people with more than average muscle mass may weigh more than normal and still not have too much fat.

As we can see, body composition is a complex issue. Often, by trying to take something complex and make it simple, we make mistakes. A height and weight chart is simple to use but may not be accurate in determining who is at risk. The Body Mass Index (BMI) is a commonly used measurement; basically, it is a height and weight chart. BMI is body weight in kilograms divided by height in meters squared. Mark McGwire of the St. Louis Cardinals is 6 feet 5 inches tall and weighs 250 pounds; his BMI is 29.7, which would label him with grade 1 obesity. A BMI of 29.7 for a male is significantly higher than that recommended for health, yet in terms of appearance or performance Mark McGwire would not be considered at risk. The point is that with BMI, height and weight can be deceiving. Further, considerable stigma can result from careless use of norms.

Muscle and bone tissues weigh more than fat and are healthy. Individuals who have large, dense bones and greater than average muscle mass are likely to appear overweight based on BMI or height and weight charts, yet they are probably not too fat. On the other side of the continuum are those who have little muscle and bones that are less dense than expected. Very low BMI is also unhealthy, particularly before 20 years of age. During growth—specifically, before 20 years of age—bones gain density. Dense bones have higher fracture points, which means the bones are more difficult to break. Bone density is a result of three factors: genetics, nutrition, and exercise (Bailey 2000, 2001). Adequate calcium and weight-bearing exercise produce healthy bones. From about 20 years of age onward, bones lose density.

Two things can be done about this loss: First, the bones should start out as dense as possible, which means that during childhood and adolescence, physical activity and calcium are critical. Second, the rate of loss should be as slow as possible; again, the critical factors are physical activity and calcium. For bone health, being underweight—especially of lean body mass—is a greater risk than being overweight.

"Study shows exercise is the best thing you can do to live longer. A new study suggests that exercising may be the single most important factor in extending your life." NBC's Robert Bazell reports the lead story on the March 13, 2002, NBC Nightly News. "A new study offers the strongest argument yet for getting fit. California researchers found that the ability to exercise—as measured on a treadmill test—is more important in predicting how long a person will live than even obesity, heart disease, or smoking."

Body Composition and Gender

Nearly from conception on, girls have more fat than boys because girls have more estrogen. At puberty, when estrogen levels increase, so do fat levels. If girls do not have enough body fat, estrogen will drop and menstruation will cease until fat levels increase. Sometimes this happens with athletes who are training; it is called secondary amenorrhea. In order to menstruate, girls and women need about 15 percent body fat (Sinning and Little 1987; Morrow, Jackson, Disch, and Mood 2000). Most girls have more than 15 percent fat. Obesity, or too much fat, begins at 20 percent for boys and 30 percent for girls (Morrow, et al. 2000). Approximately 1 in 4 children have too much fat; that is, they are obese based on percentage of body fat above 20 or 30 percent by gender. Girls are typically less active, which contributes to the higher percentage of body fat. The fact that girls are fatter than boys can be blamed partially on biology but is attributable to environment (Thomas and French 1985). Gaining fat is easier for girls, thanks to estrogen, and encouraged in girls by sociocultural norms, which suggest that girls should be less active than boys. Physical activity can facilitate weight control and healthy growth. This is an important fact to present to girls and boys.

Understanding What to Do About Body Composition

What does this mean for children who are overweight and overly fat? The cycle of being fat, avoiding activity, and becoming fatter makes the problem worse. Sometimes, teachers and coaches send negative messages to the overweight child. This can be as subtle as focusing on the lean or best performers or as obvious as saying, "If you are fat, you can't also be fit." We learned earlier that being inactive is a greater risk to health than being overweight. So, the message should be clear: Activity is important to all people. At the same time, we need to recognize that overly fat children are working harder during physical activity because they carry extra fat. Overly fat children may feel self-conscious about their bodies or may have underlying problems that have caused or contribute to their obesity.

One thing we can do to help is to make sure children understand that bodies are different and that there is not one perfect or most desirable body shape. Some differences in body shape are attributable to genetics; others are caused by what we eat and by our activity patterns. Further, we can prepare children for the bodily changes that will occur during adolescence. Finally, we can avoid using a simplistic approach to a complex problem. For example, in addition to body weight or fat, other measures of health risk can be examined. Waist-to-hip ratio (WHR), which is the circumference of the waist at the narrowest point divided by the circumference of the hips at the widest point, is a predictor of health risk. Large WHR is a predictor of risk; WHRs above 1.0 and .9 are identified as points of increased risk for males and females, respectively. Estimating body fat using skin-fold calipers is another way to examine risk. Good equipment and practice are necessary to accurately estimate fat. Some experts recommend tracking the sum of skin folds rather than calculating percent body fat (Lohman 1992). In the absence of good calipers and training, teachers should probably not estimate body fat. Under the best of circumstances, teachers should use more than one technique. Consider discussing BMI, WHR, and physical activity together to develop a risk profile. Further, we can encourage all children to seek healthy bodies that are neither too fat nor too frail nor thin.

SUMMARY

Physical activity has important health implications: Those who are physically active have less health risk than those who are inactive. Physical fitness is at the opposite end of the physical activity continuum from sedentary. Physical fitness requires specific training. Boys and girls should be motivated and encouraged to be physically active. Prior to puberty, gender differences in fitness are primarily attributable to differences in the treatment of boys and girls. In our culture, boys are expected and encouraged to be active and fit, whereas girls are not.

Children's bodies work harder during exercise than adults' bodies do, so children often fatigue sooner than adults. Further, because of biological differences between children and adults, children's fitness does not improve as much as that of adults during training. As children mature, fitness performance should improve. The long-term goal of physical education and other physical activity programs for children is developing a physically active lifestyle.

MASTERY LEARNING ACTIVITIES

1. Calculate your maximum heart rate (220 − your age). Calculate your training, or target heart rate (maximum heart rate × .7). Take your nonexercising heart rate (your heart rate while you are sitting down).

2. Locate a physical fitness test. Compare the standards across age and between the genders. What are the passing rates on the test? How were the standards selected?

3. Interview a physical education teacher. Ask about her fitness testing philosophy and the test she uses.

4. Find one newspaper article from the past week about exercise or activity and health.

5. For each of the following concepts, identify supporting facts.

   a. Lifestyles are sedentary, physically active, or physically fit.

   b. Physical activity directly influences health.

   c. Fitness has specific training criteria (aerobic, muscle strength and endurance, and flexibility).

d. Physical activity has specific criteria (moderate-to-vigorous activity).

e. Being too fat is an independent health risk; being overweight does not necessarily mean that your body has too much fat.

f. Bones and muscles are the heaviest tissues in the body. Bones must become strong during childhood and adolescence.

g. Muscle strength and muscle endurance are related but different; the training for strength is high intensity, whereas the training for endurance is high repetitions.

h. The FIT principle guides training for fitness.

i. Fitness tests vary greatly in the standards and in the passing rates set for males and females.

REFERENCES

Alliance for Health, Physical Education, Recreation and Dance (AAHPERD). 1981. *Basic stuff series I: Exercise physiology.* Reston, Va.: AAHPERD.

American College of Sports Medicine. 1995. ACSM's Guidelines for exercise testing and perscription. Philidelphia: Lea & Febiger.

Bailey, D.A. 2000. Is anyone out there listening? *Quest* 52:344–50.

Bailey, D.A. 2001. Get it right the first time: The importance of leisure activities during the growing years for skeletal health. In *Physical Activity in the Context of Leisure Education,* edited by F. Fu and H. Ruskin, 78–86. Hong Kong: Hong Kong Baptist University Press.

Blair, S. 1992. Are American children and youth physically fit? The need for better data. *Research Quarterly for Exercise and Sport* 63:120–123.

Bouchard, C., R.J. Shepard, and T. Stephens. 1994. The consensus statement. In *Physical activity, fitness and health: International proceedings and consensus statement,* edited by C. Bouchard, R.J. Shepard, and T. Stephens, 9–76. Champaign, Ill.: Human Kinetics.

Centers for Disease Control and Prevention (CDC). 1997. Guidelines for School and Community Programs to Promote Lifelong Physical Activity Among Young People. [Online.] Available: www.cdc.gov [September 8, 2002].

Council for Physical Education for Children (COPEC). 1998. *Physical activity for children: A statement of guidelines.* Reston: Va.: National Association for Sport and Physical Education (NASPE) Publications.

Faigenbaum, A.D., W.L. Westcott, R.L. Loud, and C. Long. 1999. The effects of different resistance training protocols on muscular strength and endurance development in children. *Pediatrics* 104 (1):5.

Kraemer, W.J., and S.J. Fleck. 1992. *Strength Training for Young Athletes.* Champaign, Ill.: Human Kinetics.

Lee, C.D., S.N. Blair, and A.S. Jackson. 1999. Cardiorespiratory fitness, body composition, and all-cause mortality and cardiovascular disease mortality in men. *American Journal of Clinical Nutrition* 69:373–80.

LePostollec, M. 2002. Weight training for kids. Advances for nurse practitioners: Online edition. www.advancefornurses.com/pastarticles/mar4_02feature4.html [Access date March 2002].

Lohman, T.G. 1992. Advances in body composition assessment. Champaign, Ill.: Human Kinetics.

Morrow, J.R., A.W. Jackson, J.G. Disch, and D.P. Mood. 2000. *Measurement and evaluation in human performance.* 2nd ed. Champaign, Ill.: Human Kinetics.

Park, R.J. 1988. Measurement of physical fitness: A historical perspective. *ODPHP Monograph Series:* U.S. Department of Health and Human Services.

Simons-Morton, B.G., G.S. Parcel, T. Baranowski, R. Forthofer, and N.M. O'Hara. 1991. Promoting physical activity and a healthful diet among children: Results of a school-based intervention study. *American Journal of Public Health* 81:986–991.

Sinning, W.E., and K.D. Little. 1987. Body composition and menstrual function in athletes. *Sports Medicine* 4:34–45.

Thomas, J.R., and K.E. French. 1985. Gender differences across age in motor performance: A meta-analysis. *Psychological Bulletin* 98:260–82.

U.S. Department of Health and Human Services (USDHHS). 2000. *Healthy People 2010: Conference edition.* Washington, D.C.: Government Printing Office.

Welk, G.J. 1999. The youth physical activity promotion model: A conceptual bridge between theory and practice. *Quest* 51:5–23.

Wilkinson, S., K.M. Williamson, and R. Rozsdilsky. 1996. Gender and fitness standards. *Women's Sport and Physical Activity Journal* 5:1–23.

RESOURCES

www.fitness.gov/index.html
www.acsm.org

LESSON PLANS

The six lesson plans at the end of this chapter represent several ways to incorporate fitness into elementary physical education. The lessons include circuit training, fitness challenges, and moderate-to-vigorous games. In addition, children enjoy fitness hustles (e.g., aerobic dance) and jump rope. Teachers can do fitness units, where fitness is the focus for several weeks, or do fitness days, where fitness is practiced intermittently through the year. They can include activities that are moderate to vigorous on a daily basis or assign fitness homework. Schools and teachers can further encourage physical activity and fitness at recess or after school by sponsoring walking clubs, activity groups, and similar activities. Children enjoy participating in these activities with teachers and other significant adults (e.g., parents, administrators, and counselors), so running and walking clubs are usually popular. Whether walking, jogging, cycling, or swimming, children can chart the distances; doing this on a map is educational, motivational, and fun for children.

LESSON  6.1

Moderate to Vigorous Games

Student Objectives

- Distinguish between muscular strength and muscular endurance.
- Participate in moderate to vigorous activities.
- Demonstrate cooperation when playing Reveille.

Equipment and Materials

- 4 cones or tape or, if outside, chalk
- Horn or other signal (a horn is best, but a whistle, bell, or other noisemaker will work)
- Enough carpet squares or taped or chalked Xs for half the class

Warm-Up Activities (5 minutes)

Divide the children into small groups. Have the children do crunches and push-ups.

Crunches

Tell and demonstrate for the children: *Lie on your back on a mat. Cross your legs at the ankle with your knees slightly bent. Bring your knees toward your tummy or chest until your feet are over your hips or chest. At the same time, place your hands near your ears without gripping your head. Start the crunches by lifting your head and shoulders off the floor, pointing your nose toward your knees. Lower your shoulders to the starting position but keep your head slightly off the floor. Repeat, twisting at your waist slightly so the opposite elbow and knee touch. Be sure to twist your upper body, not your elbow. One repetition is one to the left, one to the center, and one to the right.*

Push-Ups

Gather the children into an information formation.

1. Describe and demonstrate a correct push-up:

    Start with the balls of your feet and hands on the ground, hands shoulder-width apart, feet together or comfortably apart.

Stretch out (extend) your legs so that they and your upper body form a nearly straight line.

Lower your body toward the ground by bending your elbows, keeping your body straight.

When your body is nearly to the ground, move back up to the original position.

Keep your body stiff as a board.

2. Have the children practice giving you feedback on correct and incorrect push-up form. Emphasize supportive ways to offer feedback.

3. Rearrange the children into partners in scatter formation.

4. Tell the children: *One partner will do push-ups while the other watches to see that the person is performing the push-up correctly.*

5. After a few minutes, have the children switch roles. Circulate, helping children give accurate feedback.

Skill-Development Activities (20 minutes)

Select one or two games to play. Keep group sizes small to increase participation opportunities.

Reveille

Arrange children in two groups on parallel lines about 40 ft apart, defined by the four cones.

1. Describe and demonstrate the game:

   On the signal, everyone runs for the opposite line.

   The first group to line up, standing at attention, gets one point.

   Take care and cooperate when running past other children so that no one gets bumped or tripped.

2. Have the children play Reveille, repeating several times.

Sneaky Tag

Use the four cones to define a square playing area. Place the carpet squares on one side of the square. The starting line is opposite the squares. Arrange children in two groups: one group on the starting line, one group on the carpet squares or chalked or taped Xs. (On a hard surface mark Xs with tape or chalk; on soft ground, carpet squares work well.)

1. Describe and demonstrate the game:

   The children on the start line are the Sneakers, and the children on the Xs (or carpet squares) are the Taggers.

   On the signal, the Sneakers move through the Taggers trying to get to the endline without being tagged. Sneakers must stay inside the boundaries, and Taggers must keep at least one foot on the X.

   If you are tagged, jog around the end boundary during the next round, then rejoin the Sneakers for later rounds.

   Sneakers who safely get to the endline use that new line for their starting end for the next round, which will begin on the next signal.

2. Have the children play several rounds. Then have Taggers and Sneakers switch roles.

Fitness Relay

Arrange six groups of children at one end of the play area.

1. Describe and demonstrate the activity:

   The first child in each line will run to the other end of the play area (marked with cones) and do five sit-ups, then run back to the start.

   The second child will do the same thing, and so forth until all of you have had a turn.

   The first group to finish selects the exercise to be done on the next round (e.g., run and do push-ups, crunches, or reverse push-ups, or the like).

2. Play several rounds to practice a variety of fitness tasks.

Concluding Activities (5 minutes)

Physical Fitness Concept

Gather the children into an information formation.

1. Present the concept to the students: *Muscular endurance is when a muscle or group of muscles can make the same movement many times without getting too tired. Being able to do several sit-ups, push-ups, and chin-ups demonstrates muscular endurance. Muscular strength is how much work a muscle can do in one try. Muscles get stronger by exercising (for example, by moving heavy objects).*

2. Begin the discussion: *What activities have we done that call for you to repeat a movement many times?* (Crunches, sit-ups, push-ups, reverse push-ups.) *What about jogging?* (Yes.) *What about throwing a ball?* (No.) *Jumping rope?* (Yes.) *Now, everyone is going to do a muscular endurance activity. Be sure to stay in your own space.*

3. Tell the students: *Everyone switch and do a different endurance activity.* (Do this 30 to 60 seconds.) *Switch again!* (Do this 30 to 60 seconds.) *OK, sit down and relax. Usually muscular endurance activities are done for at least 10 minutes in activities like jogging and in three sets of 10 repetitions for a task like sit-ups. This kind of work helps your muscles develop endurance.*

Alternative Learning Activities

Gather the children into an information formation for this discussion.

1. Loop a rubber band around the blades of scissors. Open and close the scissors as you describe the action.

2. Begin the discussion by saying: *The rubber band is elastic, which means it stretches. When I open the scissors, the joint—the part where the blades are joined—opens wider, and the rubber band stretches. When the scissors are closed, the rubber band contracts (shortens). Your muscles are designed the same way, with muscles on one side of a joint stretching and those on the other side contracting (shortening) to make the bones move.*

3. *Put your hand on the big muscle in the front of your upper arm. This is called the biceps. Bend your arm so that your fist moves toward your shoulder. Do you feel the biceps pulling, tightening to move your arm? Now slowly lower your fist until your arm is straight. Do you feel the biceps relaxing? Muscular strength is the greatest amount of weight a muscle can lift in one try.*

4. *To train muscles and help them become stronger and able to work longer (increase endurance), we use the overload principle. Can anyone guess what "overload" means? The overload principle means you make your body do extra work—by moving either more weight at one time or the same or lower weight more times—to increase the muscle's ability to work. At your age the weight you usually move is your own body weight, so doing a few more of an exercise each time you exercise helps build your muscular strength and endurance.*

From *Physical Education Methods for Elementary Teachers, Second Edition,* by Katherine T. Thomas, Amelia M. Lee, and Jerry R. Thomas, 2003, Champaign, IL: Human Kinetics. Adapted from *Physical Education for Children: Daily Lesson Plans for Elementary School, Second Edition,* by Katherine T. Thomas, Amelia M. Lee, and Jerry R. Thomas, 2000, Champaign, IL: Human Kinetics.

LESSON

Circuit Training

Student Objectives

- Demonstrate Fitness Circuit.
- Stay on task.
- Take turns.
- State that physical fitness is exercise or sport that contributes to health and allows us to do activities throughout the day.
- State that physical activity is any movement that contributes to being healthy.

Equipment and Materials

- 6 cones
- 6 identifying signs (numbers and pictures)
- Tape (to attach signs to cones)
- Music or special signal (e.g., whistle)
- Enough short jump ropes for one-sixth of the class (see station 6 instructions)
- 2 long jump ropes (for crab walk, station 4)

Warm-Up Activities (5 minutes)

Pyramid

Arrange children along one side of the play area in a line, facing the other side.

1. Tell the students: *We are going to move across the activity area very slowly. When we come back we will speed up a little. We will continue until we are running as fast as we can. This is* called "Pyramid" because we are building from a slow to a fast speed, just as a pyramid is built from low to high. Remember to stay in your own personal space so no one gets hurt.

2. Move across the area at least six times, each time increasing the speed.

3. Repeat, moving backward, then sideways.

Skill-Development Activities (20 minutes)

Circuit Training: Fitness Circuit

Set up the six stations as described, using the cones to mark their locations. Divide the children into six groups, and assign each group to a station.

1. Explain and demonstrate the activities for each station.

2. Rotate the groups through the stations, repeating each station as follows:

Round	Time at each station (seconds)	Time between stations (seconds)
1	15 s	15 s
2	20 s	15 s
3	25 s	15 s
4	30 s	15 s

3. As you have students repeat this circuit on other days, you can increase the time at each station, decrease the time between stations, and increase the number of rounds.

Station 1: Jumping Jacks

Tell and demonstrate for the children: *Standing with your feet together and your hands at your sides, bounce up and land with your feet apart while moving your arms and clapping your hands above your head. Then jump back to the starting position. Jumping jacks help to enhance muscular endurance and cardiovascular endurance.*

Station 2: Airplane Circles

Tell and demonstrate for the children: *Standing with feet comfortably apart and arms extended to sides, circle your arms forward; count 1, circle forward (one complete circle for each count). This helps your flexibility and muscular endurance.*

Station 3: Sit-Ups

Gather the children into an information formation.

1. Describe and demonstrate a correct sit-up:

   The sit-up is really done with a rolling motion.

   Begin by lying on your back with your legs bent slightly at the knees so the soles of your feet are flat on the ground.

   Choose one of the two hand-arm positions: you can cross your hands and arms on your chest so that your hands are resting on the opposite shoulders, or you can place your hands on the sides of your head with a finger placed on each ear, keeping your elbows lined up (parallel) with the back of your head (keep them there, not pulling forward past the ears).

   Perform each sit-up slowly, rolling your chin to your chest to lift your head, your shoulders, then your lower back off the ground. During the movement, you should feel the muscles under your belly button working.

   Once your lower back is off the ground, unroll back down to the start position.

2. Have the children practice analyzing your sit-up form.

Arrange the children in scatter formation, each with a carpet square or mat.

3. As you say, *"Rollllllll,"* have each child do a sit-up, emphasizing moving slowly.

4. After one sit-up, tell the children: *Point to the muscles that did the work* (the muscles under the belly button). Repeat several times.

5. Have partners check each other's form.

Tell the children: *This helps make your abdominal muscles stronger.*

Station 4: Crab Walk

Tell and demonstrate for the children: *Assuming a back support position with your knees bent and your body straight, walk on your hands and feet from line A to line B and from line B to line A, continuing until the time is up. This helps make your arm muscles stronger.*

Station 5: Push-Ups

See lesson plan 6.1. *This helps make your arm muscles stronger.*

Station 6: Rope Jump

Tell and demonstrate for the children: *Begin with both feet on one side of the rope, then jump up and sideways so that you land on the other side of the rope moving forward slightly. Repeat, crossing back and forth over the rope. When you reach the end of the rope, turn around and continue until the time is up. This helps make your leg muscles stronger.*

Station 1
Jumping jacks

Station 2
Airplane circles

Station 3
Sit-ups

Station 6
Rope jump

Station 5
Push-ups

Station 4
Crab walk

Line A   30 ft   Line B

Concluding Activities (5 minutes)

Physical Fitness Concept

Gather the children into an information formation.

1. Explain the concept to the students: *Physical activity, like walking, house- or yardwork, contributes to health. Physical fitness is a type of physical activity that makes your body work hard; physical activity is moving that helps us be healthier.*

2. Begin the discussion by asking the students: *Can you name some jobs that require physical fitness?* Discuss the answers, identifying jobs that require energy (e.g., construction, farming).

3. Ask the students: *What after-work activities can you think of that are not sport, but are physical activity (e.g., housework, gardening)?*

Alternative Learning Activities

1. Using magazines and newspapers, make two collages: one of physical fitness activities (aerobic dance, weight training, jogging), one of physical activities (e.g., not sport or exercise). Discuss that both physical fitness and physical activities can contribute to health.

2. Make a list of ways people could add physical activity to their lives (for example, taking the stairs instead of the elevator, walking to the store instead of driving, or parking farther from stores).

From *Physical Education Methods for Elementary Teachers, Second Edition,* by Katherine T. Thomas, Amelia M. Lee, and Jerry R. Thomas, 2003, Champaign, IL: Human Kinetics. Adapted from *Physical Education for Children: Daily Lesson Plans for Elementary School, Second Edition,* by Katherine T. Thomas, Amelia M. Lee, and Jerry R. Thomas, 2000, Champaign, IL: Human Kinetics.

Fitness

LESSON  **6.3**

Moderate to Vigorous Games

Student Objectives

- Demonstrate fair play during Crows and Cranes.
- Name a muscular strength and a muscular endurance activity.

Equipment and Materials

- 4 cones or 2 long lines marked on the surface

Safety Tip

- Remind children to watch where they run so they don't hurt anyone else.

Warm-Up Activities (5 minutes)

Fitness Circuit: Stretching Routine

Arrange the children in scatter formation. Repeat each stretch 10 repetitions per minute with six seconds for each repetition: shoulder pull, arm reach-out, triceps stretch, forward straddle stretch, frog stretch.

Shoulder Pull

Slowly pull your left elbow across the front of your body toward the opposite shoulder. Hold for 10 seconds. Relax and repeat with the opposite elbow.

Arm Reach-Out

Sit on the floor. Lock your fingers together and with palms facing out, straighten your arms out in front of you. Stretch and hold for 10 seconds. Relax and repeat.

Triceps Stretch

Lift your arms up over your head and touch your elbows. Hold your right elbow with your left hand and gently pull. Let your right hand drop behind your head as you stretch. Hold for 10 seconds and relax. Repeat, pulling your left elbow with your right hand.

Forward Straddle Stretch

Sit on the floor with your legs straight and spread apart about three ft. Bend forward at the hip. Grasp your right knee, calf, or ankle (as far down your leg as you can go) and pull your body gently toward your leg. Hold for 10 seconds, then relax and repeat on the left side.

Frog Stretch

Lie down with your knees bent and the soles of your feet together. If you relax, gravity will pull your knees toward the ground and stretch the insides of your thighs. Relax for 10 seconds and then lift your knees up and toward each other, so they are no longer relaxed, for 10 seconds (knees do not need to touch at this point). Do not bounce!

Skill-Development Activities (20 minutes)

Crows and Cranes

Arrange the children in two parallel lines facing each other, with half the children on each line, 30 to 50 ft apart.

1. Explain the game:

   The children in one line are "Crows"; those in the other line are "Cranes."

   As I begin saying "Crrrr . . . ," the two lines walk toward each other.

   When I complete the word "Crow" or "Crane," the line I call is "It." The children in that line run forward and try to tag the other children, who turn and try to avoid being tagged.

   You are safe when you cross the line you started from. Tagged children join the other line and play continues.

2. Have the children play Crows and Cranes.

3. Mix up which line you call to surprise the children.

4. Remind children to watch where they run so they don't hurt anyone.

Variation: Witches and Warlocks

Instead of Crows and Cranes, call the children standing on one line "Witches," and the children on the other line "Warlocks." As you call out one name or the other, draw out the "W" sound, alternating between Witches, Warlocks, and Wizards. When you say "Wizards," everyone must freeze. Anyone who moves while frozen runs a lap before the next round of play.

Concluding Activities (5 minutes)

Physical Fitness Concept

Gather the children into an information formation.

1. Present the concept to the children: *Muscular endurance is when a muscle or group of muscles can make the same movement many times without getting too tired. The number of sit-ups, push-ups, and chin-ups a person can do helps demonstrate their muscular endurance. Muscular strength is how much work a muscle can do one time. Muscles get stronger by exercising (for example, by moving heavy objects).*

2. Begin the discussion: *Can you name some activities that call for you to repeat a movement many times?* (Crunches, push-ups, jogging, jumping rope, but throwing a ball is not.)

   Everyone show me an activity in which you repeat the movement many times. Correct anyone who is not doing an endurance activity. *Now switch to a different endurance activity!*

3. Tell the children: *Usually muscular endurance activities are done in sets of 10 to 12 repetitions, so you should build up to doing 10, resting briefly, doing 10 more, resting, and then doing 10 more.*

4. Continue the discussion: *Muscular strength varies from person to person and muscle to muscle. Different people have different strength levels, and different muscles on the same person have different strength levels. Muscles get stronger with training. Muscular strength and endurance work together to help us do all the tasks we need to do. Sometimes we lack the muscular strength to do an activity, but with training we improve and then can do the activity many times. Pull-ups are sometimes like that. At first, a person cannot do one pull-up; but with training, strength increases and one pull-up becomes easy. Then after more training, we can do many pull-ups because we have improved our muscular endurance.*

From *Physical Education Methods for Elementary Teachers, Second Edition,* by Katherine T. Thomas, Amelia M. Lee, and Jerry R. Thomas, 2003, Champaign, IL: Human Kinetics. Adapted from *Physical Education for Children: Daily Lesson Plans for Elementary School, Second Edition,* by Katherine T. Thomas, Amelia M. Lee, and Jerry R. Thomas, 2000, Champaign, IL: Human Kinetics.

LESSON

Fitness Challenge

Student Objectives

- Use equipment safely.
- Follow directions.
- Demonstrate locomotor skills.
- Define resting heart rate.

Equipment and Materials

- 4 cones or two long lines marked on ground
- 1 hoop per child

Warm-Up Activities (5 minutes)

Loose Caboose

Arrange groups of three or four in scatter formation. Scatter three or four extra children about a clearly defined play area.

1. Describe and demonstrate the game:

    In each group, form a "Train," holding one another at the waist in a line (you must stay hooked together).

    The extra children are Loose Cabooses and try to hook on to the backs of the Trains.

The Trains move around the play area, trying to avoid being hooked onto by a Loose Caboose.

If a Caboose does connect with a Train, the Engine (the first person in that train) becomes a Loose Caboose.

2. Have the children play Loose Caboose.

Skill-Development Activities (20 minutes)

Hoop Challenges

Arrange the children in scatter formation, each child with a hoop.

1. Have the children try the following challenges that develop muscular endurance and aerobic fitness:

    Spin the hoop on one arm, then on the other arm, then on one leg. Try to do 10 to 20 spins on each.

    Spin the hoop on another part of the body (waist, hips, neck).

    Spin the hoop on your body, trying to make it go slowly, then fast, then slowly.

    Spin the hoop on the ground like a top.

2. Have the children put their hoop on the ground:

    Jump in and out of the hoop slowly.

    Jump in and out of the hoop fast.

Move around the hoop, jumping in and out.

Hop in and out of the hoop.

Run and jump over the hoop.

Hop forward (then backward) around the hoop.

3. Now have the children pick up their hoop once again:

    Pick up the hoop and stretch with the hoop over your head.

    Holding the hoop, stretch to one side and then to the other.

    Roll the hoop from one line to the other.

    Roll the hoop and run around it as it rolls. Watch out for other hoops and children. Repeat several times.

    Roll the hoop and try to jump through it as it rolls.

    Roll the hoop so it returns to you (put backspin on the hoop).

Hoop Relay

Arrange the children in pairs, and give each pair a hoop. Have the pairs stand about 30 ft away from a line.

1. Describe and demonstrate the activity:

   The first child in line rolls the hoop to a line 30 ft away and back.

   The second child takes the hoop and rolls it to the line and back; this continues until time is up. The children can count the number of turns they completed if you want.

2. Have the children do Hoop Relay.

Concluding Activities (5 minutes)

Physical Fitness Concept

Gather the children into an information formation.

1. Introduce the concept: *After you have been lying still for 15 to 30 minutes (or when you first wake up in the morning) the number of times your heart beats is called resting heart rate. You can lower your resting heart rate through exercising regularly.*

2. Tell the children: *Make a fist with your hand* (demonstrate, pausing for children to close their fists); *your hand is contracted. Now open your hand* (demonstrate, pausing for the children to open their fists), *and relax. Your heart works like your hand. When the heart is relaxed (the open fist), blood enters. Then when the heart beats, or contracts (the closed fist), the blood is pushed out. The blood goes from the heart through arteries to the muscles and organs (stomach, kidneys, intestines, and so on).*

3. Tell the children: *Put your hand on your chest, be very still, and feel your heart beat.* Demonstrate and allow children to feel their heart beating. *Heart rate is the number of times your heart opens and closes in one minute. When we sleep our hearts are still beating, but more slowly. That is why it is called "resting" heart rate. When you exercise, your heart rate goes up. When you are awake but sitting still your heart rate is in between the resting and exercising heart rate.*

From *Physical Education Methods for Elementary Teachers, Second Edition,* by Katherine T. Thomas, Amelia M. Lee, and Jerry R. Thomas, 2003, Champaign, IL: Human Kinetics. Adapted from *Physical Education for Children: Daily Lesson Plans for Elementary School, Second Edition,* by Katherine T. Thomas, Amelia M. Lee, and Jerry R. Thomas, 2000, Champaign, IL: Human Kinetics.

Fitness

LESSON

Wands

Student Objectives

- Explain the health benefits of physical activity.
- Maintain continuous activity with a wand.
- Perform simple wand stunts.

Equipment and Materials

- 1 wand (30–36 in.) per child
- Optional: 2 additional wands per group
- Stopwatch or clock with second hand

Warm-Up Activities (5 minutes)

Running and Dodging Games

Arrange partners in scatter formation. Choose from Follow the Leader, Partner Dodging, and Individual Running and Dodging.

Follow the Leader

Have the children try the following activities:

Run with one person in front and one behind (in typical follow-the-leader style).

Run beside your partner.

Run back to back with your partner (one going forward, one backward).

Take turns leading.

Partner Dodging

On a signal, partner 1 runs and dodges, attempting to get away from partner 2. Partner 2 attempts to stay as close to partner 1 as possible. Take turns leading.

Individual Running and Dodging

Arrange the children in scatter formation. On a signal, have the children try the following challenges:

Run and turn quickly to the right.

Run and turn quickly to the left.

Run and make a small circle and then a large circle.

Run in a zigzag pattern.

Skill-Development Activities (20 minutes)

Wand Challenges

Keep the children in scatter formation, and give each a wand to place on the floor. Present the following tasks:

With your side to the wand, jump back and forth over it.

With your side to the wand, jump back and forth over it rapidly 20 times.

Face the wand and jump over it. Then turn completely around, and jump over it again. Try adding a turn in the air as you jump.

Jump over the wand backward.

Jump over the wand several times, increasing the height of your jump each time.

Jump over the wand several times, increasing the distance of your jump each time.

Timed Partner Jump

Arrange partners in scatter formation. Have the children try to jump for one minute.

1. Explain the activity:

   One partner holds the wand about knee high.

   The other partner jumps back and forth over the wand as many times as possible in 30 seconds.

2. The teacher signals the start and end of this time period.

   Take turns holding and jumping.

3. Have the children do the Timed Partner Jump.

Jump Over the Wand

Arrange the children in scatter formation.

> Hold the wand in front of you with both hands about shoulder-width apart. The lower you hold the wand, the easier the task will be.
>
> Jump up and over the wand.

Wand Follow the Leader

Divide children into groups of four. Give each group four to six wands. Direct each group to arrange the wands in various patterns to jump and hop into, out of, and around.

1. Tell the children: *Play Follow the Leader, changing leaders every 60 seconds.*
2. Here are some pattern suggestions:

> Place the wands in random order and jump forward, backward, and sideways over them.
>
> Place the wands in parallel lines. Jump, leap, or hop through the wands.
>
> Place the wands in a square or other geometric shape and jump, leap, or hop through the shape.

> Place the wands in other patterns. Jump, leap, or hop through the patterns.

Pass-the-Wand Cool-Down

Divide children in groups of four or five in a relay formation, with half of each group at opposite ends of the play area, facing the other part of the group. Ends should be about 60 ft apart.

1. Explain the activity:

> One child in each group holds the wand for that group. That child walks to the opposite end of the play area carrying the wand and hands the wand to the first child in that part of the line, relay fashion.
>
> The child now holding the wand walks to the part of the group where the first child began and passes the wand to the next child.
>
> We will continue until everyone has had several turns.
>
> This is not a race; it is a cool-down.

2. Have the children do the Pass-the-Wand Cool-Down.

Concluding Activities (5 minutes)

Physical Fitness Concept

Gather the children into an advanced information formation.

1. Discuss some of the health benefits of physical activity: *People who exercise tend to feel better about themselves; be less likely to experience obesity, heart disease, and high blood pressure; and be better able to cope with stressful situations.*
2. Explain that there are some things that exercise cannot do, such as increase your intelligence or change your personality.

An Exercise Quiz

Keep the children in the advanced information formation.

1. Read a list of benefits of exercise to the children.
2. Ask them to give you a "thumbs up" if the statement is true and a "thumbs down" if the statement is false.
3. *Regular exercise will do the following:*

> *Improve physical fitness.* (True; training is the only way to increase fitness.)

> *Make you taller.* (False; growth, not exercise, does this.)
>
> *Turn fat to muscle.* (False; exercise can reduce fat and increase muscle, but these are different tissues.)
>
> *Increase your IQ.* (False; but you may be able to think better if exercise helps you feel less stressed.)
>
> *Help maintain a lean body.* (True; exercise helps to reduce fat and increase muscle.)
>
> *Improve your self-image.* (True; exercise helps us be proud of ourselves.)
>
> *Reduce the risk of heart disease.* (True; exercise and diet help keep the heart healthy.)
>
> *Allow you to read faster.* (False; reading practice helps us read better.)
>
> *Improve your cardiorespiratory endurance.* (True; training is based on exercise.)
>
> *Absolutely assure you of a long life.* (False; nothing can do this, but exercise should improve the quality of your life.)

From *Physical Education Methods for Elementary Teachers, Second Edition,* by Katherine T. Thomas, Amelia M. Lee, and Jerry R. Thomas, 2003, Champaign, IL: Human Kinetics. Adapted from *Physical Education for Children: Daily Lesson Plans for Elementary School, Second Edition,* by Katherine T. Thomas, Amelia M. Lee, and Jerry R. Thomas, 2000, Champaign, IL: Human Kinetics.

Fitness

LESSON **6.6**

Moderate to Vigorous Games

Student Objectives

- Give examples of conditions that are the opposite of health-related physical fitness.
- Perform a stretching routine.
- Execute three sets of crunches, eight repetitions per set.
- Execute three sets each of regular and triceps push-ups, three repetitions per set.
- Participate in a moderate to vigorous game.

Equipment and Materials

- 4 bases
- 1 playground ball (8-1/2 in.)
- 1 parachute

Warm-Up Activities (5 minutes)

Stretching Routine

Arrange children in a large circle facing the center.

1. Describe and demonstrate each of the stretches.
2. Have children try each of the stretches.

Modified Neck Roll

Sit tall, with one hand on each side of your head covering your ears. Drop your head forward, then very slowly roll your head around in a semicircle, supporting your head with your hands, first to the left and then to the right. Do not move past the shoulders or backward. Repeat several times.

Shoulder Shrugs

Lift your shoulders to your ears, then return to normal position.

Side Stretch

Sit with feet apart and toes pointed straight ahead and knees slightly bent. Place one hand on hip and extend the other arm up over the head. Slowly bend to the side toward the hand on the hip. Hold for 10 seconds and relax. Repeat in the opposite direction.

Front and Side Lunges

Facing forward, bend to a squat with your right leg directly under your torso and your left leg extended to the side. As you bend, place your hands, palms down, on the floor on each side of your right foot to help you to balance. Keep both heels on the floor. Your left leg can be slightly bent at the knee. Your right knee should be directly over your right toes. Look forward, keeping your head up. Your back should be parallel to the floor. Hold this position for 5 to 20 seconds.

Gradually turn to your right, allowing your heels to leave the floor. Your right knee will touch or be close to touching your chest. Bend the left knee and then gradually straighten both legs to nearly extended (determine this by your comfort level—don't extend if you feel pain; knees should never be completely straight to avoid pulling the ligaments), keeping your back straight and parallel to the floor and your head up. Turn and "roll" your body over your left knee, repeating the entire sequence.

Standing Heel Stretch

Stand with one foot directly in front of the other, about one ft apart. With both feet flat on the ground and your body positioned directly above the back foot, bend your knees. Bend so your thighs are parallel to the floor without allowing your heels to leave the floor. Hold for 5 to 20 counts. Reverse feet and repeat.

3. Combine stretches into the following routine:

Head right, two, three, four; right, two, three, four; and left, two, three, four; left, two, three, four.

Shoulders up, down, two, three, four; again, two, three, four.

Reach up, left, center, right, forward; left, center, right, forward.

Heels flat on the floor—bend your right knee and hold, two, three, four, five; head up.

Turn to the right—back straight—head up and allow your heels to come up.

Stand, extending your legs—keep your back down!

Turn to the front, bend your left knee—head up, hold, two, three, four.

Turn to the left—back straight—head up and allow your heels to come up.

Stand, extending your legs—keep your back down!

Standing heel stretch (count 5 to 10). Reverse.

Skill-Development Activities (20 minutes)

Crunches and Regular and Triceps Push-Ups

Advanced Crunches

Gather the children into an advanced information formation.

1. Describe and demonstrate the exercise:

Lie on your back with your hips bent at a 90-degree angle so your feet are over your hips or tummy.

Cross your ankles and bend your knees slightly.

With your fingers gently touching your ears on each side of your head, do the crunch by lifting your head, neck, and shoulders (to the shoulder blades) off the ground.

End the lift when one elbow touches (or nears) the opposite knee or both elbows reach the knees.

Do one each—right elbow to left knee, left elbow to right knee, then both elbows to both knees—then repeat the sequence. We will use the count "Right, left, both; right, left, both."

Arrange the children in scatter formation with mats.

2. Have the children repeat this sequence six times, then rest.

3. Have the children repeat the entire sequence twice more.

Push-Ups

Gather the children into an advanced information formation.

1. Describe and demonstrate regular push-ups:

Support your body weight on your hands and feet with your hands at the side of your body, chest high. Your body should be straight with feet together.

By straightening your arms, lift your body upward; then in a smooth, continuous motion, lower your body back to starting position.

Repeat.

Do three push-ups, then rest briefly; three more and rest; three more and stop.

Arrange the children in scatter formation.

2. Have the children do three sets of three regular push-ups.

3. Describe and demonstrate triceps push-ups:

Support your weight on your hands and heels with your back facing the floor. Your body should be straight.

Gradually lower your body toward the ground, then return to starting position by bending and straightening your arms. This is a difficult skill, and at first very little motion is possible.

Repeat.

Try to do three triceps push-ups, then rest briefly; three more and rest; three more and stop.

4. Have the children try to do three sets of three triceps push-ups.

Line-Up

Divide children in two teams: one on the field and the other at bat.

1. Describe and demonstrate the game:

   The hitter bounces a playground ball and strikes it with his or her hand, then the entire team runs around the bases in a single-file line behind the hitter. Each hitter has only one chance to strike the ball—it is either an out or a run. Foul balls are outs.

   When the hitter hits the ball fairly, the players on the fielding team all line up behind the player who catches the ball. They pass the ball quickly overhead back to the end of the line, then back to the front of the line, trying to get the ball to the end and back to the beginning of the line before the members of the hitting team all reach home.

   If the ball moves to the end of the line and back to the catcher before the hitting team is home, it's an out.

   If the hitting team gets home before the ball gets to the end of the catching line and back to the catcher, it's a run.

   When the hitting team has three outs, the two teams switch positions.

2. Have the children play Line-Up (15 minutes).

Cool-Down With Exchange Positions

Arrange children around the outside of a parachute that is spread out on the ground. Assign the children numbers and instruct them to hold the parachute with the left hand and circle counterclockwise.

1. On your signal, the odd-numbered children release the parachute and move forward to take the place of the next odd-numbered player in front of them (variations can include moving up two places, three places, and so on). Repeat with even-numbered players moving.

2. Have children use a variety of locomotor skills—running, galloping, skipping, and walking—to move.

Concluding Activities (5 minutes)

Physical Fitness Concept

Divide children into groups of five or six.

1. Discuss how physical fitness is the opposite of sickness or being unhealthy: *Fitness contributes to being healthy. Fitness influences our daily lives and the length of our lives. Older people who are fit have a better chance of living longer and more active lives. Younger people who are fit say they are happier, have more energy, and are healthier than low-fit people.*

2. Ask the children: *Can you give me some examples of opposites?* (Up and down, night and day, cold and hot.) *Opposites are as far apart as possible—like living in New York and in Los Angeles is about as far apart as you can be and still be living in the United States. That's like sickness and fitness!*

3. Ask each group to discuss then describe a fit and a low-fit person. Say to the children: *Remember, looks don't tell the whole story!*

From *Physical Education Methods for Elementary Teachers, Second Edition,* by Katherine T. Thomas, Amelia M. Lee, and Jerry R. Thomas, 2003, Champaign, IL: Human Kinetics. Adapted from *Physical Education for Children: Daily Lesson Plans for Elementary School, Second Edition,* by Katherine T. Thomas, Amelia M. Lee, and Jerry R. Thomas, 2000, Champaign, IL: Human Kinetics.

chapter 7

Psychosocial Factors in Physical Education

Alexa, age 10

*C*hildren are naturally active and want to learn motor skills; however, participation in these activities and motivation to do so decline during childhood, with an accelerating decline during adolescence. Competition and rewards can have a negative impact on participation, whereas appropriate motivational techniques can encourage participation.

● ●

Learner Outcomes

The teacher will do the following:

- ▶ Define intrinsic and extrinsic motivation, ego, and task orientation.
- ▶ Describe when children are ready for competition.

- ▶ Define the four attributions.
- ▶ Compare cooperation and teamwork to competition in physical activity curriculum choices.

● ●

Glossary Terms

motivation
intrinsic motivation
extrinsic motivation
competence
social comparison
ego orientation

task orientation
competition
anxiety
role taking
self-concept
self-efficacy

● ●

Many of you can recall how excited you were about physical education as elementary students. You can probably recall a different atmosphere in high school physical education. What happened? Is the shift in attitude because high school students are "too cool" to be excited about physical education or because they really dislike physical education? One thing is clear: Participation in physical education classes and in physical activity in general declines during adolescence (the middle school and high school years). The decline is greater in girls than boys. Several factors contribute to this decline: One is the variety of new interests and time demands on adolescents. Many activities compete for their time in and out of school. Another explanation is that physical education is repetitive. That is, the curriculum is the same year after year; Siedentop (1998) suggests that physical education focuses on teaching the same beginning-level sports each year. One cure for the boredom created by that situation is to increasingly expect more from the students each year. Alternatively, many teachers opt to teach new activities at the beginning level each year. Another explanation for the decline in physical activity among adolescence could be that students are turned off to physical activity. This may be because their needs are not being met.

Teachers need to understand the psychological and sociological aspects of physical education for children for several reasons:

► So teachers will encourage physically active lifestyles

► So students are motivated

► So students learn cooperation and teamwork

This chapter will present information based on physical education, physical activity, and youth sport research. Many children (more than 20 million at any time of the year) participate in out-of-school sport programs (Ewing and Seefeldt 2002). Those experiences influence how children feel about physical activity and so influence physical education. Some of what we have learned by studying youth sport applies to physical education. A relatively new area of information is exercise psychology, which provides information about adherence and affect related to physical activity.

MOTIVATION

The goal of childhood is independence, which is achieved as we develop competence in many domains, including academics and social and physical areas. Infants, children, and adolescents are naturally driven to be independent; but adults, including teachers and parents, can facilitate or undermine this achievement of independence. **Motivation** is the reason behind making choices. Motivation can be **intrinsic** (because the child wants to), **extrinsic** (because something external influences the child), or a combination of intrinsic and extrinsic factors. Infants are motivated to develop skills in order to conquer their environment as part of a quest for independence. Children continue to learn new skills as a natural and normal part of development. Achievement motivation is the reason children (or infants) decide to learn a skill; three stages of achievement motivation have been defined (table 7.1; Scanlan 1995). **Competence** is the skill or capability to do a task. During childhood, however, the focus of learning motor skills shifts from phylogenetic (inherent) to ontogenetic (culturally transmitted; chapter 4 explains these in detail). Motivation and competence lead to independence.

As skills are mastered, children need to answer two questions:

1. Am I normal?
2. Am I improving?

Table 7.1 Stages of Achievement Motivation

Stage	Age	Description	Outcome if successful	Outcome if unsuccessful
1. Autonomous	Preschool	Exploratory behaviors and learning to cope with the environment, both self-motivated (autonomous)	Master environment, seek future tests of competence	Dependence
2. Social comparison	Primary grades	Learning about one's self by answering "Am I normal?" and "Am I improving?" Peer pressure and a quest for normalcy begin	Information about self, seeks challenging tests of competence	Dependence Bully syndrome Follows peers for most decisions
3. Mature	Upper grades	Uses correct motivation based on the situation—autonomous when peer pressure is negative and social comparison when appropriate	Independence	Dependence

Positive answers to these questions move children toward independence. To answer these questions, children compare themselves to others; this is called **social comparison.** Children are intrinsically motivated to master new skills, and they use social comparison to evaluate themselves. Teachers can help children make appropriate comparisons and track improvement. For example, children should be compared either to other children who are similar in age and experience or to their own previous performance. Children tend to use outcome information for evaluation (e.g., hitting the target or winning the race). However, as we discussed in chapter 4, progress is often slower in outcome than process. Therefore, teachers can help children recognize improvements in the mechanics and efficiency of movements or decisions rather than focus on the end product. Using comparison in this way is both informative and normative.

When children answer yes to both questions (i.e., "I am normal" and "I am improving"), intrinsic motivation to try new tasks increases. When children answer no, the outcomes vary but generally mean children do not move to stage 3 of table 7.1. Children who are unsuccessful with tests of competence—who perceive themselves as failing to improve or failing to be normal—often select easy tasks for success, or they avoid any test. This can be observed during practice, as children practice tasks that are too easy or avoid practice altogether. Another outcome is the bully syndrome, where children select opponents who are younger, smaller, or less skilled. The bully syndrome is an attempt to show competence or skill by selecting a "sure thing" as a task.

While social comparison is normal, it does not imply that competition is necessary for the comparison to occur—remember the purpose is informative and normative. Further, adults do not need to emphasize comparison to others. Teachers play a critical role in helping children see themselves as normal and improving; thus, teachers play a critical role in maintaining or increasing intrinsic motivation (Weiss 1993, 2000). Part of teaching is helping children track improvement. When teachers describe the relationship between practice and achievement, the normative function is being served. That is, most people have to work hard and practice to master this skill, so the child thinks, *I am normal because I will have to practice to learn this skill; I can't do it now but after I practice I will be able to.*

Related to the notion of intrinsic and extrinsic motivation are task and ego orientations of performers. A person can choose to do a task because it brings status and therefore feeds the ego—this is an **ego orientation.** Alternatively, a person can do a task because improving or mastering the task brings personal satisfaction, which is called **task orientation.** In youth sports, children with ego orientations tend to drop out, while children with task orientations persist. Similar patterns are observed in exercise and are expected in physical education. In other words, teachers should encourage students to participate because improving skill and mastering tasks make us feel good about ourselves. The focus should be on how we feel about ourselves rather than how others feel about us.

ATTRIBUTION

For any test of competence, there are four possible explanations for the outcome, regardless of success or failure. These attributions have two dimensions: locus of control (internal or external) and level of stability (stable or unstable), as can be seen in table 7.2. From previous chapters, you can guess that the preferred attribution is effort, because effort is related to practice. Further, effort is under a child's control and is unstable. So the objective is to have a child give maximum effort all the time.

Task difficulty is the teacher's responsibility. Recall from chapter 4 the various methods for altering a task. Teachers should make tasks challenging but doable. This means that children will have a 50–50 chance of success when giving maximum effort. Tasks that are too easy can be boring and do not help students master new skills. Tasks that are too difficult do not help students learn and may be frustrating. Ability is often viewed as talent. Talent, as we shall see in chapter 8, is not a powerful predictor of performance in many physical activities. However, talent is often presented as a major factor (Thomas, Gallagher, and Thomas 2000). If we believe talent is the most important

Table 7.2   Locus of Control

	Internal	External
Stable	Ability	Task difficulty
Unstable	Effort	Luck

factor in performance, practice and instruction become unimportant. The ability to do a task changes slowly with practice, which is why it is viewed as stable. In other words, ability does not change from moment to moment. Most children are more alike in ability than they are different; however, children do have widely varied experience and interests. The teacher should balance ability and task difficulty so that children are challenged, they improve, and they find satisfaction in achievement.

Luck is often used as an explanation for outcomes. For example, children who were on losing teams said luck explained a win. Luck is both external and unstable and therefore a poor choice. The assumption is children learn attributions, and the most appropriate attribution is effort.

GOALS

One way to help students track improvement is to establish goals and relate performance to those goals. Seeing progress and improvement is motivating. Goals should be specific and challenging. Vague or low-level goals, such as "do your best," produce the poorest performance. Goals can be for a group of students (e.g., a class) or for an individual student. Goals can focus on skill, behavior, or knowledge.

Current best practices in education focus on standards and benchmarks. These are a formal set of goals that will be discussed in chapter 15. Referring to benchmarks, standards, and goals helps students understand what is expected so students can track progress and take responsibility for learning. Whether they are informal goals for a task or a formal system of evaluation, goals are an important part of a quality physical education program. Goals should be considered during planning and be evident during practice. They are the foundation for feedback and evaluation.

COMPETITION

The earliest **competition** is between infant and the environment. This evolves into social comparison during the primary grades. Competition can be institutionalized; that is, it can take the form of tournaments, with rules and formal structure, or it can be inherent such as when one person compares herself with another. Competition is neither good nor bad (Passer and Wilson 2002). Competi-

Concepts Into Practice

Ms. Abernethy knows the value of goal setting; therefore, she sets goals for herself and her students and requires students to set goals for themselves. The goal she sets for herself is this: to verbally recognize five students in each class each day who are making progress toward the lesson's goal. She will do this by making a note at the end of class next to the names of students she has recognized. Her goal for her students is a benchmark for her program. That benchmark is for 75 percent of the students to have 30 minutes of moderate-to-vigorous activity at least five days per week reported in their journals. When she reads the journals, she will be able to determine if this goal has been met. She plans on reporting this to the students using a chart. Each week she will add a bar to the chart showing what percentage of the students met the goal. In Ms. Abernethy's class, each student is required to create personal physical activity goals. The following two samples represent goals for a less active and a more active student. "I will go for a 30-minute walk after school on Monday, Wednesday, and Friday of next week." "I will practice running the mile every day next week".

tion—especially highly structured competition—however, can create negative consequences. Among those are stress and anxiety, consistent failure, awards that undermine intrinsic motivation, and failure to meet basic goals of sport and physical activity.

Stress and anxiety increase as the importance of a performance increases and as the performance becomes public. Physical activity is important in our culture, and performance in physical education is public because classmates and teachers observe (Kimiecik, Horn, and Shurin 1996; Smith, Smoll, and Curtis 1978). Therefore, stress and anxiety are inherent in physical education as well as sport. **Anxiety** is one extreme of arousal—the negative extreme. At the opposite end of the anxiety continuum is a state as relaxed as sleep. In the middle is enough arousal to produce effort without anxiety. The performer experiences stress when he perceives an imbalance between ability and task difficulty. Stress is a result of anxiety; sometimes the heart rate is elevated, breathing may be affected, sweating can occur, or the face may flush. It may negatively affect performance.

Further, stress has emotional consequences beyond the performance. For example, general anxiety may increase. To keep stress and anxiety under control, the teacher can use three strategies:

1. Keep the importance of a performance in perspective; class participation should not be elevated to a major life event.
2. Reduce the public display as much as possible; for example, have several students participate at once or have the potential observers do something other than observe.
3. Reduce competition and focus on skill learning, short-term goals, and cooperation, rather than winning.

In the best-case scenario, half of the participants in competition lose. For example, in team sports, one team (half) wins and the other (half) loses. In individual sports, such as the 100-meter dash in track, many lose and only one wins. Unfortunately, often the same individuals are consistent losers; that is, one team never wins. When teams or individuals have similar records, competition has fewer negative consequences. In fact, the highest situation for motivation is when there is an equal chance to win or lose. Consider playing golf: If your opponent is Tiger Woods, you probably will not be motivated to play your best because you know he is so skilled at the sport. Conversely, playing your elderly aunt who has never played golf would not demand a high level of motivation or produce your best performance. Consistent losing also affects future performance. Children who are on losing teams predict future losses, even immediately after a win. Children who are on winning teams predict winning even after a

loss. You can see how children could interpret losing as failing to be normal and to improve. Teachers can eliminate these problems by making sure students have a balance of outcomes. For example, rotating students among teams so that after each game one-third to one-half of the players move to a different team, or ensuring that teams have a balanced skill pool as they are chosen, can help. Some teachers do not keep score or do not have teams compete during physical education. Another technique used by physical education specialists is to total the scores for both teams in one class and compare that to the total for both teams in a different class. Classroom teachers can compare the total score of the class (both teams) one day to the total score the next day. The key is to keep competition—and the potential negative consequences of competition—under control.

Awards and rewards are part of many competitions and can be contingent on performance—this means the award is earned. Sometimes awards are given to all participants; these are not based on performance. Finally, awards can be unexpected; that is, the award is given, but the recipient did not know prior to the performance about the award. Awards and rewards can shift the motivation from intrinsic (and task oriented) to extrinsic (and ego oriented). Generally, when students want to do something, awards are not necessary. Further, awards can undermine intrinsic motivation, which is undesirable. For young children (children seven and younger), awards are perceived as fun and tend not to undermine intrinsic motivation. However, for children older than seven, rewards and awards should be carefully considered. Use the following guidelines:

When children participate in organized sports, it is important to emphasize skill learning and enjoyment, not winning.
© Human Kinetics.

- ▶ Do not give awards to everyone for participating.
- ▶ Give contingent awards sparingly or not at all.
- ▶ Use rewards (or bribes) to get students to do something they do not want to do.

Competition—especially team sport competition—should teach several valuable skills to participants. Sportsmanship, leadership, and learning skills are among the things children and adults want sport to teach. Emphasis on competition often decreases the opportunities to learn these. It is important to remember that two major factors children cite as reasons for participating are being with friends and having fun, so when competition overshadows these factors children are likely to stop enjoying participation. In competitions run by adults, all decisions are made by the adults, so children cannot learn leadership. When competition is high, decisions are often made that focus on winning rather than on other goals of sport participation. Adults often demonstrate poor sportsmanship, and highly competitive situations set the stage for similar behaviors by children. For example, playing the best players most or all the time means other players do not have a chance to practice skills. Competition often means the players who need the most practice—the poorest players—get the least practice! In addition, it is not fun to sit on the bench. Children report a preference for playing on a losing team to sitting on the bench of a winning team. In fact, the three most frequently given reasons for participation are being with friends, having fun, and learning skills (Weiss 2000), so the teacher must organize activities that are competitive so that kids may do all three. This often means reducing the emphasis on winning and competition. Sport offers opportunities for children to practice making moral decisions. Practicing leadership, cooperation, and decision making are important aspects of sport and physical education.

The decision whether or not to cheat is another "teachable moment." If the students are allowed to cheat as long as they don't get caught, the message they receive is that cheating is okay. Children receive mixed messages from after-school experiences, professional sports, and parents. Teachers are important to children, which means that teachers can influence what children think and do. On issues related to morality (e.g., cheating, teasing), saying nothing is usually interpreted

A Teachable Moment

The catcher in a game similar to softball was holding the ball but not tagging out the runner coming toward home. The catcher would reach toward the runner, then pull the ball back as the runner hesitated between third base and home. Meanwhile, another runner reaches third base, so the first runner must go to home; however, the catcher has not yet tagged him during numerous opportunities. The teacher blows her whistle, asking, "Does anyone know why I stopped the game?" After a few seconds of consideration, a student ventures the following response: "Because the catcher was teasing the runner." The teacher says, "Okay, but why does that matter?" Another student says, "It is mean." The teacher says, "Okay; anything else?" After a pause, two students respond, "If he dropped the ball, it would let the runner score," and "He is letting the team down." The teacher says to the catcher, "Okay, *now* you know what to do. We are ready to continue to play. How do you think we should continue?"

by children as agreement, so teachers must be sure to speak up!

COOPERATION

Our society values cooperation. "Plays well with others" has meaning to us because we value the cooperation implied in the statement. Children learn to be cooperative, so it is important to provide opportunities to practice cooperative behaviors. Expecting young children (under 12 years) to consider others first is asking for behavior that is beyond their developmental capacity. Teaching them to think of others is different. Kohlberg (1971) described three stages of moral reasoning: In stage one, children make decisions based on rewards and punishment. For example, "Cheating is wrong because I was punished for cheating." Stage two is characterized by making decisions based on the expectations of significant others; in other words, "Cheating is wrong because my parents would be disappointed if I cheated." Finally, stage three finds children making a decision based on right and wrong that is internalized—"It is not fair to everyone else if I cheat."

Similarly, children do not master **role taking,** or putting yourself in someone else's place, until about 12 years of age (Passer and Wilson 2002). Cooperation without guidance is very difficult for children until they understand how someone else feels and how someone else can contribute. Part of development is learning to see the value of others and the contribution they can make and to be sensitive to their feelings. Without guidance, cooperative activities often become variations on competition. Children work together not for the joy of sharing but because it is the only way to win.

Cooperation infers everyone working together. Two ideas related to cooperation are leadership and cohesion; these help foster cooperation. First, most groups have a leader. This does not mean everyone in the group always has to do what the leader says. A leader must gain consensus from and provide guidance to the group. Second, to be cohesive, groups need to learn to work as one; the group members must work together. This happens best if each member makes a contribution to the mission of the group. Several things can facilitate cooperation: First, young children should practice cooperation with small groups, perhaps only two people. The pairs should have specific problems to solve and should contribute equally to the solution. For all ages, it is helpful to select a leader with specific duties (e.g., poll the group for opinions about possible solutions). Each member of the group should have a job that contributes to the mission. With practice, more responsibility should be shifted to the students for organizing the group activities. Group leadership can be changed frequently so that all children are leaders at some time. Competition should not always be the motivating factor for cooperation. Each day, every activity can be a venue for learning about cooperation. Cooperation is easier among those who respect one another. Children are likely to follow the lead of the teacher; thus, teachers must encourage all students, respect student contributions to the learning environment, and provide opportunities to practice cooperation.

One way to encourage this is to end class with students in a circle. Each student must say something nice or something she likes about the person on her right. Children are cued to look for the good in everyone. A variation is to have students say what they liked best in class.

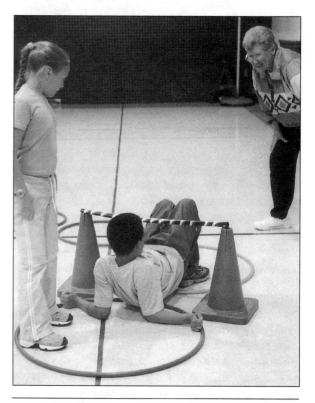

Teachers should foster a fun environment where students support each other while attempting movement activities.

SELF-CONCEPT AND SELF-EFFICACY

Self-concept is the way a person views oneself. It is an overall feeling based on specific subcomponents, such as how one feels about physical activity and sport or social settings. The quality of a child's experiences influences how that child views herself, which is translated to self-concept. Self-concept is relatively stable; that is, after about eight years of age, a child has a view of herself across a variety of settings that is translated into an overall feeling. If children receive positive reinforcement from teachers, parents, and peers about performances in physical activity and sport (and other areas), the child's self-concept will be positive. The critical element is a child's competence—or skill (Weiss 2000). The teacher's goal is simple: Increase the child's skill because this will positively influence self-concept. Three suggestions for teachers are as follows:

1. Explain success in movement and how errors and mistakes should be used to adjust movements for future success.

2. Discuss how other people should be treated when they make mistakes so that errors are viewed as a normal part of learning and are not threatening to students.

3. Be positive!

Self-efficacy is the confidence an individual has in accomplishing a specific task. For example, are you 25, 50, 75, or 100 percent confident that you can lift a 100-pound box? What about a 50-pound box? Self-efficacy is situational, whereas self-confidence is more general and stable. Self-efficacy contributes to self-concept (Weiss 2000). Confidence is related to both. Confidence is critical to continued physical activity patterns. Adults who are active report having high self-confidence and competence regarding physical activity. Their self-concept about sport and physical activity is positive and they have high self-efficacy when asked about participating in and adhering to physical activity and exercise programs. This suggests the importance of developing confidence, high self-efficacy, and movement competence (skill) during childhood.

EXERCISE ADHERENCE AND AFFECT

Being physically active is a one- or two-stage process. If you are active, the goal is to maintain an active lifestyle. If you are not active, however, the first step is to initiate an activity program; the second step is to maintain the program. Children are naturally active, so we generally think of maintaining that activity. Patterns suggest that activity drops between 9 and 13 years of age, especially for girls (Welk 1999). This means the two-stage model applies to many adolescents. Logic suggests that it would be easier to maintain activity by preventing the decline than it would be to have to initiate and maintain activity in a sedentary population. So, one goal for elementary physical education is to encourage lifelong physical activity.

Physical activity, as little as going for a walk, produces positive changes. In other words, activity can produce feelings of happiness (Ekkekakis, Hall, VanLanduyt, and Petruzzello 2000). Physical activity reduces depression and its symptoms. Some of these changes are caused by chemicals released during exercise, which promote a sense of well-being. Further, the psychological benefits of feeling in control, a sense of accomplishment, and social support are likely contributors to the improvement in affect.

A sedentary person may become depressed and avoid more activity, therefore becoming more depressed and creating a cycle. Often, sedentary people gain weight and fat. Obesity has an additive effect: being inactive and overweight leads to more depression, which leads to less activity, and so forth. Physical activity has immediate and long-term benefits for mental health.

The positive feelings associated with an active lifestyle reinforce the activity. Feeling good and being happy are translated into exercise adherence. Unfortunately, in adults approximately half of those initiating an activity program drop out within six months of starting the program (Dishman 1994). Dropping out can bring feelings of inadequacy and then depression. Clearly, keeping children active is easier than getting adults to initiate and maintain activity programs.

SUMMARY

Children are naturally motivated to be active and to learn skills. They participate because they want to be with friends, have fun, and learn skills. Focusing on the enjoyment of accomplishment and effort will encourage lifelong participation and increase motivation. Students and teachers need to use goals to monitor progress and should focus on task mastery while minimizing competition. Physical activity brings psychological as well as physiological benefits—another reason to encourage active lifestyles. Sport and physical education offer the opportunity to develop important social skills, such as cooperation and leadership. These skills are facilitated through cooperative activities.

MASTERY LEARNING ACTIVITIES

1. Select a sport. Identify the major skills in the sport. Using those skills and equipment, develop a cooperative activity for fifth-grade children.

2. Make a list of 20 things to say that would reinforce effort.

3. Write a story that portrays to children the concept of doing something because it makes you feel good about what you are doing rather than because someone else wants you to do it.

4. Find one of the articles in the reference list, read it, and write a one-page summary.

REFERENCES

Dishman, R.K. 1994. *Advances in exercise adherence.* Champaign, IL: Human Kinetics.

Ekkekakis, P., E.E. Hall, L.M. VanLanduyt, and S.J. Petruzzello. 2000. Walking in (affective) circles: Can short walks enhance affect? *Journal of Behavioral Medicine* 23 (3):245–75.

Ewing, M.E., and V. Seefeldt. 2002. Patterns of participation in American agency-sponsored youth sport. In *Children and youth in sport: A biopsychosocial perspective,* edited by F.L. Smoll and R.E. Smith, 39–60. Dubuque, IA: Kendall/Hunt.

Kimiecik, J.C., T.S. Horn, and C.S. Shurin. 1996. Relationships among children's beliefs, perceptions of their parent's beliefs and their moderate-to-vigorous physical activity. *Research Quarterly for Exercise and Sport* 67:324–36.

Kohlberg, L. 1971. Stages of moral development as a basis for moral education. In *Moral education: Interdiciplinary approaches (pp. 23–92),* edited by C.M. Beck, B.S. Crittenden, and E.V. Sullivan. Toronto: University of Toronto Press.

Passer, M.W., and B.J. Wilson. 2002. At what age are children ready to compete? In *Children and youth in sport: A biopsychosocial perspective,* edited by F.L. Smoll and R.E. Smith, 83–103. Dubuque, IA: Kendall/Hunt.

Scanlan, T.K. 1995. Social evaluation and the competitive process: A developmental perspective. In *Children and youth in sports: A biopsychosocial perspective,* edited by F.L. Smoll and R.E. Smith, 298–308. Dubuque, Iowa: Brown & Benchmark.

Siedentop, D. 1998. In search of effective teaching: What we have learned from studying teachers and students. McCloy Lecture presented at the Annual Meeting of the American Alliance for Health, Physical Education, Recreation and Dance, Portland, Ore., April 7, 1998.

Smith, R.E., F.L. Smoll, and B. Curtis. 1978. Coaching behaviors in Little League baseball. In *Psychological perspectives in youth sport,* edited by F.L. Smoll and R.E. Smith, 173–201. Washington, D.C.: Hemisphere.

Thomas, K.T., J.D. Gallagher, and J.R. Thomas. 2000. Motor development and skill acquisition during childhood and adolescence. In *Handbook of sport psychology,* edited by R.N. Singer, H.A. Hausenblas, and C. Janelle. 2d ed., 20–52. New York: John Wiley.

Weiss, M.R. 1993. Children's participation in physical activity: Are we having fun yet? *Pediatric Exercise Science* 5:205–209.

Weiss, M.R. 2000. Motivating kids in physical activity. *President's Council on Physical Fitness and Sports Research Digest* 3(11): 1–8. Washington, D.C.: President's Council on Physical Fitness.

Welk, G. 1999. The Physical Activity Promotion Model: A conceptual model to advance the promotion of physical activity in the population. *Quest* 51:5–23.

LESSON PLANS

The lesson plans at the end of this chapter focus on cooperation and minimizing competition. The first lesson requires that young children work together in a continuous relay with no winner. The second lesson focuses on developing passing and catching skills and teamwork but has an element of competition. Generally, the children do not keep score, so the emphasis on competition is very low. The game can be adapted to a variety of age groups by increasing the number of balls, calling the "fouls" more closely, or being more relaxed. Sharon's Shoot-Around provides the most practice for the least skilled students. In order for a team to be successful, the team must work together for success. Raging River requires students to cooperate and to use equipment in a unique way to solve a problem.

Most games and activities can be modified to reduce competition. Children should never be eliminated from games; they should be rewarded for teamwork, cooperation, and skill. Other cooperative activities include rhythmic activities in which partners or groups work together in partner gymnastics stunts (lessons 7.3, 7.6, and 8.1).

LESSON  **7.1**

Laundry Basket Express

Student Objectives

- Work together
- Continue the activity with little adult intervention
- Remain active for the entire time.

Equipment

- 1 laundry basket or box per pair of children
- many balls or bean bags
- 4 cones
- 1 towel or similar size cloth for each 2–4 children

Warm-Up (5 minutes)

Len's Ball Mix-Up

Arrange the children on a line in the middle of the gym. Scatter balls and beanbags around the gym on the floor. Identify two marked areas on the floor (mark with cones or use the basketball key) for the "zone". Your instructions to the children are: "Oh, dear, I made a mistake and it is a mess! When I say go I want you to pick up all the balls and beanbags and place them in the zone. You may only pick up one at a time. Once you place that one in the zone you may get another one. Here is the zone (show them one of the areas you are using as the zones—you will use the other area later). Now please quickly and carefully put all the balls into the zone!" Give the signal to start. When all or nearly all the balls are in the zone, stop the class and reassemble them on the line. You will now overact and say, "Did I say I wanted you to put those in that area? Oh my, I really wanted them at the other end (now point to the other zone). Can you do that? Ready?" Give your signal to start. This can be repeated with many "mistakes" and "oh, dears."

Skill-Development Activity (20 minutes)

Arrange the children in pairs, each pair with a laundry basket. Place the four cones in each corner of a large rectangular area.

The object of the activity is to move the balls or beanbags using the basket from one cone to the next, place the balls in a pile, and return to the original place with the basket to gather the "new" balls, which were delivered by other children. More than one pair can be stationed at a cone; just stagger their starts. The children should move balls continuously and as quickly as possible.

Concluding Activity (5 minutes)

Arrange children in groups of two or four. Give each group a towel (or cloth rectangle) and a beanbag. Each child should grasp a corner of the towel. The object is for the groups to try to move the beanbag by tossing it into the air with the towel. Give the following challenges:

- *Toss and catch.*
- *Toss it high.*
- *Toss it away from you.*
- *Can you think of other ways to move the beanbag?*

From *Physical Education Methods for Elementary Teachers, Second Edition,* by Katherine T. Thomas, Amelia M. Lee, and Jerry R. Thomas, 2003, Champaign, IL: Human Kinetics.

Games and Sports

LESSON

Len's Scooter Ball

Student Objectives

- Work cooperatively with all teammates
- Pass (throw) and catch accurately
- Follow the rules

Equipment

- 1 scooter for each child (all but 4–6 children)
- 1–3 foam 8.5″ balls
- 8 cones
- 4- 4 × 6–8 ft mats

Skill-Development Activity (25 to 30 minutes)

Arrange one cone in each corner of a rectangle (the corners of a basketball court work well). Place four more cones along the longest two sides to divide the area into three approximately equal sections. Place one mat on the floor and one against the wall (or standing like a screen) at the middle of the short end of the court.

Divide the class into two teams, divide each team into three groups. One group from each team will play in each of the three sections of the court which are marked by the cones. Each team will defend one of the two "goals," which are the mats. In order to score, the ball must hit the standing or leaning mat. Two or three players on a team will be goalies. Goalies stand on the mat that is on the floor and stop the ball from hitting the other mat. All players except goalies are on a scooter. The game is played in six or more units of time. Each unit is about one-sixth of the playing time. At the end of a unit (generally three minutes) the players in each section rotate to the adjacent section. New goalies are selected and the former goalies use their scooters (at the opposite end of the court) so that goalies rotate with their group. The object for the teacher is to have all children play goalie each time the game is played. The game begins as the teacher bounces the ball in the middle section. The rules are as follows:

- Players must pass (throw the ball) to teammates.
- The ball must be passed from adjacent areas, the ball may not be thrown over an area to the opposite end of the court.
- Players may not move scooters while holding a ball.
- Only the players in the area closest to the goal may score.
- If a player with the ball falls off the scooter, the ball goes to the other team.
- A player may only hold the ball for three seconds before passing the ball.

These rules are called more strictly with older or more experienced students. The teacher should put additional balls in play as students demonstrate skill and cooperation.

From *Physical Education Methods for Elementary Teachers, Second Edition,* by Katherine T. Thomas, Amelia M. Lee, and Jerry R. Thomas, 2003, Champaign, IL: Human Kinetics.

Partner Stunts

Student Objectives

- Work cooperatively with a partner.
- Understand the terms "base," "top," and "balance."
- Demonstrate two partner stunts and attempt other partner stunts.

Equipment and Materials

- 1 or more mats (4 ft × 8 ft) per group
- Background music (optional)

Safety Tips

- Use spotting on difficult stunts.
- Children should be as equal in size as possible when working in partners.

Warm-Up Activities (5 minutes)

Grades 2-3 Warm-Up Routine

Arrange the children in a line along one side of the mat.

1. Teach all parts of the warm-up as a routine.
2. Have the children perform the following sequence of steps:

    Head circle right, head circle left,

    Shoulder circle forward (3), shoulder circle backward (3),

    Torso stretch (side, back, side, front); repeat 3 times,

Hamstring stretch (squat to straighten); repeat 5 times,

Ankle rotations inward (3), ankle rotations outward (3),

Back arches (5),

Crunches (20),

Push-ups (10),

(Move the children into a circle formation.)

Skip 24 skips clockwise, 24 counterclockwise,

10 vertical jumps, and

Run one minute continuously around the circle.

Skill-Development Activities (20 minutes)

Wring the Dishrag

Match pairs according to size.

1. Describe and have two children demonstrate the stunt:

    Stand facing each other with hands joined.

    Lift arms (one partner's left, the other's right), turn toward and under the lifted arms, and continue turning until you are facing each other again.

2. Have the children practice Wring the Dishrag.

Partner Get-Up

Have partners sit facing each other.

1. Describe and have two children demonstrate the stunt:

   Join hands and touch toes.

   Pull until standing by balancing with each other.

   Keep your feet about shoulder-width apart.

2. Have the children practice Partner Get-Up.

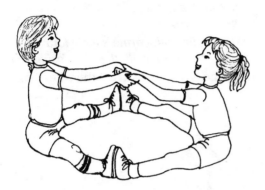

Partner Hopping

Have partners stand facing each other, about one leg length apart.

1. Describe and have two children demonstrate the stunt: *Hold each other's right (or left) leg, then hop in the same direction using only two legs of the four legs you and your partner have.*

2. Have the children practice partner hopping.

Human Top

Have partners stand facing each other with hands joined and toes touching.

1. Describe and have two children demonstrate the stunt:

   Lean backward until your arms and legs are straight and your two bodies form a "V."

   Then turn clockwise, keeping your toes together and your arms straight.

2. Have the children practice Human Top.

Back-to-Back Get-Up

Have partners sit back to back.

1. Describe and have two children demonstrate the stunt:

   Lock your elbows and bend your legs so that your heels are close to your seat.

   Push with your legs to stand with your backs still touching.

2. Have the children practice Back-to-Back Get-Up.

Quad Leg Lift

Arrange partners on the mats.

1. Describe and have two children demonstrate the stunt:

   Lie on your backs with your heads touching with your partner and extend your feet in opposite directions. Put your hands out to the side.

   Bend your knees so your feet are on the floor.

   Each of you lift one leg at the same time, until your toes touch in the air. Then lift your other leg until all four touch.

   Keep your legs up for a count of five, and then go back to the starting position.

2. Have the children practice the Quad Leg Lift.

Wheelbarrow

Continue with pairs on the mats.

1. Describe and have two children demonstrate the stunt:

   One partner lies on his tummy, arms bent, supporting the body near the chest. The other partner stands near the feet of the partner on the floor and squats down (bending knees and keeping back straight).

   The standing partner lifts the feet of her partner off the ground. Lift with your legs while keeping your back straight.

   At this point both partners walk forward—one using hands to walk, the other using feet.

2. Have the children practice the wheelbarrow.

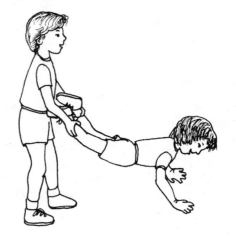

Two-Person Pyramid

Continue with pairs on the mats.

1. Describe and have two children demonstrate the stunt:

   One partner begins on all fours (with feet and hands shoulder-width apart). We call this partner the "base." The other partner stands on the hips of the base. We call this partner the "top." Both partners face the same direction.

   The top places both feet on the base's hips below the base's waist and a few inches apart.

   Take turns being the base and the top.

2. Have the children practice the two-person pyramid.

Individual Front Fall

Arrange four to six children in two to three pairs on a mat.

1. Describe and have a child demonstrate the stunt:

   Stand with your arms at your sides and feet together.

   Lean forward and fall to the mat. At the last possible second, move your arms forward to catch your body weight and break the fall.

   As your hands touch the mat, bend your arms at the elbows gradually to absorb the force as your body continues to fall to the mat.

   Finish in a face-down position on the mat.

2. Have the children practice the individual front fall. Encourage all children to try this.

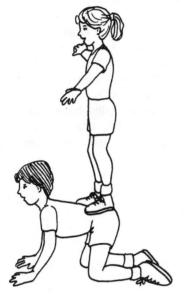

Concluding Activities (5 minutes)

Wave

Have the children stand on one side of their mat, facing the width of the mat.

1. Describe and have one group demonstrate the stunt: *Line up shoulder to shoulder and do the front fall, one after the other. The first child begins the fall, and before she hits the mat the next child begins the fall, and so forth.*

2. Have the children practice the wave.

3. Repeat with all children and mats in one long line, beginning at one end of the mats and ending at the opposite end.

From *Physical Education Methods for Elementary Teachers, Second Edition,* by Katherine T. Thomas, Amelia M. Lee, and Jerry R. Thomas, 2003, Champaign, IL: Human Kinetics. Adapted from *Physical Education for Children: Daily Lesson Plans for Elementary School, Second Edition,* by Katherine T. Thomas, Amelia M. Lee, and Jerry R. Thomas, 2000, Champaign, IL: Human Kinetics.

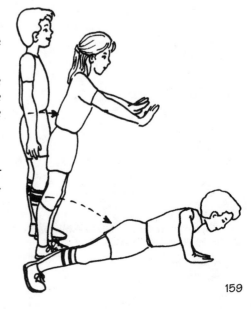

Games and Sports

GRADES **4-5**

LESSON **7.4** *Sharon's Shoot Around*

Student Objectives

- Work together cooperatively.
- Keep score for their team.
- Help others.
- Practice basketball shooting.

Equipment

- 1 basketball goal
- 4 bases
- 1 basketball or playground ball

Skill Development Activity (30 minutes)

Set four bases on one end of a basketball court.

Divide the students into two teams. One team will be scattered around the basketball goal and have the basketball. The other team will be lined up near any of the four bases (one of which you designate as home). The running team will begin running the bases—two students at a time—on the go signal. Each time a pair makes a circuit around the four bases a point is scored and another pair begins to run. The shooting team will shoot bas-

kets, beginning on the go signal. Once a student makes a basket, that student may not shoot again but will assist in retrieving balls for the remaining shooters. A point is awarded for each basket made (e.g., one for each team member). Once all players on a team have made a basket, the round ends and the teams switch positions. The game continues, ending with an equal number of rounds.

From *Physical Education Methods for Elementary Teachers, Second Edition,* by Katherine T. Thomas, Amelia M. Lee, and Jerry R. Thomas, 2003, Champaign, IL: Human Kinetics.

Games and Sports

LESSON  7.5

Raging River

Student Objectives

- Work cooperatively to solve a movement problem.
- Use equipment creatively to solve a problem.

Equipment and Materials

- 1 balance beam or line on floor per group
- 1 mat per beam
- 1 hoop per group

The following equipment is per "river" you set up. Try to keep group size around six to increase participation opportunities.

- 1 mat
- 1 cone
- 1 rope
- 2 carpet squares
- 1 ball
- 1 scooter
- Chalk or tape to mark "river"

Warm-Up Activities (5 minutes)

Select one of the following cooperative games.

Balance Challenge

Have small groups of children stand in a line on a line or balance beam, which is over a mat.

1. Describe the game:

   The object is to reverse the order of the children in your group without stepping off the beam (or line). For example, the last child on the right end of the line should reverse places with the last child on the left of the line, and so forth.

   You will have to balance while climbing over and around each other.

2. Have the children try the Balance Challenge.

Hoop Circle

Have each small group stand in a circle with hands joined, with one hoop per group.

1. Describe the game:

   Place the hoop over your heads (hands are joined through the hoop, or the like).

   The object is to move the hoop around the entire circle without releasing hands.

2. Have the children play Hoop Circle.

Circle Untangle

Have small groups stand in a close circle with hands extended inward.

1. Describe the game:

   Join hands and follow three rules; no one can join hands with the child on either side, no one can join both hands with the same child, and you may not let go of hands at any time.

   The object is to make one large circle with hands joined. Hint: Some of you may end up facing in while others end up facing out.

2. Have the children play Circle Untangle.

Skill-Development Activities (20 minutes)

Assign each small group a set of equipment, including a mat, scooter, cone, two carpet squares, one rope, and one ball. For each group define a "river" (two lines) about 30 ft apart.

Raging River

1. Describe the game:

   The object is to cross the "river" (the area between the two lines) without touching the "water" (the floor). Each group must get all group members and all equipment to the other side of the river without touching any body part to the floor. If a person touches the floor, the group must start that round over.

   Each time your group successfully crosses, you must return, using one fewer piece of equipment. Remove equipment in the following order: ball first, rope second, cone third, carpet squares fourth, scooter fifth. Your final trip will be with the mat only.

2. Have the children play Raging River. Be aware that some groups will make all seven trips, while other groups will not be able to complete one trip in the time.

3. Encourage children to work cooperatively and explore as many solutions to the problem as possible. Provide feedback as the game goes on.

Concluding Activities (5 minutes)

1. Discuss the various strategies groups used to be successful in Raging River. You may want to have groups demonstrate their strategies.

2. Expansion idea: You can use a variety of equipment to alter the game (e.g., cardboard boxes, walking cans, balance beams).

From *Physical Education Methods for Elementary Teachers, Second Edition,* by Katherine T. Thomas, Amelia M. Lee, and Jerry R. Thomas, 2003, Champaign, IL: Human Kinetics. Adapted from *Physical Education for Children: Daily Lesson Plans for Elementary School, Second Edition,* by Katherine T. Thomas, Amelia M. Lee, and Jerry R. Thomas, 2000, Champaign, IL: Human Kinetics.

LESSON

Partner Stunts

Student Objectives

- Attempt three new partner stunts.
- Name at least eight partner stunts.

Equipment and Materials

- 1 or more mats (4 ft × 8 ft) per group

Warm-Up Activities (5 to 7 minutes)

Grades 4–5 Warm-Up Routine

Keep the children in small groups on the mats. Cue the children to perform the entire routine straight through as follows:

Floor Stretching

Four straddle stretches right, four left,

Four overhead straddle stretches right, four left, and

Four pike stretches with toes pointed, then repeat four with ankles flexed.

Back Flexibility

Four back arches,

Four leg rollovers, and

Four back push-ups.

Standing Stretches

Four torso stretches, and

Four bent-leg hamstring stretches.

Endurance Exercises

One minute each of running and skipping,

20 sit-ups,

10 push-ups, and

10 dorsal back-curls.

Skill-Development Activities (18 to 20 minutes)

Triple Roll

Create groups of three, and assign each group to a mat.

1. Describe and have three children demonstrate the stunt:

   All three of you get down on all fours about three ft apart, facing the same side of the mat.

   The middle person begins to roll to the right. The right child hops over the middle person and rolls toward the left person, who jumps to the middle over the rolling person.

   Continue.

2. Have the children practice the triple roll.

Jump-Through

Continue with groups of three at the mats.

1. Describe and demonstrate the stunt:

   Hold hands to form a circle.

   One of you jumps over the joined arms of the other two children, who help lift the jumper's weight.

   Take turns jumping.

2. Have the children practice the jump-through.

Shoulder Balance

Arrange pairs of partners on the mats.

1. Describe and have two children demonstrate the stunt:

   One person (the base) lies flat on his back with knees bent.

   The other partner, the top, stands between the knees of the base, leans forward, and rests her shoulders on the extended arms of the base.

   The top holds the base's knees and kicks her legs up to a handstand position.

2. Have the children practice the shoulder balance with one pair spotting another pair.

Spotting for the Shoulder Balance

Have four children demonstrate the spotting technique:

Spotters stand on each side of the base near the waist of the base.

They guide and balance the top by holding the top's thighs and shoulders, being careful not to interfere with the base's grasp on the top.

Concluding Activities (5 minutes)

Discussion

Arrange the children in a semicircle. Discuss what the children have learned today:

What partner stunts did we learn yesterday? (Caterpillar and three-person pyramid.)

What new partner stunts did we learn today? (Shoulder balance, jump-through, triple roll.)

Which is the best stunt you and your partner can do? Which is the hardest? Show me your best!

From *Physical Education Methods for Elementary Teachers, Second Edition,* by Katherine T. Thomas, Amelia M. Lee, and Jerry R. Thomas, 2003, Champaign, IL: Human Kinetics. Adapted from *Physical Education for Children: Daily Lesson Plans for Elementary School, Second Edition,* by Katherine T. Thomas, Amelia M. Lee, and Jerry R. Thomas, 2000, Champaign, IL: Human Kinetics.

Individual Differences

Ranesha, age 8, and
Markyona, age 9

The genes we inherit set boundaries for numerous characteristics. The environment shapes us into unique individuals through those characteristics. Genes may establish our minimum and maximum height, but the environment determines what we will do with that height. All of us are unique, but we are also more alike than different.

Learner Outcomes

The teacher will do the following:

- Describe differences between experts and nonexperts.
- Discuss how variability (inclusion, gender, and expertise) enhances the learning environment.

- Explain how Title IX and IDEA influence physical education.
- Compare boys and girls in physical activity.
- Understand and appreciate differences among people.

Glossary Terms

individual differences
variability
readiness

individualized education program (IEP)
expertise
relative age effect

Individual differences are often thought of as the extremes of any characteristics (for instance, a disability or an expertise). The most interesting individual differences, however, may be those differences at neither extreme. Most of us have many similar characteristics, yet what we are like and what we accomplish is often very different. How and why does that happen? Understanding individual differences provides answers to those questions.

Teachers need to understand individual differences for several reasons:

- So that the learning environment can be individualized as appropriate for students
- To understand their own strengths, weaknesses, and interests
- As a part of understanding the contributions of nature and nurture to development
- To deliver developmentally appropriate physical education

- To meet the needs of disabled students by providing inclusive physical education programs
- To challenge the most skilled students

VARIABILITY

Developmentally appropriate practices include two components: those that are age appropriate for a group of children and those that are appropriate for the range of individual children in the group. After reading chapters 3 to 7, which presented information about the various aspects of development, you should be familiar with one of the most robust and important concepts of child development: There is a wide range of variation among individuals within the normal range; this is called **variability.** Humans are more alike than different; the variations make us unique individuals. As we consider development beyond the normal range—those with disabilities and exceptional abilities—the variation increases. Because variability is normal, teachers need to understand the individual differences associated with variability.

Readiness is the capability of a person to participate in an activity. It is determined by evaluating demands of the tasks involved, converting those to prerequisite skills, then assessing the individual's capability of performing the prerequisite skills. The saying "You have to walk before you can run" summarizes this idea. Readiness is complicated by the multiple dimensionality of most activities. For example, an activity such as a team sport requires motor skills, cognitive skills, and social interaction. To be successful, the individual must meet prerequisites from all areas. Often, a child will meet some of the prerequisites but not all of them. Consider soccer: A child may be able to control the ball and may understand the goal of scoring but may not be ready to do role taking (understanding the role of another) and therefore not be a good team member. This can be observed in the typical "beehive" soccer game, in which all the children run after the ball rather than play their respective positions on the field. Readiness for any activity should be evaluated in terms of the following task demands:

▶ Motor skill
▶ Cognitive readiness
▶ Physical characteristics (size and maturation)
▶ Psychological readiness
▶ Physiological readiness

Considering task demands in view of the normal child's development (prerequisites) helps teachers, parents, and coaches to determine if the activity is appropriate. Baseball provides a good example: The youngest children play T-ball because they cannot strike a tossed ball. Older children play while coaches pitch because it is difficult to find children who can pitch, and, even when the coach throws pitches that can be hit, striking is difficult. Next, baseball is played with a child pitching to a child batter. These alterations are made based on motor skill. Since the structure of the game does not take into account cognitive demands or psychological or physiological factors, these alterations are appropriate.

Recall the discussion about competition in the previous chapter. Competition is not obvious to young children (Passer and Wilson 2002, 1996). After a T-ball game, parents often ask, "Who won?"

The child has to ask the coach because the young players do not view this as important. As the parent continues to ask, winning becomes important to the child. If teachers de-emphasize competition, children will, too. Competition may occur at the expense of practice and therefore may have a negative impact on motor skill development that would, in turn, delay readiness and negatively affect performance. One factor contributing to children dropping out of sport is early and high-intensity competition (Gould, Udry, Tuffey, and Loehr 1996). In extracurricular sport, children have the option of dropping out and by doing so they send a message to adults. Students in physical education are not allowed to drop out directly, so they send the message in other ways. A child may send the message by sitting on the sidelines, asking to go to the bathroom, misbehaving, saying the activity is "stupid," or giving low effort. Teachers need to be very careful about competition in class. If competition causes highly skilled players to drop out, you can imagine how competition affects students with poor skills! For physical education and sport, it is important to allow young children, those 13 years and younger, to sample a number of activities and thereby avoid specializing in one sport (Côté, Baker, and Abernethy, forthcoming).

How do you know when children are ready? Generally, they will ask to compete when they are ready. Additionally, when a child can do role taking (10–12 years), attribute outcomes (10–13 years), and has the cognitive ability to understand competition (12 years), the child will be ready to compete. As children are ready for competition, programs should introduce controlled competition. This means taking care to keep winning and losing in perspective, reduce the public aspects of competition, reduce stress and anxiety, and balance winning and losing so some children are not consistently losers. Finally, it is a good idea to be sure that children have mastered cooperation before they begin competition. In sport, cooperation is observed when children help each other and share (e.g., a child who extends a hand to a teammate who has fallen to the ground or a player who passes the ball to an open player rather than keeping the ball herself).

INCLUSION

Beginning with Public Law 94-142 and continuing with recent legislation such as Americans with

Disabilities Act and IDEA (Individuals with Disabilities Education Act), an important strength of physical education has been inclusion. Inclusion is defined as meaningful participation in the least restrictive environment. The spirit of inclusion is to provide an educational setting that is "regular" or as similar to regular as possible without increasing liability or reducing learning for any students. The term *regular* refers to the regular classroom or physical education class for the age or grade of the student. Claudine Sherrill (1998) points out that adapted physical education and inclusion are "good practices" in elementary physical education. A quality program with expert instruction will individualize and adapt activities so that all students will benefit. The developmental approach suggests that inclusion is part of sound teaching. Further, everyone learns from inclusion; it is an integral part of diversity and a multicultural perspective that is inherent in education in this country.

Physical education is a direct service under federal law (Public Law 94-142 and IDEA). This means that physical education in the least restrictive environment is required for all students with disabilities (Sherrill 1998; Winnick 1995). For some students, a special class will be appropriate; for others it will be regular physical education with students of a similar age. The **individualized education program** (IEP) will describe the placement for physical education—regular PE, special (or adapted) PE, or a combination. The law requires that students with disabilities have, at a minimum, the same amount of physical education as provided for other students in the district. If the district (or state) requires daily physical education, the special needs student must have daily physical education. Providing physical education in the least restrictive environment less often than daily is a violation of these statutes. Schools are required to comply with these regulations. The law does not make exceptions for students with any health impairments or with disabilities. No one has the right to make an arbitrary decision to exclude a special needs student from physical education for a class, a week, or a year. This includes parents, classroom teachers, educational aides, and physical education specialists. The spirit of the law suggests that everyone work together to make this a successful educational experience for everyone!

Children with learning disorders (LD), behavioral disorders (BD), and mental disabilities (MD) are often placed in physical education class with developmentally normal children of the same age.

Understanding the disability and the individual child's manifestation of the disability is the first step. Reading about the disability and talking to knowledgeable people about the individual situation will help; the classroom or resource teacher, school psychologist, and parents are good sources of information. With information about the disability and the individual, you can plan ahead to manage the disability and maximize learning. Transitions and waiting are often difficult for BD students, so a reminder to "be patient" or to "wait for the signal" may help. Contracts for behavior and learning are helpful for students with learning disabilities and behavior problems (figure 8.1). Consider each lesson and determine where a student may have trouble. Plan to provide information designed to prevent problems before they occur.

Concepts Into Practice

The fall festival is about to begin and the fourth graders are very excited. The excitement is almost too much for Sam, a special needs student. Sam is in a self-contained Behavior Disorder class, but he has been placed in a regular class for physical education. Sam and Ms. Anderson, the fourth-grade classroom teacher teaching this physical education class, are very proud that Sam has earned this opportunity. Ms. Anderson has planned to play Scooter Ball (see the lessons in chapter 7). After the warm-up activity, it will take a little time to set up the equipment. Ms. Anderson anticipates that the class will become more excited, and this may be too much for Sam. She asks Sam and one other student to be her helpers. Ms Anderson asks the class to sit quietly while she and the helpers set up the equipment. This plan has made Sam feel special and has kept Sam busy, under control, and close at hand for direct supervision. In addition, Sam feels like part of the group because Ms. Anderson selected two students to help, Sam and a student without a disability.

Setting behavior goals and recording daily performance are helpful tools when working with BD children. First, identify the target behaviors as well as those to eliminate and those to reinforce. Perhaps the student has difficulty when other students do not follow the teacher's directions and

Date_____

I, (student's name), will follow instructions the first time given. I will keep my hands to myself. I will treat the

equipment with respect.

(Signature)_____

I, Ms. Helpful, will allow (student's name) to select the class choice activity when he or she has successfully met this

contract for five physical education classes.

*Ms. Helpful*_____

3 × 5 in. index card daily record

☺ = Always # = Needs work	Monday	Tuesday	Wednesday	Thursday	Friday
Instructions					
Hands to self					
Equipment					

Figure 8.1   Behavior contract and daily record card.

From *Physical Education Methods for Elementary Teachers, Second Edition,* by Katherine T. Thomas, Amelia M. Lee, and Jerry R. Thomas, 2003, Champaign, IL: Human Kinetics.

when other students do not do what he wants them to do. The student becomes upset and tries physically to force the other students to do what he wants them to do. The behaviors to eliminate are using physical force and losing control. The behaviors to reinforce are using words instead of physical force and focusing on self rather than others during class. Occasionally, the student uses an alternative to physical force when he uses a loud and frustrated voice to let the teacher know what is happening. This disrupts instruction and alienates the other students. These disruptions comprise a third target behavior to address; the teacher needs to work to reduce their frequency and redirect the focus from "tattling" to employing a calm verbal description of what is interfering with his learning. The second step is to develop a plan; older children should participate in developing it. The plan might include the following five parts:

1. Positive reinforcement when the student uses words instead of physical force
2. A reminder to focus on himself and his learning rather than the behavior of others
3. The opportunity to remove himself from a situation that may be frustrating; generally, this is limited to two to three times per class and reduced as other positive behaviors become more frequent
4. A limit of one to three times that the student may talk to the teacher; these must be in a quiet calm voice (the teacher may remind the student of this), and the number should be reduced as other positive behaviors become more frequent
5. A rating at the end of each class that identifies the student's performance on each target behavior

Teacher planning is also a major factor in dealing with both MD (mentally disabled) and LD (learning disabled) students. Identifying the supports necessary for success in a lesson or activity before the lesson and providing those supports are critical to success. Often misbehaviors are a result of frustration and can be reduced or eliminated with planning. Supports for LD and MD students are similar to the supports necessary in the classroom. Classroom teachers can typically use the same techniques in the gymnasium that they use in the classroom. Physical education specialists should discuss these supports with the classroom teacher to gain insight into the child. Both classroom teachers and physical education specialists should be part of the IEP (individualized education program) committee and have access to the IEP as necessary.

> **S**o much has been given to me that I have no time to ponder over that which has been denied.
> —Helen Keller

Students with sensory (e.g., hearing or visual) impairments need assistance coping with the environment. Adapting the learning environment is one strategy to help students with sensory impairments; several examples of this approach follow:

- Locate the student in a position to see, hear, or read lips.
- Use assistive devices, such as sound or visual signals for targets to move, throw, or kick toward.
- Provide a peer guide to help the student as necessary with environmental conditions.

Perhaps the most valuable source of information is the student with the sensory disability. Asking the student how you can help, talking to the student about what will happen during class and what you will do to help, and asking permission to talk about her disability with the other students are important strategies that can facilitate inclusion and learning.

Physically challenged students need physical education and benefit from physical activity. Children who spend their day in a wheelchair, walker, or other assistive device need time to do weight-bearing activity to stimulate bone growth and increase circulation to the lower limbs. Many activi-

Concepts Into Practice

Mr. Moore is the physical education teacher. Ryan is a student in his first-grade class. Ryan has cerebral palsy and because he is nonambulatory, Ryan is in either a wheelchair or uses a walker most of the time. Mr. Moore is starting a tumbling unit. "Today we are going to use the mats and do tumbling. There are three special things I want to tell you before we begin. These three things are important, so listen and remember. First, a special rule is that only one person can be on the mat at a time. Ryan is going to be out of his chair today and working on the mat. Second, I want to remind you to move under control. This means that we will be careful and try to do each skill correctly when it is our turn. Third, we are going to cheer for each other, so everyone will do their best. Can someone tell me one of the three special things?" Mr. Moore has provided special rules for the whole class to promote safety and learning. He is including Ryan fully in the lesson and he is encouraging students to appreciate each other's performances.

ties (such as log rolls, the seal walk, using a scooter, and parachute activities) are appropriate, safe, and beneficial and do not need adaptation for nonambulatory children. Other activities need some modification. Children with physical disabilities should be included, which means doing the same activity as the class, with the class. Inclusion does not mean doing different activities or the same activities in a different location. One of the benefits of inclusion in physical education is the social interaction that results from practicing and performing together. For able-bodied students, participating in an inclusive class helps to achieve number 6 of the content standards—Demonstrates understanding and respect for differences among people in physical activity settings.

Teaching students with physical disabilities requires extra research, planning, and communication. First, the teacher must learn as much as possible about the condition, assistive devices (walkers, wheelchairs, braces, helmets), and student as possible. Once again, the classroom teacher, parent, and physical therapist are good sources of information. Physical education specialists may have to develop these relationships to gather appropriate information. Classroom teachers have the relationships and information and thus can view their instruction of physical education as an extension of what happens in the classroom. Further, physical education is another aspect of inclusion for the special needs student. Second, the teacher must plan, focusing on including all students and mastering objectives. Many children have both walkers and wheelchairs at school. If the lesson focus is moving in patterns, the walker is a better choice. For a catching lesson, the wheelchair may work best, and for tumbling, the child is not going to use any device and may need a helmet. You can see why planning ahead and communication are critical!

Sometimes students with disabilities are accompanied to physical education by the classroom teacher or an educational assistant or aide (EA). One challenge is to take advantage of the assistant without isolating the student. Generally, spending some time planning the activity and training the EA will increase inclusion. For example, the EA can supervise her student while she is working with other students but should not replace interaction with other students, so if the activity is playing catch, the EA should assist but not actually play. The parallel play of a disabled child and his EA is no more inclusive than having the disabled child in a one-on-one class. Some-

times new teachers or physical education specialists are reluctant to tell the EA what to do. This can lead to the EA standing idle or making decisions better made by the teacher. Although most states require training to be an EA, the training is not the same as that for a certified teacher. The job of the EA is to provide the support necessary for the student to be included as is appropriate. Physical education should not be break time for the EA, nor should a child with a disability be excluded from physical education because the EA is not available, willing, or able to assist. Working with the EA so she understands the importance of physical education and how to assist is critical to this process. Use the following guidelines as you work with the EA to maximize the benefits of physical education:

▶ The student should be a part of the class formation for activities (in the circle, part of the line, a team member).

▶ The student should participate with other students (not with the aide), such as when playing catch with another child.

▶ The activity is adapted to meet the needs of the student; the student is not eliminated because of the activity.

Developmentally appropriate practices denote that teachers should select activities that are age appropriate for a group of children and those that are appropriate for the range of individual children in the group.

▶ The teacher will provide cues or instructions before or during the lesson so the EA can do an effective job.

▶ The teacher will occasionally "trade places" with the EA so that the EA will supervise the class and the teacher will work one-on-one with the special needs student.

EXPERTISE

Perhaps the greatest challenge for a teacher is dealing with a wide range of abilities in students. However, students who have exceptional skill—**expertise** (often more skill than the teacher)—can prove to be a substantial challenge. The goal of teaching is to develop expertise in our students. How does that happen? As one considers an expert, whether it is the best player on a team or the best in the world, certain characteristics come to mind. Sportswriters and broadcasters often use terms such as "quickness," "natural athlete," "talented," and "fast reaction time" to describe superstars. Less often they use the terms "hard worker"

and "dedicated." The characteristics contributing to performance are physiological (e.g., physical size, body composition, speed, and training; Thomas 1994); psychological (e.g., motivation); perceptual (e.g., visual acuity; Starkes and Deakin 1984; Starkes, Deakin, Lindley, and Crisp 1987); cognitive (e.g., declarative and procedural knowledge; Starkes 1987); and experience (e.g., practice and game play; French, Nevett, Spurgeon, Graham, Rink, and McPherson 1996; French and Thomas 1987). A person has little control over many of the biological characteristics, some control over the psychological and perceptual characteristics, and considerable control over the cognitive and experience characteristics (Abernethy, Thomas, and Thomas 1993).

World class athletes are all motivated, well trained, and well coached. A comparison of males and females in the same sports at the world-record level provides a window of the contribution of biological factors. At this level, males and females differ about 10 percent in performance—this represents a true biological difference. As you can see in tables 8.1 and 8.2, the difference between males

Table 8.1　Sex Differences in World-Record Performance in Track (100 m, 400 m)

Record as of:	Women's 100 m record (seconds)	$m \cdot sec^{-1}$ (Women)	Men's 100 m record (seconds)	$m \cdot sec^{-1}$ (Men)	Percentage difference 100 m	Women's 400 m record (seconds)	$m \cdot sec^{-1}$ (Women)	Men's 400 m record (seconds)	$m \cdot sec^{-1}$ (Men)	Percentage difference 400 m
1923	12.80	7.81	10.40	9.62	19	60.50*	6.61	47.10*	8.49	28
1933	11.70	8.55	10.30	9.71	12	56.50*	7.08	46.10*	8.49	18
1943	11.60	8.62	10.20	9.80	12	56.50	7.08	46.00	8.70	19
1953	11.40	8.77	10.20	9.80	11	55.70	7.18	45.70	8.75	18
1963	11.20	8.93	10.00	10.00	11	51.90	7.71	44.60	8.97	14
1973	10.80	9.26	9.95	10.05	8	51.00	7.84	43.86	9.12	14
1983	10.79	9.27	9.93	10.07	8	47.99	8.34	43.71	9.15	8
1993	10.49	9.53	9.86	10.14	6	47.60	8.40	43.29	9.24	9

Key: $m \cdot sec^{-1}$ = speed in meters per second

*Times extrapolated based on conversion from yards to meters.

Percentage difference = $\dfrac{\text{Men's speed (m} \cdot \text{s}^{-1}) - \text{women's speed (m} \cdot \text{s}^{-1})}{\text{Men's speed (m} \cdot \text{s}^{-1})} \times 100$

Adapted, by permission, from L.B. Ransdell and C.L. Wells, 1999, "Sex differences in athletic performance," *Women in Sport and Physical Activity* 8: 55-81.

Table 8.2 Sex Differences in World-Record Performance in Swimming (100 m)

Record as of:	Women's 100 m records (seconds)	m · sec⁻¹	Men's 100 m record (seconds)	m · sec⁻¹	Percentage difference
1923	72.80	1.37	58.60	1.71	20
1933	66.00	1.52	57.40	1.74	13
1943	64.60	1.55	56.40	1.77	12
1953	64.60	1.55	55.40	1.81	14
1963	59.50	1.68	53.60	1.87	10
1973	57.54	1.74	51.22	1.95	11
1983	54.79	1.83	49.36	2.03	10
1993	54.48	1.84	48.42	2.07	11

Key: m · sec⁻¹ = speed in meters per second

$$\text{Percentage Difference} = \frac{\text{Men's speed (m · s}^{-1}) - \text{women's speed (m · s}^{-1})}{\text{Men's speed (m · s}^{-1})} \times 100$$

Adapted, by permission, from L.B. Ransdell and C.L. Wells, 1999, "Sex differences in athletic performance," *Women in Sport and Physical Activity* 8: 55-81.

and females holding world records in 1993 for track (100 and 400 meters) and swimming (100 and 1500 meters) are between 5 and 11 percent (Ransdell and Wells 1999). However, when we compare males and females in the general population, the differences are much larger, partly because of different opportunities (e.g., training and coaching) for males and females. Another factor is evident as we examine the world records themselves, specifically the improvement from 1923 to 1993. During that 70-year span, both males and females improved; however, it is clear that the females have improved more rapidly than the males and thus are "catching up." Why? The expectations and opportunities for women are considerably different now than they were in 1923. Many women now train for sport in the same way men train—sometimes with the same coaches, using the same facilities, and with the same rewards for winning. The improvement for women between 1923 and 1993 was caused largely by factors in the environment. You as a teacher will have an impact on those same factors—opportunity, expectation, and encouragement.

The differences within gender are also large; that is, some males are much better at a particular activity than other males, and some females are better than other females. Thus, depending on the sport, biological and inherited factors make a relatively small contribution. Therefore, two impor-

tant considerations should be discussed with parents and students when discussing "talent," "natural ability," and biological factors (Thomas 1994). First, no one can control or change these factors. Second, the biological factors do not explain very much of the differences in performance at any level. Teachers, parents, and coaches need to be aware of the contribution of biological factors. No one should assume that these factors will either guarantee or deny expertise in sport. Numerous examples exist of this fact; for example, Mugsy Bogues at five feet six inches tall had a successful career in the NBA, where players are considered too short at six feet tall. Mugsy reported being told to quit at five years of age because of his height. Can you imagine how that coach feels about his early assessment of Mugsy and the advice he gave him? As teachers, we would prefer to be remembered as the person who encouraged students and provided accurate information that allowed students to maximize their potential.

Many professional athletes report being discouraged during elementary school, middle school, or high school; however, they persisted and became successful. This is likely attributable to the **relative age effect,** which means that the oldest athletes in youth sport are identified as the best. Conversely, the youngest and least mature are identified as the poorest. This age effect disappears once everyone is mature. The relative age effect was discovered by examining the age of players on youth all-star teams, where the players with birth dates just after the cut-off date were most frequently on the all-star teams (Thomas and Thomas 1999). These athletes were almost a year older than the other players (French, Nevett, Spurgeon, Graham, Rink, and McPherson 1996). Similarly, players in the most skilled positions (e.g., in baseball, the infield) were the oldest on the team. On a team with seven- and eight-year-old children, the infielders were all eight, and the outfielders and bench-warmers were all seven years old. The relative age effect suggests two things: First, being more mature than other children and adolescents is an advantage in sport. Second, being older often means having had more experience or practice, which is also an advantage. Teachers and coaches should make sure that all children—young, older, mature, and immature—have equal opportunities to learn. Remember that the latest maturing children are likely to be ectomorphic, taller, and often the superior athletes. However, they will also be the least mature during elementary and middle school. Expert physical education teachers recognize this and provide equal practice and encouragement for all students (Thomas and Thomas 1999). Further, they do not allow more mature children to dominate practice and play.

Sports range from high to low strategy, depending on the amount of offense and defense. In low-strategy sports, such as running 100 meters or swimming 100 meters, biology and motor skill are more important. Characteristics such as speed, strength, and efficient movements are critical to success. Inheritance of biological factors such as speed, cardiovascular endurance, and susceptibility to training are important in some activities such as running the marathon or the 100-meter dash. In sports where offense and defense are important, such as football, soccer, and baseball, cognition is more important. The best players at the beginning of the first year of a sport are those who know what to do. At first, most children have trouble performing the skills. Knowing what to do often precedes being able to do the skill. For example, a new badminton player is at an advantage if he knows how to play tennis. The object of the game and the format are similar. So even though the skills are different, there is an early advantage to knowing. Declarative knowledge is a foundation for playing. Experts have both declarative knowledge and procedural knowledge. Procedural knowledge is the "how to" information that is often referred to as "if, then do." Experts have good motor skills, too. How do experts acquire knowledge and skill? Practice, practice, practice! Coaches and teachers can help students perform more like experts by teaching procedures and skill together and providing lots of practice.

Experts recount hours of practice. Research identifies 10,000 hours of practice as the start of expertise (Ericsson, Krampe, and Tesch-Römer 1993; Starkes, Deakin, Allard, Hodges, and Hayes 1996). Help students understand the importance of practice and help them to be patient and allow skill to develop. Spend time on learning skills and developing knowledge. Youth sport and physical education often produce little time for practice (e.g., 10 to 13 trials during a day's practice; Thomas 1994). Experts report 200 to 300 trials per day (Thomas 1994). Good management and planning allow more time for practice. However, if children are to become experts, they must practice outside of class as well as in school.

How does one become an expert? Learning the declarative and procedural knowledge and being able to execute the skills—both of which are accomplished with lots of practice—are how expertise develops in high-strategy sport. Teachers can help children develop expertise by explaining the role of practice, understanding the influence of maturation and biology, and providing experiences that lead to skill and knowledge.

GENDER DIFFERENCES

In many of the preceding chapters, we have compared males to females on a variety of characteristics, with the conclusion that males and females are more alike than different. Teachers should expect prepubescent boys and girls to be very much alike. In fact, differences within a gender will be as large as differences between the genders on most tasks (Thomas and French 1985). Differences before puberty are largely attributable to different treatment of boys and girls. The expectations for boys are greater in sport and physical activity; opportunity may be different, and encouragement can also favor boys. Clearly, teachers and other significant adults have the opportunity and responsibility to treat boys and girls equally. This applies to all aspects of development, including the psychomotor domain. No teacher would say, "We know that girls are better in the verbal area; therefore, boys will no longer be expected to learn to write." Likewise, no teacher should say, "Physical activity is too difficult for some girls; therefore, girls do not have to participate in physical education." What we think, say, and do must be consistent—teachers must have realistic and equal expectations for all students. The biological contribution to gender differences increases at puberty and will ultimately explain a difference of less than 10 percent (Ransdell and Wells 1999). When we observe large differences between boys and girls, we must consider the factors that may explain those differences—opportunity, expectations, and encouragement. As you will see in chapter 12, not only is this the right path of action and thought, but also it is required by federal statute.

The purpose of the discussion of gender—in this chapter on individual differences—is to encourage you to consider the individual differences of each child. The point is to avoid having an expectation *because* of gender. This, of course, holds true for other factors as well—consider ethnicity, race, and culture. You need to identify students as having certain individual needs, interests, and abilities rather than as being of a specific gender or ethnicity or having a particular disability.

SUMMARY

Individual differences are a normal part of development. Good teachers approach planning and instruction knowing that children will be different from one another. Students enter each activity with different experiences and abilities, which means their readiness for activities also varies. Virtually all content—that is, all types of skills and

Girls have been encouraged to participate in physical activity at a very young age along with boys in recent years.

activities—can be adapted to challenge the most skilled students and to allow the least skilled students to learn and succeed. Practice and experience are the most important factors in developing expertise, which means that most experts are made, not born.

MASTERY LEARNING ACTIVITIES

1. Select a skill from chapter 3. Develop a readiness checklist for that skill. The checklist should include three or more criteria, in separate statements, that are prerequisites for the skill you selected.

2. Write a one-page article for the school newsletter (directed at parents) explaining why competition is not emphasized in your physical education program.

3. Select a disability. Write a one-page summary of the disability; this should include specific adaptations, safety measures, or benefits related to physical activity.

Teachers have an obligation to treat boys and girls equally in all aspects of development.

© Human Kinetics.

4. Identify two athletes in the same sport who are similarly successful. One should be the "ideal" in terms of size and other physical characteristics; the other should be atypical. Using two columns (newspaper format), one for each athlete, write an analysis of why each is successful and how each is either stereotypical or atypical.

5. Review the lessons presented in chapters 2 through 7 and describe how you would adapt the lesson to include a child with one of the following disabilities: hearing loss, visual impairment, nonambulation (using a wheelchair).

REFERENCES

Abernethy, B., K.T. Thomas, and J.R. Thomas. 1993. Strategies for improving understanding of motor expertise (or mistakes we have made and things we have learned!). In *Cognitive issues in motor expertise,* edited by J.L. Starkes and F. Allard, 317–356. North-Holland, Amsterdam: Elsevier Science.

Côté, J., J. Baker, and B. Abernethy. Forthcoming. From play to practice: A developmental framework for the acquisition of expertise in team sport. In *The development of elite athletes: Recent advances in research on sport expertise,* edited by J. Starkes and K.A. Ericsson. Champaign, Ill.: Human Kinetics.

Ericsson, K.A., R.T. Krampe, and C. Tesch-Römer. 1993. The role of deliberate practice in the acquisition of expert performance. *Psychological Review* 100 (3):363–406.

French, K.E., M.E. Nevett, J.H. Spurgeon, K.C. Graham, J.E. Rink, and S.L. McPherson. 1996. Knowledge representation and problem solution in expert and novice youth baseball players. *Research Quarterly for Exercise and Sport* 67:386–95.

French, K.E., and J.R. Thomas. 1987. The relation of knowledge development to children's basketball performance. *Journal of Sport Psychology* 9:15–32.

Gould, D., E. Udry, S. Tuffey, and J. Loehr. 1996. Burnout in competitive junior tennis players: A quantitative psychological assessment. *The Sport Psychologist* 10:322–40.

Passer, M.W., and B.J. Wilson. 2002. At what age are children ready to compete? In *Children and Youth in Sport: A Biopsychosocial Perspective,* edited by F.L. Smoll and R.E. Smith, 83-103. Dubuque, IA: Kendall/Hunt.

Ransdell, L.B., and C.L. Wells. 1999. Sex differences in athletic performance. *Women in Sport and Physical Activity* 8: 55–81.

Sherrill, C. 1998. *Adapted physical activity, recreation and sport: Crossdisciplinary and lifespan.* 5th ed. Boston: WBC McGraw-Hill.

Starkes, J.L. 1987. Skill in field hockey: The nature of the cognitive advantage. *Journal of Sport Psychology* 9:146–60.

Starkes, J.L., and J. Deakin. 1984. Perception in sport: A cognitive approach to skilled performance. In *Cognitive sport psychology,* edited by W.F. Straub and J.M. Williams, 115–28. Lansing, N.Y.: Sport Science Associates.

Starkes, J.L., J.M. Deakin, F. Allard, N.J. Hodges, and A. Hayes. 1996. Deliberate practice in sports: What is it anyway? In *The road to excellence: The acquisition of expert performance in the arts, sciences, sports and games,* edited by K.A. Ericsson, 81–106. Mahwah, N.J.: Erlbaum.

Starkes, J.L., J.M. Deakin., S. Lindley, and F. Crisp. 1987. Motor versus verbal recall of ballet sequences by young expert dancers. *Journal of Sport Psychology* 9: 222–30.

Thomas, K.T. 1994. The development of expertise: From Leeds to legend. *Quest* 46: 199–210.

Thomas, J.R., and K.E. French. 1985. Gender differences across age in motor performance: A meta-analysis. *Psychological Bulletin* 98: 260–282.

Thomas, K.T., and J.R. Thomas. 1999. What squirrels in the trees predict about expert athletes. *International Journal of Sport Psychology* 30: 221–34.

Winnick, J.P. 1995. *Adapted physical education and sport.* 2d ed. Champaign, Ill.: Human Kinetics.

RESOURCES

Côté, J., and J. Hay. 2002. Children's involvement in sport: A developmental perspective. In *Psychological foundations of sport,* edited by J.M. Silva and D. Stevens, 484–502. Boston: Allyn & Bacon.

LESSON PLANS

The first lesson plan is partner stunts for grades K and 1. The lesson would work well for students with sensory impairments with little or no adaptation. The partner can provide cues and physical guidance for each activity. The second lesson is dribbling and bouncing in patterns for grades 2 and 3. For a child with a physical disability in a walker or wheelchair, the lesson would be adapted to use taped circles on the floor rather than hoops. The wheelchair or walker would move over the tape but not the hoops. A smaller ball may help the child keep the ball under control and closer to the walker or wheelchair. A student could assist with retrieving a ball that bounces away from the chair or walker. The cones may be placed farther apart for students dribbling while in walkers or wheelchairs. If necessary, make the group smaller (three versus five children in a group) for the group with the disabled student. The third lesson is a softball lesson for grades 4 and 5. The lesson begins with a review of catching. The game is flexible to allow success for all skill levels. The most skilled players would move farthest away to catch the ball, or they could be challenged by having to run up from a distance of 10 to 20 feet from the left, the right, or behind the catching line before catching the ball. Virtually any lesson plan can be individualized for students with special needs or exceptional skill.

Partner Stunts

Student Objectives

- Learn two partner stunts.
- Cooperate with a partner.

Equipment and Materials

- 1 mat (4 ft × 8 ft) per group
- Background music (optional)

Safety Tip

- For back-to-back get-up, limit practice to the mats.

Warm-Up Activities (5 to 10 minutes)

Warm-Up Routine

Arrange the children in a large circle facing the center.

1. Teach all parts of the warm-up as a routine.
2. Have the children perform the following sequence of steps:

   Slide right (16 counts),
   Slide left (16 counts),
   Run clockwise (32 counts),
   Run counterclockwise (32 counts),
   Stretch upward (8 counts),
   Stretch forward (8 counts),
   Stretch right (8 counts),
   Stretch left (8 counts),
   Stretch downward (8 counts),
   Two waist circles (4 counts),
   Two straddle stretches (4 counts),
   Two back arches (8 counts), and
   Sit-ups and push-ups.

Skill-Development Activities (20 minutes)

Partner Walk

Designate one partner as the leader in each pair.

1. Describe and demonstrate the stunt:

   The leader stands with feet shoulder-width apart, facing his partner. The follower (the other partner) stands close to the leader with her toes on top of the leader's feet. The partners place their arms on each other's shoulders.

   The leader begins to walk (forward, sideways, or backward). The object is to keep your feet joined at all times.

2. Have the children practice the partner walk. Verbal cues are helpful.

3. Variation: Have everyone change partners on signal (music stopping, a whistle, or a hand signal). Continue, then change again.

Leapfrog

Keep the pairs in scatter formation.

1. Describe and demonstrate the stunt:

   One partner squats, with hands placed firmly on the floor, arms between the legs, head tucked against the chest.

   The other partner places both hands on the shoulders of her partner from behind, and jumps (with legs spread apart) over the squatting child.

   The jumping partner immediately gets into a squatting position, and the squatting partner becomes the leaping partner. Keep trading off.

2. Have the children practice leapfrog.

3. Once the children have mastered leapfrog with their partners, join two pairs of partners so that the leaping partner jumps three children successively, then squats, and the last child in line becomes the leaper, and so on.

4. Variations: Have the children leapfrog with the entire class in a long line! The first leaping child leaps the entire line, the second child in line begins when the first leapfrog has leapt five or more children. The game continues until everyone has had a turn leaping the line.

Wring the Dishrag

Keep pairs in scatter formation.

1. Describe and demonstrate the stunt:

   Begin facing each other with hands joined. Lift both arms on one side (one partner's right arm, the other's left arm).

   Rotate (turn) your bodies, turning in the direction of the lifted arms but keeping your hands joined.

   Keep turning so your backs are to each other, then return to the starting position.

2. Have the children practice Wring the Dishrag.

3. Variations: This stunt looks quite nice when the class (or half the class) stands in two lines with partners facing each other. The first pair in line begins to wring the dishrag; when they have lifted their lead arms, the next pair begins, and so on. You can also arrange students in a circle (one partner facing in, the other facing out) so that when the last pair finishes, the first pair begins again.

Back-to-Back Get-Up

Arrange small groups of children in pairs at the mats.

1. Describe and have two children demonstrate the stunt:

   Stand on the mat with your partner, with your backs together and arms hooked at the elbows. Place your feet at about shoulder-width apart.

   Sit down together slowly. Press your backs against each other in order to prevent bumping your heads or backs.

   You should end up sitting with your legs tucked up to your body and your feet flat on the floor, arms still locked at the elbow, and backs pressed together.

   Now push with your feet and slowly straighten your legs to stand up again.

2. Have the children practice Back-to-Back Get-Up.

Concluding Activities (5 to 10 minutes)

Simon Says

Arrange pairs of children in scatter formation.

1. Describe the game:

   Each pair, working together, does what Simon says and tries not to do the task if Simon doesn't "say" to.

   For example, suppose Simon says, "Simon says partner walk forward four steps, Simon says wring the dishrag, Simon says hop three steps backward with your partner, do leapfrog with your partner." Partners would not do leapfrog, because "do leapfrog" did not start with "Simon says."

   If you make a mistake, carefully move to the front of the play area and continue playing.

   Help your partner be a good listener!

2. Have the children play Simon Says.

From *Physical Education Methods for Elementary Teachers, Second Edition,* by Katherine T. Thomas, Amelia M. Lee, and Jerry R. Thomas, 2003, Champaign, IL: Human Kinetics. Adapted from *Physical Education for Children: Daily Lesson Plans for Elementary School, Second Edition,* by Katherine T. Thomas, Amelia M. Lee, and Jerry R. Thomas, 2000, Champaign, IL: Human Kinetics.

LESSON  *Dribbling and Bouncing in Patterns*

Student Objectives

- Dribble in a pattern.
- Demonstrate catching, dribbling, and throwing in a series.

Equipment and Materials

- 1 playground ball
- 1 hoop (30–36 in.) per child
- 15 cones or filled 2-liter plastic bottles

Warm-Up Activities (5 minutes)

Use Delivery Relay from lesson 4.2, page 79.

Skill-Development Activities (20 minutes)

Dribbling in Hoops

Arrange the children in scatter formation, each child with a hoop and ball. Have them place their hoops on the ground.

1. Tell the children: *Keep your ball close to your body; look where you are going and not at the ball.*
2. Challenge the children with these tasks:

    Bounce your ball in your hoop while standing outside your hoop. Repeat several times.

    Dribble your ball inside your hoop and walk around the outside of your hoop.

    Now change directions! Repeat several times.

Movement Tasks

Arrange small groups of three to five, still with their hoops and balls. Have each group lay their hoops on the ground in a row.

1. Have the children dribble the balls as they walk around and through the hoops.
2. Repeat.

Set up three lines of five cones, with about five ft between cones (or use hoops spaced five ft apart). Divide the children into three groups, and assign each group to a line of cones.

3. Have the children dribble a zigzag pattern around the cones.

4. Repeat.

Rearrange the hoops in a row (to dribble inside), followed by the cones spread in a row (to zigzag around). Make three sets of each.

5. Have the children dribble inside the hoops, then dribble a zigzag pattern around the cones.

6. Repeat several times.

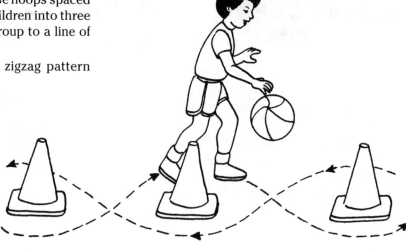

Concluding Activities (5 minutes)

Dribble-and-Throw Relay

Arrange the children into short relay lines along one end of the play area, each group with a cone about 15 ft away.

1. Have the first child in each line dribble around the cone, then throw the ball back to the next child in line, continuing through all the children.

2. After throwing the ball, each child returns to the end of their team's line.

3. Play continuously in the available time. If you wish, determine which team has gone "through the line" the most times.

From *Physical Education Methods for Elementary Teachers, Second Edition,* by Katherine T. Thomas, Amelia M. Lee, and Jerry R. Thomas, 2003, Champaign, IL: Human Kinetics. Adapted from *Physical Education for Children: Daily Lesson Plans for Elementary School, Second Edition,* by Katherine T. Thomas, Amelia M. Lee, and Jerry R. Thomas, 2000, Champaign, IL: Human Kinetics.

LESSON  8.3

Softball

Student Objectives

- Catch below the waist a ball thrown by a partner from a distance of at least 15 ft.
- Cooperate with a group to accomplish a task.

Equipment and Materials

- 1 softball per pair
- Chalk, flour, or tape to mark lines
- Signal

Warm-Up Activities (5 minutes)

Circle Conditioning

Have the students stand in circle formation. With one student as the leader, have the children perform the following calisthenics. Encourage each child to try to increase the number each day.

Bent-Knee Sit-Ups

Lying on the floor with arms folded across your chest and your hands on your shoulders, bend your knees 90 degrees and raise your body until your arms touch your knees. Perform as many as possible in 60 seconds.

Push-Ups

On hands and toes (regular push-ups) or hands and knees (modified push-ups), bend your arms and lower your trunk to touch your chin to the ground. Then raise your body back up to the starting position, performing as many as possible in 60 seconds.

Straddle Sit Stretch

Sitting with legs in a straddle position, bend at your waist, extending your arms to your right foot, touch your head to your right knee, and hold for 10 to 30 seconds. Reach up as you move to repeat to the left, performing at least three times to each side.

Lateral Jump

With feet together, jump side to side over a line as many times as possible in 30 seconds, rest 15 seconds, and repeat.

Skill-Development Activities (20 minutes)

Catching Balls Below the Waist

Arrange pairs in scatter formation, each pair with a softball, about 15 ft apart.

1. Describe and demonstrate the skill:

   Get into a ready position and move in front of the incoming ball. Your little (pinky) fingers should be coming together and your palms facing upward.

   As the ball makes contact with your hand (or glove), cover it with your other hand.

   Stand with your weight forward on the foot opposite your throwing arm when making the catch so it will be possible for you to throw quickly.

2. Have the children practice throwing and catching above and below the waist with the following variations:

   Throw so that your partner can catch above (below) the waist. Keep your little fingers together for a ball below the waist.

   Throw so that your partner must move forward (backward, to the left, to the right) to catch.

3. Gradually increase the distance between partners.

Concluding Activities (5 minutes)

Throw and Catch Game

Arrange teams of four or five along two lines, 20 ft apart. On each team, player 1 stands on one line facing the rest of his team, and the remaining players line up behind the other line, across from player 1 (see figure below). Give each team a softball. Allow the catcher to vary the distance between the thrower and catcher for each throw so that students at different skill levels can be successful.

1. Describe and demonstrate the game:

   The goal of the game is for each team to work together to make sure all students are successful.

   On the signal, player 1 selects a distance and throws the ball to player 2. Player 2 throws it back and goes to the end of the line.

   Player 1 throws to each player until all are back in their original positions. Then player 1 goes to the end of the line, and player 2 becomes the new thrower.

   Rotate through all your players.

   Score one point for each successful catch.

   The team with the most successful catches wins.

2. Have the children play the Throw and Catch Game, reminding them to help everyone succeed.

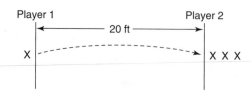

From *Physical Education Methods for Elementary Teachers, Second Edition,* by Katherine T. Thomas, Amelia M. Lee, and Jerry R. Thomas, 2003, Champaign, IL: Human Kinetics. Adapted from *Physical Education for Children: Daily Lesson Plans for Elementary School, Second Edition,* by Katherine T. Thomas, Amelia M. Lee, and Jerry R. Thomas, 2000, Champaign, IL: Human Kinetics.

Preparing to Teach Physical Education

The previous section helped you to understand *whom* you will teach and how they learn. Now you will prepare to teach. One of the first questions expert teachers ask before teaching in a new setting is, "Can I see the room?" They want to know what it looks like, what resources are available, how long they have, and other practical information that affects teaching. Experts then leverage those resources in personal ways to create a learning process that is clearly their own. Therefore, this section will begin, in chapter 9, with planning—long- and short-term (e.g., annual, unit, and lesson plans)—which will help you decide what to teach. The next question is, "How will I teach?" Factors such as group size and how information will be delivered will be covered in chapter 10. Expert teachers are good at preventing problems because problems interfere with learning—thus, expert teachers are expert classroom managers. Chapter 11 covers management, including class rules, formations, transitions, equipment handling, and getting students' attention. You may already feel the weight of responsibility that goes with being a teacher. Chapter 12 explores the responsibilities, rights, and best practices associated with becoming a professional teacher. The final chapter in this section, chapter 13, covers the "where" and "what" of physical education—playgrounds, gymnasiums, equipment, and so forth.

chapter 9

Planning Your Curriculum

Hubert, age 9

The goal of physical education is for students to become physically educated. Planning allows teachers to reach that goal and others with developmentally appropriate programs. Planning includes curricular philosophy, long- and short-term objectives, activities, and evaluation.

Learner Outcomes

The teacher will do the following:

- Explain the relationship among teacher values, learner objectives, instruction, and evaluation.
- Describe curriculum models.
- Create developmentally appropriate student outcomes.
- Define warm-up, progression, and closure activity.

Glossary Terms

proficiency barrier
progression
sequence
scope
static balance
dynamic balance
personal space

general space
speed
force
flow
objectives
warm-up
closure

Developmentally appropriate physical education is based on three principles:

1. Motor skill development is sequential and age related.
2. Motor skill development is similar for all children.
3. The rate of motor development varies.

CURRICULUM MODELS

Teachers in American schools usually have complete freedom to develop their own physical education curriculum; this includes choosing a curriculum emphasis, setting objectives and goals, selecting and sequencing content, and deciding how to assess student learning and the program.

Your curricular choices are a reflection of your values and beliefs about what students should learn and how they should spend their time in physical education classes. A teacher who is concerned about obesity and sedentary lifestyle patterns in today's children and who also believes that the primary purpose of school physical education is the development and maintenance of physical fitness will most likely emphasize a fitness education model. On the other hand, a teacher believing strongly that students should develop sport skills and understand rules and strategies of various sport activities would emphasize sports education. Regardless of the curriculum model you select, it is important to remember that with careful planning, the important outcomes of physical education can be achieved— that is, students will be physically educated. One way to achieve this is by providing developmentally appropriate lessons and instruction (see the side box on page 206 for a review of what is developmentally appropriate). A teacher is likely to have strong beliefs about the value of educational experiences and content from several different models. The result is a curriculum that reflects these preferences and is a blend of aspects from the curriculum models that match your values and objectives. A curriculum model provides you with a framework within which to design a curriculum that reflects your personal philosophy about what children should learn, but strict adherence to one emphasis is unusual and unnecessary. As discussed in chapter 2, teachers are more likely to use a blend of several curriculum theories because each teacher selects what is best for the students, what the teacher is comfortable with, and those aspects of a curriculum theory that are most important. Every teaching situation is unique, and it is impossible for a single curriculum to fit every school and every teacher. Thus, teachers must adapt or create programs for their own situations. We will examine several curricular models that will allow you to make good choices. We want to emphasize that as you develop your physical education curriculum, your primary goal should be to design developmentally appropriate experiences that will help all students become physically educated. Six elementary models are contrasted here: traditional, movement approach, fitness education, sport education, adventure and wilderness education, and developmental.

One goal of curriculum development for physical education teachers is to make physical education an integral part of the mission of the school. For classroom teachers who teach physical education, meeting the entire mission of the school—including physical education—is a goal of the curriculum. Integration of physical education into the mission of the school is important and can be accomplished by recognizing the important and unique contributions physical education makes to child development.

Teachers need to understand curriculum design for several reasons:

- ► So their programs will be based on developmentally appropriate principles
- ► So their students will understand and adopt physically active lifestyles
- ► So their programs accomplish their goals and objectives.

Traditional

Traditional activities such as games, rhythmic activities, stunts and tumbling, and sports and fitness are the basis of the multiactivity program. Meaningful participation is a key objective for this model. The multiactivity model is by far the most widely used; it is implemented by allocating a percentage of time for each activity category at each grade level. The percentages typically reflect a belief that children in lower grades should participate informally in a variety of sport and rhythmic activities, including many low-organization games. This focus on informal play progresses to specialization and competition in traditional sports in the upper grades. A primary goal is to provide opportunities for students to experience a wide variety of different activities, including team sports, individual sports, recreational games, novelty activities, adventure and outdoor pursuits, fitness, and perhaps even aquatics. Typically, the activities are organized into broad categories. Because of the scope and range of the curriculum, each activity is offered for a very short period of time (table 9.1).

Movement Approach

This thematic approach has had a tremendous influence on elementary physical education over the last 35 years. It is based on concepts derived from analysis of movement as classified into the motion factors of space, weight, time, and flow. This analysis forms the framework for selection and sequence of content. Units and lessons are structured around such themes as spatial awareness and relationships. Advocates of this kind of curriculum would generally not teach regulation volleyball or basketball but rather would organize games around themes designed to develop skills basic to many sports. For example, a movement theme for educational games could be basic body and manipulative control. Likewise, formal units of traditional gymnastics and rhythmic activities would probably not appear in a movement education program. The experiences in these areas would instead focus on the study of movement and on helping children individually discover their bodies' potential in developing rhythmic activity and gymnastics skill.

Table 9.1   Multiactivity (Traditional) Model: Percent of Time Spent in Different Activities by Grade Level

Grade level	K-1	2-3	4-5	6-8
Basic locomotor and manipulative skills	30	20	5	
Games of low organization	10	20	5	
Rhythmic activities	20	20	20	
Stunts and tumbling	20	20	20	10
Fitness	20	20	20	20
Team sports			10	10
Individual sports			5	10
Recreational games			5	10
Dance			5	10
Novelty activities			5	10
Adventure and outdoor pursuits				10
Aquatics				10

Fitness Education

A physical education curriculum emphasizing fitness focuses on facilitating many opportunities for exercise with the primary goal of developing and maintaining a level of fitness. Students will spend most of their physical education time training or working out and will learn many ways to do so. The programs are typically designed for children to gain health-related fitness benefits with the long-term goal of developing a commitment to lifelong participation in physical activity. A fitness curriculum integrates physical fitness testing and is usually organized around the four components of health-related fitness: cardiovascular endurance, muscular strength and endurance, flexibility, and body composition. Many teachers also incorporate instruction in the principles for improving and maintaining physical fitness: frequency, intensity, duration, and specificity.

Sport Education

According to Siedentop and Tannehill (2000), the purpose of sport education is to educate students in sport and to teach them to be players by allowing opportunities to practice and compete as a team. This model moves away from the typical unit approach and instead teaches sport according to the season that each sport is played. Competition between teams continues throughout the season, utilizing tournament or round robin play during the period of time. Players become a part of the team; they practice and work together to find the best assignment of personnel for team positions. Students serve as players, referees, and coaches. Competition is inherent in this model, and record keeping becomes an important aspect of the program. Students are encouraged to take an active part in all aspects of the sport experience in order to increase their sense of responsibility and appreciation for fair play.

Adventure and Wilderness Education

Activities such as rock climbing, rappeling, canoeing, backpacking, and orienteering are a part of the adventure and wilderness curriculum. The activities have an element of risk to them, which enable students to gain confidence as well as participate in problem-solving activities in a natural setting. Some programs include a ropes course, where students learn to rely on others to solve problems presented in an outdoor environment. Extended camping trips during which students are required to plan meals, entertainment, and hiking and water routes present a variety of opportunities for them to work as a part of a group and problem solve. Alternative scheduling, risk management, and utilizing community resources become important aspects of this curricular model. National and international competition in extreme sports and an increased interest in outdoor education have popularized this model among students and teachers.

Developmental

A curriculum based on developmental constructs derives its structure from research on how motor skills develop in children, as explained in chapters 3, 4, 5, 6, and 7. A learning hierarchy is designed around task complexity that develops prerequisite skills for each task and requires mastery. Recall that the stages of control in the execution of motor skills follow a rather predictable sequence; however, the rate at which motor skills are acquired varies within and across children. The program must provide opportunities for students to progress individually. Developmental physical education provides activities to enhance the rate and quality of individual development. The curriculum in the lower grades will focus on fundamental skills such as locomotion, nonlocomotion, receiving and projecting objects, and stability. These skills are combined and refined through a variety of lead-up games, gymnastics, and rhythmic activities. Eventually, more specialized skills required for traditional sports and activities are presented. Teachers who follow a developmental philosophy try to select and organize movement activities according to needs, interests, and skill capabilities of children at different ages. The developmental status of children is the basis for planning, with special attention given to the **proficiency barrier** described in chapter 4. Children who have not mastered fundamental motor patterns cannot modify these patterns to form specialized skills, because they must still focus on technique in individual movements and consequently cannot integrate them to form specific sport skills. Sport skill development begins at about third grade as fundamental patterns are combined, with both skill and accuracy stressed. At about fifth grade, emphasis shifts to developing skill in complex sport, rhythmic, and gymnastics activities. Throughout the middle-school grades (sixth to eighth), specific skills should be refined for participation in competitive and creative activities. This model is consistent with the hierarchy of the psychomotor domain presented in chapter 1.

SELECTING DESIRED OUTCOMES

Once you choose your curriculum emphasis, you can set your goals and objectives. The National Standards for Physical Education (NASPE 1995) introduced in chapter 1 are the standards for elementary students. Students who are physically educated achieve several outcomes:

1. They demonstrate competency in many movement forms and proficiency in a few movement forms.
2. They apply movement concepts and principles to the learning and development of motor skills.
3. They exhibit physically active lifestyles.
4. They achieve and maintain a health-enhancing level of physical fitness.
5. They demonstrate responsible personal and social behavior in physical activity settings.
6. They demonstrate understanding and respect for differences among people in physical activity settings.
7. They understand that physical activity provides opportunities for enjoyment, challenge, self-expression, and social interaction.

These are the desired outcomes for the developmental curriculum that we propose.

A Focus on Integration

A developmental curriculum can best achieve the NASPE standards for elementary students by using an integrated approach to planning and teaching. This approach combines skill development with an emphasis on the value of physical activity as a health benefit. For example, students work on movement skills in such a way as to stay highly physically active. Then, in teachable moments, the instructor briefly points out health-related fitness concepts. The curriculum is further designed to teach cooperation, social skills, and personal responsibility by blending these important outcomes in the overall plan. Educators have long stressed the importance of students being able to make the social adjustments necessary for success in individual and group-play environments. They need to understand concepts of cooperation, rules, fair play, and honesty in motor skill settings. Experiences in physical education should allow children to learn, solve problems, and make significant decisions about their own learning. You can see that the objectives reach all three domains—affective, cognitive, and psychomotor—and that all three domains are addressed in the NASPE standards. Finally, physical activity is integrated with other subject areas across the curriculum with the goal of helping students develop confidence and grow into responsible, self-directed, physically educated people. An instructor must plan for teachable moments to maximize effectiveness and accomplish these program outcomes. In this chapter, sample lesson plans will illustrate how this can be done.

Practical Considerations for Curriculum Planning

The physical education content you select will depend on many factors:

▶ Your school and physical education objectives and goals
▶ School and community environment and cultural influences
▶ Size of your class
▶ Student abilities
▶ Equipment and facilities
▶ Scheduling of classes
▶ Your own likes, dislikes, strengths, and weaknesses

A Teachable Moment

Ms. King's class has been playing Nose Tag on the playground for five minutes; their movement is slowing, and many children are moving to the fringe of the area. Earlier in the game, all the children were playing vigorously and staying in the center of the play area, where the action was greatest. One of the students runs to her and says, "I am really hot; can I have a drink?" Ms. King stops the activity and explains, "When we exercise our bodies produce heat. Today, the temperature is also warm, making it more difficult for our bodies to get rid of the heat from exercise. One way we cool ourselves is by sweating. The air passes over the sweat, the sweat evaporates, and our skin cools down. It is important to drink water when you sweat. If you do not drink enough water, you can become dehydrated and your body will get too hot. This is bad for your health. We will continue to play, but one student at a time may get water by using the water pass. Remember to wait for the pass and to get your drink and return promptly so others can have a turn." Ms. King has addressed the immediate health needs of her students—remaining hydrated—and she has used this opportunity to teach about heat, activity, and dehydration.

No two teaching situations are the same. You must tailor the specific content you choose to your situation in order to maximize learning for all students, based on those factors. Thus, in addition to forming your grade-level physical education objectives, answer the following questions before selecting specific units and activities:

▶ Can you manage the unit or activity, given the number of students you have?
▶ Does the unit or activity meet the needs of all your students?
▶ Is the unit appropriate for your students' developmental level (readiness)?
▶ Does your choice of unit or activity respect the cultural needs and interests of your students?
▶ Does the unit or activity have the potential to stretch your students' cultural awareness?
▶ Do you have access to a gym, all-purpose room, outdoor space, or community facility appropriate for conducting the unit or activity?

► Do you have or can you borrow or make the equipment you need to conduct the unit or activity so that all students are actively involved in learning all the time?

► How much time are you able to set aside for each lesson? Is it enough to accomplish each lesson's objective? Is block time a possibility?

► How many class periods per week are you able to mandate for physical education? Is the total time enough to accomplish your objective?

► Given your facilities, training, equipment, and individual students, can you conduct the unit or activity safely?

► Is the content meaningful, challenging, and motivating to all your students? Is the overall value of the activity equal to the cost?

► Based on the overall physical education schedule, is this activity compatible with other units and lessons being taught?

A perfect world would contain unlimited equipment, facilities, and instructional time to accomplish the goals of physical education. Unfortunately, in the real world there are issues that you must consider as you plan. Several formats are used for scheduling physical education that bring these practical issues to life:

► The school offers 25- to 30-minute back-to-back classes with a physical educator.

► Physical education is taught by classroom teachers during the last 30 minutes of the day.

► Physical education is taught by classroom teachers in rotation with art and music at each grade level.

► The school offers 25 to 30 minutes of physical education, two days per week, by a physical educator, and three days per week with the classroom teacher at the end of those three days.

When one person is teaching physical education, and classes are back to back, there is no time for extensive equipment set-up; so regardless of the grade level, activities requiring similar set-ups must be taught throughout the day. Accommodations for age and skill differences must be made, but as much of the same equipment as possible must be used in all classes. If several different teachers are teaching physical education, the use of facilities and equipment can be coordinated among those teachers. When more than one

teacher is teaching the same students, the curriculum must also be coordinated among the teachers. Where both classroom and physical education teachers are teaching the same students, the physical education teacher may be willing to create a master curriculum so that classroom teachers will know what to teach. In schools where many teachers are teaching their classes at the same time, considerable planning and coordination of facilities and equipment are necessary. Clearly, the best circumstance for children is to have physical education as often as possible—ideally five days per week for at least 30 minutes per class. This may not happen, however, and when it does, curriculum may be influenced by practical issues related to facilities and equipment. Even when there is time between classes, curriculum planning should consider equipment and facilities issues. For example, weather can influence outside activity choices; alternating gymnastics and volleyball is impractical because the equipment differs radically.

Teachers must devote time prior to physical education class to making sure that equipment is in the proper place and safe for student activity.

Developing Appropriate Content for Physical Education

Curriculum planning should consider several factors:

- Progression
- Sequence
- Scope

In a model developmental curriculum, you need to ensure that your students progress from inefficient and ineffective skill performance to an efficient and effective level. **Progression** means improvement, or mastery of increasingly difficult tasks. Generally, progression refers to steady increases in the qualitative (efficiency) and quantitative (effectiveness) aspects of the skills, and the task demands are increased. One way to observe progression is to see a task presented in a more challenging way each day of a unit. You can accomplish this goal by planning appropriate practice, regulating the difficulty of activities, and assessing children's progress along the way to assure they are learning what you want them to learn. It is important to determine exactly how much time and in what order you will teach the physical education content in order to reach your objectives. **Sequence** involves the order in which you will teach the progression of curriculum from year to year, reflecting the timing and depth of the program. Then you must define your program's **scope**, the content of the program in terms of its breadth or range throughout the academic year. Children will not develop efficient patterns in one year. Rather, the fundamental skills are emphasized over several years as teachers guide students toward skilled performance. Children are assessed to determine their status and progress and to give teachers information about when students are ready for greater challenge. The National Standards are the ultimate goal—"being physically educated" (NASPE 1995); however, NASPE provides sample benchmarks for each of the standards across the grade levels as biannual objectives (figure 9.1). This chapter should help you design your own series of checkpoints or benchmarks.

Fundamental motor skills (locomotor and manipulative skills) and movement concepts (body awareness, body parts, nonlocomotor skills, shapes, awareness of space, effort, and relation-

National standards (NASPE)

Annual or biannual benchmarks

Unit objectives

Daily lesson objectives

Figure 9.1 The NASPE standards provide a goal that physical educators want their students to reach, but that is accomplished via smaller steps: Daily lesson objectives contribute to accomplishing unit objectives, which, in turn, are directed toward mastering annual or biannual benchmarks that ultimately lead to achieving the NASPE standards.

ships) serve as organizing centers for instruction in the lower grades and provide a foundation for more complex skills and fitness activities. The Movement Alphabet (Buschner 1994) can be used to develop a sequence of developmentally appropriate movement skill and concept lessons (table 9.2). The fundamental skills are described in chapter 4 and some suggestions are provided in the following sections for incorporating the movement concepts into lesson development. Procedures are outlined for using concepts to elicit a variety of responses from children. Finally, sample benchmarks are provided to illustrate how teachers can check to make sure students are progressing.

Locomotor Patterns

The basic locomotor patterns (e.g., walking, running, and jumping) that require coordination of the body's large muscles must be practiced and mastered before children can master sport skills. Locomotor skills are considered prerequisites for many sport, dance, and gymnastics skills. Lessons involving locomotor skills should progress from movement in free space to movement requiring close control and complex interactions with objects. Because efficient performance of locomotor skills is a prerequisite to later skill development in sport activities, teachers should be able to design

Table 9.2 Movement Alphabet

Motor skills = verbs		Body awareness	Spatial awareness	Movement concepts = adverbs	
Locomotor patterns	Manipulative patterns			Effort	Relationship
Walking	Throwing	Body parts	General	Speed	Objects
				slow / fast	
Jogging	Catching	Shapes	Personal	Force	Partner
		curved / twisted		light	strong
Running	Kicking	Base	Directions	Flow	Others
		narrow / wide		left / right	
Jumping and landing	Punting	Form	forward / backward	bound	
		symmetrical asymmetrical			
Galloping	Dribbling (feet)	Nonlocomotor	up / down	free	
Hopping	Dribbling (hand)	Balance	clockwise counterclockwise		
		static / dynamic			
Skipping	Striking		Levels		
			high / medium / low		
Sliding	Volleying		Pathways		
			straight / curved / zigzag		
Leaping			Extensions		
Faking			short / long		
Fleeing Chasing Dodging			To body		
			near / far		

Reprinted, by permission, from C. Buschner, 1994, *Teaching children movement concepts and skill: Becoming a master teacher* (Champaign, IL: Human Kinetics), 10.

Scooter Ball combines catching and tossing skills with teamwork, a combination of skills that exemplifies the movement approach to physical education.

appropriate tasks and make important corrections; the rubrics in chapter 4 provide guidance for evaluating and correcting locomotor skills. Similar rubrics can be developed by teachers for combinations of locomotor skills such as walking, jogging, running, hopping, jumping, skipping, galloping, leaping, and sliding.

Manipulative Patterns

Manipulation includes giving force to objects (e.g., throwing, kicking, striking, and volleying), gaining control of objects (catching), and maintaining control of objects (dribbling). Development of efficient locomotor skills is likely to precede the mastery of manipulative skills, although they are introduced simultaneously in the program (table 9.3). Skills needed to accurately interact with stationary objects (e.g., to hit a ball off a tee) are less complex than those needed with objects moving in space (e.g., to hit a thrown ball). Thus, competency in manipulating stationary objects should precede competency in manipulating moving objects. Additional suggestions on how to design and alter tasks to increase or decrease difficulty are presented in chapter 4.

Table 9.3

Ages of children when 60% master motor skills	
Running	4–4.5 yr
Throwing	4–7.5 yr
Skipping	6–6.3 yr
Catching	6.5–7 yr
Kicking	6.5–8 yr
Hopping	7.5 yr
Striking	6.5–8.5 yr
Jumping	10 yr

Adapted from V. Seefeldt and J. Haubenstricker, © 1982, Patterns, phases, or stages: An analytical model for the study of developmental movement. In *The development of movement control and co-ordination*, edited by J.A.S. Kelso and J.E. Clark (John Wiley & Sons: New York), 309-318. Reproduced with permission.

Body Awareness

Before locomotor skills can be performed in an efficient way, children must be able to maintain their bodies in a stable position and understand what the body does while moving (e.g., how posture and balance interact and are influenced by environment). Body awareness refers to knowing the body's actions. During the early elementary years, children need to learn names, locations, and functions of the body and body parts. Tasks can be presented to challenge children to explore movement with different body parts. The grades K and 1 gymnastics lesson shown at the end of this chapter demonstrates the use of body parts, directions, and movements. Through body awareness activities, children also learn to control body shapes (curved, twisted, narrow, wide, symmetrical, asymmetrical) and nonlocomotor activities (swing, sway, twist, turn, bend, curl, stretch, sink, push, pull, and shake). **Static balance** is the ability to maintain a stationary position for a specified period of time—the center of gravity remains inside the base of support. Activities that need static balance are balancing on one foot and balancing on three different body parts. **Dynamic balance** is the ability to maintain a balanced position while moving through space. Activities requiring dynamic balance include walking on stilts and walking on a balance beam.

Body Parts

Knowing the location of body parts and surfaces is an important cognitive concept. Being able to apply these terms during movement is a basic skill necessary for understanding instruction and feedback. The movements associated with demonstrating understanding provide practice of important nonlocomotor skills. The following movement challenges combine body awareness with body parts:

- Touch the right elbow to the left knee; touch the head with both hands.
- Twist the arms; twist the right arm and the left leg; twist the whole body.
- Run and make large circles with the arms; walk and twist the trunk.
- Travel around the room; on the drum beat, balance on the right foot and the left hand.
- Balance on four body parts, three body parts, and two body parts.
- Make a complete turn while balancing on one foot.
- Balance on different body parts (knees, seat).

Nonlocomotor Skills

Nonlocomotor skills are movements done while the body remains in one location. This is contrasted with locomotor skills, where the body moves from location to location. Nonlocomotor skills include balancing tasks and other movements such as bending, stretching, curling, and swaying. The following challenges are examples of nonlocomotor skills:

- Balance on one foot and swing the opposite leg.
- Bend one, two, or three body parts.
- Bend up and down and side to side.
- Bend the neck (arms, legs, fingers) in different ways.
- Lie on the floor and bend different body parts.
- Stretch the body in different directions (up, down, to the side).
- Stretch different body parts.
- Balance on different body parts (knees, seat) and stretch.
- Shake the arms (legs, trunk, neck).
- Shake the top (bottom) part of the body.
- Shake one or both arms or legs.

- Swing the trunk from side to side.
- Swing one arm and one leg.
- Push with one or both arms (legs).
- Push from a kneeling (sitting) position.
- Pull with one hand, both hands, and one hand and then the other hand alternately.
- Pull from over the head or from the side.
- Make yourself round.
- Twist your arms, legs, trunk.
- Make a narrow shape.
- Curl your arm, back, body.
- Wiggle your arm, leg, hand, body.
- Swing your arms; swing one leg.
- Sway your body.

Spatial Awareness

Spatial awareness refers to sensing where the body moves. **Personal space** is the area around the body; it extends as far as one's reach from side to side and front to back. Personal space moves with us as we travel around a room. Children need to understand that individual space is the area around the body; the play area is **general space,** which is shared by the whole class. Through exploratory movement tasks in general space, children can learn to manage their bodies to avoid collisions. Moving under control is an important skill and safety concept that is closely related to understanding personal and general space. The concept of space also includes awareness of directions and levels.

Directions

Movement can be performed in place, left, right, forward, backward, sideways, up, down, clockwise, and counterclockwise. The concept of directions includes awareness of up, down, left, right, in front of, in back of, above, below, in, out, over, under, and around. Direction can also be referred to as the pathway or pattern of a movement. The body can move in straight, curvy, diagonal, and zigzag pathways. Fundamental movement patterns can be adapted and refined through exploring movement in different directions. The following are examples of movement tasks designed to explore directions:

- Walk (run, jump, hop, slide) and change direction on a drum beat.
- Move four slides to the right and four slides to the left.

► Jump, making a quarter, a half, and a whole turn to the left or right.

► Gallop forward four times, jump backward four times, and hop sideways four times.

► Kick one leg forward and move backward.

► Kick to the side and move sideways.

► Run around (or jump over) a hoop.

► Move through a hoop while it is rolling.

► Travel around the room in a zigzag (or curvy) pathway.

Levels

Movement can occur at high, medium, and low levels (referring to the height of the movement). Children can jump high and make wide shapes with their bodies or catch a ball high over the head. Low, medium, and high movements can be combined into a sequence to provide an array of experiences. The following movement tasks are designed to explore different levels:

► Stretch (curl, roll, rock, twist) at a low level (lying on the floor), medium level (sitting or kneeling), and high level (standing and in the air).

► Combine a roll, four running steps, and four leaps.

► Toss a beanbag over the head and catch at a high, medium, or low level.

► Make a bridge with the body using four body parts to balance.

► Walk at a low level while keeping hands at a high level.

► Jump high, "melt" to a sitting position, stretch, and balance on three body parts.

Effort

Awareness of qualities, or the effort aspect, of movement refers to sensing how the body moves. The qualities of movement are speed, force, space, and flow. Skill in movement is the ability to select the right combination of these qualities. Children must have the opportunity to experiment with varying degrees of each so they can learn to select the appropriate blend. **Speed** of the movement can range from slow to fast. **Force** is the amount of energy expended for a movement and can range from light to heavy. **Flow** is the amount of control present in a movement and ranges from free to bound. A bound movement is under complete control of the performer and can be stopped at

any moment. Free flow is a continuous movement that cannot be stopped after the action is initiated, such as a flip in gymnastics.

These are some examples of movement tasks of varying qualities:

► Run (jump, hop, skip, gallop, slide) quickly and quietly.

► Run fast, and on the signal run slowly.

► Walk or run with long, heavy steps.

► Move like a robot, a wooden soldier, or a rag doll.

► Show a hard, forceful movement (striking or hitting motion) with the arms, legs.

► Bend and stretch body parts using slow, strong movements.

Relationships

The relationship concept is movement that interacts with others or an object. Movement can be performed alone, with a partner, or in a group:

► Move toward, away from, around, or behind a partner.

► Copy the movements of a partner.

Basic locomotor, nonlocomotor, and manipulative patterns can be refined and varied by using different objects. Play objects can be adjusted in size and weight to children's developmental levels to make successful practice possible:

► Put the beanbag in front of (behind, beside, above, below, under) you.

► Walk around the hoop, stand beside the hoop, and stand in front of the hoop.

► Strike a balloon above your head and then hit it below your knees.

► Jump forward, backward, and sideward over a rope.

Developmental Progression and Benchmarks

The learning outcome is "to be physically educated" as documented by the seven NASPE content standards. Standards 1 and 2 focus on motor skills, so the developmental curriculum is first based on appropriate sequence and progression to meet standards 1 and 2. The progression from grade to grade is demonstrated as fundamental skills are combined and refined to create more complex movement patterns. When practiced in the early elementary grades (kindergarten, first, second, and third), the basic locomotor, nonlocomotor, and manipulative skills become automatic and can then be combined into a variety of higher order, more comprehensive game, gymnastics, and rhythmic activity skills. These specific skills should be acquired in the middle grades (fourth and fifth) and refined in the upper grades (sixth, seventh, and eighth). Gradually, the skills are applied to lead-up games, modified games, and specific sports; stunts; tumbling and apparatus activities; and creative, folk, social, and square dance. As a teacher, you will need to check along the way to ensure students are making progress toward becoming physically educated. For each of the fundamental motor skills and movement concepts, benchmarks should be established to indicate whether students are on track in the process. Examples of benchmarks for assessing fundamental skills and concepts are provided for four different levels (kindergarten, second, fourth, and sixth grades) in table 9.4. Each teacher should develop her own benchmarks for assessing student progress toward specific goals, but these can be used as a guide.

PROGRAM OF PHYSICAL ACTIVITY AND FITNESS

The discussion thus far has focused on the development of fundamental movement and movement concepts. It is also important, however, to plan a

Table 9.4   Sample Benchmarks for Standards 1 and 2

	Kindergarten	Second grade	Fourth grade	Sixth grade
Standard 1: Demonstrates competency in many movement forms and proficiency in a few movement forms	Walks and runs using the most effective pattern	Combines a run and a jump	Throws, catches, and kicks using an efficient pattern	Throws objects with accuracy and force from a challenging distance
	Jumps from one foot to two feet	Demonstrates the skills of skipping, galloping, and leaping	Strikes a moving ball	Strikes a ball continuously with a partner
	Catches a large ball thrown by an accurate thrower	Slides to the left and right	Dribbles a ball with the feet (or hands) around obstacles	Kicks at a moving target
Standard 2: Applies movement concepts and principles to the learning and development of motor skills	Kicks a stationary ball	Strikes a ball repeatedly with a paddle	Identifies the critical elements of throwing, catching, and kicking	Detects errors in personal movement patterns
	Demonstrates an understanding of strong and light movements	Demonstrates control in balance activities	Develops a creative jump rope routine	Performs a variety of dance activities
	Demonstrates an understanding of straight and curved pathways	Demonstrates an understanding of static and dynamic balance	Detects errors in a partner's throwing pattern	Uses offensive and defensive strategies in modified game activities

curriculum that encourages vigorous physical activity for health benefits. In defining a physically educated student, the National Content Standards (NASPE 1995) emphasize the importance of regular participation in physical activity and the development of health-related fitness as important goals. Recall that one of the predictors of physical activity in adults is learning skills as a child. Health-related fitness has four components:

► Cardiorespiratory fitness
► Muscular strength and endurance
► Flexibility
► Body composition

Using an integrated approach to curriculum planning, you can teach health-related physical fitness and physical activity in such a way as to encourage children to seek a healthful, active lifestyle long after they leave your classroom. It is important to remember that fitness is temporary: Becoming fit in class will not have lasting benefits if your students elect to be sedentary as adults. The fitness content standard focuses on learning about fitness, using individualized programs, and being active, which can be seen in the description (table 9.5).

Students must understand the differences between the terms health-related physical fitness, physical activity, skill-related fitness, and exercise. These were defined and discussed in chapter 6 and are not repeated here. The benefits of physical activity should be introduced, and children should leave elementary school understanding the basic concepts and principles of fitness education (figure 9.2).

Table 9.5   General Descriptions of Content Standards in Physical Education: Physical Fitness and Activity

Standard 3: Exhibits a physically active lifestyle	The intent of this standard is to establish patterns of regular participation in meaningful physical activity. This standard should connect what is done in the physical education class with the lives of students outside physical education. Although participation within the physical education class is important, what the student does outside of the physical education class is critical for developing an active, healthy lifestyle. Students are more likely to participate if they have had opportunities to develop interests that are personally meaningful to them. Young children should learn to enjoy physical activity. They should participate in developmentally appropriate activities that help them develop movement competence, and they should be encouraged to participate in vigorous and unstructured play.
Standard 4: Achieves and maintains a health-enhancing level of physical fitness	The intent of this standard is for the student to achieve a health-enhancing level of physical fitness. Students should be encouraged to develop higher levels of basic fitness and physical competence as needed for many work situations and for leisure participation. Health-related fitness components include cardiorespiratory endurance, muscular strength and endurance, flexibility, and body composition. Expectations for students' fitness levels should be established on a personal basis, taking into account variation in entry levels rather than setting a single standard for all children at a given grade level. For elementary children, the emphasis is on an awareness of fitness components and having fun while participating in health-enhancing activities that promote physical fitness. Middle school students gradually acquire a greater understanding of the fitness components, how each is developed and maintained, and the importance of each in overall fitness.

- Reduces the risk of heart disease, diabetes, and high blood pressure
- Promotes emotional wellness
- Enhances neural development
- Helps an individual better perform nonphysical activities
- Saves society money through improved health
- Enhances skeletal health, muscular strength, and cardiorespiratory fitness
- Improves posture

Figure 9.2 Benefits of physical activity.

U.S. Department of Health and Human Services (USDHHS). 2000. *Healthy People 2010: Conference edition.* Washington, D.C.: Government Printing Office.

Principles for Maintaining and Improving Physical Fitness

- Overload
- Frequency
- Intensity
- Time
- Type

(AAHPERD 1981)

Motivating Children in Fitness

To encourage lifelong regular physical activity, physical education activities must leave each individual feeling competent and confident. Offering praise, encouragement, and meaningful and varied activities will help motivate students to seek physical activity on their own. Criticizing, embarrassing, and shaming students will turn them off. The Council on Physical Education for Children (COPEC; 1992) has developed examples of appropriate and inappropriate practices that help teachers distinguish between what should be done and what should be avoided. Table 9.6 presents our own examples, which focus on fitness.

Individualize your fitness lessons so that students will build confidence. The following are some ideas to inspire your students:

- Instead of assigning a predetermined number of exercises, give students a range to complete, such as a choice of doing between 10 and 25.
- List several exercise for one component and allow students to choose the ones they want to do (you can set up stations).
- Instead of having all students run a mile, let each student keep track of how far he runs in 12 minutes.
- Another way to motivate students is to focus on the personal effort and improvement of all students rather than on the prowess of a few elite students. Encourage students to cheer one another on in small groups instead of having them compete to see who can do the most or run the fastest.
- Finally, praise and reward individual effort and improvement as well as group cooperation, inspiring confidence and competence in each student.

The fitness program should focus on the definition of physical fitness, the components of fitness, the benefits of exercise, and what it takes to be physically fit and maintain fitness levels (see chapter 6).

Table 9.6 Examples of Appropriate and Inappropriate Practices

Appropriate practice	Inappropriate practice
Fitness activities are used to demonstrate the concepts of fitness and the benefits of a physically active lifestyle. The activities allow the children to experience the difference between cardiovascular fitness and flexibility.	Fitness tests scores are used to identify and highlight the most fit and least fit children to the entire class. This is done in an effort to motivate the least fit students to improve and to reward the most fit children.

The Obese Child

A child who is overfat is most likely self-conscious about her body, making her reluctant to attempt to participate in physical activity. This attitude, of course, perpetuates the obesity and compounds the complications that can arise from obesity. The following guidelines are recommended for helping obese or overweight children:

▶ Create a fun physical education program to encourage all children to participate and to send the message that physical activity is worth engaging in.

▶ Always build in ways to individualize physical education lessons so that all children, including the obese child, can succeed.

▶ Approach family members privately and diplomatically and point them in the direction of professional help, such as a family physician.

▶ Privately recognize and reinforce small improvements in lifestyle choices such as eating fruit instead of potato chips with lunch or walking to school instead of riding in a car.

▶ Encourage all children to focus on how individual choices can lead to a healthy lifestyle instead of focusing on weight or body composition as the sole or most important indicator of health and fitness.

▶ Allow the obese child to choose his own intensity level. Even mild exercise is beneficial.

This approach increases the likelihood the child will continue to participate in physical activity outside of school. Increasing physical activity can have a positive impact on obesity. Activity expends energy, so if nothing changes (e.g., diet, growth), increasing activity has the potential to burn calories and therefore reduce body fat. Physical activity also reduces depression, which is often associated with obesity and being overweight.

Planning for the Year

There are many approaches to developing a schedule for the year. We recommend that you do this using a weekly calendar. The 36 weeks of the school year are listed, and a category or topic is selected for each week. You should develop an annual plan that is appropriate for your school situation. Examples for yearly programs, one for grades K through 5 and one for grades 6 through

8, are shown in tables 9.7 and 9.8. Two approaches are presented: The first plan distributes activities across the year (9.7), whereas the other blocks activities into units, which are taught during adjacent weeks (9.8). You will notice that the first week or two in each yearly plan is dedicated to the creation of a learning atmosphere. During this time, students are introduced to the rules and consequences associated with appropriate class behavior and learn efficient protocols for making transitions, creating formations, obeying boundaries, and handling equipment. More information about these protocols or management techniques is presented in chapter 11. The other categories taught during the year are games and sports, rhythmic activities, gymnastics, and fitness-related activities. The weekly units are then defined by activities that correspond to the outcome goals. Notice that the grade K through 5 plan repeats content representing locomotor, nonlocomotor, manipulative, and body management skills because the primary focus of the program at this level is on development of fundamental skills. We believe that children learn best when the topics are revisited throughout the year rather than grouped together as a long series of lessons on a topic such as locomotor skills. Locomotor skills, for example, are first introduced in week 4 or 9 and then reviewed several times during the year. In the sample plan for grades 6 through 8, the activities selected are the more traditional sport, gymnastics, and rhythmic activities and are presented in longer, theme-related units. Notice that in grades 4 and 5 we recommend introducing sport skills. The sport skills are practiced in grades 6 through 8 using lead-up games and modified games. In all grades, competition is not emphasized, allowing a focus on skill development.

Each teacher must check the annual plan to be certain it is developmentally appropriate. During a year, the activities in your plan should demonstrate the four characteristics listed in the sidebar on page 206. Progression (increased difficulty), breadth (variety), depth (improved skill development via ample time and goals), and sequence (order) should be present from year to year. This is difficult for a physical education specialist and nearly impossible for a classroom teacher because he will only teach for one year! Many states provide curricula that give the scope and sequence of activities so individual grade-level teachers can determine where they fit into the entire physical education curriculum. Your knowledge of child development is another source of information for

Table 9.7 Weekly Format for Grades K–5

Week	Category	Activity K-1	Activity 2-3	Activity 4-5
1	Creating a Learning Atmosphere	Organizational protocols	Organizational protocols	Organizational protocols
2	Fitness	Hustles	Hustles	Hustles
3	Fitness	Assessment	Assessment	Assessment
4	Gymnastics	Locomotor skills	Pretumbling and review	Tumbling
5	Gymnastics	Pretumbling	Stunts and tumbling	Tumbling
6	Games and Sports	Body parts, throwing, and catching	Throwing and catching	Tossing, throwing, and catching
7	Games and Sports	Throwing, catching, and moving objects	Tossing and kicking	Frisbee
8	Gymnastics	Tumbling	Stunts and tumbling	Tumbling
9	Games and Sports	Running, dodging	Locomotor skills	Vigorous games
10	Games and Sports	Moving objects with feet	Kicking and striking	Soccer
11	Fitness	Circuit training	Circuit training	Circuit training
12	Gymnastics	Tumbling	Stunts and tumbling	Tumbling
13	Gymnastics	Partner activities	Partner activities	Partner and group stunts
14	Games and Sports	Kicking	Striking and dribbling	Soccer
15	Rhythmic Activities	Body shapes, nonlocomotor, and locomotor	Locomotor skills	Locomotor and nonlocomotor
16	Rhythmic Activities	Singing games	Nonlocomotor skills	Folk dances
17	Rhythmic Activities	Lyrics and action words	Singing games and folk dance	Country dances
18	Games and Sports	Striking with hand	Frisbee	Basketball
19	Games and Sports	Manipulative skills stations	Parachute	Volleyball
20	Gymnastics	Small equipment	Small equipment	Small equipment

(continued)

Table 9.7 *(continued)*

Week	Category	Activity K-1	Activity 2-3	Activity 4-5
21	Games and Sports	Striking with extension	Manipulative skills	Basketball
22	Gymnastics	Large equipment	Large equipment	Large equipment
23	Games and Sports	Locomotor skills, jumping	Locomotor combinations	Basketball
24	Rhythmic Activities	Rhythm sticks	Rhythm sticks	Rhythm sticks
25	Rhythmic Activities	Long ropes	Rope jumping	Rope jumping
26	Rhythmic Activities	Short ropes and marching	Folk dances and singing games	Tinikling
27	Games and Sports	Manipulative skills stations	Manipulative checklist	Juggling
28	Games and Sports	Locomotor skills and combinations	Locomotor checklist	Track and field
29	Games and Sports	Locomotor games	Locomotor games	Track and field
30	Games and Sports	Manipulative games	Manipulative games	Softball
31	Games and Sports	Cooperative games	Cooperative games	Cooperative games
32	Fitness	Moderate and vigorous games	Vigorous games	Vigorous games
33	Rhythmic Activities	Parachute play	Scarves	Juggling
34	Fitness	Challenges	Challenges	Rope jumping
35	Fitness	Assessment	Assessment	Assessment
36	Field Days			

decision making, as are the lessons, activities, and material in this book. Optimally, classroom teachers who are responsible for physical education will have either the time to plan together, a specialist to plan the vertical (grades K through 5) curriculum for them, or a state or district curriculum to guide this process. Physical education specialists may have similar resources. In either case, the vertical nature of the curriculum is demonstrated in this chapter and is a concern for all teachers.

Is Your Program Developmentally Appropriate?

Teachers should use these four criteria to judge whether physical education programs are developmentally appropriate (COPEC 1992):

1. Orderly sequence of motor skill learning
2. Allowing for individual differences
3. Appropriate goal structures
4. Ample learning time

Table 9.8 Weekly Format for Grades 6-8

Week	Category	Activity
1	Creating the Learning Environment	Protocols (organization)
2	Creating the Learning Environment	Protocols (organization)
3	Fitness Assessment	
4	Fitness	Circuits
5	Fitness	Hustles
6	Fitness	Rope jumping and Chinese ropes
7	Games and Sports	Football
8	Games and Sports	Soccer
9	Games and Sports	Volleyball
10	Rhythmic Activities	Dance steps
11	Rhythmic Activities	Folk dances
12	Rhythmic Activities	Tinikling
13	Rhythmic Activities	Tinikling
14	Rhythmic Activities	Advanced tinikling
15	Rhythmic Activities	Rope jumping
16	Gymnastics	Tumbling
17	Gymnastics	Tumbling
18	Gymnastics	Partner stunts
19	Gymnastics	Partner stunts
20	Games and Sports	Basketball
21	Games and Sports	Basketball
22	Games and Sports	Cooperative games
23	Fitness	Circuits
24	Fitness	Hustles
25	Games and Sports	Juggling
26	Gymnastics	Small equipment

(continued)

Table 9.8 *(continued)*

Week	Category	Activity
27	Gymnastics	Large equipment
28	Recreational Games	Bowling
29	Games and Sports	Tennis
30	Games and Sports	Softball
31	Games and Sports	Track and field
32	Games and Sports	Track and field
33	Fitness	Circuits
34	Fitness	Hustles
35	Fitness Assessment	
36	Field Days	

Another way to approach the annual plan in elementary school is to devote a day of the week to a specific type of activity. Three examples are presented in table 9.8. The activity categories are the same as in the first method—games and sports, fitness, gymnastics, and rhythmic activities. The "free choice" technique can be used in any curricular organization. The "day-of-the-week" method guarantees that activities will be revisited throughout the year, and it is consistent with the format of after-school activities, in which children have dance one day and soccer another. The order of activities should provide progression and follow a sequence; this is presented in table 9.9 as well. Free choice days are earned by the entire class for skill mastery, good behavior, or both. Teachers offer choices as a reward or recognition of student performance. Two ways to do this are to allow the class to select one activity for the free choice or for the teacher to provide several activities from which individual students select a choice.

There is no one right way to go about selecting the activities for a year, as long as the choices you make are consistent with your outcome goals. We have provided three examples, but feel free to adjust them in any way that will work for you and your class and that is consistent with developmentally appropriate physical education.

Guidelines for Writing Objectives

The NASPE Standards (1995) specify the knowledge, skills, and ways of thinking that students are expected to master in elementary physical education. Understanding these long-term goals is important, but a more immediate concern for teachers is the ability to work backward to set daily lesson objectives. Learner outcomes for daily lessons are usually stated in three domains: cognitive, affective, and psychomotor. Regardless of the domain, the following guidelines should be used to write good objectives:

1. The **objectives** should be stated in terms of observable student behavior. For example, appropriate verbs for the psychomotor domain include dribble, jump, trap, and throw. A meaningful objective describes the end desired behavior so well that no mistake in judgment can be made as to whether the student performed in the desired manner.

2. The expected behavior must be defined in terms of the important conditions under which it is to occur. Catching a ball thrown overhand from a distance of 50 feet is more difficult than catching a ball thrown underhand from 10 feet. Describing the conditions is essential because this component

Table 9.9 Daily Approach to Curriculum: Day-of-the-Week Plan

Monday	Tuesday	Wednesday	Thursday	Friday
Games and Sports	Gymnastics	Fitness	Rhythmic Activities	Games and Sports
Games and Sports	Gymnastics	Games and Sports	Rhythmic Activities	Free choice
Games and Sports	Gymnastics	Fitness	Rhythmic Activities	Free choice

Activity Progression and Sequence

	K–1	2–3	4–5	6–8
Games and Sports	Locomotor Manipulative Low-organization games Combination skills	Locomotor Manipulative Lead-up games Combination skills Novelty skills	Locomotor and manipulative skills, combinations Beginning sport skills	Soccer Football Basketball Volleyball Softball Frisbee Tennis Track and field
Gymnastics	Locomotor Pretumbling Tumbling Partner stunts Small equipment Large equipment	Tumbling Partner stunts Small equipment Large equipment	Tumbling Partner stunts Small equipment Large equipment	Tumbling routines Partner and group stunts Apparatus routines
Rhythmic Activities	Locomotor Nonlocomotor Singing and word tasks Folk dances	Locomotor and nonlocomotor Folk dances Rhythm sticks Ropes	Folk dances Rhythm sticks Ropes	Folk dances Country dances Rhythm sticks Ropes
Fitness	Fitness assessment Hustles Challenges Circuits Games	Fitness assessment Hustles Challenges Circuits Games	Fitness assessment Hustles Circuits Ropes Wands	Fitness assessment Hustles Circuits Ropes Resistance

determines the level of difficulty. The type and size of the equipment, the size of the area, and whether the movement is initiated by the learner or by another person are all examples of conditions that must be defined.

3. The criteria of acceptable performance must be described. The level of performance for success can be subjective (e.g., using correct technique) or objective (e.g., hitting the target 8 out of 10 times). Both subjective and objective criteria for mastery are important and often are included together in a student objective. The following is a sample objective that includes both criteria:

Without losing control, the student will dribble the ball 10 yards and back using the dominant hand and exhibiting the following technique:

- Head up and eyes forward
- Knees slightly bent
- Elbows close to body
- Force applied with fingers of cupped hands

The teacher may shorten the objective by not stating the specific points of technique. In the following example, subjective criteria for the child's technique are implied but not spelled out precisely:

The student will dribble the ball 10 yards and back using the dominant hand with good form.

Writing Objectives in Three Domains

In chapter 4, we discussed the factors to consider when establishing a simple-to-complex sequence of movement tasks. With the instructional sequence established during preplanning and the criteria for specific objectives, writing objectives for motor skill instruction (psychomotor domain) should be a simple task. Stating objectives in the cognitive and affective domains is also important. As in the psychomotor domain, learning outcomes for these two domains need to be sequenced. For example, a student cannot be expected to make good decisions in a game situation if the basic rules and strategies have not been taught. To dribble the ball down the basketball court and pass off to a teammate without traveling, the child must be proficient in dribbling and must have both declarative and procedural knowledge of traveling. The same is true for the affective domain. If children are expected to work effectively as a team toward a common goal, then learning to work cooperatively with a partner should be stressed at an early age. The learning outcomes in these two

domains are hierarchical, which means that lower-level skills and attitudes must be developed before the higher-order outcomes can be expected. To assist teachers in writing cognitive and affective objectives, Bloom and associates (Bloom 1956; Krathwohl, Bloom, and Masia 1964) have established a taxonomy for these domains. The following are sample objectives for content standards 6 and 7:

- The child demonstrates cooperation by working with a partner (K).
- The child gives two or more examples of sharing and cooperation in physical education (grade 2).
- The child names dances or activities from at least two countries other than the United States (grade 4).
- The child describes how team members of different skill levels can contribute to the team effort (grade 6).
- The child uses movement to correctly express the feelings of happy, sad, and angry (K).
- The child names one new activity that he enjoyed as a result of trying it for the first time with the class (grade 2).
- The child lists one accomplishment in physical education for herself and one for a classmate (grade 4).
- The child identifies two emotions felt and provides sport (or physical activity) examples of those emotions (grade 6).

Writing a Daily Lesson Plan

When getting ready to write daily plans, you should realize that there is no specific or correct way to write them. Although the format for a lesson plan may differ according to the book you are reading, all lessons should have the same general components for effective learning. The lesson plan outlines expected learning outcomes (objectives) and describes the procedure to be used daily to reach the outcomes. It outlines the learning activities to be introduced, how these experiences will be presented and organized (instruction and demonstration), what cues need to be emphasized (feedback), and how success will be determined (evaluation). The format we recommend includes a warm-up at the beginning of each lesson. The **warm-up** activities usually focus on moderate-to-vigorous movement designed to get the body ready for the activities to follow. Our plans also list all equipment and materials you will need for each lesson, any important safety tips, and a concluding activity.

Depending on the teacher's level of experience, lesson plans for a particular activity written by different teachers can look quite different from one another. Veteran teachers will not have to write as much on paper as the novice teacher will. You can compare writing and teaching from lesson plans to cooking. When you first attempt to make a dish, you must consult a cookbook, purchase and prepare the ingredients, and then carefully follow the order of activities laid out for you in the recipe. As you make this dish over and over, you need to consult the recipe less often and you also begin to add your own ideas to the mix. Planning and teaching are much like this. You will become more comfortable as you teach the lessons

year after year; then you will be able to add your own touch to the lessons, making the experience more exciting and enjoyable. The lessons presented in previous chapters demonstrate one format for developing lesson plans. Each teacher will find a format that works best. Table 9.10 presents another format new teachers can use for planning. Teachers should develop a format acceptable to their supervisors and one that suits the teachers' individual preferences. Both of these formats have similar components. Having written lesson plans is essential for several reasons:

▸ To guide instruction
▸ To reduce liability via careful planning
▸ To improve planning for future lessons
▸ To serve as a reminder of past activities

Table 9.10 Sample Lesson Plan

Objective	Activity	Formation (draw)	Equipment	Cues	Evaluation
Demonstrate slow and fast movements	Move about the area walking or running, slow or fast as instructed	Scatter	None	"Move under control" "Walk/run, slow, fast"	Observe children changing as instructed.
Name 3 locomotor skills	Practice run, hop, gallop, and slide	X--------o (×5)	Poly-spots	"Fast" "One foot" "One foot leads" "One side"	Ask children to name a skill as teacher demonstrates.
Demonstrate 3 locomotor skills	Practice run, hop, gallop, and slide	X--------o (×5)	Poly-spots	"Fast" "One foot" "One foot leads" "One side"	Observe children doing the skills.
Identify feelings resulting from movement	Demonstrate favorite locomotor skill individually.	X--------o	None	Children's names	Ask why this is a favorite.
Understand straight and curved movement patterns	Move using any locomotor pattern in the appropriate pattern based on cue; switch with drum signal	Scatter	Drum Pencils and paper	"Straight" "Curve" "Move under control"	Children draw lines indicating straight and curved on paper.

The objective is specified first, then an activity is designed to accomplish the objective. The formation (the position and location of students for the learning activity) and the equipment for each activity are specified; then teacher cues and an evaluation for each activity follow.

It is important for the teacher to know the content of the lesson very well. By being familiar with many different activities and understanding developmental progressions, the teacher can then adapt the learning activities according to the needs of each child. These activities can be noted in the daily plan as alternative activities to use "just in case." They will still help meet the objectives in the lesson plan but perhaps with a different approach.

Several essential components should be included in every lesson plan: objectives, equipment, warm-up, skill-development activities, and closure.

Objectives

Objectives should describe precise learner outcomes for the day. When writing objectives, keep in mind the amount of time available to practice the skill. Too often, teachers write objectives that are impossible to achieve in just a 30-minute period. Objectives should be written according to what the student should know and be able to do by the time the class has ended. The sample benchmarks for specific grade levels provided by the NASPE standards can be used as a guide when writing objectives.

Equipment

All items needed for the lesson should be listed, such as mats for gymnastics, music for dance lessons, sport equipment for skill development, and cones for boundaries. You should use all equipment you have available so that each child will get maximum participation and practice.

Warm-Up

A three- to five-minute vigorous activity should be included in each lesson. This provides the students with immediate activity to get the heart pumping before settling down into the learning activities. The warm-up may or may not relate to the lesson for the day.

Skill-Development Activities

The skill-development phase of the lesson plan simply describes how the teacher will progress through the lesson. This should include a description of the learning tasks and a diagram of formations, groupings, and the arrangement of each learning activity. This part of the lesson plan addresses how the content will be communicated to the students as well as the progression used to teach each skill.

To meet the needs of all developmental levels in the class, the teacher should be prepared to offer a wide variety of skill practice activities. Cue words or major points in technique that need to be emphasized are included in this part of the plan. If concepts or strategies need to be stressed, a note could be included as a reminder to the teacher. Keep in mind that all activities planned for the day should directly relate to the objectives of the lesson.

Closure

The **closure** summarizes the day's learning and allows you to do a quick check for understanding. An effective lesson closure should firm up student learning by reviewing the purpose and objectives of the lesson and reflect on or review what was learned. It allows students a chance to cool down after the activities. It also gives the teacher the chance to check for understanding by asking questions or administering some form of assessment. Finally, it should give the teacher the opportunity to "bait" the students and get them excited and looking forward to the next lesson.

SUMMARY

The curriculum is a plan for the physical education program. The first step in creating a curriculum is to develop goals and objectives that are based on the teacher's values. The seven National Content Standards for physical education provide a framework to begin planning the curriculum. Activities and instruction should be developmentally appropriate. This means that although the overall learning outcome (goal) of physical education is the same for all students, the learning activities and expectations are different. Younger children should experience a wide variety of movements that begin with fundamental skills as well as combinations of fundamental skills. With age and skill development, children are introduced to sport-specific skills, fitness, and other leisure time-specific skills. The overall goal is to enable children to be physically active adults who are competent, confident, and knowledgeable.

MASTERY LEARNING ACTIVITIES

1. Locate a unit plan. Does it meet the four criteria for a developmentally appropriate program?

2. Find a Web site that has physical education lesson plans. Critique one lesson plan. Does it include all the important components?

3. Select one of the lesson plans in another chapter. Determine which Content Standard the lesson best addresses.

4. What do you value and how does that influence what you will teach in physical education? Which curricular model best meets your values? How will you ensure that your program will meet the content standards for physical education?

5. Considering the weather, typical school facilities, and your personal interests, develop a yearly plan for grades K, 3, and 5.

6. Write five lesson plans that demonstrate progression and that are developmentally appropriate. Each lesson should cover at least three content standards.

REFERENCES

American Alliance for Health, Physical Education, Recreation and Dance (AAHPERD). 1981. *Basic stuff series I: Exercise physiology.* Reston, Va.: AAHPERD.

Bloom, B.S., ed. 1956. *Taxonomy of educational objectives: Handbook 1. The cognitive domain.* New York: McKay.

Buschner, C. 1994. *Teaching children movement concepts and skill: Becoming a master teacher.* Champaign, Ill.: Human Kinetics.

Council on Physical Education for Children (COPEC). 1992. *Developmentally appropriate physical education practices for children.* Reston, Va.: National Association for Sport and Physical Education (NASPE) Publications.

Krathwohl, D., B. Bloom, and B. Masia. 1964. *Taxonomy of educational objectives: Handbook 11. Affective domain.* New York: McKay.

National Association for Sport and Physical Education (NASPE). 1995. *Moving into the future: National standards for physical education.* Boston: WCB/McGraw-Hill.

Siedentop, D. and D. Tannehill. 2000. *Developing teaching skills in physical education.* Mountain View, CA: Mayfield.

RESOURCES

International Life Sciences Institute (ILSI). 1997. *Improving children's health through physical activity: A new opportunity, a survey of parents and children about physical activity patterns.* Washington, D.C.: ILSI.

Melograno, V. 1996. *Designing the physical education curriculum.* 3d ed. Champaign, Ill.: Human Kinetics.

Seefeldt, V., and J. Haubenstricker. 1982. Patterns, phases, or stages: An analytical model for the study of developmental movement. In *The development of movement control and co-ordination,* edited by J.A.S. Kelso and J.E. Clark, 309–18. New York: Wiley.

LESSON PLANS

The following sample lesson plans demonstrate how learning experiences can be designed to accomplish the desired outcomes for a developmental curriculum. The first three lessons are fashioned to develop movement competency in locomotor skills, with a special emphasis on movement concepts and principles. The grades K and 1 lessons are focused on walking, running, and jumping within the context of personal and general space. At this level, students are asked to adapt the fundamental patterns by moving forward, backward, and sideways. The plan for grades 2 and 3 extends the work on locomotor skills and concepts by incorporating galloping, sliding, and skipping with the effort concept. At this level, locomotor skills are also refined and varied by performing with a partner. In grades 4 and 5, students are asked to combine locomotor and nonlocomotor movements into a sequence and work cooperatively with a group to achieve a goal. The intent of these lessons is to provide experiences for children to achieve the National Content Standards 1 and 2.

The second set of lessons is designed to emphasize the importance of regular participation in physical activity and the development of health-related fitness. Students are introduced to cognitive information that will develop an awareness of the relationships between activity and its effects on the body. Activities are incorporated that will provide students with an understanding of a healthy lifestyle. These lessons are developed to ensure that students achieve National Content Standards 3 and 4.

The intent of the next set of lessons is to encourage patterns of behavior that promote personal and group success in an activity setting by providing opportunities for students to participate in cooperative activities and self-expression. Students are asked to share their feelings about physical education and to participate in cooperative discussion groups on a variety of health-related topics. These lessons are developed to achieve National Content Standards 5, 6, and 7.

LESSON

Body Parts, Positions in Space, Directions

Student Objectives

- Identify body parts and spatial directions.
- Explain the signals per direction.
- Participate in gymnastics activities.
- Follow instructions.
- Cooperate when playing Identify the Body Part.

Equipment and Materials

- Whistle
- 1 hoop (30–36 in.) per child or pair
- Music: "Hokey Pokey" (with and without words) from *Hokey Pokey,* Melody House (MHD 33)

Warm-Up Activities (5 minutes)

I See

Arrange the children in scatter formation.

1. You begin by saying *I see.* The students respond with "What do you see?"
2. You give a movement command such as *I see everybody running in place.* The children run in place.
3. After a short time you begin again with *I see.* The students freeze and respond with "What do you see?" and so on.
4. Some other activities are clowns marching, children running fast, children jumping, children chopping wood, horses galloping, and children skipping.

Skill-Development Activities (20 minutes)

Movement Challenges

Arrange the children in scatter formation or in a semicircle, with all children visible to you.

1. Tell the children: *Touch your foot (head, chest, knees, toes, elbows, legs, thighs, calf, back, shoulder, arm, hip, wrist, ankle, finger, front, bottom, neck, tummy, forearm, face) with both hands.*
2. Repeat step 1 with: *Wiggle (or move) your foot.* Continue with the remaining body parts. Give each child or pair of children a hoop. Keep the children in scatter formation or in a semicircle, standing near their hoops.
3. Have the children perform the following challenges:

   Put your elbow (leg, knee, head, foot) inside your hoop.

   Get inside the hoop (in front of the hoop, beside the hoop, part in and part out of the hoop, under the hoop).

   Walk around the hoop.

   Move the hoop around you.

   Next, arrange partners in scatter formation.
4. Tell the children: *Touch your partner's foot.* Continue with the body parts previously listed. Continue with modified formations: *Stand beside (back to back with, elbow to elbow with) your partner.*

Identify the Body Part

Keep partners in scatter formation. Designate one partner as the caller and the other as the mover.

1. Describe the activity: *The mover moves a body part, and the caller says the name of the part out loud. We will repeat this several times, then switch caller and mover.*
2. Have the children play Identify the Body Part.

Movement Challenges

Arrange children in scatter formation. Challenge the children with the following tasks:

Raise your right (left) hand.
Move your left (right) foot.
Walk to your right (backward to the left).

Concluding Activities (5 minutes)

Hokey Pokey

Arrange the children in a circle, facing center.

1. Play a record or tape of the music. Try the first few times with a voice singing the words, then let the children sing to an instrumental version. As they follow the directions, have the children rock, or move back and forth as one would in a rocking chair, with the music.

2. On the chorus *(You do the Hokey Pokey and you turn yourself around; that's what it's all about!)*, direct the children to turn in individual circles while pointing fingers to the sky and shaking hands. Then *(You do the Hokey Pokey, H-o-o-key P-o-o-key)* have the children get on their knees and bow with their arms extended and hands wiggling.

From *Physical Education Methods for Elementary Teachers, Second Edition,* by Katherine T. Thomas, Amelia M. Lee, and Jerry R. Thomas, 2003, Champaign, IL: Human Kinetics. Adapted from *Physical Education for Children: Daily Lesson Plans for Elementary School, Second Edition,* by Katherine T. Thomas, Amelia M. Lee, and Jerry R. Thomas, 2000, Champaign, IL: Human Kinetics.

Gymnastics

LESSON **9.2**

Locomotor Patterns and Combinations

Student Objectives

- Demonstrate various locomotor patterns and at least one combination of two patterns.
- Distinguish between personal and general space.
- Cooperate while playing Partner Follow the Leader.

Equipment and Materials

- None

Safety Tip

- Remind the children of personal and general space.

Warm-Up Activities (5 minutes)

Point and Run

Arrange the children in scatter formation; stand at the front of the area facing the children.

1. Have the children run through general space. Have the children continue to run in one direction until you signal them to change direction.

2. Whistle to call their attention, then use a hand signal to indicate a change in direction: Signal with the thumb (toward you so the thumb points in the direction the children are to move front) or finger (left, right, or away from you so the finger points in the direction the children are to move back).

3. Remind the children not to bump into each other.

Skill-Development Activities (20 minutes)

Movement Challenges

Keep the children in scatter formation.

1. Tell the children: *Walk from your space to another space.*

2. Describe the route taken (for example, from your classroom to the physical education area). Call it a "pathway," "pattern," or "route."

3. Describe an alternative route from your classroom to the physical education area. Call it a pathway, pattern, or route, too.

4. Tell the children: *Walk back to your space a different way, using a different route or pathway. Are there more ways to travel between spaces, other than a different route or path? We might use different levels (high, low) or walk backward.*

5. *Walk backward on your toes (on heels, bent over, sideways).*

Sliding

Keep the children in scatter formation.

1. Describe and demonstrate the skill: *Sliding is a kind of walking in a sideways direction with a slight hop in the middle, in which the following foot never passes the leading foot.*

2. Have the children practice sliding. Add: *Slide with your arms out.*

3. Have them practice sliding at various speeds in both directions.

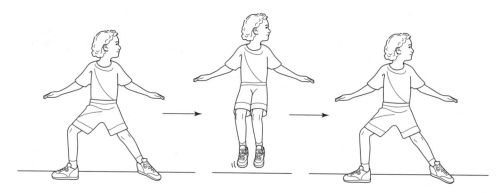

Galloping

Arrange the children in scatter formation.

1. Ask the children: *What is the name for the kind of running a horse does?* (Galloping.) *Galloping is like sliding. Can you tell me how? Can you show me galloping?*

2. Have the children practice leading with each foot.

3. Ask the children: *Who can gallop with one foot leading, then switch to the other foot leading?*

4. Discuss and demonstrate "right," "left," "front," and "back."

5. Challenge the children with the following tasks:

   Slide right.
   Gallop forward.
   Run backward.
   Slide to the right.
   Gallop with your left foot leading.

Movement Challenges

Arrange partners in scatter formation.

1. Tell the children: *One partner stands still; the other partner walks around your partner. Stop!*

2. Have the pairs switch standing-still partner and moving partner.

3. Repeat; then continue with: *Move until you are in front of your partner.*

Concluding Activities (5 minutes)

Partner Follow the Leader

Keep partners in scatter formation.

1. Have partners alternate being leader every one minute.

2. Direct the leader to use one of today's locomotor patterns to move about the area with the partner following using the same pattern: *Leaders, you can walk, slide, or gallop. Change which foot you lead with. Partners, follow the leader!*

From *Physical Education Methods for Elementary Teachers, Second Edition,* by Katherine T. Thomas, Amelia M. Lee, and Jerry R. Thomas, 2003, Champaign, IL: Human Kinetics. Adapted from *Physical Education for Children: Daily Lesson Plans for Elementary School, Second Edition,* by Katherine T. Thomas, Amelia M. Lee, and Jerry R. Thomas, 2000, Champaign, IL: Human Kinetics.

Fitness

LESSON

Circuit Training

Student Objectives

- Demonstrate Fitness Circuit 1.
- Stay on task.
- Take turns.
- State that regular exercise means exercising three times every week.
- State that physical fitness means having enough energy to move all day and be healthy.

Equipment and Materials

- 6 cones
- 6 identifying signs (numbers and pictures reminding children of what to do at the stations; photos of previous or older students performing the exercises are helpful)
- Tape (to attach signs to cones)
- Music or special signal (e.g., whistle)

Warm-Up Activities (5 minutes)

Use Pyramid in lesson 6.2 on page 131.

Skill-Development Activities (20 minutes)

Fitness Circuit

Place six cones with either numbers or pictures for identification in a circle with 30 ft between each cone. Divide the children in six small groups, and place one group at each cone.

1. Spend five to six minutes explaining how to use the circuit and how to do each exercise. (When this is a repeat lesson, quickly review the circuit by describing and demonstrating the activities for only one to two minutes.)

2. At first, have the children spend about one minute at each station, with 30 seconds to travel between each station.

3. Over time as the children gain experience and strength and endurance, have them spend two minutes at each station and 15 seconds between. In addition, altering the time frames makes this fun; for example, sometimes go slowly between cones (one minute) and short (5 seconds) at cones.

4. Tell the students:

   At each cone you will do a different exercise until the signal. When the music stops (or the whistle blows) you will run to the next cone and do the exercise for that cone.

   Everyone will run clockwise, in this direction (point).

   When you hear the music, what should you be doing? (Exercising.)

   When the music stops what should you be doing? (Running to the next cone.)

   If you get to the cone and the music has not started, run in place until the music signals for you to start the exercise.

5. Have the children practice running between and stopping at the cones on the signal. Alter the amount of time between the cones by saying: *Change, move s-l-o-w-l-y, at normal speed,* or *fast.* You may want to accompany the verbal instruction with an arm signal. For example, move your arm in a circle so that the children can judge the amount of time to move between stations by the speed of your arm (e.g., slow arm circle for long times between).

6. Begin the activity, continuing as time permits.

Station 1: Big Swing

Tell and demonstrate for the children: *Stand with your feet shoulder-width apart and knees slightly bent. Bending at the waist and knees, swing both arms between your legs, reaching backward as far* as possible. *Change directions of the arm swing, moving both arms in front of your body and then up and over your head and back as far as possible. Do this as continuously as possible in a rhythmic motion.* This exercise helps your body bend or become more flexible.

Station 2: Big Steppers

Tell and demonstrate for the children: *Standing and staying in one place, take big marching steps* (exaggerate, bringing knees toward chest).

Station 3: Big Curls

Tell and demonstrate for the children: *Standing with feet shoulder-width apart, arms hanging relaxed to the side, look at your belly button by curving your backbone slightly. Tighten your abdominal muscles and hold for five counts; then stand straight, relax five counts, and repeat.*

Station 4: Big Jumps

Tell and demonstrate for the children: *Pretend you are standing at the back of an imaginary box. Jump over the box going forward; then jump to the side, backward, and to the other side, in a pattern like you were jumping over the edges of the box.* (Note: A picture of a box may be a good reminder of what to do at this station.)

Station 5: Big Apples

Tell and demonstrate for the children: *Stand with feet shoulder-width apart and hands on waist. Reach with one hand as far to one side as possible, and pretend you are picking an apple off of a high branch on a tree beside you. Now move the apple above your head and put it in the pretend basket on the opposite side of your body. Remember to stretch all through the movement. Repeat with the other hand to the other side.* (Note: A picture of an apple may be a good reminder of what to do at this station.)

Station 6: Big Circles

Tell and demonstrate for the children: *Jog in your own circle forward, backward, sideways facing in, sideways facing out. Repeat. Remember to stay in your own space!* (Note: You may need to have groups practice this all at once [spread out through play area] before sending students through the circuit.)

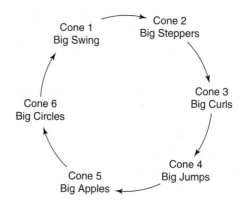

Concluding Activities (5 minutes)

Physical Fitness Concept

Gather the children into an information formation.

1. Explain the concept to the students: *Regular exercise helps you develop physical fitness. Physical fitness means that you are healthy and have enough energy to move all day without becoming too tired. Regular exercise means that you do moderate to vigorous exercise at least three times a week for at least 10 minutes at a time, three times each exercise day.*

2. Discuss these concepts: *"Moderate to vigorous" means that the movements make you breathe hard and possibly sweat. Can you name some things you do that are moderate to vigorous exercise?* Allow children to respond, helping them distinguish between moderate to vigorous and sedentary activities.

3. Continue the discussion:

   Do members of your family exercise regularly? How? (Long walks, tennis, jogging.)

   Being healthy and having enough energy to move all day long without becoming too tired probably mean you are physically fit.

   Can you name someone from the movies or television who is physically fit? (Michael Jordan, Sylvester Stallone, Mia Hamm.)

   Why do you think these people are physically fit? (They exercise regularly, they look healthy, and they appear to have a lot of energy, so it is a combination of exercise and energy.)

4. Finish the discussion: *Can you walk like a person with a lot of energy?* Encourage children to move about the area with a lot of energy, and

point out children who are especially energetic. Ask the children: *Can you move like a person with little or no energy?* Children should move slowly, with poor posture, sad faces, and so on.

Alternative Learning Activities

1. Ask the children to bring in or select from magazines and newspapers you provide pictures of "fit" and "not fit" people. Those who are fit should be demonstrating high energy. Make a collage of the two types of pictures and draw a large circle with a slash through it on those of "not fit."

2. Ask children to draw pictures of people doing moderate to vigorous activities.

3. Invite a parent or person from the community to talk about their exercise program. *(Hint:* Police and firefighters are good sources.)

From *Physical Education Methods for Elementary Teachers, Second Edition,* by Katherine T. Thomas, Amelia M. Lee, and Jerry R. Thomas, 2003, Champaign, IL: Human Kinetics. Adapted from *Physical Education for Children: Daily Lesson Plans for Elementary School, Second Edition,* by Katherine T. Thomas, Amelia M. Lee, and Jerry R. Thomas, 2000, Champaign, IL: Human Kinetics.

Physical Activity and Fitness

Student Objectives

- Name a benefit of physical activity.
- Name two or more components of health-related physical fitness.

Equipment and Materials

- Magazines, scissors, glue, paper, markers/crayons for collages

Health Concept (30 minutes)

Gather the children into an information formation for the entire discussion.

Physical Activity

1. Introduce the concept: *Physical activity is a part of a healthy life; physical fitness means being able to do a specific amount of physical activity.* Introduce the following definitions:

   A sedentary person is one who sits and rests most of the time.

   A physically active person is one who walks or moves around. For example, a "physically active person" may have three 10-minute bouts of activity each day. A physically fit person is one who trains his body so it can do certain physical tasks, including everyday living tasks. Physical fitness has five parts: cardiovascular (aerobic) fitness, muscular strength and endurance, flexibility, and a healthy amount of body fat.

2. Ask the children: *Can you name some jobs that are sedentary?* (Typist, bus driver, cashier.) *Can you name some jobs that are physically active?* (Construction worker, train conductor, janitor.) *Who can you name that is physically fit?* (Michael Jordan, Tiger Woods.) *How do you know?* (They are able to perform well in their sports because they have trained their bodies.)

Identify Sedentary Versus Active Activities

1. Tell the children: *For each activity listed, say "active" or "sedentary":*

   Using the elevator

   Riding the bus
   Cleaning the house
   Watching television
   Taking the stairs
   Walking to school
   Playing basketball
   Taking a nap
   Mowing the grass

2. Ask the children: *Can you name some ways you could be more physically active?* (Take several responses, making sure the children understand that chores and other nonsport and nonplay activities, such as yard work and house cleaning, can be good for health.)

Physical Fitness and Health

1. Introduce the idea: *A physically fit person should be able to do the following:*

   Jog (or any other combination of aerobic activity) for three 10-minute continuous segments three days each week, do 10 sit-ups and 10 push-ups,

   Touch his or her toes (with knees slightly bent for safety), and have some body fat, but not too much fat.

2. Tell your students: *Being physically active regularly leads to being physically fit, reducing health risks. People who are sedentary are often sick and sometimes die when they are young. What could a person with a sedentary job do to be healthier?* (Exercise after work to be more physically active.)

3. Have the children draw or cut pictures out of magazines to make a collage of sedentary and active people.

From *Physical Education Methods for Elementary Teachers, Second Edition,* by Katherine T. Thomas, Amelia M. Lee, and Jerry R. Thomas, 2003, Champaign, IL: Human Kinetics. Adapted from *Physical Education for Children: Daily Lesson Plans for Elementary School, Second Edition,* by Katherine T. Thomas, Amelia M. Lee, and Jerry R. Thomas, 2000, Champaign, IL: Human Kinetics.

Rhythmic Activities

LESSON **9.5**

Galloping, Sliding, and Skipping

Student Objectives

- Distinguish between galloping, sliding, and skipping.
- Gallop, slide, and skip in different directions.
- Gallop, slide, and skip with a partner.

Equipment and Materials

- 1 drum
- 1 parachute

Warm-Up Activities (5 minutes)

Magic Movements

Arrange the children in a circle.

1. Explain the activity:

   You run in a circle.

   On "Freeze!" stop and create a movement to express a feeling, such as happy, sad, frightened, ugly, gentle.

2. Name some feelings and have the children try to express them, and then ask the children for additional suggestions.

Skill-Development Activities (20 minutes)

Locomotor Tasks

Arrange the children in scatter formation.

Galloping

1. Describe and demonstrate galloping: *To "gallop" you step, leap (one leg leads, the other joins).*
2. Use a drum for your start and stop signal. Challenge the children with the following tasks:

   Gallop freely in general space.

   Gallop so that your body goes high with each step. Push off hard with your back leg, and swing your arms.

   Take very large steps as you gallop.

   Gallop backward. This is very hard. Use your arms.

   Think of a movement to do with the arms (head, shoulders) as you gallop.

   Gallop with a partner.

Sliding

Make sure the children are still in scatter formation.

1. Describe and demonstrate sliding: *To slide means you step, then close (move your foot up to the other foot) going sideways.*
2. Challenge the children with the following tasks:

   Slide to the right (left).

   Look in the direction in which you're sliding.

   Try looking in the opposite direction.

   Try different pathways.

   Slide while holding both hands with a partner.

Skipping

Make sure the children are still in scatter formation.

1. Describe and demonstrate skipping: *To skip you step-hop.*

2. Challenge the children with the following tasks:

   Skip freely in general space.

   Skip and think of different positions for your arms (in front, to the side, folded in front of chest, behind back).

   Skip high (low, fast, slowly).

   Skip with a partner (two other people).

Concluding Activities (5 minutes)

Parachute Activities

Space the children around the parachute, each holding the edge with one or both hands. Moving clockwise or counterclockwise, have the children gallop, slide, and skip, stopping on the start/stop signal.

From *Physical Education Methods for Elementary Teachers, Second Edition,* by Katherine T. Thomas, Amelia M. Lee, and Jerry R. Thomas, 2003, Champaign, IL: Human Kinetics. Adapted from *Physical Education for Children: Daily Lesson Plans for Elementary School, Second Edition,* by Katherine T. Thomas, Amelia M. Lee, and Jerry R. Thomas, 2000, Champaign, IL: Human Kinetics.

Fitness

LESSON

Moderate to Vigorous Games

Student Objectives

- Cooperate with two other children when playing Three-on-Three.
- Demonstrate correct technique in stretching.
- Define *cardiorespiratory, or aerobic, fitness.*

Equipment and Materials

- 4 cones
- 10 playground balls

Warm-Up Activities (5 minutes)

Fitness Circuit: Stretching Routine

Arrange and mark six stations in the center of a large rectangle defined by four cones. Divide the children into six groups, and assign each group to a station.

1. Describe and demonstrate the stretching exercise at each station. The first time the children do the circuit, use five to six minutes to explain the stations and rotation, and allow two minutes at each station. In subsequent lessons, allow three minutes at each station after a brief review of the six stretches and safe-stretching guidelines.

2. Remind students of the importance of stretching slowly to the point of tension, not pain. No bouncing!

3. After the first station, signal the children to leave their station, run to the outside boundary, and return to the next station in order. Continue until each group has visited each station.

Station 1: Shoulder Pull

Slowly pull your left elbow across the front of your body toward the opposite shoulder. Hold for 10 seconds. Relax and repeat with the opposite elbow.

Station 2: Arm Reach-Out

Sit on the floor. Lock your fingers together and with palms facing out, straighten your arms out in front of you. Stretch and hold for 10 seconds. Relax and repeat.

Station 3: Triceps Stretch

Lift your arms up over your head and touch your elbows. Hold your right elbow with your left hand and gently pull. Let your right hand drop behind your head as you stretch. Hold for 10 seconds and relax. Repeat, pulling your left elbow with your right hand.

Station 4: Forward Straddle Stretch

Sit on the floor with your legs straight and spread apart about three ft. Bend forward at the hip. Grasp your right knee, calf, or ankle (as far down your leg as you can go) and pull your body gently toward your leg. Hold for 10 seconds, then relax and repeat on the left side.

Station 5: Shoulder Lift Stretch

Lie on the floor with your knees bent and fingertips touching your ears. Slowly lift your head forward, stretching your upper back and neck. You should feel a gentle pull along your spine (backbone) to the shoulder blades. Hold for 5 seconds, then slowly relax to the starting position. Relax for 10 seconds and repeat.

Station 6: Frog Stretch

Lie down with your knees bent and the soles of your feet together. If you relax, gravity will pull your knees toward the ground and stretch the insides of your thighs. Relax for 10 seconds and then lift your knees up and toward each other, so they are no longer relaxed, for 10 seconds (knees do not need to touch at this point). Do not bounce!

Skill-Development Activities (20 minutes)

Three-on-Three

Define a large rectangle with the cones. Divide the children into groups of three, and give a ball to each of one-half of the groups. Have this half of the class line up along one short side of the rectangle. Have the remaining groups of three stand in the rectangle about one-third of the way from the short side where the other groups are lined up. Pair each group of three on the line with a group of three inside the rectangle.

1. Describe and demonstrate the game:

   The object of the game for the team with the ball is to move the ball from the starting line across the far end line.

   You may take five steps carrying the ball, then you must stop and pass, bounce, or roll the ball toward the end line.

   The ball must go over the end line carried by a group member or passed to a group member. Remember to use no more than five steps when carrying the ball.

   The object of the game for the other team is to take the ball away.

   When and if you take the ball away, by catching or a tie (taking ahold of the ball when an opponent is holding the ball), you immediately go to the start line and from there try to get the ball over the end line.

Whenever the ball goes over the end line, your team will trade roles with the other team.

2. Have the children play Three-on-Three.

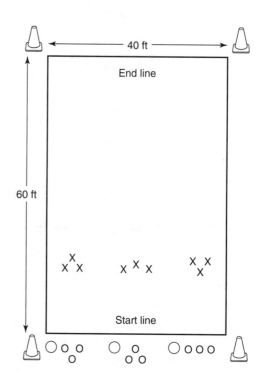

Concluding Activities (5 minutes)

Physical Fitness Concept

Gather the children into an information formation.

1. Present the concept to the children: *Cardiovascular fitness, or heart fitness, is also called "aerobic fitness." A person who can jog, ride a bike, or swim for 20 minutes is demonstrating aerobic fitness. Cardiovascular, or aerobic, fitness has three major benefits:*

   A trained heart has a lower resting heart rate, because the heart pumps more blood each beat, and so fewer beats are needed to pump the same amount of blood.

   A trained heart has more pathways for blood to travel in and around the heart.

   Training lowers blood pressure (how hard the blood pushes against the artery walls).

2. Tell the children: *All these reduce the risk of illness related to the heart.*

3. *When I say, "Start," count the number of beats your heart makes. You can count your heartbeats by putting your fingers on each side of your Adam's apple and pushing gently. Swallowing helps you to locate the Adam's apple. Start.*

4. Stop the count at 10 seconds.

5. Tell the children: *Now, jump up and down quickly 20 times.* Have the children count their heart rate again. The heart rate should be higher.

Creative Movement

Student Objectives

- Combine several locomotor skills while moving.
- Duplicate a partner's movement sequence.
- Work cooperatively with a group to achieve a goal.

Equipment and Materials

- 2 rhythm sticks
- 1 drum
- 1 tambourine
- Chalk, tape, or flour (outdoors) to mark lines

Warm-Up Activities (5 minutes)

Use Movement to Sounds from lesson 4.4, page 82. Variation: Have students gallop.

Skill-Development Activities (20 minutes)

Movement Combinations

Make sure the children are still in scatter formation.

1. Have the children perform the following movement combinations:

   Leap forward (four counts), leap backward (four counts), leap turning (four counts), jump in place (four counts), and collapse.

   Hop right (four counts), hop left (four counts), run forward (four counts), stretch (two counts), and curl (two counts).

   Swing right leg forward and back (eight counts), swing left leg forward and back (eight counts).

   Hop in place (four counts), hop forward (four counts), hop backward (four counts), hop in place (four counts).

   Walk forward (eight counts), jump in place (eight counts), walk backward (eight counts), jump in place (eight counts).

   Slide right (eight counts), slide left (eight counts).

   Run (three counts), leap (one count). Repeat several times.

   Run (two counts), leap (two counts). Repeat several times.

2. Repeat challenges as time allows.

Partner Copy Activity

Arrange partners in scatter formation.

1. Select two or more locomotor or nonlocomotor skills you wish to target and a variety of counts (e.g., 4, 8, 12, 16, 24).

2. Explain the activity:

   The goal of the activity is for the leader to use the skills in a sequence with the specified number of counts. For example, the task might be to use walk, hop, and jump for 16 counts. The sequence could be walk (eight counts), hop (four counts), and jump (four counts).

   One of you creates the movement sequence and the partner watches.

   The partner then repeats the sequence.

   Then trade roles and repeat the activity using other skills and counts.

3. Present the following tasks for partners:

   Walk, run, stretch, and twist for 12 counts.

   Gallop forward, gallop backward, jump forward, jump backward for 24 counts.

   Walk forward, walk backward, hop in a circle for 12 counts.

   Skip and slide for 16 counts.

4. After several practice trials, have the children select their own movements and number of counts.

Advanced Movement Sequences

Divide the children into groups of four to six and place each group behind a line. If your space is large enough, create smaller groups so more students can move at once.

1. Describe and demonstrate the following sequence: *Three jumps forward; five walking steps backward; eight galloping steps with the right foot leading; eight galloping steps with the left foot leading.*

2. Have children take turns in their groups helping each other learn and practice the sequence. Practice the sequence with the children moving across the floor until it becomes easy.

3. Repeat with the following sequences:

   Three hops forward on right foot; three hops forward on left foot; six leaps forward; four jumps forward; eight walking steps backward.

   Four walking steps forward; four walking steps backward; two hops right; two hops left; four jumps forward.

   Two galloping steps with right foot leading; two galloping steps with left foot leading; four walking steps forward; eight jumps side to side.

Concluding Activities (5 minutes)

Movement Sequences

Ask each group to create a movement sequence to perform while moving across the floor.

From *Physical Education Methods for Elementary Teachers, Second Edition,* by Katherine T. Thomas, Amelia M. Lee, and Jerry R. Thomas, 2003, Champaign, IL: Human Kinetics. Adapted from *Physical Education for Children: Daily Lesson Plans for Elementary School, Second Edition,* by Katherine T. Thomas, Amelia M. Lee, and Jerry R. Thomas, 2000, Champaign, IL: Human Kinetics.

LESSON

Rope Jumping

Student Objectives

- Explain how to use the overload principle to develop strength.
- Maintain continuous activity with a long rope.
- Jump a short rope cooperatively with a small group for 10 minutes.

Equipment and Materials

- 4 jump ropes per group (12 to 16 ft long)
- 1 short jump rope per trio of students

Warm-Up Activities (5 minutes)

Jumping Through Long Ropes

Divide the children into groups of six or eight, and assign each group to a rope pattern made with four parallel long jump ropes.

1. Explain the activity:

   Starting at one end, jump over the ropes into the spaces between the ropes, first going forward, and then sideways.

   Repeat several times, hopping on the right foot, hopping on the left foot, and leaping.

   Play Follow the Leader with each child getting a turn to lead your group.

2. Have the children do the activity.

Skill-Development Activities (20 minutes)

Jumping Long Ropes

Divide the children into groups of four or five, each group with a long jump rope, in a scatter formation. Establish a rotation system for each group, with two children turning and two or three jumping.

1. Describe and demonstrate swinging: *In swinging, the turners swing the rope slightly from side to side. Jumpers stand next to the rope and jump over it as it swings.*

2. Have the children practice swinging, rotating so turners get a chance to practice jumping.

3. Describe and demonstrate swing and turn: *In swing and turn, turners swing the rope over the head of the jumper. Jumper jumps over the rope.*

4. Have the children practice swing and turn, rotating jumpers and turners. Continue practice until most children can jump at least three jumps without missing.

5. Describe and demonstrate front door: *In front door, you turn the rope toward the jumper. The jumper runs under the turning rope (runs in the "front door") and either jumps or runs out.*

6. Have the children practice front door, rotating jumpers and turners.

7. Describe and demonstrate back door: *In back door, you turn the rope away from the jumper. The jumper begins to run as the rope leaves the ground, entering when the rope is at the top (runs in the "back door"). The jumper stays and jumps once, then jumps out while the rope is at the top.*

8. Practice back door, rotating jumpers and turners.

Continuous Jumping to Chants

Divide the children into pairs, each pair with a rope in scatter formation.

1. Say each chant, then have children practice it. Explain that jumping rope continuously is good aerobic exercise.

2. Have each pair select one of the chants and jump continuously up to 50 or until a miss occurs.

10-Minute Jump

Divide the children into groups of three, and give each group a short jump rope. Have the groups get into scatter formation.

1. Explain the game:

   The object of the game is for one team member to be jumping at all times.

   One person should start jumping. When she begins to tire, the second child should begin jumping.

   When the second child begins to tire, the third child should begin jumping. Continue taking turns and resting for 10 minutes.

2. Have the children play 10-Minute Jump.

Cool-Down

Walk one lap forward, one backward.

Concluding Activities (5 minutes)

Physical Fitness Concept

Gather the children into an advanced information formation.

1. Review the definition of muscular strength: *Do you remember what "muscular strength" is?* (The greatest amount of weight your muscles can lift in one try.)

2. Review the meaning of overload: *Do you remember what the overload principle is in muscular strength and endurance terms?* (Exercising with more weight than usual.)

3. Discuss exercises for strength training: *Overload training is a way to help your muscles get stronger. You want to make your muscles work harder. If you can lift a 5-lb weight easily with one hand but a 10-lb weight is very hard to lift, then you want to use a 10-lb weight to exercise for strength. You won't be able to perform many repetitions because you have overloaded your muscles.*

4. Ask the children the following questions:

   If you can lift a 10-lb weight easily, can you develop strength by using a 5-lb weight and performing many repetitions? (No.)

   If a person can lift a 30-lb weight but can only do one or two repetitions, can he develop strength using the 30-lb weight? (Yes.) *What does overload training mean in muscular strength and endurance terms?* (Increasing weight to develop strength or number of repetitions to develop endurance.)

From *Physical Education Methods for Elementary Teachers, Second Edition,* by Katherine T. Thomas, Amelia M. Lee, and Jerry R. Thomas, 2003, Champaign, IL: Human Kinetics. Adapted from *Physical Education for Children: Daily Lesson Plans for Elementary School, Second Edition,* by Katherine T. Thomas, Amelia M. Lee, and Jerry R. Thomas, 2000, Champaign, IL: Human Kinetics.

Organization

LESSON

Signals, Boundaries, Groupings, and Rules

Student Objectives

- Change direction on a visual signal.
- Move diagonally, lengthwise, and crosswise across an area.
- Move in an area within an area.
- Give situational examples of rules.
- Cooperate in a discussion group.

Equipment

- Physical Education Rules poster
- Four cones

Warm-Up Activities (5 minutes)

Moving to Visual Signs

Arrange four cones to form a rectangle. In response to the following visual signals, the students move in the indicated directions and stop. Movement should be continuous unless the stop signal is given.

Thumb pointed over your shoulder. (Students move forward.)

Finger pointed right. (Students move left.)

Finger pointed left. (Students move right.)

Finger pointed straight ahead. (Students move backward.)

Hand held up with palm facing front. (Students stop.)

Finger pointed to either back corner. (Students move diagonally.)

Hand held up with palm facing front. (Students stop.)

Skill-Development Activities (20 minutes)

Form Two Teams

Students form a line on a boundary line and count off by twos.

1. The number ones move across the area to the other boundary line.
2. The ones are Team 1 and the twos are Team 2.

Touch Down

Team 1 lines up on a boundary line with each player holding both hands out in front, hands placed together to form a pocket. Team 2 lines up on the opposite boundary line. You hold a small object that is used as the bait.

1. Holding the small object, walk to each student pretending to drop the object in the student's hands.
2. Give the object to a student, but don't let the opposing team know who that person is.
3. On a signal the teams run to the opposite boundary lines, with each player on Team 2 attempting to tag a player on Team 1.
4. If the player with the object gets to the opposite boundary line without being tagged, Team 1 scores a point.
5. Repeat with Team 2 as the carrying team.

Moving Within a Rectangle

Arrange the students in four groups. Divide the rectangle into quarters (point out imaginary lines), and place one group in each of the quarters.

1. Ask the students to move within their own areas.

2. The students stop on a signal, and on the next signal they move together to another area.

3. Repeat, with the rule that they cannot go to the same area twice.

Concluding Activities (5 minutes)

Rules

Ask the students to recall and verbally list the rules. Watch for situations in the remainder of the organization lessons that are examples of good rules behavior; stop the class and point them out.

Cooperative Discussion Groups

Arrange the students in groups of four to six to form heterogeneous discussion groups. Have equal representation of students of different races, ethnic origins, social classes, and gender.

1. Establish guidelines for cooperative discussion groups. Tell the children that

   everyone must participate in the discussion;

   only one student can talk at a time, and the others must listen; and

   everyone must show respect for others.

2. Present a topic for the groups to discuss. Here are some examples:

   Describe a student who takes responsibility for his or her own behavior.

   What should we do with students in our class who fail to take responsibility for their own behavior?

   How should we deal with students who do not follow the class rules?

   How should we deal with students who do not try?

   How should we deal with students who do not take care of the equipment?

From *Physical Education Methods for Elementary Teachers, Second Edition,* by Katherine T. Thomas, Amelia M. Lee, and Jerry R. Thomas, 2003, Champaign, IL: Human Kinetics. Adapted from *Physical Education for Children: Daily Lesson Plans for Middle School, Second Edition,* by Amelia M. Lee, Katherine T. Thomas, and Jerry R. Thomas, 2000, Champaign, IL: Human Kinetics.

Organization

LESSON **9.10**

Forming Groups and Journal Writing

Student Objectives

- Use task cards in a station formation.
- Share their feelings about physical education in writing.

Equipment

- Task cards
- A notebook and pencil for each child

Warm-Up Activities (5 minutes)

Forming Groups

Review forming groups with adaptations. Cards are made before class and distributed to the children as they enter the gym. Each card should be either red, blue, yellow, or green; cards should have different team names printed on them (e.g., Cubs, Cardinals, Rangers, or Orioles). Cards should be numbered from 1 to 28 or the number of children who are in the class. With 28 students in the class, there should be 7 red, 7 blue, 7 yellow, and 7 green cards. Each team name should be printed at least once on each color.

1. Present the following tasks:

   Find a partner who has the same color card. Students should ignore the team name and the number.

Now find a partner who has the same number on the card. Students should ignore the team name and the color.

2. Form two groups. Cardinals and Cubs make up one grup, and Rangers and Orioles make up the second group. Students should ignore the color and the number.

3. Continue with other combinations.

4. Form two groups. Group 1 = numbers 1 through 14 and Group 2 = numbers 15 through 28.

5. Form four groups. Group 1 = Cardinals, Group 2 = Cubs, Group 3 = Rangers, and Group 4 = Orioles.

Skill-Development Activities (20 minutes)

Task Cards

Fitness tasks are printed on cards large enough for the students to read (8-1/2 by 11 inches or larger).

1. Place one of the cards at each of the four stations.

2. Students are assigned to a station and on a signal move to the next station. Allow two or three minutes at each station.

   Task Card #1: Run in place 50 steps or more without stopping.

Task Card #2: Moving in circles or figure-eights, gallop or skip for 50 steps without stopping.

Task Card #3: Hop 25 times on the right foot and 25 times on the left foot.

Task Card #4: Jump in place at least 50 times.

Partner Relay

Arrange the students in pairs and assign each pair to one of five relay teams. Mark a starting line and a return line.

1. At the return line, place a stack of cards for each relay team.
2. The cards (one for each pair) should specify how the pair will return to the starting line. Here are some examples:

Run with one person going forward and one going backward.

Hold hands, face each other, and slide.

Gallop with opposite feet forward.

Concluding Activities (5 minutes)

Feelings About Physical Education

Arrange the children in scatter formation. Each child needs a notebook and a pencil.

1. Ask the children to think about their own feelings when they were in physical education last year.
2. Stimulate the students' thinking by asking some of the following open-ended questions:

    I feel good in physical education when I . . .

    My favorite activity is . . .

    If I were the teacher, I would change . . .

    Some things I do not like about physical education are . . .

3. This should be a serious activity; students' responses should be private and not discussed in class.
4. You should read the journals to get ideas about how the students think and feel about their experiences in physical education.

From *Physical Education Methods for Elementary Teachers, Second Edition*, by Katherine T. Thomas, Amelia M. Lee, and Jerry R. Thomas, 2003, Champaign, IL: Human Kinetics. Adapted from *Physical Education for Children: Daily Lesson Plans for Middle School, Second Edition*, by Amelia M. Lee, Katherine T. Thomas, and Jerry R. Thomas, 2000, Champaign, IL: Human Kinetics.

Organization

LESSON

Cooperative Teams and Discussion Groups

Student Objectives

- Work successfully in a student learning group.
- Cooperate in a discussion group.

Equipment

- Six playground balls

Warm-Up Activities (5 minutes)

Forming Groups

Review forming groups with adaptations. See lesson plan 9.10, page 233.

Skill-Development Activities (20 minutes)

Cooperative Learning Groups

Arrange the students in groups of four to six to form heterogeneous learning teams.

1. Review the guidelines for cooperative group work (see lesson plan 9.9, page 232).
2. Discuss that in group work, cooperative effort is important.

   Each student is responsible for her own work and the work of the team. The group is not successful unless all students accomplish the goal.

   Students must help each other.

   Each student must try hard.

3. Present a problem for the groups to solve. Here are some examples:

   Create a ball game that uses throwing and catching.

   Create a ball game that uses kicking.

   Discover ways to explain the meaning of balance.

   Discover ways to explain the meaning of strength.

Concluding Activities (5 minutes)

Cooperative Discussion Groups

1. Continue work with cooperative grouping by asking students to discuss a variety of topics.
2. Present open-ended questions for the groups to discuss and arrive at a solution. All groups discuss the same question. Here are some examples:

   What should we do about students in our class who do not like physical education?

   Why is physical education important?

   What are the most important things we can learn in physical education this year?

   What does playing fair mean?

   Why is it important to follow the rules when playing a game?

3. A representative from each group shares the solution with the entire class.

From *Physical Education Methods for Elementary Teachers, Second Edition,* by Katherine T. Thomas, Amelia M. Lee, and Jerry R. Thomas, 2003, Champaign, IL: Human Kinetics. Adapted from *Physical Education for Children: Daily Lesson Plans for Middle School, Second Edition,* by Amelia M. Lee, Katherine T. Thomas, and Jerry R. Thomas, 2000, Champaign, IL: Human Kinetics.

chapter 10

Organizing for Teaching

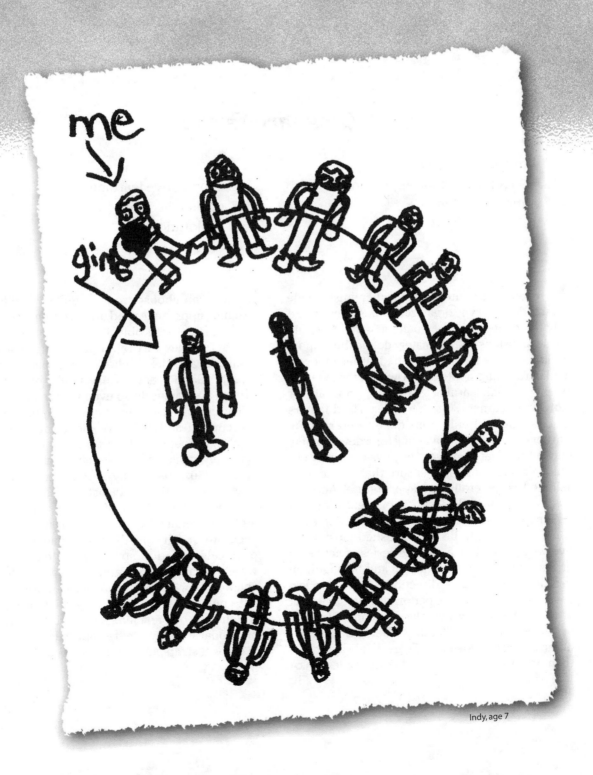

me

ging

Indy, age 7

Many instructional strategies are available to teachers. One way these strategies can be described is in terms of learner involvement in decision making. Effective teachers employ a variety of teaching strategies.

Learner Outcomes

The teacher will do the following:

- ► Define indirect and direct styles of teaching.

- ► Distinguish among station teaching, guided discovery, exploration, contracts, cooperative learning, and task sheets.

Glossary Terms

direct instruction approach
indirect instruction approach
station teaching
task sheets

learning contracts
cooperative learning
guided discovery
exploration

After selecting content, the teacher must decide how students will be organized for instruction and how the content will be communicated to them. These decisions will ultimately define the responsibilities of the teacher and the learner in a particular teaching context and will determine the extent to which learning tasks are appropriate for individual learners. Chapter 8 discussed factors that teachers should consider in determining learner outcomes and planning for a developmentally appropriate program of physical activities. This information should ensure that the content selected is generally age appropriate. Another teacher responsibility is to implement a quality lesson for individuals within each class. Some lesson objectives can be accomplished most effectively by presenting a specific series of activities or tasks to a group of students and having them respond according to directions. For these lessons, all students will be performing the same task at the same time. Some class periods might be organized to allow different students to practice different tasks, however. There is always more than one way to organize and deliver a lesson. A teacher can choose from a number of different teaching approaches and organizational patterns, depending on the objectives of the lesson, the characteristics of the students, the resources available, and the teacher's own abilities and interests. Good teachers use more than one approach and might do so even within one lesson.

This approach—using a method appropriate to the content and objective—is no different than what classroom teachers do every day in math, science, reading, and other academic subject areas. The approach may be different than what physical education specialists are used to. In fact, you can probably think of several stereotypes of a physical education teacher. These may not be accurate or fair, but they do demonstrate why physical education specialists should model a variety of approaches and patterns. In the next chapter, we will present management routines. Do not confuse having routines—which are good—with having one teaching approach and one organizational strategy. Limited approaches and organizational strategies are not the best practice.

Teachers need to understand how to organize for teaching for several reasons:

► So that lessons can be individualized as necessary to optimize student learning

► So that numerous instructional approaches are available to the teacher

► So that different instructional approaches are selected based on the content, the learner, and the teacher characteristics

TEACHING APPROACHES

Teaching approaches, teaching styles, and instructional strategies all refer to the ways teachers go about delivering the content of the lesson to students. Different styles or approaches are usually defined in terms of the amount of teacher control versus learner involvement in the lesson. A teacher might select a **direct instruction approach,** in which the emphasis is on class control, with little opportunity for students to choose between alternatives and make decisions about their own learning. Using this style, a teacher would give explicit instructions and provide a clear description of what learners are to do. They would specify how students should respond and direct all aspects of the class. Think of teaching styles on a continuum with a direct approach at one end and an indirect approach at the other (figure 10.1). An **indirect instruction approach** is characterized by opportunities for student involvement with teachers establishing a learning environment that helps students discover solutions on their own. Indirect teaching would involve students in decision making at a maximum level. Teachers can select an approach that falls anywhere along the continuum from direct to indirect, depending on the goal of the lesson and the intended outcome. Examples that fall between direct and indirect are station teaching, individualized instruction, and cooperative learning. Indirect approaches are consistent with the constructivist approach and active learning discussed in chapter 2.

Approaches With No Learner Involvement: Direct Teaching

Many lessons are taught most appropriately with the direct style. If the lesson objective is for all students to perform a particular movement in a particular way and learning can be enhanced by listening to a verbal description and observing a model, then direct teaching is appropriate. Skills such as the forward roll, the standing long jump, or three-beanbag juggling can be taught effectively by the direct style. The organizational arrangement for direct approaches is usually teaching the whole class, but other formations can be used, such as partners or small groups. The goal is for the teacher to direct all aspects of the class, but movement tasks of varying difficulty can be offered for students at different developmental levels. Students should be arranged so that all can see and hear, because the teacher delivers all the content and determines the pace of the class. The teacher explains the movement or movement sequence, remembering to include well-selected cues; demonstrates all or part of the skill; signals the learners to repeat the movement demonstrated one or more times; observes the performance of students and provides feedback; and, eventually, evaluates the final achievement. In a direct approach, the teacher controls all aspects of the class.

The direct style is a good choice for teachers when the lesson involves introduction of a new skill or when safety is an issue. This format allows complete teacher control and is useful with classes that are difficult to manage. Often, after students spend some time in controlled practice, they should be able to manage their own behavior well enough to be provided with more opportunities for decision making and individualized practice. Several guidelines are important for successful use of direct teaching:

► Always have a signal (e.g., a drumbeat or a verbal command) to get the attention of the class.

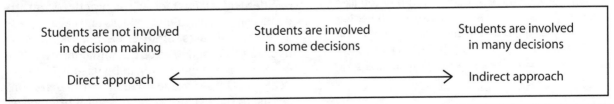

| Students are not involved in decision making | Students are involved in some decisions | Students are involved in many decisions |

Direct approach ⟵————————————————⟶ Indirect approach

Figure 10.1 Continuum of teaching styles.

From J.R. Thomas, K.T. Thomas, and A. Lee, 1988, *Physical education for children: Concepts into practice* (Champaign, IL: Human Kinetics), 107. Reprinted by permission of J.R. Thomas, K.T. Thomas, and A. Lee.

▶ Try to provide for maximum practice (e.g., use small groups for drills). Never have children stand in long lines.

▶ Most important, remember the responsibilities of the teacher in motor skill learning, discussed in chapter 4. These include identifying the skill level of the child on a task and providing for developmentally appropriate practice so that every child finds success.

The direct style can also be applied in lessons where students play a new game of low organization, learn an aerobic dance or jump rope routine, or practice a folk or square dance. In these situations, it is desirable to guide the class through the steps or sequence using a structured approach.

Direct teaching is a helpful style when safety is an issue. It allows the teacher the opportunity to organize and control the learning environment when new skills are being taught.

Concepts Into Practice

Kimi is student teaching. The first lesson she will teach to her fourth-grade class is the grapevine step. She recognizes the importance of the students mastering this step, because she will use it in line dances during the next two lessons. As she discusses her teaching options with her cooperating teacher, she decides to use a direct approach to introduce and practice the grapevine. Then, at the end of the lesson, if students have mastered dancing the step to music, she will conclude with a challenge for the students to create ways to use the grapevine step in small groups. If the students have not mastered the step, she can use the concluding time for additional practice. Everything goes smoothly using the direct style, and Kimi can see that all the students can do the grapevine step. She presents the challenge to her class. Most of the groups begin trying ways to use the step, but two groups are standing still, arguing and becoming frustrated. Kimi visits those groups. The first group has no idea what to do, so she says, "See if you can do the grapevine step and put a turn at the end, so each time you change directions." The second group has many ideas but cannot agree on what to do first. Kimi says, "Try Erin's idea first, then Joe's, then Carrie's. See which one you like best." Kimi's cooperating teacher praised her for identifying the problem and trying two styles of teaching. Kimi realized that the indirect approach may work better for some groups than others.

Teaching Approaches With Some Learner Involvement

As mentioned earlier, some teaching approaches fall between the two extremes of the direct and indirect approaches; these are station teaching, individualized instruction, and cooperative learning. Many movement tasks and sport skills can be practiced effectively using a station approach to teaching. With this format, the teacher usually decides which activities will be practiced, but students can practice different tasks and can progress at individual rates. **Station teaching** is an effective way to practice after the initial introduction of a skill or movement. It can be used in both primary and upper grades. When learning stations are used, the teacher sets up several practice areas in the gymnasium or on the playground. This arrangement is similar to learning centers in a classroom and circuit training in physical fitness. Lessons can be designed for practicing different skills or different levels of a particular skill. Students are divided into groups, and each group is assigned to a station. The teacher usually signals when the groups are to rotate. After children have some experience working independently at completion of all the tasks or activities, they can progress individually to the next group. (Tasks are usually communicated to the learners with task sheets or posters.) This frees the teacher to work with children who are having trouble or to evaluate individual students.

One example of a station learning arrangement is shown in figure 10.2. The tasks shown in the figure are appropriate for second-grade children. Each station should have enough equipment for five children to participate at the same time. To make sure students understand what to do at each station, the teacher should explain and demonstrate. The task sheets, posters, and other reminders at each station are also helpful. The same activities can be used effectively for practice of sport skills in the upper grades. Ability grouping for sport-skill practice allows a range of skill levels within an age group. Usually, each station is planned with progressive tasks, but it is also desirable to have some stations designed specifically for those students who would benefit from modified (lower-level) or extended (higher-level) tasks. In most sport-skill lessons, students tend to accomplish more if grouped with children of similar skill (Thomas 1994). This is especially important if safety is a concern. Figure 10.3 shows a layout for soccer stations and provides sample tasks.

#1 Throwing and catching	#2 Kicking	#3 Dribbling
#6 Rope jumping	#5 Striking	#4 Jumping and landing

Station 1—Throwing and catching
- Toss the beanbag over your head and catch it with your right hand (five times).
- Repeat, using your left hand.
- Stand on the red line and hit the red target on the wall 5 out of 10 times.
- Repeat, using the blue line and the blue target.

Station 2—Kicking
- Kick the ball with your right foot from the red line so that it goes between the cones and hits the wall (five times).
- Repeat, using your left foot.
- Kick the ball with your right foot from the blue line so that it goes between the cones and hits the wall (five times).

Station 3—Dribbling
- Dribble the ball in place 10 times using your right hand.
- Repeat, using your left hand.
- Dribble the ball in place five times with your left hand and then five times with your right hand.
- Dribble 10 times alternating right and left hands.

Station 4—Jumping and landing
- Using two feet, jump through the hoops on the floor.
- Repeat, going backward and sideways.
- Run and jump for distance.

Station 5—Striking
- Strike the balloon up and over your head five times using your right hand.
- Repeat, using your left hand.
- Stand on the red line and strike the large ball so that it hits the red target on the wall (five times).
- Repeat, using the blue line and the blue target.

Station 6—Rope jumping
- With your rope on the floor, jump back and forth over it 10 times.
- Jump rope forward 10 times without missing.
- Repeat, jumping backward.

Figure 10.2   Skill stations.

Goal

#1 Goalkeeper punting	#6 Dribbling and passing with a partner
#2 Dribbling around cones	#5 Heading
#3 Throw-in	#4 Passing and trapping

Goal

Station 1—Goalkeeper punting
- Punt the ball 10 times to a partner who is 30 yards away.
- Punt to the right 10 times and to the left 10 times.

Station 2—Dribbling around cones
- Dribble the 30-yard course several times, weaving in and out of the cones.

Station 3—Throw-in (two-hand overhead)
- Throw for accuracy at the targets placed at 10, 15, and 20 yards (five times at each distance).

Station 4—Passing and trapping
- Using the inside of the foot, kick a stationary ball to a partner 10 feet away 10 times. Partner will trap using the sole of the foot.
- Repeat, using nondominant foot.

Station 5—Heading
- Head a ball thrown by a partner 10 times.
- While moving to your right, head a ball thrown by a partner 10 times.
- Repeat while moving to your left.

Station 6—Dribbling and passing with a partner
- Running with a partner at moderate pace 10 yards apart, dribble and pass with the partner while running a distance of 20 yards.
- Repeat several times with rest.

Figure 10.3   Soccer stations.

From J.R. Thomas, K.T. Thomas, and A. Lee, 1988, *Physical education for children: Concepts into practice* (Champaign, IL: Human Kinetics), 111. Reprinted by permission of J.R. Thomas, K.T. Thomas, and A. Lee.

Individualized Teaching With Task Sheets and Contracts

Task sheets can also be used to communicate the activities to be accomplished to individual students. Students can work alone or with partners, but there is always opportunity for individual progression. The sheets can be designed for varying lengths of time, and students can work on the same or different skills. Task sheets may provide some tips for performance, but initial instruction and demonstration should be given for new skills. Task sheets are more often used to refine skills. In working with a partner, this approach allows for valuable evaluation and feedback. Figures 10.4 and 10.5 show two types of task sheets.

Learning contracts provide an excellent way to begin shifting decision-making responsibility from the teacher to the learner. A teacher–student contract is a written agreement of what the student is to accomplish in a specified time period. There are several types of contracts; each requires a different amount of student responsibility. Contract teaching should allow varying amounts of time for completing tasks and should provide opportunity for independent work. The student choice contract provides a list of activities, and each usually has a point value. Students can choose from the tasks and work at individual rates, but they should be encouraged to select tasks that match beginning competency levels. Figure 10.6 shows an example of a student choice contract.

An open-ended contract gives the student the most responsibility: The student simply lists the skills to be mastered and the time needed to accomplish them. Figure 10.7 is an example of a contract designed for basketball by a fifth-grade student. Open-ended contracts can also be used for doing physical fitness activities outside class.

Balance Beam Task Sheet

Name _____

	Completed	
	Yes	No
1. I can walk the beam slowly without falling.	❐	❐
2. I can walk the beam slowly with my hands on my hips without falling.	❐	❐
3. I can walk forward, balance on one foot at the center, and continue walking to the end without falling.	❐	❐
4. I can walk the beam with a beanbag balanced on my head without falling.	❐	❐
5. I can walk the beam sideways with my right foot leading without falling.	❐	❐
6. I can walk the beam sideways with my left foot leading without falling.	❐	❐
7. I can walk the beam backward without falling.	❐	❐
8. I can walk forward, pick up a beanbag at the center, and continue to the end without falling.	❐	❐
9. I can walk to the center, make a half turn, and continue to the end of the beam without falling.	❐	❐
10. I can walk to the center, perform a swan balance on my left foot, and continue to the end of the beam without falling.	❐	❐

Figure 10.4 Sample individual task sheet.

From *Physical Education Methods for Elementary Teachers, Second Edition,* by Katherine T. Thomas, Amelia M. Lee, and Jerry R. Thomas, 2003, Champaign, IL: Human Kinetics.

From J.R. Thomas, K.T. Thomas, and A. Lee, 1988, *Physical education for children: Concepts into practice* (Champaign, IL: Human Kinetics), 113. Reprinted by permission of J.R. Thomas, K.T. Thomas, and A. Lee.

Cooperative Learning

Cooperative learning is a teaching approach designed to encourage students to take responsibility for their own learning and to work cooperatively with a group to accomplish a goal. Using this format, students are usually assigned to heterogeneous groups with equal representation of students of different races, ethnic origins, social classes, and gender. Students are presented with a problem or a question and given time to solve the problem or answer the question. The problem might be to create a ball game that uses throwing and catching or discover ways to explain the meaning of balance. It is important to establish guidelines for cooperative work. Everyone in the group must participate in the assigned work; however, only one student may talk at a time, and the others must listen quietly. Everyone must show respect for others. It is important that each student assume responsibility for her own work as well as the work of the entire group. The group is not successful unless all students accomplish the goal, so students are encouraged to help each

other. Before assigning a cooperative activity, teachers should set the stage by discussing the following concepts with the class:

► Why groups fail to solve the problem (the problem is too difficult; group members fight with one another)

► How group members have their feelings hurt (others are not listening; they are unable to help)

► What makes groups successful (taking turns, sharing responsibility, respecting others)

After the activity, discuss what worked and what did not with the class. Focus on groups with positive interactions and results.

Cooperative discussion groups can be used to get students to think about the importance of individual effort and social responsibility. For example, the following topics could be used at the beginning of the school year to emphasize the importance of working hard and following the rules set for the class:

Soccer Task Sheet

Name _____   Partner _____

Skill   Dribble and pass with a partner

Checkpoint

• Keep the ball in front of your partner when passing.
• Control the dribble and the pass.
• Pass using your right foot and your left foot.
• Pass using the inside and the outside of your foot.

Task 1   Run at a moderate pace, approximately 10 yards apart; dribble and pass with your partner for 50 yards. (Repeat three times with rest in between.)

Evaluation   Place an X in the space that you think best represents *your* performance in dribbling and passing.

Rating	Trial 1	Trial 2	Trial 3
Poor			
Fair			
Good			

Task 2   With your partner, dribble and pass for 50 yards. After passing the ball, move behind your partner. Your partner then moves to where you were and passes to you. Partner moves behind you, and you take his/her place. (Repeat three times with rest in between.)

Evaluation   Place an X in the space that you think best represents *your* performance in dribbling and passing.

Rating	Trial 1	Trial 2	Trial 3
Poor			
Fair			
Good			

Figure 10.5   Sample task sheet for soccer.

▶ Describe a student who doesn't try in physical education.

▶ What should we do if some students don't try?

▶ What would our class be like if nobody tried?

▶ How should we deal with students who always want to argue with other students and the teacher?

▶ How should we deal with students who shove or hit other students?

Other topics for discussion might be the following:

▶ Why is physical education important?

▶ What does "playing fair" mean?

▶ Why is it important to follow the rules when playing a game?

During a fitness lesson, cooperative groups can be asked to discuss and make decisions about ways to increase activity levels or burn calories. After you explain target heart rate to them, older students (grades 4 and 5) could be asked to calculate a training heart rate range for a particular student. The following topics or problems are provided as examples:

▶ Name some ways a person who wants to lose weight can increase the amount of physical activity he gets. (Walk to school instead of riding, plan an exercise program, or use the stairs rather than the elevator.)

▶ Name some ways to increase your activity level after school each day. (Take a bike ride, mow the lawn, walk to the park, go roller-skating, play sports, or rake leaves.)

Jump Rope Contract

Your objective is to earn 20 points this week. Select from the list of options the tasks you want to accomplish. To compete an option, you must perform the activity without error.

I, _____ will earn 20 points from the list below.

Points		Options	Times
2	1.	Two-foot doubles: jump on both feet twice for each turn of the rope.	20
2	2.	One-foot doubles: jump on one foot twice for each turn of the rope.	20
2	3.	Two-foot singles: jump on both feet once for each turn of the rope.	10
2	4.	One-foot singles: jump on one foot once for each turn of the rope.	10
2	5.	Alternate: jump on each foot for each turn of the rope.	10
2	6.	One-foot continuous: jump on the same foot for each turn of the rope.	10
2	7.	Leg swings: jump using a one-foot single while the free leg swings across.	10
2	8.	Ski twists: jump two-foot singles with knees and ankles together and twisting.	10
2	9.	Two foot, one foot: jump on two feet and then on one foot for each turn of the rope.	10
5	10.	Straddle jumps using two-foot double rhythm: first jump is out, rebound is in.	10
5	11.	Straddle cross using two-foot double rhythm: first jump is out, rebound is in with feet crossed.	10
5	12.	Rock: place one foot in front of the other. Jump on front foot leaning slightly forward, then jump on back foot.	10
5	13.	Arm cross: jump continuously, crossing and uncrossing arms after each jump.	10
5	14.	Make up a routine using at least four different jumps.	10

Figure 10.6 Sample jump rope student choice activity.

From *Physical Education Methods for Elementary Teachers, Second Edition*, by Katherine T. Thomas, Amelia M. Lee, and Jerry R. Thomas, 2003, Champaign, IL: Human Kinetics.

From J.R. Thomas, K.T. Thomas, and A. Lee, 1988, *Physical education for children: Concepts into practice* (Champaign, IL: Human Kinetics), 112. Reprinted by permission of J.R. Thomas, K.T. Thomas, and A. Lee.

► Calculate a target heart rate range. Give each cooperative group a card or sheet of paper with the following formulas:

Training heart rate = 220 – age $\times$ .75 (lower end)
Training heart rate = 220 – age $\times$ .90 (upper end)

For a 12-year-old, the range would be

220 – 12 = 208 $\times$ .75 = 156 (lower end) and
220 – 12 = 208 $\times$ .90 = 187 (upper end).

The cooperative task is to calculate the training heart rate range for each student in the group. Students should be reminded that everyone in the cooperative group must understand the formula and how to use it before the group is successful.

Teaching Approaches Involving Learners in Many Decisions: Indirect Styles

Indirect teaching styles involve discovering, exploring, selecting from alternatives, and seeking solutions to problems or tasks designed and presented by the teacher. The teacher usually preplans a sequence of challenge tasks or movement questions with more than one answer. Indirect teaching calls for varied responses, whereas the direct style would call for a particular response from each child. As the children are solving a given problem in a series, the teacher may move around the playground and give individual assistance, which may include some direct teaching. Students

Basketball Contract

Activity_____

Date _____

I will	Goal	Time
1. Practice one-hand set shots from the foul line.	At least five from each area	15 minutes
2. Practice dribbling around cones using alternate hands.	Complete the course five times without losing control of the ball.	10 minutes

Signed _____

Evaluation

Did you reach your goal today?
What do you need help with?

_____

Figure 10.7   Sample open-ended contract (basketball).

From J.R. Thomas, K.T. Thomas, and A. Lee, 1988, *Physical education for children: Concepts into practice* (Champaign, IL: Human Kinetics), 112. Reprinted by permission of J.R. Thomas, K.T. Thomas, and A. Lee.

can be arranged in any formation and can work alone, with a partner, or in groups. The teacher presents the problem, provides time for students to experiment and explore, and encourages students to think critically about a solution.

At the primary level, an indirect approach can be quite effective in teaching lessons designed to vary movement patterns using the elements of movement (space, qualities, and relationships). Older children can explore relationships, direction, and variations using basic sport skills. Examples of movement problems for younger children and possible responses and extensions are presented in table 10.1. The problems and the extensions are designed from the movement concepts presented in chapter 9. Movement problems for older children might be designed for a specific sport. Table 10.1 presents problems for soccer.

Guided discovery is an indirect approach used when the teacher wants the students to discover a solution through a series of questions. This approach is a convergent, problem-solving process in which a predetermined answer or response is wanted by the teacher. With a series of well-designed questions, the teacher leads the students

Table 10.1   Examples of an Indirect Approach

Teacher	Responses	Extension
Show me three ways to travel around your hoop.	Walking backward Jumping sideways Crab walk	Try again. This time show me how your three movements can be made at a low level.
Discover different ways to toss your ball to your partner.	Underhand using two hands Underhand using one hand Overhand using two hands	Can you send the ball to your partner with other body parts?
Can you find three ways to send the soccer ball a short distance to a partner with your foot?	Kick with inside of foot Kick with outside of foot Kick with heel	Continue practice. Decide which part of the foot provides a more accurate kick.
How can you stop a soccer ball coming toward you in the air?	With the head With the body With the leg	Can you find other ways?

to the desired movement response. Another indirect approach used by teachers is **exploration,** which is an open-ended, divergent, problem-solving process. In this style, there are no predetermined or correct answers; the goal is for students to explore and create solutions on their own. Figure 10.8 shows sample activities for the direct approach, guided discovery, and exploration.

Physical education teachers have recently been encouraged to promote a learning environment that will encourage students to think critically (Werner 1995). It is believed that the more indirect styles of teaching are needed to accomplish this goal (Anderson, Reder, and Simon 1998). Critical thinking involves choosing from alternatives, applying knowledge in new situations, and analyzing and evaluating information. Students who think

critically process information at a higher level. Figure 10.9 shows some examples of ways to encourage critical thinking in physical education.

SUMMARY

A number of different teaching approaches can be used in physical education. Each one has a set of assets and liabilities. Students can become competent in many movement forms, can learn to apply concepts and principles to learning, and can achieve a health-enhancing level of physical fitness in classes using either a direct or an indirect approach. They can demonstrate responsible personal and social behavior, develop respect for differences

Sample Activities

Direct Approach

Follow the Leader, mirroring, finger plays, and Simon Says (played without the elimination process, of course) are examples of developmentally appropriate activities taught with a direct style of instruction. Also in this category are songs accompanied by unison clapping or movement, and rituals like the Mexican Hat Dance and the Hokey Pokey. If these activities are to be performed in a traditional manner, with all children doing the same things at the same time, the only expedient way to teach them is with a direct approach using demonstration and imitation.

Guided Discovery

The ultimate goal of the following questions and challenges is a forward roll. However, because guided discovery allows students to respond to challenges at their own developmental level and rate, even if children don't manage to perform the desired forward roll, their responses should be accepted. Ultimately all children can be led to the "correct" answer through convergent problem solving.

Specific challenges and questions will vary according to the responses elicited, but the following is an example of the process:

- Show me an upside-down position with your weight on your hands and feet.
- Show me an upside-down position with your weight on your hands and feet and your tummy facing the floor.
- Can you put your bottom in the air?
- Can you look behind yourself from that position?
- Can you look at the ceiling? Try to look at even more of the ceiling.
- Show me you can roll yourself over from that position. Can you do it more than once?

Exploration

Any challenge that results in a number of responses falls under the heading of exploration, or divergent problem solving. For example, a challenge to the children to make a crooked shape can result in as many shapes as there are students. A challenge to balance on two body parts can result in one child balancing on the feet, another on the knees, and still another, who may be enrolled in a gymnastics program, doing a handstand. Teachers must encourage children to continue producing divergent responses, but that encouragement should take the form of neutral feedback (e.g., "I see your two-part balance uses one hand and one foot").

Figure 10.8 Sample activities for teaching with different methods.

Reprinted, by permission, from R. Pica, 1995, "Exploration guided discovery and the direct approach," *Teaching Elementary Physical Education* 6(5): 5.

Direct Style

1. Hop forward five times. Then jump sideways three times.
2. Run straight across the room. Hop on one foot back.
3. Bounce the ball with your fingerpads.
4. Rise suddenly, directly, and with a lot of power (explode up), then slowly, directly, and gently sink as you make your body come to rest on the floor.
5. Balance on one foot in a scale position. Then do a forward roll.
6. Hit the ball with a flat racket as you hit your tennis forehand.
7. When dribbling the ball against the opponent, protect the ball by keeping your body between it and the opponent.

Indirect Styles

1. **Select:** Travel around the gymnasium using the steplike weight transfer actions. Each time you hear the drum, change the way you travel. Now each time you hear the drum, change the direction of your travel. Finally, change both your method of travel and direction when you hear the drum.
2. **Classify:** Today we are going to work on different ways to use our feet to travel, as we move in general space. You may use only your feet to travel. Ready, go . . . stop. Who can tell me one way? Yes. Walk, run (one foot to the other, alternating). Hop (one foot to the same). Can you try other ways? Yes, I see two to two (jump).
3. **Compare:** Try bouncing the ball with stiff fingers and slap at it with your palm (made lots of noise). Now try pushing the ball down with your fingerpads. Keep your fingers spread and try not to make any noise as you push the ball down to the floor. Which way seems to give you the most control?
4. **Explain, compare, contrast:** Try different rising and sinking actions. Vary the way you use time, force, and effort. Make the way you rise very different from the way you sink. Perform your sequence for a partner by taking turns. Then, compare and contrast your solutions. How were they the same? Different?
5. **Sequence:** Use a roll of your choice to link two balances smoothly.
6. **Apply:** I'm noticing that as you hit your forehand strokes, a lot of balls kind of pop up and go high into the air. Others often hit their ball down into the net. What can you do to change this and hit the balls over level but close to the net? How would this change your grip? Swing?
7. **Analyze:** Dribble a ball against an opponent in this space (15' x 40'). Start at one end and try to get to the other end without your opponent stealing the ball from you. How can you best protect the ball while dribbling down the court?

Figure 10.9   Examples of ways to encourage critical thinking.

Reprinted, by permission, from P. Werner, 1995, "Moving out of the comfort zone to address critical thinking," *Teaching Elementary Physical Education* 6(5): 7.

among participants, and develop an awareness of the intrinsic values of participation with a combination of the two approaches. If critical thinking is a goal, then more indirect approaches should be incorporated.

MASTERY LEARNING ACTIVITIES

1. Write three paragraphs: the first a summary of what you value, the second a contrast of direct and indirect styles of teaching, and the third matching a teaching style to your values. The reader should understand what you value, the direct and indirect styles, and why one style is better for you based on your values.
2. Select a concept based on one of the National Content Standards (NASPE). Develop a cooperative learning or critical thinking activity that would help students understand the concept.
3. Using kindergarten, third, and fifth grades, contrast the advantages and disadvantages of the direct and indirect methods for each age level.
4. Select a skill and a grade level. Develop either a contract or an individual skill sheet for that skill.

5. Develop a station teaching lesson for a specific grade. Make a time line for the lesson that indicates how much time you will spend introducing the stations, how long a group will stay at each station, and how long it will take to rotate. Be sure that the total time is less than or equal to a class period so that all students can rotate through all stations during one lesson. Describe how you will stay on time.

REFERENCES

Anderson, J.R., L.M. Reder, and H.A. Simon. 1998. Radical constructivism and cognitive psychology. In *Brookings papers on education policy: 1998,* edited by D. Ravitch, 227–55. Washington, D.C.: Brookings Institution.

Thomas, K.T. 1994. The development of expertise: From Leeds to Legend. *Quest* 46:199–210.

Werner, P. 1995. Moving out of the comfort zone to address critical thinking. *Teaching Elementary Physical Education* 6:7.

RESOURCES

Metzler, M.W. 2000. *Instructional models for physical education.* Needham Heights, Mass.: Allyn & Bacon.

Mosston, M., and S. Ashworth. 1994. *Teaching physical education.* 4th ed. New York: Macmillan College Publishing.

Pica, R. .1995. Exploration, guided discovery and the direct approach. *Teaching Elementary Physical Education* 6:5.

Siedentop, D., J. Herkowitz, and J. Rink. 1984. *Elementary physical education methods.* Englewood Cliffs, N.J.: Prentice Hall.

LESSON PLANS

The lesson plans at the end of this chapter show examples of the various approaches to teaching. The first lesson uses a direct teaching approach for introducing vigorous games. A fitness concept is introduced as a concluding activity. The second lesson uses a station formation, but the teaching approach is direct. The next two lessons use a direct approach to teach jumping rope and stunts. The following lessons illustrate a station approach and an individualized contract. The Games and Sports lesson uses stations to teach soccer skills, and the Fitness lesson combines stations and a fitness contract.

LESSON **10.1**

Moderate to Vigorous Games

Student Objectives

- Demonstrate stretching in a warm-up routine.
- Play a moderate to vigorous game.
- Describe how much exercise is needed to be physically fit.
- Demonstrate cooperation by playing one of the games.

Equipment and Materials

- 4 cones or tape, or if outside, flour or chalk
- 1 hoop or carpet square per group
- 1 playground ball
- 1 foam or small playground ball per group

Warm-Up Activities (5 minutes)

Arrange the children in scatter formation.

Stretching Routine

Shoulder Shrugs

Lift your shoulders to touch your ears, then return to relaxed position.

Side Stretches

Sit with your feet apart and knees slightly bent. Place one hand on your hip and extend the other arm up over your head. Slowly bend to the side toward the hand on your hip. Hold for 10 seconds and relax. Repeat in the opposite direction.

Ankle Rotations

Standing on one leg, make as large a circle as possible with the foot of the opposite leg. Your knee and hip should not move—only your ankle.

Stretching Routine 2

Keep the children in scatter formation.

1. Describe and demonstrate the four stretches.
2. Direct students to do the stretches in the following order:

   Eight shoulder shrugs

   Eight side stretches (four each side)

   Eight side lunges (four each side)

   Eight ankle rotations (four each ankle)
3. Repeat entire sequence.

Skill-Development Activities (20 minutes)

Select one or two games to play. Keep group sizes small to increase participation opportunities.

Leader Ball

Divide the children into groups of four to five children. Each group has a leader and a ball.

1. Describe and demonstrate the game:

   You will take turns being the leader.

Everyone stand behind the starting line shoulder to shoulder, facing the leader, who should stand about 10 ft away.

Jog in place all during the activity.

The leader throws the ball to the first child at one end of the line, who throws the ball back to the leader.

The leader throws it to the second child, who also throws it back to the leader. This continues until each child has caught and thrown the ball.

When the leader catches the ball tossed by the last child, the entire group runs to the end line (point to a line parallel to the starting line), and the child who was originally first in line becomes the new leader.

Keep playing until everyone has had a turn being the leader.

2. Designate a spot to put the ball while the children are running, such as a hoop or carpet square.

3. Have the children play Leader Ball.

Pair Tag

Arrange children, each holding hands with a partner, in equal numbers on two facing lines, 50 to 60 ft apart. One pair (also holding hands) is in the center between the two lines. These two are "It."

1. Describe and demonstrate the game:

With hands joined, the It pair tries to tag other pairs, who run from It to the opposite side of the play area on the go signal.

As pairs are tagged they also become It and join the other taggers in the middle.

When all pairs have been tagged, the last pair stands alone in the center for a new game. Any pair that drops hands must also join the taggers in the middle. Work with your partner so that when you're running one of you doesn't drag the other around.

2. Have the children play Pair Tag.

Delivery Relay

Divide the children into groups of four, and have two groups stand across from each other on each side of two lines, 60 ft apart.

1. Describe and demonstrate the game:

One child in each group will get a ball (or other small object).

On the signal, that child carries (delivers) the ball to a teammate at the other line. That child returns the ball to a child at the first line and so on until each child has carried the ball over the distance.

Jog in place while waiting for your turn.

2. Have the children play Delivery Relay, repeating as time allows.

Concluding Activities (5 minutes)

Physical Fitness Concept

Gather the children into an information formation.

1. Present the concept to the children: *A physically fit person exercises regularly, jogging, cycling, or swimming, doing sit-ups and push-ups, and stretching. These exercises can help our muscles stay healthy and keep our bodies from storing too much fat. To be physically fit we must exercise at least three times each week. It is best to spread the exercise throughout the week, rather than do three days in a row. But, if you can, exercising more than three days a week is great! Fun, active games also improve our health-related physical fitness.*

2. Ask: *How could we do this?* Discuss possible scenarios; for example, do fitness Monday, Wednesday, and Friday or Tuesday, Thursday, and Saturday.

3. Discuss activities that the children could do at home in addition to the program at school.

Alternative Learning Activities

1. Make a fitness contract and help the children fill it out.

2. Make a fitness calendar. For the current month, have each child mark days when they have done 30 minutes of total activity (at least 10 minutes at a time). Children may write the actual activities or parents may help.

From *Physical Education Methods for Elementary Teachers, Second Edition*, by Katherine T. Thomas, Amelia M. Lee, and Jerry R. Thomas, 2003, Champaign, IL: Human Kinetics. Adapted from *Physical Education for Children: Daily Lesson Plans for Elementary School, Second Edition*, by Katherine T. Thomas, Amelia M. Lee, and Jerry R. Thomas, 2000, Champaign, IL: Human Kinetics.

LESSON **10.2**

Jumping and Hopping With Hoops

Student Objectives

- Demonstrate jumping and hopping with good control.
- Work cooperatively with a group on hopping and jumping tasks.

Equipment and Materials

- 1 hoop (30–36 in.) per child

Warm-Up Activities (5 minutes)

Tortoise and Hare

Arrange the children in scatter formation.

1. Describe the activity:

   Run very slowly when I say, "Tortoise" and very fast when I say, "Hare."

   We will start with running in place, and move on to running in general space.

2. Have the children play Tortoise and Hare.

Skill-Development Activities (17 minutes)

Tasks for Hoops

Keep the children in scatter formation, and give each child a hoop.

1. Challenge the children with the following hoop tasks:

   Balance on your right (left) foot in the center of your hoop.

   While balancing on one foot, try to stretch your body tall (bend over and touch the ground, stretch your arms wide, swing your free leg).

   Jump around your hoop, forward (backward).

   Jump in and out of your hoop.

   Jump forward into your hoop. Jump backward out of your hoop.

   With one foot inside the hoop and one foot outside the hoop, jump around the hoop. Repeat, going backward.

   Hop inside your hoop five times on your right (left) foot.

   Hop forward around the outside of your hoop.

   Hop in and out of your hoop.

   Jump around the outside of your hoop, jump into the hoop and balance on one foot.

   Rearrange children in groups of three or four, each group with one hoop.

2. Challenge the groups with the following tasks:

   Jump around the hoop with your right side toward the hoop (clockwise).

   Take five giant steps away from the hoop, then hop back toward the hoop.

   Everyone stand in the hoop. (Combine groups to see how many children can fit into one hoop!)

Concluding Activities (8 minutes)

Jumping and Hopping Through Hoop Patterns Stations

Set up the four stations as shown in figure on this page. Divide the children into four groups, and place each group at one of the four stations.

1. Briefly describe and demonstrate each station.
2. Have the children perform the tasks.
3. Rotate the children to a new station every two minutes.

Station 1

Jump forward and backward through the hoops. Hop forward and backward through the hoops.

Station 2

Straddle jump (one foot in each hoop) forward and backward through the hoops. Hop through the hoops, creating a pattern.

Station 3

Hop forward and backward through the hoops. Jump through the hoops.

Station 4

Jump sideways through the hoops. Hop sideways through the hoops.

Station 1

Station 2

Station 3

Station 4

From *Physical Education Methods for Elementary Teachers, Second Edition*, by Katherine T. Thomas, Amelia M. Lee, and Jerry R. Thomas, 2003, Champaign, IL: Human Kinetics. Adapted from *Physical Education for Children: Daily Lesson Plans for Elementary School, Second Edition*, by Katherine T. Thomas, Amelia M. Lee, and Jerry R. Thomas, 2000, Champaign, IL: Human Kinetics.

Rhythmic Activities

LESSON  **10.3**

Rope Jumping

Student Objectives

- Perform two-foot singles and doubles (forward and backward) with a short jump rope.

Equipment and Materials

- 1 short jump rope per child
- Signal

Warm-Up Activities (5 minutes)

Use High, Low, Medium from lesson 5.3, page 106.
Variation: Specify a different locomotor skill or allow the children to select a skill.

Skill-Development Activities (20 minutes)

Two-Foot Singles

Arrange the children in scatter formation, each with a jump rope.

1. Describe and demonstrate the activity: *To do two-foot singles, jump on both feet once for each turn of the rope.*
2. Have the children practice two-foot singles, starting slowly, then going faster.

Two-Foot Doubles

Keep the children in scatter formation, each with a jump rope.

1. Describe and demonstrate the activity: *To do two-foot doubles, jump on both feet twice for each turn of the rope. The rope turns slower for two-foot doubles.*
2. Have the children practice two-foot doubles.

Basic Jump Backward

Keep the children in scatter formation, each with a jump rope.

1. Describe and demonstrate the activity: *For this jump, throw the rope backward and jump with both feet together as the rope hits the floor. This is a variation of the two-foot single.*
2. Have the children practice the basic jump backward.

Helicopter

Keep the children in scatter formation, each with a jump rope.

1. Describe and demonstrate the activity: *With both ends of the rope in one hand, swing the rope in a circle overhead. Make sure you keep a tight grip on the rope and watch out for your classmates.*
2. Have the children practice the helicopter.

Single-Side Taps

Keep the children in scatter formation, each with a jump rope.

1. Describe and demonstrate the activity: *With both ends of the rope in one hand, swing the rope in a circle to the side of your body.*
2. Have the children practice single-sided taps.

Double-Side Taps

Keep the children in scatter formation, each with a jump rope.

1. Describe and demonstrate the activity: *Holding both ends of the rope in one hand, swing the rope in a circle once on one side of your body and once on the opposite side of your body.*
2. Provide a drumbeat, and have the students practice double-side taps to a drumbeat with each hand.
3. Have the students practice jumping in place to a drumbeat while doing double-side taps.

Extension Activities

Have the children create routines using helicopters, single- and double-side taps, and two-foot single and double jumps.

Concluding Activities (5 minutes)

Don't Miss

Divide the class into four groups, each child with a jump rope. Each group should have jumpers of all achievement levels.

1. Describe the activity:

    Each of you will choose a type of jump and on the signal jump as many times as possible without a miss. Jumps can be two-foot singles or doubles or basic backward jumps.

    I will time you for one-minute periods, and you must each count the number of misses during each session.

    The group with the lowest number of misses wins. You are on your honor to count accurately.

2. Have the children do the activity. Repeat several times.

From *Physical Education Methods for Elementary Teachers, Second Edition,* by Katherine T. Thomas, Amelia M. Lee, and Jerry R. Thomas, 2003, Champaign, IL: Human Kinetics. Adapted from *Physical Education for Children: Daily Lesson Plans for Elementary School, Second Edition,* by Katherine T. Thomas, Amelia M. Lee, and Jerry R. Thomas, 2000, Champaign, IL: Human Kinetics.

LESSON **10.4**

Tricky Stunts

Student Objectives

- Attempt individual stunts.
- Have fun!

Equipment and Materials

- 1 or more mats (4 ft × 8 ft) per group

Safety Tips

- Children who have identified or complain of lower back problems should not do the double-jointed walk.

- The double-jointed walk should only be done for short distances.

Warm-Up Activities (5 minutes)

Follow the Leader

Arrange the children in a line.

1. Ask the first leader to perform locomotor skills, such as skipping, running, and jumping, as the group follows.

2. Ask a second leader to lead additional locomotor skills that the first leader did not think of.

3. If there are no additional locomotor skills, ask the new leader to do the grades 2–3 warm-up routine from lesson 7.3, page 156.

4. When that exercise is finished, ask the next child in line to lead another warm-up exercise, and so on, until the children have done all the warm-up exercises.

Skill-Development Activities (21 minutes)

The stunts and skills today are special—each is unique. Encourage the children to learn and have fun with these activities!

Around the World

Create small groups, and assign each group to a mat.

1. Describe and have a child demonstrate the stunt:

   Begin sitting with legs tucked tightly against your chest, knees apart, and ankles together. Put your upper arms between your legs, and wrap your lower arms around your lower legs. Keep your wrists flexed so that your hands meet in front of your ankles.

   Tuck your chin tightly against your chest, and roll your body to one side.

Continue the circular motion by lifting and rolling your torso.

2. Have the children practice Around the World.

Walking in Place

Continue in small groups with each group to a mat.

1. Describe and demonstrate the stunt:

    The object is to appear to walk while actually staying in one place.

    Move your arms back in an exaggerated way while stepping forward, dragging the supporting leg backward.

    You must get the support leg back a step before putting the swing leg down or you will move across the floor.

2. Have the children practice walking in place.

Heel Click

Continue in small groups with each group to a mat.

1. Describe and demonstrate the stunt: *Jump as high as possible into the air, tap your heels together one or more times, and land on both feet.*

2. Have the children practice the heel click.

Double-Jointed Walk

Remember, children with lower back problems or those who complain of discomfort when attempting this stunt should not do this stunt.

1. Describe and demonstrate the stunt:

    Begin squatting with your knees apart, feet together, and arms threaded through your legs. Try to clasp your hands in front of your ankles.

    Keep your shoulders close to your knees, with both upper arms between your legs.

    Wrap your forearms around your lower legs, with your wrists bent so that you can join your hands in front of your ankles.

    While holding your head high and looking forward, walk using a side-rocking motion.

2. Have the children practice the double-jointed walk.

Knee Touch

Continue in small groups with each group to a mat.

1. Describe and demonstrate the stunt:

    Standing on one leg, hold the foot of the opposite leg behind your seat.

    Dip down until the knee of your bent leg touches the floor.

2. Have the children practice the knee touch.

Scoot-Through

Continue in small groups with each group to a mat.

1. Describe and demonstrate the stunt:

   Begin in the push-up position with your arms supporting your body weight and your legs extended to the rear with your body in a straight line.

Without moving your hands or arms, slide your legs forward, keeping your legs as straight as possible until they pass between your arms. Continue sliding your legs through until your body is extended in front of your arms.

2. Have the children practice the Scoot-Through.

Concluding Activities (4 minutes)

Simon Says

Divide the students into small groups and scatter the groups around the play area, each group at a different mat. If there is room on the mats, all children can perform at once; otherwise, have the children perform in order. Pick one child in each group to start as Simon.

1. Describe the game:

   Simon tries to trick the group into doing something that Simon does not "say" to do. Use the individual stunts learned in this lesson.

   Simon gives commands, some of which begin "Simon says" (and then Simon names individual stunts from this lesson). The group should perform those tasks.

When Simon gives a command without saying "Simon says" (e.g., if Simon were to say, "Do the heel click"), the group should not perform the task.

Take turns, in order, for being Simon.

A turn ends as soon as Simon tricks someone.

When a different child becomes Simon, the old Simon moves to the end of the order.

A child doing a task that Simon did not say moves to the end of the order for performing and for being Simon, but keeps playing.

2. Have the children play Simon Says.

From *Physical Education Methods for Elementary Teachers, Second Edition,* by Katherine T. Thomas, Amelia M. Lee, and Jerry R. Thomas, 2003, Champaign, IL: Human Kinetics. Adapted from *Physical Education for Children: Daily Lesson Plans for Elementary School, Second Edition,* by Katherine T. Thomas, Amelia M. Lee, and Jerry R. Thomas, 2000, Champaign, IL: Human Kinetics.

Games and Sports

LESSON **10.5**

Soccer

Student Objectives

- Make progress toward refining the instep kick.
- Kick a ball in various directions.

Equipment and Materials

List is for one station circuit. If you set up more than one station circuit, you will need more equipment. See relevant text.

- 1 soccer ball per pair
- Station 1: 2 goals or targets
- Station 2: 1 cone
- Station 3: 1 large cardboard box
- 1 jump rope per child
- Chalk, flour, or tape to mark lines
- Signal

Warm-Up Activities (5 minutes)

Rope Jumping

Arrange the children in scatter formation, each with a jump rope.

1. Describe and demonstrate the activity: *Turn the rope at a slow tempo and use the two-foot double step (two jumps on both feet simultaneously for each rope turn).*

2. Have them do this 2 minutes, rest 30 seconds, jump rope for two more minutes, followed by another 30-second rest.

Skill-Development Activities (20 minutes)

Instep Kicking Stations

Assign a group of three or four to each station, each child with a ball. (Duplicate stations as needed to keep group size small.)

1. Describe and demonstrate each instep kicking station.
2. Have the children practice instep kicking at the stations.
3. Signal groups to rotate to a new station every five minutes.

Station 1: Passing for Goal

Mark a kicking line 25 ft from a goal line on which you have set up two targets or goals.

Kick to the right and to the left so that the ball travels between the goal markers, practicing until you can hit the target three times in a row before moving to a longer distance. (Distance can vary according to skill.)

Station 2: Kicking to Hit an Object

Mark a field about 30 by 30 ft and place a cone in the center of the field.

Kick from any boundary of the square and attempt to hit the cone in the center. Gradually increase the distance you kick from.

Station 3: Kicking the Ball off the Ground

Mark a field 20 by 20 ft and place a large cardboard box in the center of the field.

Kick a ball so that it travels off the ground and lands in a box. Gradually increase the distance you kick from.

Station 4: Kicking for Distance

Mark two kicking lines 30 yd apart.

Take turns with a partner kicking a ball as far as possible.

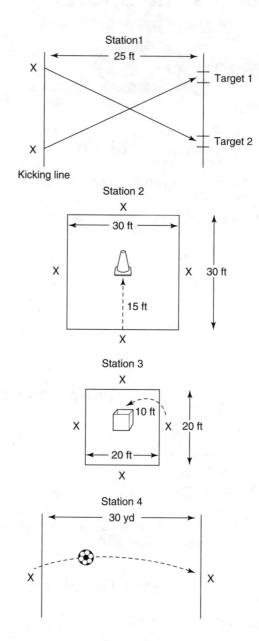

Concluding Activities (5 minutes)

Kickover

Create fields that are 10 by 20 ft, with a 5-ft goal marked by cones at one end. Mark kicking lines at 5, 10, 15, and 20 ft (see figure at right). Place two teams of three or four on each playing field, one ball per team.

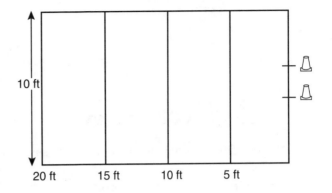

1. Describe the game:

   Give each player a chance to kick the ball (using the instep kick) toward the goal.

   Your team scores one point if the ball goes over the end line and two points for a successful hit into the goal area.

   Begin at the 5-ft line. After each player gets a kick from the 5-ft line, both teams move to the 10-ft line, and so on.

   The team with the most points at the end of the playing time wins.

2. Have the children play Kickover.

From *Physical Education Methods for Elementary Teachers, Second Edition,* by Katherine T. Thomas, Amelia M. Lee, and Jerry R. Thomas, 2003, Champaign, IL: Human Kinetics. Adapted from *Physical Education for Children: Daily Lesson Plans for Elementary School, Second Edition,* by Katherine T. Thomas, Amelia M. Lee, and Jerry R. Thomas, 2000, Champaign, IL: Human Kinetics.

LESSON

Developing a Fitness Contract

Student Objectives

- Make a fitness contract based on fitness evaluation.
- State one reason fitness is important.
- Participate in fitness activities independently.

Equipment and Materials

- Fitness Contract form
- Equipment needed for fitness stations
- Large task cards (at least 8 1/2 in. × 11 in.); if using stations, one per station

Skill-Development Activities (30 minutes)

Learning About Fitness Plans

Set up enough stations to create a circuit with task cards for groups of four to six students. To begin the lesson, however, first gather the children into an advanced information formation.

1. Discuss the importance of exercising on a regular basis, and work with students so they can develop realistic goals for exercise.

2. Show the children a sample set of fitness test scores. Ask the following:

    In what areas does this person need to improve to enjoy a basic level of health-related fitness? (If the flexibility score was low, this would be a target area.)

    What might be a realistic, specific goal in each of those areas? (Goals can range from participation for low-fit individuals, to a specific time or score.)

    What activities might this person do to reach each goal? (Walking and other aerobic activities are good, as well as stretching.)

How often should this person do those activities to have a good chance of reaching her goals? (Three or more times per week.)

3. Help the children work to develop a similar personal fitness plan.

4. Divide the children into groups of four to six. Have the groups rotate through a circuit, practicing fitness activities while you meet with each child at one station to discuss his personal plan and to sign a written agreement to try to improve their fitness level outside of class. Use the fitness contract shown on page 263 or develop one that meets your needs.

5. Explain that you will give the fitness tests again later during the year so that they can see improvement.

CARDIOVASCULAR ENDURANCE PROGRAM CONTRACT

I, _____, do hereby contract to exercise for 20 minutes three times a week for 10 weeks. My exercise heart rate will be _____.

Week	Days	Type of exercise	Duration
1			
2			
3			
4			
5			
6			
7			
8			
9			
10			

Approved by _____

Date _____

From *Physical Education Methods for Elementary Teachers, Second Edition,* by Katherine T. Thomas, Amelia M. Lee, and Jerry R. Thomas, 2003, Champaign, IL: Human Kinetics. Adapted from *Physical Education for Children: Daily Lesson Plans for Elementary School, Second Edition,* by Katherine T. Thomas, Amelia M. Lee, and Jerry R. Thomas, 2000, Champaign, IL: Human Kinetics.

chapter 11

Managing Students

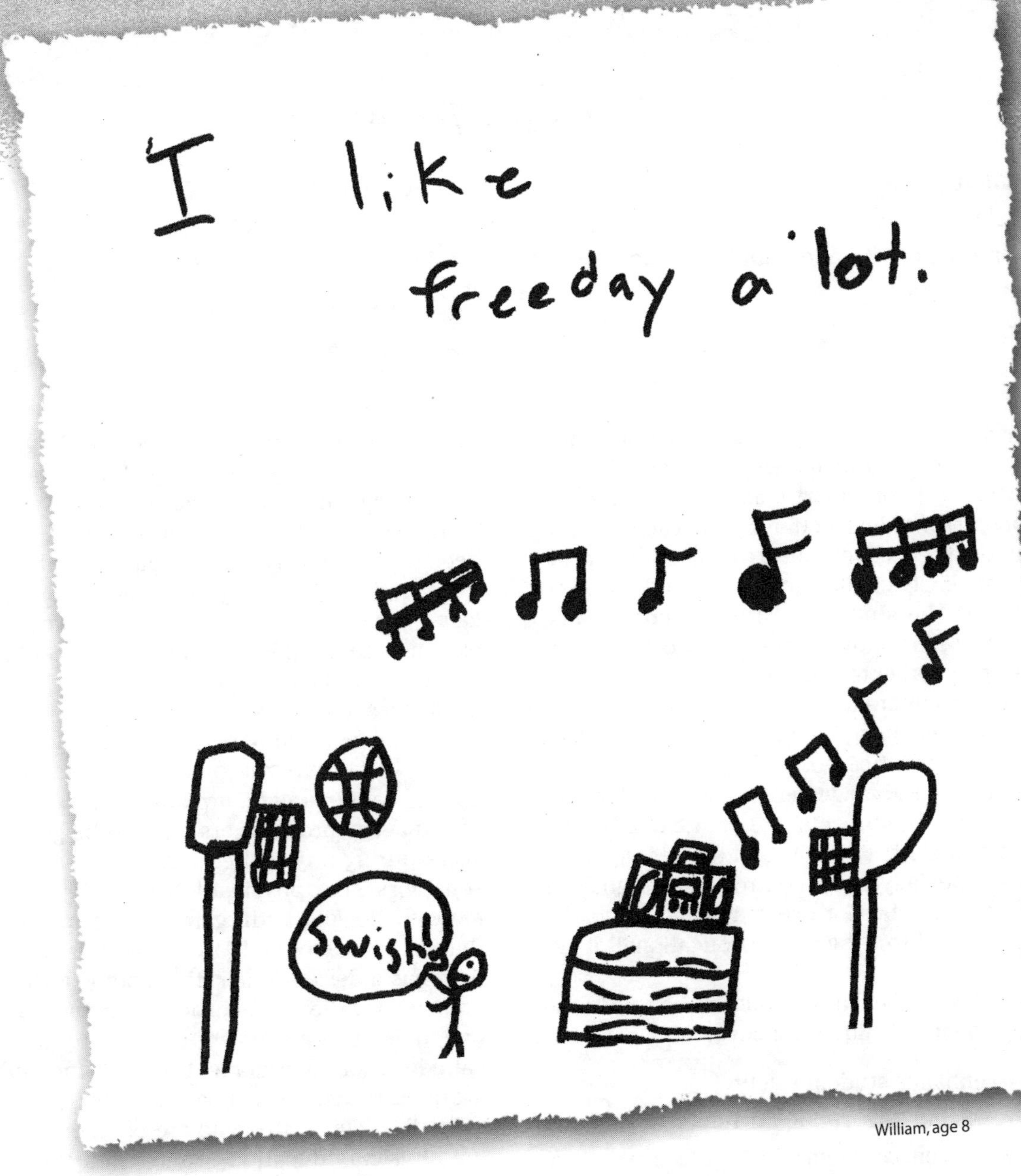

William, age 8

M anagement is a precursor to instruction. It allows teachers to prevent problems, keep students safe, and maximize time for instruction and practice.

Learner Outcomes

The teacher will do the following:

- Describe the relationship and differences between management and instruction.

- Define and demonstrate at least five management techniques.
- Explain how to adjust management techniques for use with various grade levels of students.

Glossary Terms

management
class signals
initial activity and concluding activity
transition

formations
class rules
desist
time-out

D arryl Siedentop (1998) has said that all expert teachers are good managers; however, all good managers are not expert teachers. Management is a precursor to instruction. Some teachers manage students effectively but do not provide instruction (especially challenging tasks, feedback, and practice). The students are under control and seem busy and happy, but this does not mean they are learning. Other teachers use management techniques to facilitate teaching and learning. Teaching includes planning, instruction, directions, demonstrations, practice, goal setting, cues, feedback, and evaluation. **Management** is a set of techniques used to control students and create a safe environment, including routines and rules. Management—especially class control—is the goal for some teachers; but for expert teachers, management is a tool to achieve the educational objectives.

Teachers need to know about and be able to use management techniques for several reasons:

- To enhance student safety
- To ensure time and opportunity for learning
- To prevent problems during physical education

The most basic skill of teaching is managing students, including keeping them safe and under control, taking care of administrative tasks (e.g., attendance), and holding their attention. Perhaps because these tasks are obvious and inherent in the description of being a teacher, or perhaps because expert teachers make management look easy, novice teachers assume management of students is easy. Planning for management is critical for successful teaching and learning; it is what makes management look effortless! Physical education, because of the facilities and activities involved, requires careful planning and execution of management. Teachers need to be good managers during physical education for several reasons. First, the physical location of students is more challenging in the gym or on the playground than in a classroom. In the classroom, each student has a desk or chair; that spot is a clear and personal location, unlike location in the gym. Second, noise and movement complicate the physical education environment; even if the children are quiet, the equipment often is noisy (e.g., bouncing balls). Third, students are often excited during physical education, where both the performance and emotions are on public display. In a classroom, student work is often private—no one can see it—whereas in physical education, performance is conducted in front of others—often important others. As discussed in chapter 1, movement skills are important; this places additional stress on students to do well in front of others. The additive effect of these factors can make physical education a volatile subject that demands good management. Good management can also help students achieve the fifth national content standard: "Demonstrates responsible personal and social behavior in physical activity setting."

MANAGEMENT COMPONENTS

Management has six components: class signal, initial and concluding activities, transitions and

Management is important for teachers to create a comfortable, safe, and successful learning environment. It can include posting physical education rules on the wall and giving students enough space to participate in the movements.

formations, handling equipment, class rules, and intrusive events. Those components will be discussed in this chapter. As children are introduced to your management system, positive reinforcement of good behaviors is recommended, such as, "I really like the way you lined up today," "Thank you for stopping and listening so quickly," or "Chris did a great job putting away our equipment today, let's say 'thanks.' "

Class Signal

Getting the student's attention in the gym is a challenge; doing so outdoors is even more challenging. The purpose of most **class signals** is for students to stop, look, listen, and be quiet as quickly as possible. Signals include noise makers (e.g., tambourine, bell) and hand signals. Many of you recall physical education teachers using a whistle. In elementary school, a whistle is generally not the best signal. Teachers sometimes become dependent on the whistle and use it rather than planning carefully. Whistles are often used for starting and stopping activities, refereeing games, and expressing dissatisfaction. A raised hand is a popular signal; students like to be among the first to notice. A variation is the give-me-five signal, where the teacher's raised hand is mirrored by students. The five fingers mean feet still, hands at sides, eyes looking, ears listening, and brain thinking. Another signal that requires students to respond is the mirror clapping signal. In this case the teacher claps a pattern and the students respond with that pattern. Signals that require students to respond with an answer (e.g., with raised arm or clapping) are fun and inclusive but usually take more time.

Some teachers use the same signal every day and all year. Other teachers use a variety of signals. As long as children know the signal and what to do when the signal is given, either technique works well.

Initial and Concluding Activities

Classroom teachers usually escort students to the gym for physical education, turning the students over to the physical education teacher. The first thing students do at or in the gym is the **initial activity.** Some teachers use squads, others a line, but at some point the class has a routine that signals the beginning of physical education. When classroom teachers teach physical education, the same type of initial activity signals the beginning physical education. Opening the door to the gym and having children run chaotically around the gym is not an initial activity. Students need to know what to do first, where to go, and what to expect. If attendance is part of the routine, it can be handled during this initial activity. The following are some ideas for initial activities:

▶ On a 20-foot square on the floor, marked with four tape lines of different colors, children are grouped by color at the beginning of the year. For grades 2 through 5, instructions for challenges are written on a dry erase board (e.g., balance on your right foot for 10 counts, 10 jumping jacks); for grades K and 1, the challenges remain the same for several weeks (e.g., touch toes 10 times; stretch to the sky 10 times).

▶ Three rows and 25 columns of symbols are taped to the wall. Row 1 is shapes (square, triangle, or circle, which are red, blue, green, and yellow); row 2 is numbers (1 through 25); and row 3 is balls (tennis, basketball, football, or soccer). Children

are assigned a spot (one of the columns) to stand in front of after entering the gym. Attendance is taken by recording the numbers without students. This system helps manage class later, too, as groups are made by selecting the row that forms the size and number appropriate to the activity. If the teacher wants four groups, she simply says, "Footballs to station 1, tennis to station 2, basketball to station 3, and soccer to station 4" or "Squares and triangles are in the field; circles and rectangles at bat" (figure 11.1).

▶ Students enter the gym and run (or hop, skip, or gallop) until the music stops. The pattern (cones, lines, circle) is predetermined and remains the same for every class.

Each of these activities establishes a routine, so students know exactly what to do once they enter the gym. Class ends in a similar way, with a routine. Students transition from physical education teacher to classroom teacher (or gym to classroom) in the same way each class. The following are ideas for **concluding activities:**

Figure 11.1   One of the ways a teacher can help manage students is to use wall markers of shapes and numbers to group students quickly.

▶ A set of footprints marks a spot for the line leader to stand (away from the door); other students line up behind the line leader. The teacher gives students "high five" as they leave the gym.

▶ The students stand on a line, and the teacher asks them to rate themselves on skill, behavior, and cooperation for the day. Once the teacher and students agree on the ratings, the students walk quietly out of the gym.

▶ Students sit on markers. The class must add a physical education vocabulary word to the word list on the wall. The word must have been used in class and must be new (not already on the wall). The teacher writes the word and tapes it to the wall.

Notice these activities are not the same as an instructional warm-up or a concluding activity. These are part of the class routine, established to make children comfortable and to keep control. The initial and concluding activities do not have to be long; 10 to 60 seconds is enough time to set a clear beginning and ending point to the physical education class.

Transitions and Formations

Two types of **transition** occur in physical education: the physical transition and the cognitive or activity transition. The physical transition moves students from one location, or **formation,** to another. The cognitive or activity transition changes "gears"; students may stay in one place but be expected to do something very different after the transition. Both transitions require planning. Generally, the cognitive transition starts with closure on the previous idea or activity, then provides an anticipatory set or introduction to what will come next. This is easier if the two activities are related or can be related. If the activities have nothing to do with each other, teachers help students to make the transition by saying, "Now we are changing gears; we are going to do something completely different."

Formations that groups of children can take include shapes, groups, and spacing. The easiest are those made with a landmark—a line on the floor, a cone, carpet square, or poly-spot. Poly-spots can be purchased from physical activity equipment companies. These come in a variety of shapes and colors. Children often use landmarks, like the line or circle formation, to create shape formations. Formations include boundaries; that is, where

does the line end? Establishing boundaries is important; they should not be by default. Often, boundaries are the walls. This may be inadequate for running activities, however, where running to the wall may cause injury. Cones, lines, and other markers can be used to establish boundaries. Outdoors, the edge of the hard surface often makes a good boundary. Teachers should clearly mark and state boundary locations for any space and sometimes for each activity.

Groups come in all sizes, from 2 (partners) to 10 or more. Spacing can be either close or far and personal or general. Close spacing occurs when students are near enough to each other to touch; far spacing occurs when students are far enough apart so that touching is not possible. Personal space is the area around your body, defined by extending your arms in all directions. General space is all the space that is not personal space. Scatter formation is when students are randomly placed in far spacing.

To spend as little time as possible when moving students into formations, note the following hints:

▶ Have a system in place to put students in groups of various sizes (e.g., squads, marks on the wall, alphabetical groups).

▶ Use physical landmarks to form lines, circles, and other shapes.

▶ Change formations as few times as possible.

▶ If possible, order the activities so that those using the same formation are presented together.

Poor cognitive or activity transitions are apparent when children answer questions with off-the-topic comments, an answer appropriate for the previous topic but not the current topic, or a motor response that is no longer appropriate. Three things will keep students with you during these transitions:

1. An overview at the beginning of class that outlines the content for the day (this alerts students that there will be transitions)

2. Reminding students during the transition of the change (e.g., "now we are changing gears")

3. Using different terminology or a different voice (e.g., tone or loudness) after the transition

Handling Equipment

Equipment creates two problems for management. First, equipment can change the excitement, noise, or self-control of students to an inappropriate level. Second, equipment can take too much time from instruction and practice. Distribution of playground balls is often irresistible, even for college students, and the balls are bounced as the teacher tries to give directions. One strategy is to keep the equipment out of sight and out of reach until it is needed. Another is to separate equipment and students but have equipment ready and distributed around the gym. A constant tension exists between the time available to distribute equipment and class control. The type of equipment, class routine, and student characteristics (e.g., age, experience, self-control) influence the decisions teachers make about how to handle equipment.

The most efficient way to handle equipment is to have it located where it will be used and ready for use, although this can be tempting to students. For older students and classes with well-established routines, this method is preferred. Alternatively, one student can get equipment for several students. This works especially well when a group will be using the equipment but can also work when each child in a group needs equipment. Finally, the most conservative and time-consuming method is for the teacher to distribute equipment to each student or for students to get their equipment one at a time.

Practice with distributing and returning equipment improves the process if the teacher provides instruction and feedback. Clear instructions and expectations, with cues and reminders, are also helpful. Learning how to deal with equipment is an important part of physical education. Students can learn self-control, listening, sharing, and helping when teachers make these learning objectives.

Class Rules

Class rules have two purposes: to keep students safe and to allow learning. Class rules should be centered on those two purposes. The sixth National Content Standard is that the student should demonstrate understanding and respect for differences among people in physical activity set-

tings. One way that a teacher can help students achieve this goal is through comprehensive rules that are clearly explained. Students cannot follow the rules unless they know them. Rules should be stated in the positive rather than the negative. Rules should be broad enough to handle a variety of situations. For example, "Hands to self" rather than "Don't hit, don't kick, don't touch, and don't take." Older children can help make the rules for the class; however, teachers may have to guide students to cover all the necessary areas. Therefore, before allowing students to make up their "own" rules, outline the rules yourself. If the students do not mention one of your rules, you may be able to guide them to suggest it by giving an example of a situation calling for the rule. For example, if students do not propose a rule related to equipment, you might stimulate thought by saying, "What happens at home if one of your toys is broken?" Usually, this means the child has less to play with, and thus the child will suggest being careful with equipment. Often management is a direct approach to instruction, but this is a clear opportunity for indirect instruction by guiding or questioning students. Most children prefer to know and follow the rules. For many children (and adults), it is embarrassing to do something wrong. This means that it is important to explain the rules, give examples, and help children understand why rules are important (e.g., to keep the students safe and allow them to learn). Posting the rules is helpful (table 11.1).

When children are disruptive or break a rule, several options are available:

► Ignore the child and behavior.
► Give a general reminder.
► Desist.
► Issue a warning.
► Punish the child.

Hint

To improve student behavior, catch students doing something right and reinforce the good behavior.

Teachers should handle misbehavior by adhering consistently to school or school district discipline plans. Generally these policies focus on punishment systems; for example, issue a warning, declare a time-out, send the student to the office, and call the parent. However, management and class rules should be preventive and reduce the need for punishment. The first thing a teacher must do is to determine why the child is breaking the rule. If it is to gain the attention of the teacher, ignoring may be the best solution. Catching students doing something right and recognizing or reinforcing the good behavior are the best ways to encourage good behavior. It is possible that the student does not remember the rule or know that the rule applies in this behavior situation. In that circumstance, a general reminder to the class about the rule may work best. A **desist** is another way to handle problems; it is used, when a student is talking while the teacher is talking or a student is touching another student. The teacher simply moves close to the offending student without interrupting instruction. In a desist, the teacher gains proximity, does not point out the infraction, and continues with class as though nothing happened. There are several useful variations on the desist:

► The teacher looks at the offending student and attempts to make eye contact until the target behavior stops.

► A pat on the back—the teacher touches the student (e.g., on the shoulder) as a reminder that the teacher is paying attention.

► Changing the subject—the teacher asks the student a question or for assistance with a task.

Deciding how to change student behavior is based on several factors. The first guideline is to interrupt instruction as little as possible. That is the advantage of a desist. Second, change the behavior with as few consequences as possible. Consequences range from embarrassment to punishment. The desist and its variations meet these requirements; that is, instruction is not interrupted and the consequences are very low, although behavior is often changed immediately.

In situations where students or classes are a continual source of disruption, an action plan may be the best solution. Behavior letters (figure 11.2), awards (figure 11.3), monitoring-reporting forms (figure 11.4), and behavior contracts (figure 11.5) all work toward changing behavior in the long term. Teachers should recognize and reinforce good behavior out loud and in writing. Typically, bad behavior is difficult to ignore, so it is recognized and reported; but recognizing good behavior is also important. Reporting disruptive behavior can be a reminder to report good behavior, so each time a bad behavior is noted at least one good behavior is also noted.

The time-out is often recommended to change student behavior. **Time-out** is isolating a student physically and in terms of instruction. In physical education, a time-out allows a student time to calm down, which is often what is needed. However, some students may prefer to sit on the sidelines, so time-out is not a punishment. For any conse-

Table 11.1 Sample Class Rules

	First grade	Fifth grade
1	Be nice.	Avoid hostile gestures, fighting, and game disruptions.
2	Hands off.	Keep hands, feet, and objects to yourself.
3	Be careful.	Use equipment only as it is intended.
4	Listen and do.	Follow instructions the first time they are given.
5	Do your best.	Stop, look, and listen on the signal.

quence to be effective, the consequence must actually force the student to change the behavior. Therefore, consequences—even for the same behavior—must be individualized for each student. For the student who really wants to play, time-out works; however, for the student who does not care about playing, time-out will not be effective. This principle applies to all consequences (e.g., send to office, call parent). Physical activity is never an appropriate punishment because that is what we want students to learn and enjoy.

Intrusive Events

Intrusive events interfere with teaching. Two examples are when students get a drink of water or go to the bathroom. In chapter 6, we learned that water is important. If students must leave the instructional area to get water, student safety is a primary concern; secondary to that is maintaining continuity of class. Assuming it is safe, how will you allow students to get a drink without having each student ask individually? Another consideration is having more than one student gone at a time; this can increase risk and can disrupt play or instruction. Many teachers use a pass system. This works well until the pass is lost. A recommended method

is to put a two-sided sign in a pocket on the wall. One side says "stop" and is red, the other side says "go" and is green. When a child goes for a drink or to the bathroom, he switches the sign to "stop"; upon returning, he switches it back to "go." The teacher can glance at the sign, as can all other students, and know a student is gone.

Other intrusive events include messages, delivered either over the public address system or directly to the teacher, and emergencies. Some emergencies are covered by the school plan (e.g., fire drills, tornado drills); others are part of the class first aid and emergency plan. The procedure for an injury should be written and posted on the wall of the gym. Critical information includes the 911 emergency phone information (and the school name, address, and phone number for use when making 911 calls), whom to notify in the school (e.g., the nurse or principal), the location of first aid supplies, and what the students should do during the emergency. Once you develop a plan, share the plan with the principal and school nurse, then revise the plan after talking to them. Once everyone agrees with the plan, share and discuss it with your students. Ice packs, a first aid kit, accident reports (figure 11.6), and a phone are essential emergency supplies (see chapter 12 for a more complete list).

Dear (parent name):

You will be pleased to know that your child, (child's name), has been exhibiting the following good behavior in physical education class:

- Following instructions
- Using equipment appropriately
- Participating in all activities
- Being courteous to other students

You and your child are to be commended. Thank you for your cooperation.

Sincerely,

(teacher's name)

Figure 11.2 Sample letter to notify parent of good behavior.

Teacher's Award for Good Behavior

presented to

_____

for
following behavior rules

_____
Principal

_____
Teacher

Figure 11.3 Award for good behavior.

Behavior Contract

I, (student's name), will do the following:

1. Practice the skills at each station.

2. Not push or hit other students during physical education this week.

_____
(student's signature)

I, (teacher's name), will do the following:

1. Allow (student's name) to select the game for the day.

2. Appoint (student's name) equipment manager for the day, next week.

_____
(teacher's signature)

Figure 11.5 Behavior contract.

Name of child	(Date)

Behavior Report

Fails to follow instructions.	❑
Is verbally hostile.	❑
Physically abuses another student.	❑
Disrupts a game or activity.	❑
Misuses equipment.	❑
Fails to stop on the signal	❑

Teacher's signature

Figure 11.4 Observation form for monitoring and reporting behavior.

Incident Report Form

Name of student _____ Grade _____ Age _____

Date of incident _____ Time of incident _____

Did the incident occur during
- ❏ Class? If checked, what class? _____
- ❏ Recess?
- ❏ Other? If checked, please explain. _____

Nature of incident
- ❏ Injury (accidental)
- ❏ Injury (not accidental)
- ❏ Verbal abuse
- ❏ Other (explain) _____

Describe the incident:

Location _____

People involved _____

What happened _____

Immediate action taken _____

Was there an injury?   Yes ❏   No ❏   If yes, describe the degree (nondisabling, temporarily disabling).

_____

Was a teacher present at the time?   Yes ❏   No ❏   Name _____

Other witnesses: Name   Class

_____

_____

Was the parent notified?   Yes ❏   No ❏

What could be done to prevent similar incidents? _____

_____

Signature _____

Figure 11.6   Accident and incident report.

From *Physical Education Methods for Elementary Teachers, Second Edition,* by Katherine T. Thomas, Amelia M. Lee, and Jerry R. Thomas, 2003, Champaign, IL: Human Kinetics.

LEGAL LIABILITY

Chapter 12 provides greater detail on legal liability. The purpose of this section is to demonstrate the relationship between management and liability. Teachers are responsible for the care and safety of their students. Because teachers care about students and therefore want them to be safe, teachers need to understand their legal responsibility. A teacher's legal responsibility is based on negligence. Negligence is defined as an act that does not meet the standards established by law for protection of children against unreasonable danger or risk of injury. This is often called the "standard of care" in legal terms and refers to "best practices" in educational terms. To establish negligence, it must be proven in court that a teacher failed to take necessary action to ensure the safety of a student and that this failure to act resulted in an injury. Negligence may also be established if a teacher commits an act that a reasonable person would have realized involved risk of injury, and an injury did result. Thus, a teacher can fail to act, can act inappropriately, or can act in a way that falls below a certain standard required by law and be considered negligent. In fulfilling the responsibility to maintain a safe environment for children, the teacher should provide adequate supervision, plan activities appropriate for the participants, maintain a safe play area, provide adequate instruction, and establish procedures for emergency care. Four factors influence negligence. These are adequate supervision, safe environments, adequate instruction, and appropriate emergency procedures.

Teachers should never leave children unsupervised on a playground or in the gymnasium—just being in the area is not enough. Supervisors need to be aware of what is going on, make students aware of safety factors, and be accessible to any student needing help. Children must learn to move under control and to think about their actions. Teachers must select a location for observing students that provides the best view of the most children. Two other factors influence the location a teacher selects for observing: first, the risk associated with the activity or equipment, and second, student characteristics. If the activities or equipment used in a lesson are generally low risk, but one activity is of greater risk, the teacher should consider locating near the highest-risk activity. Sometimes, however, risk is associated with students—those most likely to misuse equipment or move out of control. Then the teacher must decide where the risk is greatest and locate there.

One technique to facilitate supervision is orientation with the "teacher's back to the wall." This means no students can get behind the teacher and out of view. Teachers can walk the perimeter, trying to view as much as possible of the class. When it is impossible to see the entire area, the teacher should constantly scan the area. Typically, an experienced teacher's vision is captured by an out-of-boundary activity—something that looks different than expected. For example, the teacher is expecting to see all the children moving across the gym floor in about the same way; however, three boys in the back row are several steps behind the group—a sure sign they are not on task. If no harm has been done, and the boys are back on track, the teacher continues to scan. On the other hand, the teacher needs to intervene if the boys continue misbehaving by pushing and shoving each other. Good scanning captures these events; the teacher decides how to handle them, and scanning continues. Even when the teacher must respond to the event that captured her vision, the scanning should continue as soon as possible. When teachers are forced to stop scanning, they may need to stop all activity until it is possible to begin scanning again. With the previous example, the teacher may stop all activity and say, "Why did I ask everyone to stop?" hoping for someone to share; or she may say, "There is no reason for anyone to touch another student during this activity." The teacher may reorganize students so that the three boys are no longer together, or she may decide to stand closer to the boys but still in a position to see the whole class. At times, teachers will need to leave the perimeter, moving through or into the instructional area. Teachers should know that this can increase risk, especially if students will then be behind the teacher. Teachers scan in the classroom, too, and in fact it may be more difficult to identify inappropriate behaviors there—for example, children off task—than in the gym. Scanning is an important skill any time children are present (e.g., playground, bus duty, cafeteria, classroom, gym).

Teachers should examine small equipment for damage and inspect large equipment regularly. An excellent source of information about equipment and facilities is the National Playground Safety Commission Web site (www.cpsc.gov). Guidelines on the site for safe equipment and recall information are updated regularly. When ensuring a safe environment, teachers should check surfaces, making sure indoor surfaces are clean and dry and outdoor hard surfaces are dry and free of debris. Soft outdoor surfaces should be appropriately maintained (e.g., grass mowed and reasonably dry, sand deep and raked, bark or shavings deep). Even under the best circumstances, accidents can happen. The point is to avoid injuries that *can* be avoided. Teachers need to find out who at the school is responsible for checking equipment and maintaining facilities. Although it would be ideal to have these duties assigned to maintenance staff, this should not be assumed. A checklist of the times and dates that equipment and facilities are checked is helpful. In any case, do not let your students use equipment or facilities that are unsafe; do everything reasonable to prevent anyone from being injured.

Adequate instruction has two components: instruction for skill and instruction for safety. This applies to both free play (e.g., recess) and class time. Good management practices cover this instruction for class time. Teachers should be proactive, making sure that recess and other free play are safe by instructing students about safety and skill.

Teachers must use good judgment when making decisions based on natural hazards such as weather conditions (e.g., heat and humidity), insects, and animals. It is better to be too conservative than to increase risk for students. Generally, when teachers are trying to do the "right thing" and have reasons for their decisions, their liability will be low. Using good management reduces liability.

SUMMARY

Management is important because it reduces risk, increases safety, and allows more time for learning. Routines, a basic component of management, make students comfortable. Good management reduces teacher liability. Management also allows children to develop the skills necessary to be physically educated as they learn to demonstrate responsible personal and social behaviors and to show respect for differences among people by following class rules.

MASTERY LEARNING ACTIVITIES

1. Examine lesson 11.1 for grades K and 1 and lesson 11.4 for lessons for 4 and 5. What are the differences between the grades? List the management techniques used in the lessons.
2. Write an emergency plan to be posted on the gym wall.
3. Fill in the following matrix.
4. Describe the four factors determining legal liability (negligence).

	Definition	Example 1	Example 2	Example 3
Signal				
Rules				
Formations				
Boundaries				
Intrusive event				
Initial activity				
Concluding activity				
Emergency procedure				

REFERENCES

Siedentop, D. 1998. In search of effective teaching: What we have learned from studying teachers and students. McCloy Lecture presented at the Annual Meeting of the American Alliance for Health, Physical Education, Recreation and Dance, Portland, Ore. April 7, 1998.

National Playground Safety Commission. www.cpsc.gov.

U.S. Consumer Product Safety Commission. *Handbook for public playground safety,* Publication 325. Washington, D.C: United States Government Printing Office.

RESOURCES

Siedentop, D., J. Herkowitz, and J. Rink. 1984. *Elementary physical education methods.* Englewood Cliffs, N.J.: Prentice Hall.

LESSON PLANS

The four lesson plans at the end of this chapter demonstrate how to teach students about rules, formations, handling equipment, and other management techniques. The lessons are fun and teach important skills. Notice how the techniques and practice change as children mature. Teachers should cover the basics of class organization at the beginning of the school year and again as necessary throughout the school year. The investment of time in planning is worthwhile because in the long run it prevents problems and increases instructional time.

LESSON **11.1**

Signals, Rules, and Boundaries

Student Objectives

- Identify safety and learning as benefits of having and following rules.
- Identify the class signals.
- Practice starting and stopping on signal.
- Move into information formation on a signal.
- Move within and around boundaries.

Equipment and Materials

- Chalkboard or flip chart (or poster board, large paper) for writing
- 1 carpet square per child
- 5–10 beanbags

Warm-Up Activities (5 minutes)

Islands in the Ocean

Arrange carpet squares so that there are six or more ft between each square. Each child should be sitting on a carpet square.

1. Explain that each carpet square is an island, so each child has her own island. The islands are small, and the children must try to stay "dry" by staying on the carpet square.

2. Call out the following movements and positions, reminding children to stay on the squares: *Stand up, walk, lie down, sit on your knees, sit down and touch your feet, stand up and touch your feet, jump, turn around, and sit down.* You can repeat any of the movements and speed up or slow down the changes in movements, depending on how successful the children are at each movement.

3. Compliment children who stay on the squares.

Skill-Development Activities (20 minutes)

Physical Education Rules

Arrange the children in a close group sitting on the floor on the carpet squares.

1. Explain the formation: *This is called an "information formation." When I say, "information formation," you should move to this close group, sitting on the floor. We will practice this again later.*

2. Ask the children: *What might happen if we did not have rules or laws? For example, how do traffic rules help us?* (If there were no stop signs or cars did not stop at the signs, there would probably be many accidents. Many people could be hurt. Having rules and following rules keep us safer.)

3. *What rules should we have in physical education so everyone can be safer?* Lead a discus-

sion to rules 1 through 3. Write the rules on the chalkboard or paper:

- *Rule 1: Hands off. This means we do not put our hands, feet, or other body parts on anyone else so that everyone will be safe.*

- *Rule 2: Be careful. Do not hurt equipment; do not move wildly so everyone will be safe and so the equipment will stay in good condition for physical education.*

- *Rule 3: Listen and look for the stop signals. When you hear or see the signal, stop, listen, and look at the teacher.* Demonstrate the stop signal. Say to the children, *Show me the stop signal. Good remembering! Following the stop signal helps everyone hear instructions and stay safe.*

4. *These rules give everyone the same opportunity, or chance, to learn. What other situations should we have rules for?* (When one child does not hear the instructions because another child is talking, when one child keeps a piece of equipment [e.g., a ball] too long so other children do not have the chance to practice, and so on.) Lead the discussion to rules 4 through 6.

   • *Rule 4: Be nice. Do not fight; do not bother others; be helpful. Being nice keeps everyone safe, learning, and having fun!*

   • *Rule 5: Listen and do. When the teacher is talking, you should not talk; when another student has permission to talk, please don't talk; it is OK to talk quietly at other times; do what you are instructed to do.* Some teachers prefer to have a signal for quiet that differs from the stop signal, such as a raised hand or finger over the mouth. If you wish to have a separate quiet signal, explain and demonstrate it now.

   • *Rule 6: Do your best. Always try everything and work hard. This rule makes sure everyone will learn and feel good about physical education.*

5. Continue the discussion about the importance of following rules until you think the children have a good understanding of acceptable behavior in the physical education setting. Most "rules" the children will come up with will be variations or examples of the six rules already listed. Help the children to categorize these as such. Write any further rules on the chalkboard or paper.

6. *Note:* After class, make a poster of your final version of class rules for future reference.

Moving Within and Around Boundaries

Using the four cones, mark a large rectangle in the playing area.

1. Relate this activity to rule 5: Listen and do. Tell the children: *Having boundaries helps us to be safe and learn, because if you are too far away, you might not be able to hear what to do or you might be in danger.*

2. Walk the entire class around the sides of the rectangle formed by the four cones.

3. Show them the boundary lines between the cones. Describe the boundary lines: *These are like invisible walls, and the area "inside" is like a room. On the other side of the wall is the "outside."* Scatter the children inside the "room."

4. Signal the children: *Move carefully but freely (randomly) inside.* Signal stop. Compliment those who stop quickly and quietly.

5. *Move along the boundaries on the outside of the line.* Signal stop. Offer compliments.

6. *Move along the boundaries on the inside of the line.* Signal stop. Offer compliments.

7. *Move along the boundaries on the outside.* Signal stop. Offer compliments.

8. Repeat steps 4 through 7 as time permits.

Concluding Activities (5 minutes)

Physical Education Rules

Signal the children to create the information formation.

1. Compliment those who remember the formation and gather quickly and quietly.

2. Repeat the rules that were written earlier and ask: *Can you give a reason for each rule?*

3. *Do you have any questions?* Allow children to raise any concerns they have.

4. If this is your last class, ask one child to gather the cones and two or three others to gather the carpet squares and bring them to you.

From *Physical Education Methods for Elementary Teachers, Second Edition,* by Katherine T. Thomas, Amelia M. Lee, and Jerry R. Thomas, 2003, Champaign, IL: Human Kinetics. Adapted from *Physical Education for Children: Daily Lesson Plans for Elementary School, Second Edition,* by Katherine T. Thomas, Amelia M. Lee, and Jerry R. Thomas, 2000, Champaign, IL: Human Kinetics.

Organization

LESSON  11.2

Rules, Consensus, and Formations

Student Objectives

- Recognize the rules.
- Give examples of the rules.
- Reach consensus on the class rules.
- Move from a line to a circle formation.
- Participate in a game.

Equipment and Materials

- Physical Education Rules poster
- 1 carpet square per child plus a few extra
- 4 cones or other markers
- Flour, line chalk, string, or tape circle
- 5-10 beanbags

Warm-Up Activities (5 minutes)

Wild One

Use four cones to define a rectangular play area. Scatter carpet squares and beanbags randomly in the play area, leaving spaces between them. Have each child begin by standing on a carpet square. There should be extra squares.

1. Review and emphasize rule 2: Be careful before introducing the game.

2. Designate one child as the Wild One ("It") and direct him or her to move randomly about the play area, making faces, waving arms, and generally acting wild while the other children walk from carpet square to carpet square. Tell the children: *Only one child may be on a square at a time. Keep moving all the time from square to square.*

3. After a while, signal stop and select a new Wild One. Stop the game if more than one child ends up on a square to remind them to move to a different square.

4. After the children have learned to moved continuously from square to square, tell them to run between squares.

5. Repeat the game with new Wild Ones, stopping as necessary to remind the children that there is only one Wild One or that only one person may be on each square.

Skill-Development Activities (20 minutes)

Rules Consensus

Gather the children into an information formation.

1. Show the children the rules. Ask the children:

   Who remembers a rule? Continue until the children have repeated each one.

   Why are rules important? (Stay safe; save time.)

2. Give an example of when each rule might apply:

   - *Rule 1: Hands off. If a person is a Wild One, other people may not be able to listen, do, and learn.*
   - *Rule 2: Be careful. If our equipment is broken, no one will learn; a student who is hurt cannot learn.*

- *Rule 3: Listen and look for the stop signals. Remember yesterday when we practiced moving in and out of our area? If everyone had not stopped when I signaled, some people might not have heard the directions.*
- *Rule 4: Be nice. People fighting can keep many from learning.*
- *Rule 5: Listen and do. As a new activity begins, we must listen for instructions, then do them in order to learn as much as possible.*
- *Rule 6: Do your best. Each of us must try everything, even if we think we are not very good at the activity.*

3. Ask if children understand each rule. Discuss if necessary:

   Are these good rules?

   Can you agree with them? If yes, continue; if no, discuss and resolve any problems or misunderstanding so all children can agree with the rules.

   Can you follow the rules? We are all counting on you.

4. Ask one child to gather the beanbags and two children to gather the carpet squares for you.

Circle and Line

Arrange children in a line between two cones. Mark a large circle with cones, chalk, or flour (for the playground) 20 or 30 ft from the line.

1. Describe the line formation. Tell the children:

   Look at your present location and remember it.

   Look for some special landmark, like a line, clover, or bare spot.

2. Describe and point out the circle.

3. Signal the children: *Move in any way you want to the circle and stand still on the line.* Adjust the children's positions in the circle as necessary. Signal the children: *Move back to your positions on the line.*

4. Repeat several times until the children master the skill.

Moving Within and Around Boundaries

Using four cones, mark a large rectangle in the playing area around the circle. Create the rectangle in a different position from the previous lesson.

1. Remind the children what they have learned about boundaries.

2. Ask the children: *Who can show me the boundaries marked by the cones?* Allow one child to demonstrate by running between the four cones marking the boundaries of the rectangle.

Concluding Activities (5 minutes)

Circle Boundaries Game

Arrange half the children in a circle, inside the rectangle formed by the four cones. Scatter the remaining group outside the circle, but inside the rectangle.

1. Explain that there are three places the scattered children can move on your command: (1) inside the rectangle but outside the circle, (2) inside the circle, and (3) around the boundaries.

2. Explain the activity: *When I say, "rectangle," "boundaries," and "circle," walk or run until I signal for you to stop or change locations.* Repeat several times, then reverse the roles of the two groups.

For additional steps, place a line somewhere in the rectangle.

3. Expand the activity: *Now let's add another word. When I say, "Line!" form a line as quickly as possible.*

4. Have the circle group walk along the circle. Each time you signal for the other group to change locations, have these children change the direction in which they are walking.

5. If this is your last class, ask one to four children to gather the cones.

From *Physical Education Methods for Elementary Teachers, Second Edition*, by Katherine T. Thomas, Amelia M. Lee, and Jerry R. Thomas, 2003, Champaign, IL: Human Kinetics. Adapted from *Physical Education for Children: Daily Lesson Plans for Elementary School, Second Edition*, by Katherine T. Thomas, Amelia M. Lee, and Jerry R. Thomas, 2000, Champaign, IL: Human Kinetics.

LESSON

Equipment and Spacing

Student Objectives

- Practice getting and returning equipment.
- Demonstrate near and far spacing.

Equipment and Materials

- 4 cones
- Enough beanbags for one-fourth of the class
- Enough hoops for one-fourth of the class
- Enough balls for one-fourth of the class
- Enough jump ropes for one-fourth of the class
- 6 carpet squares

Warm-Up Activities (5 minutes)

Formations Review

Arrange the children in scatter formation inside a large rectangle defined by the four cones.
  Ask the children to complete the following tasks:

Move into a circle formation around me.

Jog clockwise.

Freeze!

Jog counterclockwise.

Freeze!

Move to a line formation between me and that cone (point).

Jump up and down in personal space.

Freeze!

Move to a scatter formation.

Run in general space inside the boundaries.

Freeze!

Jog around the outside of the boundaries clockwise.

Freeze!

Move to the line I'm pointing to (on one side of the rectangle).

Hop across the rectangle to the opposite line.

Make a circle around me.

Skill-Development Activities (20 minutes)

Station Rotation

Place the carpet squares one on each of the long sides of the rectangle and one in each corner.
  Divide the children into six groups.

1. Assign each group to a carpet square.

2. Number each carpet square, saying the numbers for each group aloud as you point to the square: *Say each number aloud with me.*

3. *On the signal, each group should move from their carpet square to the next higher number; number 6 should go to number 1. Continue un-*til the groups are back to their starting positions.

4. *Repeat in reverse (1 goes to 6, 6 to 5, 5 to 4, and so on).*

Giving Out Equipment

Divide the children into four groups, and assign one group to each corner of the play area.

1. Assign each group a type of equipment (e.g., beanbags to group 1, hoops to group 2, balls to group 3, and ropes to group 4).

2. Name a group. Have each child in the group get one piece of equipment from you, return to the group's station, and sit down with the equipment.

3. Repeat with the other three groups.

Concluding Activity (5 minutes)

Nose Tag

Arrange the children in scatter formation. Designate two players as "Its."

1. Describe and demonstrate the game:

    Two children begin as Its and try to tag the other children, who run, trying to avoid being tagged by the Its.

    You are safe from being tagged if you are standing on one leg with the other leg looped over one arm while the hand on that arm holds your nose.

    If you let go of your nose, lose your balance, or begin to run, you are no longer safe and can be tagged by an It.

    Once tagged, you become an It and switch places with the original It.

2. Have the children play Nose Tag.

From *Physical Education Methods for Elementary Teachers, Second Edition,* by Katherine T. Thomas, Amelia M. Lee, and Jerry R. Thomas, 2003, Champaign, IL: Human Kinetics. Adapted from *Physical Education for Children: Daily Lesson Plans for Elementary School, Second Edition,* by Katherine T. Thomas, Amelia M. Lee, and Jerry R. Thomas, 2000, Champaign, IL: Human Kinetics.

Organization

LESSON  **11.4**

Stations and Rotations, Rules and Consequences

Student Objectives

- Help decide the consequences for rules infractions.
- Move to station formation and rotate.

Equipment and Materials

- 4 cones
- Enough hoops for one-fourth of the class
- Enough balls for one-fourth of the class
- Enough carpet squares for one-fourth of the class
- Enough jump ropes for one-fourth of the class

Warm-Up Activities (5 minutes)

Near–Far Concepts

Arrange partners in scatter formation. Ask the children to respond quickly to the following statements:

Stand close to your partner.

Move as far away from your partners as possible.

Class, make a double circle, one partner standing beside the other, so one partner is on the inside and the other is on the outside circle.

Move sideways so that the inside circle is smaller, the outside circle is larger, and you and your partner are in far position.

One partner moves outside the boundaries while one partner stays inside the boundary in near position.

One partner moves outside the boundaries while one partner stays inside the boundary in far position.

One partner makes a line on this side (point); *the rest of you make a line over there* (point).

Make the lines as short as possible so you are in near position.

Make the lines longer so you are in far position.

Skill-Development Activities (20 minutes)

Consequences

Gather the children into an information formation.

1. Read the rules.
   - *Rule 1: Follow directions.*
   - *Rule 2: Hands off other students.*
   - *Rule 3: Be careful of equipment and others.*
   - *Rule 4: Stop, look, and listen on the signal.*
   - *Rule 5: Do not fight or stop practice or play.*
2. Ask: *Are there any questions about the rules?* (Pause.) *We have talked about why it is important*

to follow the rules. Following rules makes it easier for everyone to learn, saves equipment, and keeps us safe. What happens if someone breaks a rule? (It interferes with learning, it may be dangerous, equipment may be broken, and there should be consequences for the rule breaker.)

3. Ask the children: *What consequences would be fair?* Discuss. Suggested consequences include the following:
   - First offense: three-minute time-out.
   - Second offense: six-minute time-out.

- Third offense: Call parents.
- Fourth offense: Send to principal.

4. *Note:* Remember to use behavior contracts, good behavior rewards, and good or poor behavior letters to parents. After class, make a poster of the consequences.

Stations

Use the cones to define a rectangle. Divide the children into four groups, and assign one group to each corner of the play area. Assign one type of equipment to each group.

1. Name a group and have one member of that group get the equipment for the entire group.

2. Allow the children to do creative movements with the equipment for one to three minutes.

3. Have each group rotate to the next station and repeat.

4. Continue until all four groups have been at all four stations.

5. Have one child from each station return the station's equipment.

Concluding Activities (5 minutes)

Movement Patterns

Arrange the children in scatter formation in the middle of the play area. Tell the children to move in the following patterns, changing on the signal:

Hop forward (backward, left, right). Repeat.

Jog in a circle (clockwise), turn and jog in a circle the opposite direction (counterclockwise).

Skip forward, then jump backward.

Walk forward, change direction, change direction, change direction (any direction).

Move in a zigzag pattern.

Move in a straight line.

Move in a curved line.

Unit Plan for Grades 2–3: Organization

Week 1: teach and review rules

Monday: signals and information and line and scatter formations

Tuesday: formations and boundaries

Wednesday: signals, formations, and boundaries

Thursday: equipment and spacing

Friday: stations and rotations and rules and consequences

From *Physical Education Methods for Elementary Teachers, Second Edition,* by Katherine T. Thomas, Amelia M. Lee, and Jerry R. Thomas, 2003, Champaign, IL: Human Kinetics. Adapted from *Physical Education for Children: Daily Lesson Plans for Elementary School, Second Edition,* by Katherine T. Thomas, Amelia M. Lee, and Jerry R. Thomas, 2000, Champaign, IL: Human Kinetics.

Organization

GRADES **4-5**

LESSON

Signals, Boundaries, Groupings, and Rules

Student Objectives

- Move diagonally across an area.
- Move in an area within an area.

Equipment and Materials

- Physical Education Rules poster
- 8 cones or markers
- Large sign cards (8 1/2 in. × 11 in. or larger)
- 8 foam balls
- Chalk, flour (outdoors only), or tape for marking lines

Warm-Up Activities (5 minutes)

Single File

Arrange the students in squad formation. Designate a leader of each squad. Practice working in single file:

On the signal, the last person in each line runs to the front of that line and becomes the new leader.

All leaders jog or walk around (across, inside) the area as you hear me call out the pattern.

Skill-Development Activities (20 minutes)

Rules

Arrange the children in an advanced information formation.

1. Ask the children to recall and state the rules.
   - Rule 1: Follow directions.
   - Rule 2: Hands off.
   - Rule 3: Be careful.
   - Rule 4: Stop, look, and listen on the signal.
   - Rule 5: Do not fight.
2. Watch for situations during the remainder of the lesson that are examples of good behavior; stop the class and point them out.

Changing Direction to a Verbal Signal

Arrange the children in scatter formation within a large rectangle marked with four cones.

Have the children move to the following commands, giving a signal when each change of direction should occur: *run (walk, hop, jump) left (right, back, forward, sideways).*

Task Cards

Print movement tasks on cards large enough for the children to read (8 1/2 in. by 11 in. or larger).

1. Show the cards to the entire group or place the cards at the activity stations. Direct the children to read the tasks and respond with the appropriate movements.
2. Task card instruction examples (or choose other tasks that fit with your skills-development plans):

   Slide right, slide left, hop in a circle.

   Jump forward, jump backward, spin, sit down.

   Run 10 steps backward, leap back to starting place.

   Gallop in a circle, hop three times, jump high.

286

Station Formation

Place one of the cards at each of four stations. Direct the children:

> Move to the stations, forming squads with no more than eight (or, one fourth of the class) per squad.
>
> Rotate (1 goes to 2, 2 to 3, and so on).

Partner Relay

Arrange the children in pairs, and assign each pair to a four-person relay team. Mark a starting line and a return line. At the return line, place a stack of cards for each relay team, one card for each pair of students. The cards should specify how the pair will return to the starting line. Task card instruction examples (or choose other tasks that fit with your skill development plans):

> Hold one hand with your partner and hop on opposite feet.
>
> Run backward.
>
> Skip with one person in front of the other.
>
> Join both hands and slide.

1. Explain the activity:

> On the signal, travel with your partner, using any type of movement to the return line. Then select a card from the stack of cards and read the task.

> Travel back to the starting line, using the movement specified. This is not a race.
>
> Continue until each pair in your group has had a turn.
>
> Shuffle the cards and repeat the game until time is up.

2. Run the Partner Relay.

Moving Diagonally

Have the children get back into four groups, and place one group in each corner of a large rectangle defined by four cones.

1. Have group 1 switch with group 3.
2. Have group 2 switch with group 4.
3. Repeat steps 1 and 2.
4. Have the children move to scatter formation.
5. Present the following tasks:

> Can you move diagonally? Stop when you hit a boundary.
>
> Move to a corner if you are not in a corner.
>
> Move diagonally.

Concluding Activities (5 minutes)

Moving Within an Area

Use a second set of four cones to mark out a square in the center of the large rectangle. Divide the children into five squads. Send squads 1 and 2 to one end of the large area. Send squads 3 and 4 to the other end of the large area. Send squad 5 into the small square.

1. Explain the activity:

> Squads 1, 2, 3, and 4 will throw the foam balls over the small square, playing catch between those squads. Squad 5 players will try to catch the balls.
>
> If a member of squad 5 catches a ball, that child switches places with the thrower.

2. Run the activity. If squad 5 is having trouble catching the balls, enlarge the center square.

From *Physical Education Methods for Elementary Teachers, Second Edition,* by Katherine T. Thomas, Amelia M. Lee, and Jerry R. Thomas, 2003, Champaign, IL: Human Kinetics. Adapted from *Physical Education for Children: Daily Lesson Plans for Elementary School, Second Edition,* by Katherine T. Thomas, Amelia M. Lee, and Jerry R. Thomas, 2000, Champaign, IL: Human Kinetics.

LESSON **11.6**

Signals, Boundaries, Groupings, and Rules

Student Objectives

- Move among line, circle, scatter, pair, and station formations.
- Form squads.
- Start, listen, and stop on an auditory signal.
- Move in, across, around, and outside boundaries.
- State rules for class behavior.
- Work cooperatively with a group to accomplish a goal.

Equipment and Materials

- Physical education rules poster
- 4 cones or markers
- 1 carpet square per squad
- 1 basketball or 8 one-half in. playground ball per group

Warm-Up Activities (5 minutes)

Boundaries

Divide the children into four groups. Arrange one group on each boundary line of a large rectangle defined by the four cones. Name or number the boundaries (1 to 4, or North, South, East, and West).

1. Call out the following exchanges; students on the boundaries named exchange places with each other:

1 and 3 (North and South)
2 and 4 (East and West)
1 and 4 (North and West)
3 and 2 (South and East)
1 and 2 (North and East)
3 and 4 (South and West)
3 and 1 (South and North)
4 and 2 (West and East)

2. Tell the students: *Everyone back to starting position!*

Skill-Development Activities (20 minutes)

Advanced Information Formation

Arrange the children in concentric semicircles with the first row seated, the next row kneeling, and the last row standing. Tell the children: *This as an "advanced information formation."*

Physical Education Rules

Keep the children in the advanced information formation.

1. There are two ways to handle this section: read the rules or work with the students for a consensus on the rules. Read the rules to the students.

   - *Rule 1: Follow directions (the first time they are given).*
   - *Rule 2: Hands off (keep hands, feet, and objects to yourself).*

- *Rule 3: Be careful of equipment and others.*
- *Rule 4: Stop, look, and listen on the signal.*
- *Rule 5: Do not fight or interfere with the practice or play of others (avoid hostile gestures, fighting, and game disruption).*

2. *Are there any questions about the rules?* Discuss.

Cooperative Groups

Arrange the children in groups of four to six heterogeneous learning teams every time you create cooperative groups. Place the students wisely by combining students who lack social skills with others who are more socially mature. Separate the students who tend to be disruptive by placing them in different groups. Also strive to create equal representation of students of different races, ethnic origins, social classes, and gender in each group. Finally, keep group sizes as small as possible to increase participation opportunities. Have each squad line up at a carpet square, arranged at one end of the play area.

1. Assign a role for each member of the group. Roles can include organizer or leader, timekeeper, encourager, praiser, equipment handler, facilitator, and summarizer. Explain the roles you wish the students to use:

   The "organizer" is the student who gets the group started on the group project and serves as the group leader.

   The "timekeeper" keeps time and makes sure the task is completed in the allotted time.

   The "encourager" encourages each student to work productively and reminds each student that their role is important.

   The "praiser" encourages positive interaction by making supportive remarks to each student.

   The "equipment handler" is responsible for getting and returning the equipment the group needs.

   The "facilitator" asks the teacher for help if it is needed.

   The "summarizer" keeps mental notes of the process and provides a summary at the end of the session.

2. Establish guidelines for cooperative work:

   Everyone must contribute to the work.

   Only one student can talk at a time, and the others must listen.

   Everyone must show respect for the others.

Remember that each person has a unique role to fill.

Problem Solving

Continue with small groups.

1. Present a problem for the groups to solve; for example:

   Create a ball game that requires a circle and uses the skills of throwing, catching, and running.

   Design a play to be used in half-court basketball.

   Design an exercise plan for a week.

2. Share how you will score the work of each group on a five-point scale, ending with: *Your group can earn five points only if you collaborate and work according to the guidelines and if all students fulfill their assigned roles.*

Squad Formation

Teach the children to divide themselves into their small groups (assigned in previous section) with a designated meeting place and a set formation (short parallel lines at each carpet square arranged at one end of the play area).

1. Tell the children: *On the signal, move behind the squares, forming lines with the groups I've already assigned.*

2. Adjust children, if necessary, so that the lines are straight and nearly equal in length. Tell the children: *Remember your squad and your position in your squad.*

Concluding Activities (5 minutes)

Formations

Start this activity with the children still in their squads. Define the play area with the four cones. Ask the children to create the following formations:

Make a line facing me.

Move to scatter formation.

Make a circle around me.

Find a partner and stand back-to-back.

Move to scatter formation.

Move to squad formation.

Squad 1 go to station 1. (Point to a corner; Stations 1 to 4 are corners of a rectangle.)

Squad 2 go to station 2, (and so on; use the long sides or center of the rectangle if you have more than four squads).

Rotate (squad 1 goes to station 2, squad 2 to station 3, and so on).

Players at each station make a circle.

Make one big circle with the entire class.

Move back to squad formation.

Move to scatter formation.

Select a partner and get back in scatter formation.

Move back to squad formation.

Single File

Continue in squad formation. Designate a leader of each squad. Practice working in single file:

On the signal, the last person in each line runs to the front of that line and becomes the new leader.

All leaders jog or walk around (across, inside) the area as you hear me call out the pattern.

From *Physical Education Methods for Elementary Teachers, Second Edition,* by Katherine T. Thomas, Amelia M. Lee, and Jerry R. Thomas, 2003, Champaign, IL: Human Kinetics. Adapted from *Physical Education for Children: Daily Lesson Plans for Elementary School, Second Edition,* by Katherine T. Thomas, Amelia M. Lee, and Jerry R. Thomas, 2000, Champaign, IL: Human Kinetics.

Teachers' Rights, Responsibilities, and Best Practices

Jane, age 7

At least three levels of rules, regulations, and responsibilities apply to teachers; these include criminal laws, professional standards, and best practices. We expect teachers, as professional educators, to be held to a higher standard than the general public. In fact, teachers are expected to establish challenging standards for themselves. Meeting or exceeding these expectations provides a safe and nurturing environment for students.

Learner Outcomes

The teacher will do the following:

- Define the terms liability, negligence, standard of care, and best practice.
- Explain the three levels of responsibility for teachers.
- Discuss teacher responsibilities as these relate to safety.
- Describe why best practices and beyond is important.
- List expectations for professional teachers.
- Describe the characteristics of a professional educator.

Glossary Terms

breach of contract
professional ethics
statutes
Buckley Amendment
tort
negligence
liability

standard of care
instruction
supervision
active supervision
chain of command
best practice

Unfortunately, the media presents almost daily accounts of teachers and schools being criticized or involved in legal action. The accounts may tell of poor student achievement or illegal behavior by a professional educator. In many cases, what would not be newsworthy for the typical citizen creates a media frenzy for a teacher because teachers are held to a higher standard as professionals and as caretakers of children. Teachers appreciate the recognition that goes with their reputation for shaping the future by teaching tomorrow's leaders, but with that recognition comes considerable responsibility. Teachers are expected to be exemplary models for children! Because most schools are supported by tax monies from the state government, the legislatures of each state have the opportunity to set criteria for teacher behavior and licensing. Usually these are expressed in codes of professional conduct as part of state rules and regulations. Professional organizations also outline performance and ethical codes for teachers and identify best practices. In addition, federal statutes (laws) require schools and teachers to meet a variety of requirements. Finally, teachers must also abide by the civil and criminal codes that apply to every person.

Teachers need to understand their rights and responsibilities and the laws, statutes, and regulations that apply to teachers for two reasons:

1. To provide the optimal educational environment for their students so that they can be professional educators

2. To protect themselves and their schools from litigation

This chapter will provide an overview of legal concepts, prevention, safety, and liability issues and will introduce your rights, responsibilities of professional conduct, and best practices. Prevention and knowledge are critical tools for you to avoid problems with the law. Professional legal problems for teachers can result from three areas of law: contracts, statutes, and tort. In addition, teachers, as citizens, may have personal legal problems when their behavior falls under the realm of the criminal code.

CRIMINAL CODE

A teacher is bound and guided by several sets of laws, regulations, and expectations. Civil and criminal laws apply to teachers just as they apply to everyone else. Laws, whether we agree with them or not, allow our democratic society to operate in a reasonably safe, secure, and smooth manner. These laws are similar to your class rules, which are designed so that the class will run in a smooth and orderly manner. As citizens in a free country, we can lobby to change the laws, but we are expected to abide by those laws until the law is changed. Our values and moral development influence our beliefs, and society protects our right to hold different values and beliefs. Our society also protects the majority, however, by expecting citizens to follow laws.

Laws and regulations about automobile operation, taxes, substance use, and public conduct, among many others, apply to everyone. We may not agree with the speed limit, but we have the right to lobby for changes in speed limits and are subject to punishment if we are guilty of breaking it. You may be thinking, *How does this matter if I am a teacher?* Under most circumstances, speeding would not be relevant to your professional life. However, it could be if you were speeding while you had students in your car or if you were operating a school district vehicle.

Any criminal or civil law might affect your professional life, especially as a prospective or new teacher. For example, many states (e.g., Iowa) require teachers to report any convictions (other than a parking ticket) on the application for a license. Some states (e.g., Missouri) require you to report arrests or charges even when there has been no conviction. There is no clear answer as to how this information is used in determining who will be licensed. Schools require similar self-reporting on job applications. Once again, it is not clear how this information influences who is employed. Many teachers and prospective teachers must undergo a criminal background check for licensing and employment. Although these specific laws do not focus on teachers or school-related activities, they can influence your opportunity to be hired as a teacher. The use of criminal background information will undoubtedly evolve during your career because these procedures are new and changing rapidly.

Areas of the law that are most likely to influence your opportunity to teach are those that deal with minors, such as providing alcohol to a minor or having an illegal personal relationship with a minor. One of the reasons behind self-report and criminal background checks is to keep child predators out of the schools. It is important to understand that breaking a law with a minor or breaking a law designed to protect a minor does not have to happen on school property. Whether on or off the school premises, these behaviors are likely to have serious legal and professional consequences. Convictions less likely to create a problem are status crimes. Status crimes are acts that are illegal when you are of one age but not illegal when at an older age. Breaking curfews is one example.

Our culture and government are based on the notion that society is better served by people who act responsibly and who adhere to rules that were created for the greater good. Public education is expected to teach and follow that notion. Thus, teachers, as citizens and as a part of a public entity, are bound in two ways to the laws. Further, codes of ethics for teachers may require other teachers to intervene when students or colleagues are not abiding by the law. Therefore, teachers are bound to the criminal laws in three ways—as citizens regulating their own behaviors, as professionals meeting professional standards, and as enforcers who may be obligated to report illegal acts committed by students or colleagues.

CONTRACTS

Generally teachers should not have legal problems related to contacts. A contract is a promise, and breaking the promise, or **breach of contract,** is cause for legal action. Teachers do have connections to contracts in three areas: their personnel contracts, school activities related to a district contract, and contracts that they initiate for their school.

Most school districts use contracts to describe a teacher's duties and the responsibility of the district to compensate the teacher (e.g., salary and benefits). Educators and school districts are expected to live up to the contract from the moment of verbally accepting a job through the time the job is completed. Once you sign a contract with a school, you are obligated to work for that district for the duration of the contract, even if a better job is offered to you after you sign the contract. You can be sued for failing to meet the obligations of the contract, but schools may agree to release you from a contract at your request. This is a matter of **professional ethics** as well as a legal issue. Professional ethics would suggest that once you verbally agree to accept a job offer, you should follow through. Think about loyalty, why loyalty is important, and how breaking a contract reflects on your loyalty.

Schools and districts often have contracts with businesses or individuals, such as a food service contract with a company to provide the school meals or a contract with a sporting goods store to provide equipment. Sometimes these contracts have special provisions, such as "exclusive rights." Exclusive rights means no competing business or individual will be allowed to do business with the school during the time of the contract. Teachers are expected to respect these contracts. Often, teachers are not aware of these contracts and breach the contract out of ignorance. It is best to check with the principal or business manager before purchasing anything because you might not be reimbursed for purchases outside the contract or you could involve the school in a lawsuit.

Finally, teachers are not usually allowed to commit the school or district to a contract. An official of the agency must sign contracts, or else the contract will be invalid or the signer will be responsible for the contract obligations. This may seem like a small matter, but consider a field trip that may have a contract for transportation, food, and admission for a group of students. If you sign the contract, you are likely to be responsible for the costs. Part of the reason for district policy about who can make a contract is to protect individual teachers from financial debt; another is to avoid conflict of interest. A teacher might go to a business to purchase equipment because her cousin owns the business, yet another business may have better prices. The fact that the chosen business benefited someone the teacher knew is a conflict of interest. Beware of purchasing if gifts are associated with the purchase. If you order materials—even through regular school channels—and are given a free gift as a result of the order, the gift belongs to the school, not to you.

STATUTES

Statutes are established by the government and guide operations of many entities. Three examples are the Americans with Disabilities Act, Title IX, and the Buckley Amendment. These affect all teachers—classroom teachers and physical education specialists. We will discuss each briefly as related to physical education.

Inclusion of Special Needs Students

For more than 30 years, schools have been charged with finding, identifying, and educating people with disabilities. Physical educators have been proud that physical education was classified as a direct service from the inception of laws defining special education (e.g., P.L. 94-142). This means that all students with identified disabilities will have physical education in the most inclusive and appropriate setting. The setting for physical education is determined at the individualized education program (IEP) meeting and should be stated, along with any restrictions or necessary supports, on the IEP. Therefore, every teacher—whether a classroom teacher or a physical education specialist—providing physical education to the student with a disability must understand the IEP and ideally should attend the IEP meeting. Physical education is a valuable and viable part of every child's education, as recognized in the original legislation and continuing with the most recent version of the Americans with Disabilities Act. In a "regular" physical education class that includes students with disabilities, the teacher faces three challenges. The first is meeting the potentially wider range of abilities. The second is ensuring the safety of all students in the class. The third is meeting the demands set forth in the statutes. The learning environment is enriched with diversity, so the first challenge is one that enhances learning and should be the focus for the teacher. Unfortunately, the remaining two often are the focus of a teacher's efforts. Chapter 8 presented information on individual differences and disabilities. Help with adapting activities was covered in chapter 4. If you meet the first challenge, it is unlikely you will have trouble with the other two. However, some suggestions might help.

When the IEP specifies inclusive placement in regular physical education, the assumption is that any limitations to regular physical education participation or supports necessary for participation are specified in the IEP. Supports include special equipment, an education assistant, and other modifications to allow the student to be successful. Unfortunately, this may not always be true. For example, the physical education department may not have been represented at the IEP meeting. Alternatively, the special needs child may not need any supports and may perform well in physical education but could cause a threat to other children in the class. So, first, do not assume anything. Second, gather as much information about this situation as possible from the IEP, the parent, persons who were at the IEP meeting, and from the student. Third, keep an open line of communication with parents and the student. As with all physical education students, apprising the students and parents of your plan for activities, expectations, and approach is helpful. You may want to meet with the student and her parents to discuss the plan of activities. Clarify what you know based on the IEP and what you need to know from the parents and others. At this point, you should have all the information necessary to satisfy the IEP and offer a safe learning environment to your special needs student. If at any time you have concerns for the safety of this student or others, use a backup plan: Change the class activity and seek help as soon as possible. For example, you are supervising a throwing and catching activity with tennis balls, and a wheelchair-bound student is hitting other students or being hit with the tennis balls. You are concerned because the hits are to the head. Stop the activity quickly, and—as seamlessly as possible—move into a safe rhythmic activity. Good teachers have a selection of backup activities that can be used at any time. An example for young children might be the action song "Head, Shoulders, Knees, and Toes"; for older children, "Hi, My Name Is Joe" would be an example.

"Hi, My Name Is Joe"

Chant or sing the following lyrics; the actions are in parentheses.

Hi, my name is Joe (wave left hand and arm)

and I have a wife and kids and a dog and work at a button factory (still waving).

One day

My boss said to me, "Hey, Joe" (now wave both hands),

"can you push this button with your right hand?"

I said sure (now pretend to push a button with the right hand while waving).

(Continue pressing the button with your right hand.)

Hi, my name is Joe (wave left hand and arm, push button with right hand)

and I have a wife and kids and a dog and I work at a button factory (still waving and pushing button).

One day

My boss said to me, "Hey, Joe" (wave between pushing with right hand),

"can you turn this dial with your right foot?"

I said sure (now twist right foot, push button with right hand).

Repeat adding a new body part on each verse, as follows:

▶ Left foot tapping pedal

▶ Left hand turning knob

▶ Head pressing lever

Gender Inclusion

Since Title IX, schools have been obligated to provide equal opportunities for boys and girls. Title IX has had the greatest impact on competitive sport opportunities. In part II of this book, we presented a great deal of information that suggests that boys and girls are more alike than different. As a result of Title IX, you are able to put that knowledge into action! We do not recommend separating boys and girls during elementary physical education for any reason. Children can be grouped for instruction and practice by skill level but not by gender. When the opportunity is not equal because of gender, a lawsuit can ensue based on Title IX. Doing what is right, however, is more important than the possibility of a lawsuit. Allowing all children the opportunity to reach their potential is optimal.

A Student's Right to Privacy

The **Buckley Amendment,** also called the Family Right to Educational Privacy Act, may be violated more than any other statute. This law stipulates that educational information must be confidential. Only students and their parents are to be aware of most information about student progress. The following are examples of violations:

- Posting of student grades by name or social security number
- Casual discussions of student performance, even among teachers
- Discussing student performance over the phone without being able to verify the caller's relationship to the student
- Providing parents of students over 18 years of age with educational record information.

Does this mean that teachers cannot discuss a student? No, but the teachers should be doing so in a professional context. If the identity of the student is not important (i.e., if you are asking a more experienced teacher for help and the teacher does not know the student or the student's identity is not critical to the problem), you should not identify the student. On the other hand, you may seek advice from the student's previous teacher as long as this is done in a professional manner. Casual discussions about students in the teachers' lounge are not appropriate. Nor are conversations about a student with another student. You need written permission from the parents and additional permission from students over seven years of age in order to report any information about academic performance to someone other than your school administration, the parents, or the student. The permission should include what can be discussed or provided, to whom, and for what period of time. If you have questions about requests, you should ask your principal for advice. It is always okay and usually safer to respond to a request by saying, "I do not have that information in front of me; can I get your name and number and call you back?" This allows you to make sure it is permissible to provide information. Noncustodial parents, insurance companies, and coaches often seek information without permission.

Look for a problem in the place where you may least expect it. Mentioning the highest grade or best score on a test or measurement may embarrass the best student. This is a violation of that student's rights. So, while your intention was to share the joy of the great performance, you need to do so privately. In physical education, many performances are public. You'll find that it is easier to maintain a student's privacy in a classroom situation. Examples are the movement away from reading aloud or the care taken to maintain privacy when handing back graded work. There is no reasonable way to keep each performance private in physical education. However, you can be sensitive to the students, especially when you are doing assessments and grading.

TORTS

Circumstances arise when a teacher may have legal problems but has not broken a criminal law. When a student is hurt, someone gets blamed. The result can be a lawsuit where the plaintiff (the student or his parents) alleges a breach in the standard of care (or duties of care). Usually, the teacher and the school are the defendants (the ones being sued). These lawsuits are examples of a **tort,** which is civil legal action. Sometimes criminal actions accompany these civil actions. Teachers are often the first to ask the question "Could I have prevented this?" An accident is an unintentional and unavoidable event. Accidents happen everywhere, including in school. Because physical education is a high-risk activity, accidents are a concern. Every educator must consider four sources of risk for students—the activity, the equipment or facility, the teacher's behaviors, and the other students' behaviors. Careful planning will reduce the risk in physical education and other physical activity experiences because you will consider all four sources of risk. Chapter 13, "Equipment and Facilities," tells how to increase safety on the playground and in the gymnasium. The focus there is how to reduce risk while facilitating learning. Chapter 11, "Managing Students," helps with controlling students—again reducing risk and increasing learning. Answering the question "Is this developmentally appropriate?" also assists teachers in reducing risks. Finally, other teaching behaviors, such as supervision and your response to an injury, prove important. As a teacher, you want to be able to answer, "Yes, I did everything possible to prevent this injury, and I responded appropriately after the injury."

Negligence occurs when you are responsible for an injury; that is, you did not act in a reasonable and prudent way to prevent the injury based on the situation. **Liability** cases attempt to prove that the responsible person did not meet the standard of care and damage resulted from the injury. The law recognizes the **standard of care** as the test for liability cases. Standard of care is defined as what a reasonable and prudent person would do under the circumstances. Negligence, the most frequent level of all tort lawsuits, is a result of a specific relationship, in this case between you and your student. As a teacher, you are expected to provide both instruction and supervision while avoiding acts or omissions that could hurt your students. The standard of care depends on the relationship and what should be expected. Three other levels of torts exist: intent to cause harm, knowledge of potential harm, and recklessness that causes harm. Anyone, including teachers, can be charged with or found guilty of any of the four levels of torts. However, intent, knowledge, and recklessness do not require a special relationship. For example, a person who punches a stranger can be sued for intent. The key to educational negligence is this: Because teachers are trained and are in a position of trust, the standard of care is greater for teachers than many other people.

In physical education, the idea of assumed risk is a moderating variable. Every physical activity (and everything else) has some risk; for example, even when wearing appropriate shoes and clothing, a normal, healthy child can fall down and be injured running across a clean, perfectly maintained gymnasium floor. That type of risk is assumed in any physical activity. Add another well-behaved child to the scenario; they bump and fall, and an injury results. This is also a likely part of assumed risk. However, if we add water to the floor, the risk has changed, and the questions become, "Did the teacher know about or do anything about the water?" "Was it reasonable for the teacher to know about the water?" If yes, "Was it reasonable for the teacher to do something different?" Teachers can help parents and students understand the risk inherent in physical education by informing them about the types of activities planned. As a part of this, you can inform parents of rules—especially the reason for the rules. Send home a letter that explains the rules and the activities. Have the parent sign the letter and return it to you. End your letter with an offer to answer any questions the parent may have. This will open the lines of

Active supervision by a teacher means being constantly aware of dangerous situations.

communication. This letter will not eliminate all chance of a lawsuit, but it is good practice.

Reading about lawsuits and injuries could be a bit overwhelming. Instead, consider this: Teachers are generally reasonable and prudent people. Thus, you are in a position to make good decisions about the risk for your students. When you suspect that something is not safe, follow up and make a good decision. You can prevent injuries and the resulting legal complications. If you think equipment is faulty (e.g., the bolts on the playground climber are loose) or a facility looks unsafe (e.g., the gym floor is damp, wet, or slippery), do not use it; rather, report it to the appropriate authority, and try to follow up to be certain repairs are made. Use an appropriate level of concern about liability and injuries to guide your careful planning. Part of your desire to be a teacher stems from your concern for children; that concern combined with knowledge about safety will reduce your chances of negligent behavior. The next section examines the teacher's duties of care in more detail.

STANDARD OF CARE (DUTY OF CARE)

Although all aspects of teaching are important, the first obligation is safety. Fortunately, doing a good job in the other aspects of teaching generally enhances safety. Recall the four sources of risk for your students. These educational concerns are aligned with the five duties of care representing the legal perspective: proper instruction, proper supervision, proper classification, a safe environment, and response to an injury (Pettifor 1999).

Instruction

Instruction begins with a plan. A written lesson plan demonstrates that you have considered what to teach and how to teach it. Specifically, your plan should fulfill several objectives:

- It should be developmentally appropriate.
- It should allow for differences among children.
- It should consider both progression (improvement) and previous experience.
- It should identify the objective of the lesson, safety issues, and equipment needed.

- It should note management and safety because both are important parts of a lesson plan and should be included in writing.
- It should include demonstrations and questions to determine understanding, use corrective feedback, and note this on the lesson plan.
- It should be consistent with district, state, or national guidelines.

Chapters 9 and 14 provide greater detail for planning and instruction. Three concepts can guide you: Do not assume anything, plan for the worst, and be more rather than less careful. Assumptions are not a legal or moral defense. Do not assume that your students have had previous experience or that all students will listen and be careful. Having all children active as much of the time as possible is ideal for learning and health but may be problematic for safety. As a new teacher or the teacher of a new class, exert more control at first. As you learn which students need more guidance or which activities have lower risk, you can gradually allow more freedom and reduce your control. In the classroom, having children sit is a great way to keep control. As classroom teachers increase in confidence (and control), they gradually allow more freedom of movement around the room. The same principle works here! Let your students know that you ask them to go one at a time, to sit or stand still, or to follow other safety rules because you care about them. Your message to them is "Many activities that are fun are also risky, so we must be responsible and earn the opportunity to participate in fun and challenging activities." Do not teach an activity unless you feel competent and confident. If you are unsure, ask another teacher for help or substitute a different activity.

During instruction, a fine line exists between a student who is rebellious and one who is afraid. As you saw in chapter 11, fear of failure often breeds behavior problems in physical education. Another type of fear is related to failure and also to injury: Occasionally a student will refuse to participate in a risky activity because he is afraid. Generally, when a student says, "I'm afraid," it is true. Students often encounter negative outcomes for admitting fear. These are learned at an early age, so children are often reluctant to admit fear. Do not try to force a student who is afraid. Encourage, break the task down, offer help, but never say, "Oh, come on, it is easy"—this only makes the student feel worse about the fear! Look for signs of fear, such as holding on tightly to a source of security. Children who are afraid will grab onto something—including you—and not let go! It is difficult to force a fearful child to do a task. It is wrong, especially if the child is hurt in the attempt, and it is not a productive educational procedure. Instead, be patient, help the child gain confidence, and reduce the pressure on the student. Also, be sensitive to how the child is portrayed to the other students. Being afraid is difficult, but being afraid in front of your peers is much worse. Once again, you may reduce the stigma and gain a student's confidence by recognizing the fear as valid, identifying the difficulty of the task, and even admitting personal fears of a similar nature.

Checklist for Instruction

- ❏ Parents and students were informed of the class rules and rationale for the rules (in writing).
- ❏ The rules are posted at the venue, and additional activity-specific rules are reviewed before each class.
- ❏ Parents and students were informed of the curriculum plan (over the semester or year).
- ❏ Parents were offered the opportunity to ask questions and to communicate about the curriculum and rules.
- ❏ A written lesson plan is available (see chapter 9 for more detail).
- ❏ The activity is developmentally appropriate.
- ❏ The students have been adequately prepared for the activity.
- ❏ The lesson accommodates a variety of skill levels and groups students appropriately.
- ❏ Alternative activities are available as needed.
- ❏ An emergency and accident procedure is posted at each activity venue.
- ❏ A first aid kit is readily available.
- ❏ The equipment and venue are checked regularly for hazards (see chapter 13 for more detail).
- ❏ Incident reports are kept on file.
- ❏ The principal (and other teachers as appropriate) are notified about the incident.
- ❏ After an accident, follow-up with the student and parent are completed.

Supervision

Supervision is the most basic of teacher responsibilities. Teachers are responsible for supervising students in the classroom, before school, at recess, and at many other times. Although being present is the prerequisite for **supervision,** being present does not guarantee adequate supervision. When you physically (direct removal) or mentally (indirect removal) leave the area, your students are at greater risk. Most teachers think very carefully before leaving their students alone. Most of the time nothing happens—no one is injured and no one discovers the students were alone. If a student is injured, however, the teacher may be held responsible because she failed to provide proper supervision. At other times, a teacher may be in the area with the students physically, but he may not be fully aware of what is happening. Of course, this may be the goal of a student—to do something inappropriate without the teacher's being aware! Examples of indirect removal include talking to a class visitor during class, handling a disruptive or injured student, and fixing a piece of equipment. It is best to be with your students at all times, but sometimes a teacher must leave a class unattended. What happens if a student gets hurt when you are not present? Pettifor (1999) suggests, "Courts will consider these factors in determining liability":

- ▶ Reasons for the absence
- ▶ Length of the absence
- ▶ The age and maturity level of those students left unsupervised
- ▶ Location of the injured student when left unsupervised
- ▶ The activity the students were engaged in immediately prior to the teacher's absence
- ▶ The teacher's ability to foresee the potential dangers compared with a reasonable person (p. 289)

Provide active rather than passive supervision for children in your care (Hudson, Thompson, and Mack 1999). What does this mean? **Active supervision** has three characteristics:

1. Proximity——the distance you are from the activity
2. Scanning—looking at the entire area regularly
3. Positioning—placing yourself so you can see everyone and everything

Active supervision applies to any supervision. The courts recognize three types of instructional supervision in physical education (Dougherty 1993). General supervision means the teacher is physically present. Specific supervision means the teacher is assisting a student or group of students. Transitional supervision occurs when there is a change in activity or change in venue. You can see that the teacher (or a qualified substitute) should be present at all times during physical education. Supervision is constant, and the teacher should provide assistance such as spotting when necessary. Spotting is physical guidance provided to a learner by another person for the purpose of increasing safety. Thus, students will be under continuous supervision by a qualified adult. For example, when going from the playing field to the classroom, the students should not be sent ahead while the teacher is putting away equipment.

Tips for Proper Supervision

1. Have everything you need with you before you begin to supervise.
2. Enter the venue with the students or be present when the students are brought to you for supervision.
3. Plan the activity so that you can see all the students, so you are close to the high-risk activities or problematic students, and so you can look around the entire area frequently.
4. Make supervision a priority; attend to interruptions only when it will not interfere with supervision.
5. Have an emergency plan.
6. Use appropriate student–teacher ratios.

Classifying Students

Teachers frequently need to group students for activity. For most activities, teachers should group students per logical criteria. For example, in partner activities, size may be important; so students of similar size may be paired, or one large and one small student may work together on partner balances where the larger student serves as the base. Skill level is another way to pair students. Except when peer tutoring and utilizing equalized teams, students are usually paired by skill level. A very strong and well-skilled thrower paired with a weaker

and less-skilled catcher is a formula for disaster in a catching activity. For many activities, random groups or pairs work well because one student is unlikely to hurt another student. Rhythmic activities are good examples of relatively low-risk activities and thus are good for randomizing the groupings. Generally, you won't want to group by gender (e.g., all boys in one group or boy–girl pairs). Also avoid allowing students to make up their own groups. Certain combinations, pairings, or groups can create trouble regardless of the activity. As the teacher, it is your job to form pairs, groups, or teams in a way that will be safe, productive, and efficient. A note of caution: You may be the biggest "kid" in the class, so consider whether it is safe for you to participate. Your size may endanger a student, you must serve as a role model, and you must be able to supervise. It is unlikely that your participation is justified in view of those three points.

Safe Environment

Equipment, facilities, or venues must not contribute to an injury. Poor maintenance and developmentally inappropriate uses of equipment and facilities frequently lead to injuries. Schools should inform students (and parents) about playground and facility rules. Equipment and facilities need to be checked routinely—that is, on a regular, documented schedule. Upkeep and repairs should be conducted in a timely and efficient manner, and someone should be responsible for these activities. Maintenance also includes routine cleaning of the areas. Sand on a gym floor, rocks on asphalt, water on surfaces, and dirt and debris in fans and ventilating systems can all contribute to risk. Don't assume that someone else has taken care of these responsibilities, however. View yourself as the last line of defense in ensuring the safety of your students. If you find equipment or a facility unsafe, do not use it! Report the problem—preferably in writing—and follow up to be sure repairs have been made.

Select small equipment, such as balls and bats, based on the size and skill of the students. Similarly, large equipment, including outdoor play structures, should be appropriate for the age of the students. Playgrounds should have areas designated for different age groups (or grades). Chapter 13 offers more information and sources for playground regulations. Thus, a teacher who takes older children to an area designated for younger children, or vice versa, may be placing those students at risk because the new area does not meet their developmental needs.

Venues and facilities are subject to another category of potential safety hazards. Weather and other transient factors such as overcrowding increase risk for students. The weather itself can be a risk (too cold or hot) or can create a risk (water on the field). Scheduling physical education during lunch or recess, when the area is crowded, or scheduling more than one class in an area both increase risk. Even in a large gymnasium, having a volleyball game at one end and dance or gymnastics at the other is not a safe practice. Stray balls can trip students concentrating on another activity. Chapter 13 includes examples of environmental factors to consider as you determine the appropriateness of a venue or facility.

If you know of a hazard, you are obligated to report it to your supervisor. Say you see a hole in the outdoor court and decide not to use the area for your class. When the next physical education class enters the area, a child is hurt when she steps into the hole. In this case, you will be partially at fault because you did nothing to prevent the injury! So, you should report the hazard to the principal, mark the hazard (e.g., post a "keep out" sign or mark the area with yellow hazard tape), and inform anyone else that may use the area about the hazard.

When an activity requires safety equipment (e.g., protective eye wear for floor hockey), make sure you and all the students have and use the safety gear. Be a good role model! Allowing children to bring equipment from home can be a good solution to equipment shortages. However, two problems can arise when using equipment from home: The equipment can be lost or stolen, or it can fail to be maintained properly. Before deciding to allow students to bring equipment from home, you might want to check with the principal.

RESPONDING TO INJURIES

Unfortunately, there is no way to avoid all injuries. Therefore, you'll need to have a plan for dealing with them, should they occur. Your plan should include the following:

► Getting help
► Having a first aid kit on hand
► Receiving first aid training.

With cell phones and intercoms, it should be easy to get help; but when a crisis arises, everything that can go wrong will. First, have a written plan posted at each venue (e.g., the playground and the gym). Include in the plan whom you will

contact first and how. Make sure there is a backup plan, if, for example, you call the office but the line is busy or no one answers. Include the school nurse's number. In your instructions, include the school address and phone number so when calling for emergency medical help you can say where you are located. This plan should be developed by a team (e.g., the principal, school nurse, and one or more teachers) and should be clearly understood by everyone. Each school will differ in whom to call first and how the emergency should be handled. The point is to have a plan, in writing, and have the materials necessary to carry out the plan available at all times. The school gymnasium is likely to have a phone available; many have an intercom. You can use a student messenger in older grades. Clearly, in an emergency the first two obligations are to get help and to stabilize the injured student. Thus, you need to have current first aid training, and you must have a first aid kit readily available.

Contents of a First Aid Kit

► Copy of the emergency plan
► Emergency contact numbers for fire, police, and ambulance
► Disposable gloves
► Blanket
► Antibacterial hand cleaner
► Adhesive bandages, tape and gauze pads, elastic wraps
► Antiseptic and burn ointment
► Insect sting kit
► Eye wash kit
► Scissors and tweezers
► Cotton pads and cotton-tipped applicators
► Cold pack
► Splints and triangular bandages

A third issue concerns the rest of your class while you are occupied with the emergency. Again, a plan is helpful. The students would be safest sitting quietly a reasonable distance from the injured student; do not allow the class to gather around the injured student. A reasonable plan is to discuss with your students what should happen if there is an injury before an injury happens. Children are often curious and afraid, and they want to be helpful. Let them know how they can help. A sample of what you might present to students follows.

Responding to an Emergency

- ▶ Tell the teacher immediately if you or someone else is hurt.
- ▶ All students who are not injured should continue working until the teacher says, "Stop."
- ▶ When the teacher says, "Stop," move to a safe place and sit quietly until a grown-up tells you what to do.
- ▶ Be a helper by waiting patiently.
- ▶ If the teacher asks you to do something, listen carefully and do it immediately.

PROFESSIONAL RESPONSIBILITY

As previously mentioned, educators are held to higher standards than other people. Teachers are expected to meet certain responsibilities in order to maintain their jobs and teaching licenses; in doing so, they also avoid being sued or arrested. Sometimes, a teacher will no longer be allowed to teach after she has failed to meet professional standards. Many states offer two or more levels of a teaching license. The first license allows you to teach for a set period of time; in order to qualify for your next license, you may have to meet specific additional requirements. For example, you may have to be observed while teaching or take additional courses. The following list provides examples of professional responsibilities, though it is not complete:

- ▶ Keeping up to date (keep learning!)
- ▶ Doing your job as an instructor and supervisor
- ▶ Doing mandatory reporting
- ▶ Demonstrating ethical behavior
- ▶ Seeking help when necessary

You are familiar with the need to continue to learn and to do your job as an instructor and supervisor, and you have probably heard of mandatory reporting. Mandatory reporting includes teachers who are obligated to report suspected abuse (e.g., physical, sexual, emotional) to the appropriate authority (usually the principal). You should also intervene or report instances in which you have reason to believe a student is breaking the law. This frequently happens with substance abuse—a student will talk about using an illegal substance. The fact that you overhear this or that a student takes you into his confidence does not relieve you of your duty to do something. Schools have different policies; you must find out how you are obligated to handle the situation. Many times, students confide in teachers as a plea for help. Allowing the student to continue endangering his life is not helping. Let the student know you care and that you are obligated to help. Hopefully, you will feel comfortable telling the student that you will provide support during this time and be able to follow through. The first step in helping is reporting.

From an ethical standpoint, the teacher needs to follow the **chain of command.** If you have a problem or concern, your first obligation is to address this with the person. You may observe a colleague doing something that seems inappropriate, such as giving a student a ride home from school, appearing to be under the influence of alcohol or drugs at school, or using equipment that is unsafe. Ethical behavior demands that you discuss this first with the colleague. There may be a logical explanation that will satisfy your concern. The explanation may even teach you something!

Sometimes the colleague is clearly doing something that seems wrong, has no explanation, and seems determined to continue. If students are not in immediate jeopardy, you should express your concern and provide a reasonable time period for change. However, if students are at risk, you will want to seek help at a higher level immediately. Discuss the situation discreetly with your supervisor or a trusted senior colleague; under most circumstances, you should follow her advice. You always have the right to continue moving up the administrative ladder with your concerns, but you should be certain of the facts and know that you have informed all persons in the chain. The first question most school superintendents will ask is, "Have you discussed this with your principal?" If you have not, the superintendent may not speak with you. You have two obligations in this regard under ethical behavior—follow the chain of command and do not gossip or complain casually about colleagues or school policy.

Professional responsibility recognizes that everyone needs help—even professionals. Standards encourage you to seek help from colleagues and supervisors as necessary. This is not viewed as a sign of weakness but of strength and determination to do what is right.

BEST PRACTICES AND BEYOND

Most of this chapter has been devoted to the minimum expected of teachers. You probably entered education to be the best, not to do the minimum. Therefore, a brief discussion of best practices is appropriate. A **best practice** is a way to do something that maximizes the opportunities to be gained from the experience. Several best practices have been presented in previous sections of this chapter. For example, although it is acceptable to cancel a physical education class because of unsafe conditions (and this is certainly better than continuing under unsafe conditions), there is a better way. Have a backup plan. Identify and learn several activities that do not require equipment or a specific venue. Use one of those activities instead of canceling class.

We suggested earlier in the chapter that teachers inform parents and students of rules and activities via a letter. This is clearly better than not informing them at all. However, including parents and students in the planning of rules is even better. This helps them to buy into the rules and encourages greater understanding between you and them. Afterward, parents and students will see rules as a means to safety and maximum learning. Rather than viewing a special shoe requirement as an inconvenience and unnecessary expense, parents may see it as a way to protect their children from injury. This, again, is a best practice rather than meeting the minimum!

SUMMARY

One of the many responsibilities teachers face is keeping their students safe. Most teachers enter teaching because of a caring attitude and concern for children that translates into a desire to make and keep students safe. In addition to these values influencing teachers' behaviors, the laws that regulate our society also apply to teachers. Professional organizations and state regulations reiterate this responsibility for teachers. A teacher's desire for continuous improvement leads many teachers to seek the best practice in each situation, including student safety. In addition to student safety teachers accept many other responsibilities, such as arranging field trips, purchasing equipment for the school, and managing school events. These activities often require teachers to have some understanding of laws, statutes, contracts, and torts.

MASTERY LEARNING ACTIVITIES

1. Search the newspaper for an article on a lawsuit against a school or teacher. In 100 words or fewer, describe the case. Was it negligence, intent, knowledge? Were criminal charges filed? What are the professional issues involved?

2. Find the code regulating teacher behavior for your state or a state where you hope to teach. (Look on the Internet or ask the State Department of Education for a reference.) What is covered in the code?

3. Observe a teacher during physical education class. Where did the teacher stand and why? In your description, consider proximity, scanning, and position of the teacher as well as the activity and the age and skill of the children.

4. Search the literature and find an article on best practice (in the classroom or gymnasium). How did reading this change your view?

5. Using the Department of Education Web site, select two states and identify the similarities and differences in each in applying for a teaching license. Do both states require self-reporting? Do they perform criminal background checks?

REFERENCES

Dougherty, N., ed. 1993. *Principles of safety in physical education and sport.* Reston, Va.: American Alliance for Health, Physical Education, Recreation and Dance (AAHPERD).

Hudson, S.D., D.M. Thompson, and M.G. Mack. 1999. Prevention of playground injuries. *The Journal of School Nursing,* 15(3): 30-33.

Pettifor, B. 1999. *Physical education methods for classroom teachers.* Champaign, Ill.: Human Kinetics.

RESOURCES

Hart, J., and R. Ritson. 1993. *Liability and safety in physical education and sport.* Reston, Va.: American Alliance for Health, Physical Education, Recreation and Dance (AAHPERD).

www.uni.edu/playground/home.html

chapter 13

Equipment and Facilities

I love Pacer run.

Andy, age 9

Equipment and facilities enhance student learning but present safety challenges for teachers and schools.

Learner Outcomes

The teacher will do the following:

- Evaluate the appropriateness of equipment for skill development.
- State and apply safety guidelines for equipment and facilities.
- Plan instructional or free time to maximize physical activity when using equipment and facilities.

- Distinguish between structured and unstructured physical activity.
- State the benefits of unstructured physical activity.

Glossary Terms

proximity
visual angle
scanning

decision making
structured physical activity
unstructured activity time

Equipment and facilities present unique challenges for teachers and schools. Trade-offs exist between practical issues and potential for learning. Practical issues include cost, maintenance, space, and storage; these must be balanced with the ideal for engaging students in meaningful play and instruction to facilitate student learning. Further, teachers—even physical education specialists—may not have the expertise or the time to effectively plan and monitor physical education equipment and facilities. Finally, the same equipment and facilities are usually multipurpose; that is, these are used for instruction (physical education), free time (recess), recreation (before and after school), and often at lunchtime or assemblies. Different people may supervise the use of facilities, with varying degrees of ownership or investment. For example, the physical education teacher may take great care in managing the gym and equipment compared with someone who is renting the gym after school. Consider what a common practice this is and how a classroom teacher might feel if the school rented her classroom to someone else for use after school!

Knowing about equipment and facilities enables teachers to do several things:

- Enhance student learning
- Make the environment as safe as possible
- Balance practical concerns and learning issues

SMALL EQUIPMENT

Small equipment falls into three general categories: manipulatable objects (e.g., balls), single-use equipment (e.g., batting tee), and support materials (e.g., cones, music). Practical issues such as cost and storage must be balanced with instructional issues (e.g., developmentally appropriate, variety, specificity, practice) when considering small equipment. For example, in a class of 25 students, the ideal situation would be to have one piece of equipment for each student. However, when you begin to purchase 25 footballs, volleyballs, basketballs, soccer balls, bats, baseball gloves, goals, and bases, storage and cost are clearly practical issues. You may find it is better to purchase 25 playground balls and only a few of each other type. Consider what is necessary for instruction at all grade levels and across activities. For example, organizational equipment is used in all physical education classes, so it makes sense to purchase one set of cones, poly-spots, and carpet squares for the school. Every teacher does not need a set of cones in her classroom. The same would be true for playground balls; each classroom teacher does not need to keep 25 in the room. Generally, the decision will be to invest in multi-use rather than single-use equipment. For example, purchase and store playground balls rather than soccer balls, if you must choose; or purchase many playground balls and a few specialty balls. Physical education specialists face equipment issues as well; storage and expense are at the top of the list. In addition, many specialists travel from school to school, so transporting equipment is an additional problem.

Support materials include management items and other equipment that facilitates learning. Schools should have enough markers (poly-spots) so that at least one is available for each student in a class. Cones are another necessity. Sometimes homemade equivalents are helpful, such as colored masking tape to mark spots on the floor and two-liter plastic bottles (filled with sand or water and sealed) for cones. A CD or tape player can be used to play music for fitness, dance, and gymnastics (NASPE 2001a). When purchasing a player, select one that is as adaptable as possible. For example, choose one that works with a remote microphone so the teacher's voice can be amplified when necessary.

For the lower grades, playground balls (rubber 8.5 and 13 in. [21.5 cm and 33 cm]), foam balls (8.5 in. [21.5 cm] with plastic coating), hoops, and beanbags are essential. Sport-specific balls are helpful in the upper grades (these include volleyball trainers, footballs, softballs, soccer balls, and junior basketballs). Other helpful equipment includes carpet squares and hoops (30- to 36-in. [76-cm and 91-cm] size). Have one for each student, if possible; but class can still be effective with one for each two or three students. Selecting equipment for a variety of students can help meet individual needs. For example, rather than order a dozen identical bats, order three or four each of two or three types of bats, selecting from traditional metal bats to large plastic bats. Younger and less skilled children will be more successful with the larger plastic bats, whereas well-skilled and older children will be challenged by the "regular" bats. The variety meets the needs of students

within and between classes. If you are the physical education specialist, you need to have equipment on hand that is appropriate for all grades. Classroom teachers may want to pair up by grades as a practical approach to equipment. In both cases, the information here is a guide to what you will need for the school, your class, or your grade.

Some specialty equipment is used less often but is helpful; this includes items that enhance manipulative skills, balance, and teamwork. Examples include scooters, foxtails, batting tees, nets, walking cans, wands, rhythm sticks, beanie launchers, jump ropes, bowling balls and pins, quoits, Frisbees, fluff balls (yarn), Hacky-Sacks, beach balls, balloons, rackets, bats, bases, goals, targets, and floor hockey sticks. Music for dance, fitness, and gymnastics is also considered specialty equipment. Sample equipment lists are presented in tables 13.1 to 13.3. The National Association for Sport and Physical Education (NASPE 2001a), an association of the American Alliance for Health, Physical Education, Recreation and Dance (AAHPERD), provides a list of equipment (table 13.4) as part of their guidelines for elementary physical education materials.

A sign over an "attractive nuisance" will dissuade students from getting into unsafe situations.

Table 13.1 Necessary Equipment (shading identifies appropriate grades)

	K-1	2-3	4-5	6-8
30-40 poly-spots	■	■	■	■
30 wands	■	■	■	■
8-12 cones	■	■	■	■
6 gymnastics mats (6 × 12')	■	■	■	■
1 balance beam (4" × 10')	■	■	■	■
30 playground balls (8.5')	■	■		
4 batting tees	■	■		
30 beanbags	■	■		
30 foam balls (8.5')	■	■	■	
30 hoops (30-36")	■	■	■	
1 parachute	■	■	■	
12 long jump ropes (16')		■	■	
30 jump ropes (5-7')		■	■	■
30 Frisbees		■	■	■
2 volleyball nets			■	■
12 junior or foam footballs			■	■
12 trainer volleyballs			■	■
12 softballs			■	■
12 junior basketballs			■	■
4 junior bats			■	■
1 set of softball bases			■	■
8 batons			■	■

Table 13.2 Suggested Equipment

	K-1	2-3	4-5	6-8
4 shapes (to climb through)	■			
3 pairs of walking cans	■	■		
3 jumping cubes (2' square)	■	■		
30 ribbon streamers	■	■		
2 sets of pillow polo (24 sticks total)	■	■		
30 carpet squares	■	■	■	
60 rhythm sticks	■	■	■	■
30 scooters	■	■	■	■
1 drum or tambourine	■	■	■	■
1 climbing rope	■	■	■	■
1 vaulting mat	■	■	■	■
2 sets of floor hockey sticks (24 total)			■	■
2-6 soccer goals			■	■
6 bowling balls			■	■
6 sets of bowling pins			■	■
30 tennis rackets (half short handle)			■	■
90 tennis balls			■	■
4 sets of bamboo poles (for tinikling)			■	■

Table 13.3   Optional Single-Use Equipment

	K-1	2-3	4-5	6-8
Juggling scarves	X			
Scoops and balls	X			
Buddy walkers (2 person)	X			
Foxtails		X	X	
Kosh-kosh balls		X	X	
Juggling beanbags		X		X
Ominkin ball or Earth ball	X			X
Hacky-Sacks			X	X
Pogo sticks			X	X
Stilts			X	X
Buddy walkers (4 person)			X	X

So, how do you decide what you need? First, think about what you will teach and what you have on hand. Next, prioritize the list so that those things you need most often are at the top of the list. Finally, consider budget and storage issues. Buy what you will use most frequently and is within your budget and that you have room to store. Each year, add to the equipment on hand, remembering to replace items that need to be replaced because of wear and tear.

HOMEMADE EQUIPMENT

Once again, a trade-off exists, this time between the cost effectiveness and the safety of homemade equipment. Homemade is usually less expensive, but it may present problems in maintaining safety. Equipment manufacturers are responsible for making their products safe, and manufacturers stand behind their products as long as the product is used as intended. You are the only person standing behind homemade equipment, however! Certain items, such as fluff or yarn balls, are relatively safe; thus, if these are less expensive to make than to purchase, homemade is a good substitute. Some items present safety issues, however, such as coat hangers covered with nylon used instead

Homemade equipment is an inexpensive way to provide for your class.

Table 13.4 NASPE (2001) Elementary Physical Education Equipment

General equipment	Quantity
Chalk or white board	1
Bags to carry balls	6
Ball inflator	1
Ball repair kit	1
Bulletin board	1–2
Clipboards	Enough for one-half of class
First aid kit	1
Measuring tape (100', 50')	1
CD/tape player	1
Crates or baskets for storage	5
Field marker (for chalking lines)	1
AV cart with electrical outlet for CD/tape player	1

Educational games

Skill themes: bounding, striking, kicking, catching, throwing

Equipment items	Equipment size	Quantity for class size of 20–25
Playground balls	5", 6" and 8.5"	17, 17, and 30
Balls for striking w/body	8" and 9"	15–18 of each
Beach balls	24", 45"	18, 25
Foam balls	7" or 8"	25
Fleece or yarn balls	3" (get washable)	25
Balloons	11"	36–72
Squish balls	3"	17–18
Foam balls—bounceable	4.75"	30
Beanbags	4", 5"	30
Flying disks	11"	30
Deck rings	7" diameter	17–18
Rag balls	9"	17–18

(continued)

Table 13.4 *(continued)*

General equipment	Size	Quantity
Plastic bottle bats	11.5" handles	17–18
Soft bat	24", 27", and 29"	5 of each
Lollipop paddles (styrofoam heads)	8"and 10" diameter with 12" handles	17–18 of each
Scoops		30
Youth tennis rackets	21" and 24"	30, 30
Foam blade hockey sticks with styrofoam pucks	40", 45" sticks	30 of each
Portable gym standards (150 lb)		Minimum 8 (or 4 pairs)
Net for standards		4
Cones or jug markers	12",18", 24"	26, 14, 14
Pinnies, sashes, or vests (3 or more colors)		30
Scooter boards w/handles		30
Spotmarkers		20
Basketballs (junior size)		30
Adjustable basketball goals	7"–10"	4–6
Soccer balls	Sizes 4 and 5	18 and 30
Parachute		1

Educational dance

Skill themes: locomotor and nonlocomotor skills

Equipment items	Equipment size	Quantity for class size of 20–25
Plastic hoops	30" and 36" diameter	20, 20
Styrofoam hoops holders (2 per hoop)		30
Rhythmic equipment—		
• Ankle wrist bells		
• Rain stick		
• Rap stick		
• Drum w/mallet		
• Lummi sticks	12" L and .75" diameter	30
Stretchy material bands	36" L and 6" W	30

Table 13.4 *(continued)*

General equipment	Size	Quantity
Nylon scarves	54" × 54"	30
Tinikling sticks/boards and jump bands		15 pairs
CD/tape player		1
Cordless microphone		1
Sound system		1

Educational gymnastics

Skill themes: rolling, jumping/landing, balance, transfer of weight, hanging/swinging

Equipment items	Equipment size	Quantity for class size of 20–25
Foam vaulting trapezoid	(3–4 sections)	1
Styrofoam shapes (circles, triangles, ovals, wedge)		8
Mats	4' × 6' or 5' × 10' c, 2" thick, 100	ILD foam 7–8 mats (3-4 students per mat)
Landing mats	4" thick	Minimum of 1
Incline mats	36"W × 72"L	1
Balance beams/benches	12' L, 12" W	1 or more
Jumping boxes (foam shapes of varying heights)	12"–24"	4–6
Trestles	5', 6', and 7'	2 of each
Sliding boards to connect to trestles	12" L, 10–12" W	2
Connecting ladder		1
Hanging ropes		1–2
Jump ropes (plastic segments for beginners; speed rope for experienced jumpers)	7', 8', 9' and 16' length	13, 13, 13, 13
Stretch jump ropes ("magic ropes")		8–12
Wands		12–13

Physical fitness assessment

Sit-and-reach box for measuring flexibility		2–4
Stopwatches		4–6
Skin-fold calipers		6
Modified chin-up bar and standards		
Fitness assessment package		

Reprinted from *Guidelines for Facilities, Equipment and Instructional Materials in Elementary School Physical Education* (2001) with permission from the National Association for Sport and Physical Education (NASPE), 1900 Association Drive, Reston, VA 20191-1599.

of paddles. The coat hanger is a hazard and should not be substituted for purchased paddles or rackets. Other typically safe, inexpensive, homemade items include wands from broom handles and rhythm sticks from dowels. You can create a foxtail by putting a tennis ball inside a tube sock. Generally, things that are soft can be made at home, whereas items that inflate or have hard surfaces should be purchased.

Items that are available readily, but are not specific to physical education, are also helpful. For example, cardboard boxes, laundry baskets, and milk crates make excellent storage containers and targets. The school cafeteria staff may be able to supply you with boxes; if you have a ready supply, you can dispose of those you are using after use (e.g., using one for a target) rather than having to store them for reuse.

Another source of low-cost (and sometimes free) help is the local bowling lanes. Bowling lane personnel can add additional holes to purchased gymnasium balls so the balls fit more children. They may be able to donate bowling pins as well. Because the children will use their facilities, these businesses are usually willing to help. Other businesses will often donate things you need—for example, carpet squares from the flooring store, dowels from the lumber yard (to make wands and rhythm sticks), and storage containers (garbage cans on wheels, milk crates, laundry baskets) from the local discount or home supply store.

LARGE EQUIPMENT

Large equipment falls into three categories: outdoor equipment, such as playground structures; indoor moveable equipment, such as mats and balance beams; and indoor fixed equipment, such as climbing ropes, rock walls, and chinning bars. As you will see from the next section, there is some overlap between large equipment, and facilities—that is, playground structures are considered both a facility and large equipment. Playground equipment will be discussed in the next section.

The same practical challenges (cost, storage, and number) that apply when considering small equipment also apply to large equipment. Large fixed equipment also presents safety hazards, since often these items are an attractive nuisance. Once large fixed equipment is installed, the teacher and school are responsible for its supervision and maintenance. Many schools use the gym for other purposes or allow outside groups into it after school. A student at lunch or a visitor may find it impossible to resist climbing up and hanging from the chinning bar—it is very attractive; thus, it is a nuisance. Making matters worse, we know it is attractive and therefore we are responsible for making sure it is safe. If a student or visitor is injured while trying to use the chinning bar, we are likely to be sued! To make such equipment less of an attraction, when given the option, select large fixed equipment that can be

Playground equipment is considered both a facility and large equipment.

stowed out of the way. For example, choose chinning bars that can be raised or removed from the wall, nets and ropes that can be raised to the ceiling when not in use, or rock walls where the rocks can be removed when not in use. Care should be taken when placing large equipment. Do not place fixed equipment in walkways, especially near exits. Have a plan for securing equipment when it is not being used. At the very least, post a sign that indicates potential danger (figure 13.1). Additional information about fixed hazards is presented in the next section.

FACILITIES

Three or four different facilities are found in most schools: indoor physical education facilities and outdoor grass surfaces, playground structures, and hard surfaces. Inside are the gymnasium or multipurpose room, which were designed for physical education, and other spaces such as hallways and classrooms that can be used when other facilities are not available for physical education. Gymnasiums or multipurpose spaces should provide 110 square feet of space per child in an area approximately 70 × 100 feet (NASPE 2001a). The ceiling should be at least 20 feet high; the room must have adequate lighting, sound absorption, and walls that are smooth and hard at least 10 to 15 feet above the floor. Windows may be present higher than that, and mats are used for padding below that height. Depending on the age and original design of indoor facilities, safety hazards may exist, even in facilities that were designed specifically for physical education. One of the most common safety issues indoors is the size of the space. For example, a gym may be large enough for a basketball court, but the out-of-bounds lines are very close to the wall. Children running to catch a ball may not be able to stop. This means that the walls become a hazard. Walls with doorknobs protruding or hanging equipment present even greater hazards. In small facilities, it is often good practice to establish boundaries inside the court lines. Teachers should consider the size of the facility, the size of the children, the number of children, and the type of activity to decide what is safe. Games of chase (e.g., tag) may be appropriate in the gym for younger children (grades K through 3) who are slower and smaller, but unsafe for older children (grades 4 through 6) who are larger and faster. A distance of seven to nine feet between the activity and a hazard (e.g., the wall or stored equipment) is recommended. Further, both drinking water and restrooms should be nearby.

Danger
No Climbing

Figure 13.1 Warning sign.

Concepts Into Practice

Mr. Astor, a fourth-grade teacher, realizes that the gym is too small and dangerous for his large class of older students. The new gym will be ready for next semester. He wants to teach physical education every day, but rainy days are a challenge. After a lot of thought, he decides to split his class in two and teach 30 minutes of physical education to each group. One group will work on physical activity journals and have free reading time while the other group is doing activity. Then the groups will reverse roles. This works well because bleachers are available for the writing group to use, and Mr. Astor can position himself across the gym from the bleachers. This way he can see all the students.

Other indoor hazards include the surface, permanent objects, and moveable objects. Debris or water makes nearly any surface dangerous. This means that the floor should be dry-mopped frequently and wet-mopped regularly (i.e., with water or a cleaning solvent). Dry mopping should remove sand, dirt, and other debris. Wet mopping is appropriate for regular cleaning and for sanitizing the surface. Once the floor has been wet-mopped, it should dry thoroughly before being used. One way to reduce sand and other debris on the floor is for children to have athletic shoes used only for physical education. Although this creates expense for parents, it can reduce risk. Constantly wearing one pair of shoes reduces their tread, which can cause slipping, even on a clean floor. In addition, shoes worn outdoors track in dirt, sand, and debris. So, indoor-only shoes specifically for physical education are helpful. Alternatively, the floor could be cleaned after every class.

Virtually anything that protrudes into the gym or other indoor area creates a hazard. Doorknobs are common in older facilities, and so are drinking fountains. Sometimes physical education equipment is positioned so that it protrudes into the activity area. Chin-up bars, bleachers, fire alarms, and storage cabinets are examples of possibly protruding items. Sometimes the problem can be solved simply by moving the chin-up bar to a position that is taller than any student. At other times, there is no way to move the equipment. In that case, padding is helpful. Mats that protect children from doorknobs, posts, the edges of stages, and other equipment that protrudes into the space can be purchased or custom made. NASPE (2001a) provides guidelines for facilities; these include specific recommendations for avoiding many problems with facilities that can create dangerous situations (figure 13.2).

---

1. Boards of Education, through their school budget process, fund
   (a) the purchase and maintenance of appropriate and sufficient physical education supplies and equipment, and
   (b) equitable physical education facilities and maintenance of these facilities for each school.
2. Physical education teachers, physical education program administrators, and school administrators should jointly
   (a) develop standards for appropriate supplies and equipment and procedures for purchasing, and
   (b) provide input to plans for new physical education facilities.
3. School and community facilities and programs are designed and implemented to support and complement one another in serving children's needs.
4. There is a dedicated facility for the physical education instructional program.
5. Adequate space, ranging from 110 square ft to 150 square ft per child, for learning movement activities in which children can move freely and safely. The student-to-teacher ratio should be 25:1 per class. Intact classes should not interfere with one another.
6. Adequate space, ranging from 400 to 600 square ft with a height of 12' to 15', is available for safe and proper storage of physical education equipment.
7. Physical activity space is designed to facilitate instruction free of distractions and pass-through traffic patterns.

8. Restrooms and drinking fountains should be located close to the instructional facilities; if drinking fountains are in the instructional area, they should be recessed.
9. Office space, ranging from 120 to 240 square ft in size, for the physical education teacher is provided to allow students convenient access to their teacher for consultation and assistance.
10. A learning environment with adequate acoustics ("sound baffles") permits children to participate safely in all phases of instruction.
11. Indoor facilities, with proper flooring and lighting, are clean and sanitized on a daily basis. Floor surface should be either hardwood with cushion or a roll-out synthetic product. The minimum amount of light should be 30-foot candles.
12. All-weather outdoor surfaces are properly marked with circles, lines, and courts to permit participation in a wide variety of activities and are appropriate for students with varied ability levels.
13. Outdoor areas are available for teaching and
    (a) are free from safety hazards (such as glass, debris, water),
    (b) located away from occupied classrooms,
    (c) have clearly defined physical boundaries,
    (d) are far away from parking lots or streets (no closer than 100 yd) or are separated by barriers that prevent vehicles from entering the area,
    (e) are close enough to school building to permit access to equipment, and
    (f) provide shelter in case of inclement weather.
14. Natural play areas are available to facilitate and encourage creative and exploratory play.

Figure 13.2   NASPE facilities guidelines.

Reprinted from *Guidelines for Facilities, Equipment and Instructional Materials in Elementary School Physical Education* (2001) with permission from the National Association for Sport and Physical Education (NASPE), 1900 Association Drive, Reston, VA 20191-1599.

Even in the newest of facilities, storage is at a premium. The solution is often to store some items along the edge of the gym, but a rack of folding chairs pushed against the gym wall the morning after a meeting seems harmless until a child is injured falling into the chairs. Placing a stack of mats in a corner seems like a good solution because the mats are padded. However, the mats are an attractive nuisance. Unsupervised children may climb on the pile, in which case they may risk falling and injuring themselves. Thus, moveable items may be a hazard. If possible, remove the items; if not, create a safety zone around them so children are less likely to injury themselves. NASPE suggests 400 to 600 square feet of storage with 12- to 15-foot ceilings to avoid problems associated with storage.

Outdoor hard surfaces (asphalt, concrete, or synthetic) should be separated from general playground areas so instruction is not interrupted by recess and other events. The area should be 50 × 80 feet or greater and provide 110 square feet of space per child. Outdoor field space should be well drained, with appropriate turf that is cared for regularly. The permanent equipment on fields (such as backstops) should be checked regularly for wear or disrepair and serviced as needed. Generally, the playground of a typical elementary school should measure 8 to 10 acres.

The playground, specifically the playground equipment, can be a learning center used during instruction. Children will find challenges in using the equipment to solve problems, develop upper-body strength, and practice jumping and landing. Traditional single-use playground equipment (e.g., swings, slides, and merry-go-rounds) is being replaced by multi-use structures. Many playgrounds have both types, and the safety issues are generally the same for both. Selection of the equipment should be based on the age of the students and its general use. Is the purpose to develop skill, to promote social interaction or fitness, or to foster creativity? What age range will use the equipment? Equipment catalogs provide helpful information in making decisions about what to purchase. A separate area for pre-K and kindergarten should be provided. The size and skill of this age group demand different, specifically smaller equipment when compared with older children. Further, younger children may be injured by older children simply because younger children get in the way or cannot get out of the way of older children during vigorous play. Once user-appropriate equipment has been selected and the acceptable locations identified, three additional areas of concern arise.

The first area of concern is proper installation, the second is maintenance, and the third is the surface. The manufacturer's instructions for installation of playground equipment should be followed carefully and monitored for compliance after the equipment is installed. Updated

Playground equipment can be a learning center where children find challenges to solve problems, develop upper-body strength, and practice jumping and landing.

information is available from the National Playground Safety Commission (NPSC; www.cpsc.gov, then search for playground safety) on the current standards for various ages of children and maintenance of equipment. These standards change, and safety warnings and recalls occur; therefore, it is important to check with the NPSC regularly to be certain your playground is in compliance. Regular maintenance is critical for safety. Equipment may be damaged during use, or bolts and other parts may wear or become loose. Monthly inspections will generally catch these problems. The surface of the equipment is the most difficult feature to maintain. Each material has advantages and disadvantages, and all require regular maintenance. Sand is a good surface, but it requires regular raking and replacement. Pea gravel works well in wet weather but is dangerous when children throw it. For all materials, the depth determines absorption during impact from falling or jumping. Guidelines for the proper depth of each material are provided by the NPSC.

SAFETY

Safety is a result of proper installation, maintenance, supervision, and training. Planning is essential for safety. Selection of the facilities and equipment for the age, skill, and ability of the children is the first step. Second is planning for maintenance so that equipment and facilities are checked regularly. For example, the gym floor may need to be cleaned between classes if shoes are dirty or wet. The NPSC safety checklist outlines 10 steps to a safer playground; the checklist is presented in figure 13.3. Remember that this checklist is a starting point for safety; teachers, schools, and parents should strive to go beyond these minimums!

Concepts Into Practice

Ms. Blount has taken her class to the playing field for a lesson on soccer. The field is very wet, even though it is late in the afternoon. She decides that it is unsafe and moves her class to the hard-surface play area that is nearby and dry. She knows the soccer lesson will not work—or be safe—on the hard surface. Fortunately, she has a back-up plan. She uses the extra playground balls she brought and teaches Four Square.

1. Make sure surfaces around playground equipment have at least 12 in. of wood chips, mulch, sand, or pea gravel, or mats are made of safety-tested rubber or rubberlike materials.
2. Check that protective surfacing extends at least 6 ft in all directions from play equipment. For swings, be sure surface extends, in back and front, twice the height of the suspending bar.
3. Make sure play structures more than 30 in. high are spaced at least 9 ft apart.
4. Check for dangerous hardware, such as open "S" hooks or protruding bolt ends.
5. Make sure spaces that could trap children, such as openings in guardrails or between ladder rungs, measure less than 3.5 in. or more than 9 in.
6. Check for sharp points or edges in equipment.
7. Look for tripping hazards, such as exposed concrete footings, tree stumps, and rocks.
8. Make sure elevated surfaces, such as platforms and ramps, have guardrails to prevent falls.
9. Check playgrounds regularly to see that equipment and surfacing are in good condition.
10. Carefully supervise children on playgrounds to make sure they are safe.

Figure 13.3 CPSC (NPSC) public playground safety checklist.

Supervision begins with training of the personnel who will supervise the use of equipment and facilities. Supervision must be adequate in quality and quantity; this means having enough trained supervisors to manage the size of the area and the number of children. Training applies to the children and often to their parents. Children should learn the rules for the equipment and facilities and why each rule is important. It helps for parents to be informed about the rules, too, because parents can reinforce the school playground rules after school and on weekends. In addition, parents should be informed about playground safety before safety becomes an issue. Children must learn to move under control when using the equipment and facilities. Safety prevents accidents, but it does not eliminate risk. Children, their parents, and the supervisors need to understand the risk involved and work as a team to promote safety.

Supervision has four aspects: proximity, visual angle, scanning, and decision making.

1. **Proximity** means the distance between the supervisor and the object of supervision. The need for proximity is based on the risk or hazard presented by the equipment or activity and on the

individual children. For example, a large piece of playground equipment might require the teacher to stand nearby, or a group of risk-taking children might demand the teacher's presence.

2. **Visual angle** is the range or percentage of the area the teacher can see from a particular location. Generally, standing at one corner and farther away from the area provides the greatest angle.

3. **Scanning** means sweeping the area with the eyes to observe. Scanning is preferred over fixed vision, in which a person looks at one object or event. Scanning the entire area every six seconds is recommended (Thompson, Hudson, and Mack 1999).

4. **Decision making** occurs when you observe something that seems out of range, such as a child who is higher than normal, a large cluster of children, or a ball where it should not be. Generally, you fixate on the out-of-range area to determine if the situation demands intervention. If the decision is no, scanning continues; if the answer is yes, you increase proximity (e.g., move toward the situation). The aspects interact, so in order to gain proximity, you reduce visual angle; or to identify a problem and make a decision, you may have to stop scanning.

With training and practice, supervision improves. Consider the position you select from which to begin supervision. Move as the situation demands. When you must stop scanning, return to scanning as soon as possible. As children talk to you, continue monitoring playground behavior. Generally, it is best not to stand near other supervisors. First, this can be distracting to all of you, and second, this is not the way to provide optimal supervision.

RECESS

Physical education and recess cross paths in two dimensions: facilities and goals. Although each serves a unique role in a child's education and each is important, practical and educational issues arise because of the two crossed paths. Both recess and physical education contribute to the amount of physical activity children receive during a school day. Remember that children need at least one hour of physical activity each day, including 30 minutes of moderate-to-vigorous activity in that hour. When physical education is a sequential instructional program that focuses on skill acquisition, it is **structured physical activity**. Recess is **unstructured activity time** in which children practice using skills learned in physical education as well as social skills and have the opportunity to release stress

(Pellegrini and Smith 1993; Pellegrini and Davis 1993). Consider that three 10-minute recesses and one 30-minute physical education class daily provide the minimum of one hour of activity children need each day. Evidence suggests that children who do not have recess may be more distracted, less able to concentrate, and more restless than children who have recess. Children may learn social skills in solving problems and conducting conflict resolution during recess (Thomas, Lee, McGee, and Silverman 1987). NASPE and the National Association of Elementary School Principals support recess as an essential part of a child's learning (NASPE 2001b). The Council for Physical Education for Children (COPEC) provides eight recommendations for recess that specifically establish that recess and physical education are both important and independent components of a quality educational program (figure 13.4).

SUMMARY

Consider the size of the children, class, and facility when deciding the appropriateness of an activity for that facility. When selecting equipment, consider the size, ability, and age of the students and the match of equipment to the intended learning outcome. Prevent injuries by regular maintenance of equipment and facilities and appropriate supervision. Using a variety of equipment and facilities can enhance student learning. Allowing students both structured and unstructured opportunities to learn and create when using gross motor skill is an important part of child development. Being safe means reducing risk as much as possible.

MASTERY LEARNING ACTIVITIES

1. Using a catalog or Internet site, find a physical education equipment list and determine the cost of such equipment for class.

2. Travel to an elementary school playground. Conduct a safety inspection using the 10 points from the Consumer Product Safety Commission (CPSC) Public Playground Safety Checklist.

3. Identify the physical education facilities in the elementary school you attended (or one where you have observed as a college student).

- Physical education provides a sequential instructional program with opportunities for children to learn about and participate in regular physical activity, to develop motor skills, and to use skills and knowledge to improve performance.
- Schools should develop schedules that provide for supervised, daily recess in grades pre-kindergarten through grades 5 or 6. The use of facilities for recess activities should not interfere with instructional classes (separate locations for each activity). If possible, recess should not be scheduled back to back with physical education classes.
- Recess should not be viewed as a reward but a necessary educational support component for all children. Students should not be denied recess as a means of punishment or to make up work.
- Periods of moderate physical activity should be encouraged and facilitated while recognizing that recess should provide opportunities for children to make choices. NASPE recommends that children ages 6 to 11 participate in at least one hour and up to several hours of physical activity each day. This activity may occur in periods of moderate-to-vigorous, activity lasting 10 to 15 minutes or more. Recess may provide some of this activity time.
- Schools should provide the facilities, equipment, and supervision necessary to ensure the recess experience is productive, safe, and enjoyable. Developmentally appropriate equipment, as outlined in the NASPE Guidelines for Facilities, Equipment, and Instructional Materials, should be made available. Adults should regularly check equipment and facilities for safety.
- Physical education teachers and classroom teachers should teach children positive skills for self-responsibility during recess.
- Adults should direct or intervene when a child's physical or emotional safety is an issue. Bullying or aggressive behavior must not be allowed, and all safety rules should be enforced.

Figure 13.4 COPEC recommendations for recess.

NASPE 2001b.

4. Using the CPSC Web site (www.cpsc.gov), determine the following for slides:

    a. Rung sizes, stair treads, and ramp slopes

    b. Heights of guardrails

    c. Angle and guardrail sizes

REFERENCES

National Association for Sport and Physical Education (NASPE). 2001a. *Guidelines for facilities, equipment and instructional materials in elementary education.* Council of Physical Education for Children. A position paper from the National Association for Sport and Physical Education. Reston, Va.: NASPE Publications.

National Association for Sport and Physical Education (NASPE). 2001b. *Recess in elementary schools.* Council of Physical Education for Children. A position paper from the National Association for Sport and Physical Education. Reston, Va.: NASPE Publications.

Pellegrini, A.D., and P.D. Davis. 1993. Relations between children's playground and classroom behaviour. *British Journal of Educational Psychology* 63: 88–95.

Pellegrini, A.D., and P.K. Smith. 1993. School recess: Implications for education and development. *Review of Educational Research* 63: 51–67.

Thomas, J., A. Lee, L. McGee, and S. Silverman. 1987. Effects of individual and group contingencies on disruptive playground behavior. *Journal of Research and Development in Education* 20: 66–76.

Thompson, D., S.D. Hudson, and M.G. Mack. 1999. Who should supervise the children? *Childcare Information Exchange* 127: 74-7.

U.S. Consumer Product Safety Commission. 2002. *Handbook for public playground safety. Publication 325.* Washington, D.C.: Government Printing Office.

RESOURCES

Bruya, L.D. 1988. *Play spaces for children: A new beginning. Children play: Elementary school playground equipment.* Reston, Va.: American Alliance for Health, Physical Education, Recreation and Dance (AAHPERD).

Burya, L.D., and S.J. Langendorfer. 1988. *Where our children play: Elementary school playground equipment.* Reston, Va.: American Alliance for Health, Physical Education, Recreation and Dance (AAHPERD).

Herkowitz, J. 1984. Developmentally engineered equipment and playgrounds In *Motor development during childhood and adolescence,* edited by J.R. Thomas, 139–173. Edina, Minn.: Burgess.

Mack, M.G., S.D. Hudson, and D. Thompson. 1999. Playground safety: Using research to guide community policy. *Journal of Health Education* 30: 352-7.

Sallis, J.F., T.L. McKenzie, B. Kolody, M. Lewis, S. Marshall, and P. Rosengard. 1999. Effects of health-related physical education on academic achievement: Project SPARK. *Research Quarterly for Exercise and Sport* 70: 127.

Thompson, D., S.D. Hudson, and M.G. Mack. 1998. Keep school playgrounds safe. *The Education Digest* 64: 60-4.

LESSON PLANS

The first two lessons demonstrate the use of large equipment in gymnastics and games as children use balance beams and other climbing or jumping apparatus. The third lesson adapts several facilities (indoor and outdoor) for use in fitness testing and training.

The final four lessons demonstrate the use of small equipment in lessons. For younger children, the lesson is using stations to practice manipulative skills. The parachute is used to foster cooperation and following directions. Beanbags are used for juggling in grades 4 and 5; scarves can be used first, then balls once juggling is mastered.

Gymnastics

LESSON **13.1**

Large Equipment

Student Objectives

- Practice independent work.
- Practice following rules.

Safety Tip

- Emphasize following the rules. Sit all the children on carpet squares before rotating and as necessary to calm them.

Equipment and Materials

- Station 1: 1 low balance beam (e.g., 2 each: 2 in. × 4 in.; 4 in. × 4 in.; 4 in. × 6 in.) and beanbags or 1 rope per child (optional: 2 wands per child)
- Station 2: 1 jumping cube (24 in.) per child
- Station 3: 1 2-in.-diameter climbing rope (10–20 ft) attached to the wall
- Station 4: 1 tunnel, or 2 or 3 other shapes, several beanbags
- Station 5: 1 vaulting cube (wider at bottom than top, 24–30 in. high, or large paper boxes stuffed with paper) and 1 beanbag per child
- Station 6: 1 wooden climbing ladder, a wall, mats, and several beanbags
- Mats (4 ft × 8 ft) as needed for safety
- Carpet squares (if too many children per spot at stations)

Warm-Up Activities (5 minutes)

Use grades K–1 warm-up routine from lesson 8.1, page 180.

Skill-Development Activities (24 minutes)

Stations

Set up the stations as described in the text and shown in the figures on pages 323-324. Arrange small groups at the six stations.

1. Use six to seven minutes to describe and demonstrate the six stations.
2. Review the stop and rotate signal.

3. Have the children practice at each station three minutes, then rotate. (When revisiting this lesson, you will be able to use more time at each station, because explanations will take less time.)
4. Move from station to station spotting, observing, and managing.

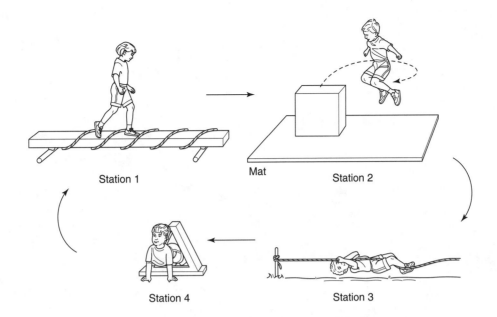

Station 1

Mat   Station 2

Station 4   Station 3

Station 1: Balance Beams

Step over the objects on the balance beam (bean-bags spaced on a beam or a rope wound around the beam). Wands (broomsticks) make good aids for children who are having trouble on the beam. Allow children to use them as canes (one in each hand) to facilitate balance.

Station 2: Jumping Cubes

Perform the following activities while jumping from the cubes:

> *Clap hands in flight.*
> *Spin all the way around (360 degrees) in the air.*
> *Jump higher. (Someone can hold an arm up as a target or barrier.)*

Station 3: Climbing Rope

Practice climbing the rope:

> *Go feet first.*
> *Go no-legs (hold them in the air).*

Station 4: Shapes or Tunnel

Try these tasks while navigating the shapes:

> *Carry an object (a beanbag).*
> *Go with your eyes closed.*

Station 5: Vaulting Cubes

Practice the following vaulting skills:

> *Use only one arm.*
> *Use no arms.*
> *Carry an object (a beanbag).*

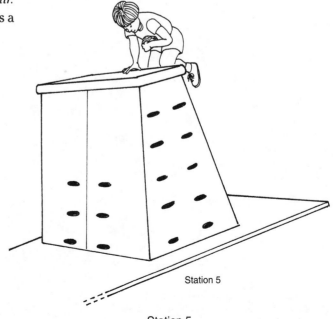

Station 5

Station 5

Station 6: Ladder

Practice ladder-climbing skills:

Carry an object (a beanbag).
Climb at a steeper angle (by raising the ladder).

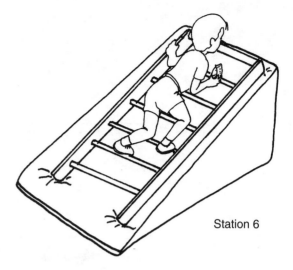

Station 6

Concluding Activities (1 minute)

Have the children either help set the stations in order for the next class or help put the equipment away.

From *Physical Education Methods for Elementary Teachers, Second Edition*, by Katherine T. Thomas, Amelia M. Lee, and Jerry R. Thomas, 2003, Champaign, IL: Human Kinetics. Adapted from *Physical Education for Children: Daily Lesson Plans for Elementary School, Second Edition*, by Katherine T. Thomas, Amelia M. Lee, and Jerry R. Thomas, 2000, Champaign, IL: Human Kinetics.

LESSON  **13.2**

Large Equipment

Student Objectives

- Practice skills on large apparatus.
- Follow other children.
- Cooperate with a large group.

Equipment and Materials

List is per obstacle course you set up. Try to keep group sizes small to increase participation opportunities.

- 1 jumping cube (24 in.)
- 3 balance beams (2 in. × 4 in.; 4 in. × 4 in.; 4 in. × 6 in.; 8–14 ft long)
- 2 vaulting cubes (wider at top than bottom, 24–30 in. high, or large paper boxes stuffed with paper)
- 1 tunnel, or 2 or 3 other shapes
- 1 wooden climbing ladder
- 1 2-in.-diameter climbing rope (10–20 ft) attached to the wall
- 1 triangle mat
- Mats (4 ft × 8 ft) as needed for safety
- Carpet squares (if children must wait turns)

Warm-Up Activities (5 minutes)

Use grades K–1 warm-up routine from lesson 8.1, page 180.

Skill-Development Activities (24 minutes)

Obstacle Course

Set up the courses as shown. Divide the children into the same number of groups as obstacle courses. Try to keep groups small to increase participation opportunities.

1. Describe and demonstrate the obstacle course.

2. Have the children go through the obstacle course using the skills shown in the figure.

3. Send one child at a time (or space the children so no child catches another).

4. Repeat for all the children as many times as possible.

Start

Concluding Activities (1 minute)

Have the children either help set the stations in order for the next class or help put the equipment away.

From *Physical Education Methods for Elementary Teachers, Second Edition,* by Katherine T. Thomas, Amelia M. Lee, and Jerry R. Thomas, 2003, Champaign, IL: Human Kinetics. Adapted from *Physical Education for Children: Daily Lesson Plans for Elementary School, Second Edition,* by Katherine T. Thomas, Amelia M. Lee, and Jerry R. Thomas, 2000, Champaign, IL: Human Kinetics.

LESSON **13.3**

Manipulative Skill Stations

Student Objectives

- Practice independently.
- Record own progress.
- Improve performance in the six tasks as a result of practice.

Safety Tip

- Remind children of the signals that will be used to stop activity, change stations, and so on.

Equipment and Materials

Plan to set up two complete sets of stations.

- Station 1: tennis balls, targets, rope, 2 standards (or other supports to suspend the rope from 5 to 15 ft high)
- Station 2: bowling pins or weighted plastic bottles, playground balls
- Station 3: 4 barrels, 5 hoops, rope, beanbags, tennis balls, foam balls, 2 standards (or other supports to suspend the rope 5 ft high)
- Station 4: playground balls, launchers, beanbags
- Station 5: playground balls, rope and 2 standards, wall or fence
- Station 6: balloons, foam balls, playground ball, wall or fence
- 4 student progress sheets per child (see end of this lesson for sample)
- Tape, flour (outside only), cones, or chalk to mark lines as needed
- Signal

Warm-Up Activities (5 minutes)

Slap Tag

Arrange the children into two equal groups on two parallel lines, about 50 ft apart. Designate one group as the Runners and the other as the Chasers. Have the Chasers stand with their backs to the play area and their hands stretched out behind.

1. Describe the game:

    The Runners sneak across and slap the hands of the Chasers.

As soon as the hands are slapped, both the Runners and the Chasers turn and run for the Runners baseline at the other side of the play area.

The Chasers try to tag the Runners before they reach base.

Every Runner who is tagged moves to the other side and joins the Chasers.

Each round we will switch who starts as the Runners and Chasers.

2. Have the children play Slap Tag.

Skill-Development Activities (25 minutes)

Ball Stations

Set up two complete sets of stations. Arrange the children into 12 groups of two or three. You may want to group the children in the classroom (e.g., red, blue, gold, silver, orange, and green stars); this will help you send groups to their starting stations quickly (red stars to station 1, blue stars to station 2, and so on).

1. Spend six to seven minutes explaining stations. Then send the children to the stations the first day.
2. Rotate each group to a new station after six minutes the first day (eight or nine minutes on subsequent days). Rotate the children through three stations each day.

Station 1

Mark lines 10, 15, 20, 30, 40, 50, and 60 ft from the wall. Suspend a rope 5 ft above the ground at 30 ft back from the wall.

Throw tennis balls at the wall. Throw tennis balls over the rope from the different distances.

Station 2

Set up a bowling pin and mark lines 5, 10, and 15 ft from the pin.

Play one-pin bowling (from increasingly difficult distances of 5, 10, and 15 ft) *using a playground ball.*

Station 3

Place ice cream barrels (marked a, b, c, and d) 2 ft apart with the nearest one 5 ft away. Place hoops (marked a, b, c, d, and e) 5 ft apart with the nearest hoop 5 ft away. Mark lines 5 and 10 ft away from the hoops and barrels. Suspend a 5-ft-high rope and mark a line 10 ft away.

Toss balls into the barrels. Toss foam balls into five hoops. Toss over and under a 5-ft-high rope from 10 ft away.

Station 4

Mark lines 5, 10, and 15 ft from a wall.

Bounce the ball to the wall, let it rebound, and catch it from 5, 10, and 15 ft. Launch the beanbag and catch it with both hands (same hand as launching foot, opposite hand as launching foot). Toss the beanbag in the air and catch it.

Station 5

Mark lines 10, 20, 30, and 40 ft from a wall. Suspend a rope 3 ft above the ground in front of the wall.

Kick the ball to the wall from each line. Kick the ball above the rope from the 10-ft line. Kick the ball under the rope from 10-ft line.

Station 6

Mark lines 5, 10, and 15 ft away from a wall.

Hit the balloon up as many times as possible. Hit the foam ball from your palm. Hit the playground ball on a bounce from the ground to the wall from the lines.

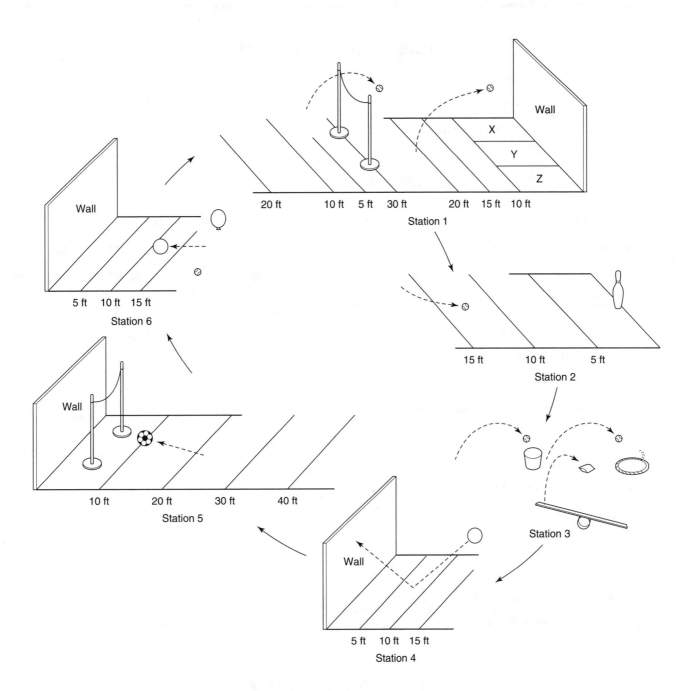

Wall

X
Y
Z

20 ft   10 ft   5 ft   30 ft   20 ft   15 ft   10 ft

Station 1

15 ft   10 ft   5 ft

Station 2

Station 3

Wall

5 ft   10 ft   15 ft

Station 4

Wall

10 ft   20 ft   30 ft   40 ft

Station 5

Wall

5 ft   10 ft   15 ft

Station 6

Student Progress Sheet

Have one sheet per child to use each day. Have a red pencil at each station the first two days, and a blue pencil the second two days. Have or help each child circle her best score for the day at each sta- tion. Using the different-colored pencils allows you, the children, and their parents to see progress.

STUDENT PROGRESS SHEET

Station 1: I can hit the wall with the ball standing on the line marked 10, 15, 20, 30, 40, 50, and 60 feet.

I can throw the ball over the rope to zone X, Y, Z, from the line marked 10, 15, 20, 30, 40, 50, and 60 feet.

Station 2: In 10 rolls I hit the pin _____ times from 5 feet; _____ times from 10 feet; and _____ times from 15 feet.

Station 3: I can throw the foam ball into hoop a, b, c, d, e.

I can throw the tennis ball into barrel a, b, c, d.

I can throw the ball over the rope: Yes _____ No _____

I can throw the ball under the rope: Yes _____ No _____

Station 4: I can bounce the ball to the wall and catch it from 5, 10, 15 feet.

I can launch and catch the beanbag: Yes _____ No _____

I can toss the beanbag over my head and catch it: Yes _____ No _____

Station 5: I can kick the ball 10, 20, 30, and 40 feet.

I can kick the ball high (over the rope): Yes _____ No _____

I can kick the ball low (under the rope): Yes _____ No _____

Station 6: I can hit the balloon _____ times.

I can hit the foam ball _____ times.

I can hit the playground ball 5, 10, 15 feet.

Concluding Activities

No concluding activity, because the children should spend all their time at the stations. As you rotate students to the last station, however, tell them you will give a three-minute warning that class is ending and for them to circle their last best score and replace the equipment so it is ready for the next class.

From *Physical Education Methods for Elementary Teachers, Second Edition,* by Katherine T. Thomas, Amelia M. Lee, and Jerry R. Thomas, 2003, Champaign, IL: Human Kinetics. Adapted from *Physical Education for Children: Daily Lesson Plans for Elementary School, Second Edition,* by Katherine T. Thomas, Amelia M. Lee, and Jerry R. Thomas, 2000, Champaign, IL: Human Kinetics.

LESSON  **13.4**

Locomotor Skills Obstacle Course

Student Objectives

- Travel through an obstacle course using various locomotor skills without touching the obstacles.

Equipment and Materials

- Flour, chalk, or tape for marking lines

For each obstacle course:

- 4 cones
- 10 hoops
- 8 milk crates
- 2 low balance beams

Arrange obstacle courses as shown below, 1 course per group.

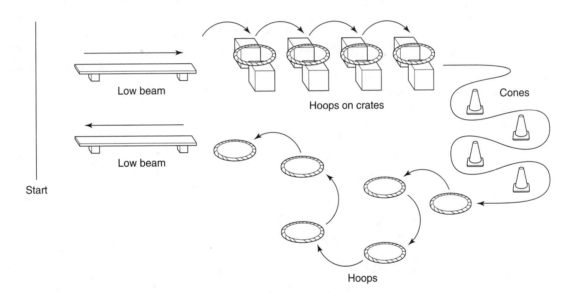

Warm-Up Activities (5 minutes)

Reveille

Arrange the children in two groups along parallel lines as in the figure.

1. Describe the game:

   On the signal (a horn is best, but a whistle, bell, or other noisemaker will do), everyone runs for the opposite line.

The first group to line up, standing at attention, gets a point.

Take care when running past other children so that no one is bumped or tripped.

We will play several rounds.

2. Have the children play Reveille.

Skill-Development Activities (20 minutes)

Obstacle Course

Divide the children into groups of four to six, and arrange each group at the beginning of an obstacle course.

1. Describe the activity: *Hop (on right foot) down the balance beam, jump through the elevated hoops, weave around the cones, hop (on left foot) through the hoops on the ground, and walk backward down the second balance beam.*

2. Have them repeat, using different arrangements of the equipment and other locomotor skills (e.g., gallop, slide, skip).

3. Have each group make a pattern for their course, learn it, and teach it to the other groups.

Concluding Activities (5 minutes)

Crows and Cranes

Arrange two groups facing each other on lines 20 ft apart. Two additional lines are needed 30 ft outside the first pair of lines (adjust starting lines closer together or farther apart as needed). Designate one group as "Crows" and the other as "Cranes."

1. Describe and demonstrate the game:

   I will call out "Crows" or "Cranes" (extend the first consonants of the word so the children do not know which name will be called, C-r-r-r-rows or C-r-r-r-ranes).

   The team whose name is called turns and runs to its goal line as the other team chases, attempting to tag the runners.

   All tagged players become members of the other team, and play continues. Play ends when all the runners cross the line or are tagged.

2. Have the children play Crows and Cranes.

3. Variation: Have both groups walk toward each other; as they get close together the group called runs back to the goal line.

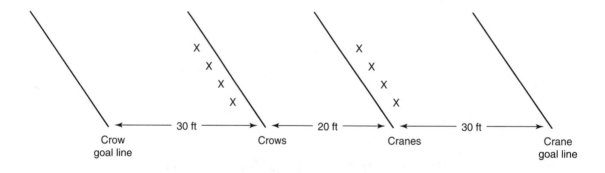

LESSON  **13.5**

Parachute Games

Student Objectives

- Perform parachute activities, demonstrating cooperation.
- Follow verbal instruction to learn new activities.

Equipment and Materials

- 1 parachute
- Several fluff balls
- Several large (13 in.) playground balls
- Several smaller (6 in.) balls (2 or more colors)
- Stopwatch or clock with second hand
- Chalk, flour, or tape to mark lines

Warm-Up Activities (5 minutes)

Use Sneaky Tag from lesson 2.2, page 26.

Skill-Development Activities (20 minutes)

Parachute Activities

Arrange the children around the outside of the parachute, which is spread out on the ground.

Exchange Positions

Assign the children numbers, one through number of children.

Tell the children to hold the parachute with the left hand and circle counterclockwise. Remind them of which numbers are odd and which are even. Tell the children: *On the signal, the odd-numbered children release the parachute and move forward to take the place of the next odd-numbered player in front of them* (variations can include moving forward two places, three places, and so on). Repeat with the even-numbered players moving. Have the children use a variety of locomotor skills (walk, run, skip, gallop, slide) to move.

Run Under

Assign the children numbers from one to four.

Tell the children: *Begin in a squat position, holding the parachute with both hands. When you hear the signal, lift up the parachute to form an umbrella. I will call a number from one to four. All of you let go of the parachute, and the players with the num-*

ber called must move across the circle under the parachute to the opposite side (and into the former position of another player with the same number) before the parachute floats down. You can specify the type of movement you want the children to use (e.g., different locomotor skills, animal walks, moving backward).

Popping Popcorn

Place several fluff balls on the parachute.

Tell the children: *Shake the parachute up and down, attempting to "pop" the balls into the air but not off the parachute.*

Ball Roll

Have the children grasp the parachute, which you have laid on the ground. Place a large playground ball on the parachute.

Explain and have the children try the activity: *I will tell one child to stand and raise his or her part of the parachute. Then the next child counterclockwise* (point) *in the circle raises the parachute, and so on. The object is to keep the ball rolling around the edge of the parachute.* After the ball passes, the children may lower the parachute to keep the ball going. After children gain some proficiency include changing the direction of the ball or add additional balls.

Parachute Games

Keep the children around the outside of the parachute, which is spread out on the ground.

Popcorn Game

Place several fluff balls on the parachute. Assign the children numbers, one through the number of children.

Describe and have the children play the game: *The odd numbers form one team and the even numbers another. The odd-numbered team releases the parachute and each member takes two or three steps backward. The even-numbered players have 30 seconds to pop all the balls off the parachute. Players then exchange places, and the odd-numbered team has a turn. The team with fewer balls on the parachute after the 30-second time period wins.*

Center Ball

Have two teams stand on opposite sides of the parachute (you can use the teams already created, but they don't need to remember their numbers), holding it about waist high. Place two 6-in. balls (of different colors) on the parachute.

Describe and have the children play the game: *Each team tries to shake the opponent's ball into the center pocket and at the same time keep their own ball from going into the pocket. Your team scores a point every time it puts the opponent's ball in the pocket.*

Ball Shake

Two teams stand on opposite sides of the parachute (keep teams from Center Ball or make two new teams). Place several different (e.g., one foam, one playground, etc.) balls on the parachute.

Describe and have the children play the game: *On a signal to begin, each team tries to shake the balls off the other team's side of the parachute. You may not use your hands to keep the balls on the parachute. Your team will earn one point each time a ball leaves the parachute on your opponent's side and touches the ground.*

Concluding Activities (5 minutes)

Parachute Games

Let the children choose one of the parachute games to repeat.

From *Physical Education Methods for Elementary Teachers, Second Edition,* by Katherine T. Thomas, Amelia M. Lee, and Jerry R. Thomas, 2003, Champaign, IL: Human Kinetics. Adapted from *Physical Education for Children: Daily Lesson Plans for Elementary School, Second Edition,* by Katherine T. Thomas, Amelia M. Lee, and Jerry R. Thomas, 2000, Champaign, IL: Human Kinetics.

LESSON

Practicing the One-Mile Run and Sit-Ups

Student Objectives

- Practice pacing in the one-mile run.
- Practice correct sit-up form.

Equipment and Materials

- Cones for marking one-mile running course (the figure shows several layouts of fields you can use to administer the run)
- Stopwatch
- Mats (optional)

Areas suitable for distance run test

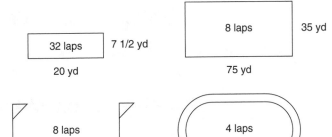

Reprinted by permission from the American Alliance for Health, Physical Education, Recreation and Dance, 1900 Association Drive, Reston, VA 20191.

Skill-Development Activities (30 minutes)

One-Mile Run and Sit-Ups

Divide the children into two groups.

1. Discuss the need for pacing in the one-mile run.

2. Describe and demonstrate a correct sit-up:

   The sit-up is really done with a rolling motion.

   Begin by lying on your back with your legs bent slightly at the knees so the soles of your feet are flat on the ground.

   Choose one of the two hand-arm positions: You can cross your hands and arms on your chest so that your hands are resting on the opposite shoulders or you can place your hands on the sides of your head with a finger placed on each ear, keeping your elbows lined up (parallel) with the back of your head (keep them there, not pulling forward past the ears).

   Perform each sit-up slowly, rolling your chin to your chest to lift your head, then your shoulders, then your lower back off the ground.

   During the movement, you should feel the muscles under your belly button working.

   Once your lower back is off the ground, unroll to the start position.

3. Have the children practice analyzing your sit-up form.

4. Have one group practice the pacing of the one-mile run. Encourage each child to find the fastest pace she can maintain while running the total distance.

5. Have the other group select partners. One partner in each pair does sit-ups for 60 seconds while the other partner holds feet; then have them switch roles.

6. After 15 minutes in each activity, allow a 2-minute rest; then have groups switch activities.

7. If the weather is hot, make sure the children have opportunity to get water when they want it.

From *Physical Education Methods for Elementary Teachers, Second Edition,* by Katherine T. Thomas, Amelia M. Lee, and Jerry R. Thomas, 2003, Champaign, IL: Human Kinetics. Adapted from *Physical Education for Children: Daily Lesson Plans for Elementary School, Second Edition,* by Katherine T. Thomas, Amelia M. Lee, and Jerry R. Thomas, 2000, Champaign, IL: Human Kinetics.

LESSON

Juggling

Student Objectives

- Attempt to juggle two, then three, beanbags.

Equipment and Materials

- 3 beanbags per child

Warm-Up Activities (6 to 8 minutes)

Use Walk/Jog from lesson 4.3, page 81.

Skill-Development Activities (17 minutes)

Note: Repeat as lesson 13.8 for children who did not learn to juggle during lesson 13.7.

Juggling

Arrange the children in scatter formation, each child with three beanbags. Describe, demonstrate, and have the children practice only one or two steps of juggling at a time (see next section for descriptions of each step).

1. Describe and demonstrate steps 1 and 2.
2. Have the children practice steps 1 and 2 until they achieve some skill.
3. Encourage them to establish a good rhythm.
4. Describe and demonstrate steps 3 and 4.
5. Have the children practice steps 3 and 4 until they achieve some skill.
6. Describe and demonstrate step 5.
7. Have the children practice step 5 until they achieve some skill.
8. Describe and demonstrate step 6.
9. Have the children practice step 6 until they achieve some skill.

Steps in Juggling

Describe, demonstrate, and have the children practice only one or two steps of juggling at a time (see outline in previous section):

Step 1—*Using your right hand, throw one beanbag up and catch it. The beanbag should go slightly above your head.*

Step 2—*Using your left hand, throw one beanbag up and catch it.*

Step 3—*With one beanbag in each hand, toss the right-hand beanbag and then the left-hand beanbag, catching each with the same hand as tossed it. This should be toss right, toss left, catch right, catch left. Now after tossing the beanbag in your right hand, toss the one in your left hand under it, catching each beanbag with the same hand that tossed it.*

Step 4—*Repeat step 3, but catch each beanbag with the opposite hand.*

Step 5—*Hold two beanbags in your right hand. Toss one in the air, then the other. Catch the first and toss it again. Catch the second and toss it again; continue.* Cue the children: *Toss the beanbag underneath (toward the left side) each time. Repeat with your left hand.*

Step 6—*Hold two beanbags in your right hand and one in your left. Toss one beanbag from your right hand, toss the beanbag from your left hand, and then toss the third beanbag. Repeat.* Cue the children: *Toss each beanbag underneath (toward the inside of the body) the one in the air.*

Concluding Activities (5 minutes)

Children who cannot do step 6 will not be able to do this activity; for those children, go back and help them practice the needed skills during this time.

Continuous Juggling

Arrange the children in scatter formation, each child with three beanbags.

1. Explain the following modification: *In step 6 (previous section), after tossing and catching the third beanbag, you stop and begin again. But in continuous juggling, you keep tossing until you miss or stop.*

2. Have the advanced children practice continuous juggling while you help the other children master step 6 (see previous section, steps in juggling).

From *Physical Education Methods for Elementary Teachers, Second Edition,* by Katherine T. Thomas, Amelia M. Lee, and Jerry R. Thomas, 2003, Champaign, IL: Human Kinetics.

Teaching Physical Education

Finally you are ready to teach! Now what? This section focuses on what you do when children are present—what you do to facilitate learning during class. Close your eyes and picture a physical education class. What do you see? Teachers often give instructions, demonstrate, and provide feedback to students, so that may be what you picture. Teachers also spend time watching students, as you will see, and observation is an important part of teaching. The first chapter in this section is about those very activities. Teachers also evaluate students as an integral part of the learning process; thus evaluation is the next chapter. Finally, we explore ways to grow as a teacher through the use of reflection, portfolios, continuing education, and professional engagement.

chapter 14

Instructing Students

Demetrius, age 10

Instruction includes teaching behaviors such as positioning, scanning, observing, interacting, cuing, demonstrating, reinforcing, and giving feedback. These are enhanced by personality variables: voice, body language, eye contact, and facial expression. Teaching and learning are dynamic processes that require constant monitoring so that optimal learning takes place. Teachers can learn to optimize these behaviors and thereby have an impact on student learning.

Learner Outcomes

The teacher will do the following:

- Define and demonstrate appropriate teaching behaviors (directions, cues, demonstrations, reinforcement).
- Discuss and enhance instruction with personality variables.

- Define and use observation for skill and behavior.
- Identify a plan for improving observation.
- State how and when teaching expertise develops.

Glossary Terms

volume
tone
pace
body language
facial expression

location
scanning
directions
demonstrations
teachable moment

Just as the phrase "natural athlete" is used to describe expert athletes, "she is a natural" has been applied to teachers. However, expert teachers recognize that hard work and practice contribute to teaching expertise. Expert teachers make it look easy! Teachers *learn* to be expert instructors; they are not born to teach. We believe that no one wants to be a poor teacher. Unfortunately, most of us can identify at least one teacher who was not effective. With knowledge and practice, anyone can be a good teacher. The goals of methods courses, practical experience, and student teaching are to help you develop the skills necessary to teach and to continue improving as a teacher. This chapter will describe important behaviors for teachers during instruction and much of what has been learned about expert teachers. Table 14.1 provides a guide for effective instruction. It in-

cludes everything in this chapter, plus elements of planning from the previous chapters. Refer to the table as your read this chapter.

Teachers need to understand and apply information about instruction for several reasons:

- So that student learning is optimal
- So that the teacher is ready to assume the responsibility of teaching
- So that continuous improvement of teaching is a realistic goal

PRACTICE

Practice and feedback are two of the most important learning variables. Generally, practice is considered a planning variable. The assumption is that

Table 14.1 Rubric to Guide Instruction

	Novice	Emerging	Mastery
Initial activity (not warm-up)	Routine is not evident	Eventually students organize	Immediate initial activity with little or no instruction
Transition	Planning is not evident	Some time spent moving into formations or groups	Smooth, brief transitions for groups or formations planning evident
Equipment	Planning is not evident	Plan evident, could improve	Quick and efficient, planning evident
Special events	Restroom or water requests, behavior problems, and other events interrupt instruction	Plan is evident but some interruptions occur, behavior problems, are handled with desist or other techniques	The plan is evident and minimizes interruptions, behavior problems are generally prevented
Concluding activity (not cool-down)	Routine is not evident	Students organized to leave after instructions	Clear routine is evident and requires few or no cues
Voice	Inappropriate—too soft, loud, assertive	Occasionally too loud or not loud enough, generally good	Appropriate—clear, loud enough
Body language	Negative or low energy	Generally reflective of the message and energetic	Consistently energetic, reflective of the message
Eye contact	None	Some	Consistent
Facial expression	Negative, neutral	Neutral or smiling	Smiling most of the time—occasionally reflective of situation
Student interaction	Unclear whether you like the students or activities	Generally clear that you like the students and activities	Clear that you like the students and activities
Enthusiasm	Low energy, seems tired or apathetic	Demonstrates sufficient energy	High energy, seems disappointed when time is over, appears to be able to go on indefinitely
Positioning	Poor choice, cannot see or be seen by all students	Back to the wall most of the time	Selects optimal location for each phase of lesson
Focus	Consistently distracted	Occasionally distracted	Focused on students and learning
Scanning	Not evident	Looks every 6 seconds and identifies some problems	Constantly scanning (every 6 seconds), identifies most problems

(continued)

Table 14.1 *(continued)*

	Novice	**Emerging**	**Mastery**
Instructions	Not clear	Generally clear	Clear and concise
Demonstration teacher or peer	Fails to demonstrate or incorrect demonstrations or more than than 3 demonstrations	Correctly demonstrates no more than 3 times	Correctly demonstrates (no more than 3 times) with appropriate cues
Reinforcement	Fails to provide verbal or physical reinforcement	Uses same phrase or physical reinforcement repeatedly	Consistently applied using varied phrases and physical reinforcements
Feedback	No performance-contingent feedback	At least 2 performance-contingent statements	At least 2 contingent, uses both corrective and reinforcing, uses the sandwich technique (encourage, correct, encourage)
Evaluation	Not evident	Attempt to evaluate skill or lesson	Clearly relating objectives, practice, feedback, and assessment
Objectives	Not clear	Somewhat clear	Evident and related to the instruction, practice, and feedback or evaluation
Practice organization	Inappropriate or ineffective	Acceptable (multiple trials)	Optimal (random, student-paced)
Warm-up activity	Not evident or inappropriate	Appropriate	Facilitated mastery of the objectives or supported skill development
Skill-development activity	Not evident or inappropriate	Children active	Learning (skill or knowledge acquired) evident or fitness objective met
Closure or culminating activity	Not evident or inappropriate	Somewhat related to lesson	Takes skill development to a higher level (e.g., use in game or evaluate, increase understanding)

when practice is well planned, learning activities go smoothly and instructional variables are the focus for the teacher. Unfortunately, this assumption can be wrong. Even the best plans, by the most expert teachers, sometimes fail. Therefore, teachers need to monitor practice organization to determine whether the practice is helping students to learn. The key variables in practice are type of practice (e.g., constant, blocked, variable, and random), amount of practice (e.g., number of trials), and content of practice (e.g., whole skill, part or progressive part, contextual).

Motor skill learning takes time—and lots of practice. This means that regardless of the quality of practice, students may not improve during a lesson. Therefore, teachers have difficulty determining whether the problem is with the amount of practice, the organization of practice, or some other factor. One way to evaluate the effectiveness of practice is to examine the range of performance on a task. If some students are improving and others are not, practice organization and content are probably fine. However, when no one is successful or improving, you need to reorganize either the practice or the content. Likewise, when everyone has mastered the task, it is time to move on in the content. The teacher may need to provide additional practice for those who are struggling or may need to alter the task for individuals or groups so that practice challenges those students who are mastering the skill and allows success for those who are struggling. Another way to evaluate practice is to determine whether the quality of the skill is improving or student understanding is increasing. Recall that these variables are more sensitive to change than outcome variables. If understanding of the skill has increased or if performance of the skill has become more efficient, then practice is working.

Several events should cause teachers to reorganize practice quickly:

► Students are having trouble following instructions; for example, they do not know what to do, they do the wrong thing, or they do nothing.

► None of the students are making progress in qualitative aspects of the skill.

► Students cannot explain what they are trying to accomplish with the practice.

► After considerable time, skill is not improving.

Students learn new skills through effective practice. Teachers provide effective practice and instruction. The next section will focus on instruction.

PERSONALITY VARIABLES

Discussion of personality generally includes such characteristics as outgoing, shy, and reserved. Your personality may influence how you teach and will certainly influence how easy it is for you to learn to be an effective teacher. A shy person may have to overcome anxiety about being in front of a group. A quiet person may have to develop enthusiasm. A loud and assertive person may need to quiet, calm, and control natural tendencies in order to be effective with young children. A person who is enthusiastic, friendly, humorous, caring, and expressive may have a head start as a teacher when compared with a person who is shy, quiet, solemn, and low keyed. However, to be an effective teacher, one needs to develop specific skills related to instruction.

Voice is important because the size of a gym and the environment on the playground tend to dissipate **volume,** so students have trouble hearing. There is a balance between being loud enough and yelling. Yelling often influences the tone of

Humor and enthusiasm can be effective teaching tools.

your voice, making you seem angry when you are just trying to be heard. Often, those with deeper voices are heard more easily, so if your voice is not deep, practice using a deeper voice. If volume is still a problem, try using a microphone (the wireless kind works well in the gym) or whispering so that students get in the habit of listening carefully. The **tone** of your voice is especially important in elementary school. Children are very sensitive to anger, frustration, sarcasm, and apathy in voices. Be sure your voice expresses what you want to convey. Talking too fast makes it difficult for students to understand, so **pace** what you have to say. Pause occasionally to allow students to reflect. Silence from a teacher is not always a bad thing. We suggest listening to an audiotape to identify aspects of your voice that may need to be changed.

Body language is more important than words to most listeners. If you stand with your arms crossed, the observer may think you are angry or unapproachable. Other body language might reflect fatigue (slouching), impatience (hands on hips), or disinterest (turning away). Teachers generally do not want to seem unapproachable or disinterested and should not ever appear that way to students—even when true! Using your hands to emphasize a point or to maintain student interest is one form of positive body language. Walking around—without pacing—demonstrates enthusiasm and shows concern for all students. A videotape can help you evaluate your body language.

Using eye contact does two things: First, it sends a positive message to students—you like them and feel comfortable with them. Second, it helps keep students focused on you. For younger children, you may have to kneel or squat down to have eye contact; being at eye level with your students is helpful. You will want to practice making eye contact with every student during class.

Facial expression—primarily, smiling—is one of the most powerful tools you have. Young children (those seven years and younger) interpret a neutral facial expression and an angry expression the same way (e.g., The teacher is angry with me or doesn't like me) (Passer and Wilson 2002). Smiling sends positive messages to children: "I like what I am doing, I like you, I am happy." Other facial expressions can be used to convey informa-

tion or to emphasize a point. For example, surprise, concern, and excitement are useful. Many expert teachers entertain their students—at least part of the time; somewhere inside those teachers is an actor or comedian. Every teacher does not have to entertain; however, it is a useful tool for those teachers who are comfortable using it.

Teachers have many interactions with students; this is probably why you decided to become a teacher. The interactions are positive for you and the student. Therefore, interact with all students and learn to do so in a variety of ways. If we began each class with individual greetings, the class would be over before the greetings ended. Similarly, teachers have multiple ways—some general and others specific—to interact with students. That means simply that sometimes we recognize the student for no particular reason; at other times the contact is a reaction to a specific event. Both recognitions are important—especially to the student. So, how do teachers interact? Smiles, comments, a touch, and a look (not "the look") are all interactions (table 14.2).

Enthusiasm is most often expressed as energy. However, it is also observed in careful planning, feedback, and every phase of instruction. In physical education, energy is an implied teacher characteristic. A teacher who is tired, lazy, or ill would have trouble portraying enthusiasm for physical activity and the health benefits related to physical activity. Enthusiasm for what you do helps others see why it is important and why they should participate. Passionate teachers have enthusiasm; we see this in every phase of their teaching. Their energy is transmitted to their colleagues and students, and their mission is to create the same passion in everyone.

A teacher is not required to have a sense of humor, but it is useful. Humor directed at oneself is especially helpful. Making fun of students or others is not an acceptable educational practice, however. Humor can be used as an effective teaching tool. Remember that children like physical education and sport because they are fun, and humor can make learning fun. Humor brings novelty to class; for example, throwing a rubber chicken into the parachute as children shake the edges of the parachute to make "popcorn fluff balls" with foam balls is fun and funny.

Table 14.2 Teacher–Student Interactions

List the students' names in the left column. Each time your observer notices you looking, speaking, touching, or smiling at a student, a mark is placed in the appropriate box. The goal is to have at least one interaction with each student in a class and balance the interactions among students.

Name	Looked at	Spoke to	Touched	Smiled at

Using Humor

Ms. Heath is going to play Len's Ball Mix-Up (as seen in chapter 7). She saw Len teach this game to kindergarteners when she was a student. He held the students' attention by walking in front of the students carrying a box with the balls and beanbags. The box had a hole; when he tipped the box backward, the balls fell out through the hole. This left a trail of balls behind him. When he turned, he looked surprised to see the balls! The children laughed and were very excited to pick up the balls as part of the game. She decides to try using humor to make the activity more fun, even though she is usually a quiet and serious teacher.

Teaching requires that you juggle several things at once—lesson content, student management and safety, and instruction. The balance between being aware of what is happening generally and concentrating on student learning is a challenge. Teachers need to focus on students and student learning and not be distracted by unimportant events. At the same time, teachers need to pay attention to important events—within the class and outside it. For example, a signal for a fire drill is important and demands a teacher response, whereas a stray bell going off should not interfere with learning. One of the most difficult times for a teacher occurs early in student teaching, when observers are more likely to be present. Your focus needs to be on the students and what they are learning, so making eye contact with or monitoring the cooperating teacher or other visitors is an example of "loss of focus." On the other hand, a teacher should notice when someone enters the gym or playground. The teacher immediately makes a quick visual check to decide if the event is important. Most of the time, focus should immediately return to instruction. For example, you see someone enter the gym; it is your principal. You glance at the principal and notice she has just stopped by to see what you are doing. Class continues as though she is not there. Alternatively, when you glance at the principal, she signals that she needs you. Immediately you give the students something to do and move toward the principal as you continue to observe your students.

TEACHING BEHAVIORS

Instructions, cues, feedback, and demonstrations are among the teaching behaviors that are most important to physical education. Teachers can learn to do each of these and with practice improve the effectiveness of each. The first step is understanding each behavior so you know what you eventually want to accomplish.

It seems obvious that teaching is directed at students; therefore, teaching is a series of teacher–student and student–teacher interactions. However, although this is logical and seems obvious, student–teacher interactions are not as frequent as one might expect (Rink 1996). Consider only interactions that are related to learning, eliminating management interactions; now eliminate all group interactions (e.g., the teacher giving instructions to the class). Student–teacher interactions, those times related to skill learning when a teacher speaks to, looks at, or touches a student, are often infrequent. The overall message that one-on-one, skill-related interactions send is "I like you; I like this activity." It is helpful if the teacher truly likes the students and the activity, but what really matters is that the students believe this to be true. Teachers should try to have many interactions with students that portray these positive ideas.

Teachers, in the gym and probably in the classroom, spend more time with group interactions than one-on-one interactions. In the classroom, the teacher has the opportunity for one on one through written work, whereas in the gym the feedback, reinforcement, and encouragement must come directly and often one on one. At the same time, teachers must instruct and supervise the whole class. Optimally, teachers will provide instruction to the class and interact one on one as frequently as possible.

Location

Where should you stand when you teach? In part, this is related to the formation in which you have placed students. For example, when students are arranged in a circle, a teacher is usually well positioned by becoming part of the circle because standing in the middle of the circle places at least half the students behind the teacher. Three guidelines determine **location,** or where you should position yourself for an activity. First, try to position yourself so you can see as many students as possible, and preferably all students. Standing with your back to the wall (or to the boundary), you will keep all students in front of you. Second, you will want to position yourself nearest to the activity with the highest risk; and, third, you will need to be close to the highest-risk students. Recall that when a teacher temporarily moves out of position to stand near a student who is misbehaving, this is called a desist (chapter 11). A desist is temporary, and the teacher typically moves back immediately to the best location. Classroom

teachers use this technique frequently by moving from the front of the room to stand near a student or group of students; once they return to the task, the teacher moves away. Sometimes optimal location (deciding which is the greater risk) is a difficult decision and may require a change in the lesson. For example, you need to spot an activity. You place that activity near the boundary, so as you spot you can see most of the class. However, you have one student who often moves out of control. Once that student leaves the activity you are spotting, you must ask, "Am I close enough to monitor and maintain a safe environment?" You may need to have that student stay with you, sit out for a while, or alter the activity so that it is safe for students to do without spotting. For example, you could switch from handstands, which generally need spotting, to Donkey Kick, which does not need spotting. Moving among students is often a positive; you should consider the cost-to-benefit trade-off. The benefits are increased opportunities for student interactions, better vision of individual performances, and possibly more effective evaluation for feedback. The cost is that you will not be able to see all of the students. As you do low-risk activities with students who move and work under control, you will have more freedom to move among the students. The optimal position is one that allows you to see all the students and is near the highest-risk activity and the highest-risk students (figure 14.1).

Scanning

Scanning is visually searching the learning area. Specifically, you are looking at students and what students are doing, pausing only when something demands your attention. You should try to make a visual sweep of the entire area every few seconds (six seconds is a good goal). When something captures your attention, you should decide quickly, "Do I need to do something?" Safety issues are a major concern in your scanning, which means you are looking for "out-of-bounds" movements. Examples include a student moving too fast or out of control, improper use of equipment, students touching or interacting when they should not be. As your scanning improves you will be able to capture other behaviors, which are related to instruction rather than safety. These include students who are off task, trying but doing the wrong skill, or errors in skill execution. Expert teachers can scan to monitor student behavior while maintaining focus on learning. A teacher would be able

Figure 14.1 Optimal position to guide students and activities.

to spot or provide feedback to one student while monitoring the rest of the class. To use scanning effectively takes practice. One way to gain this practice is during observation of other teachers. Scanning and observation are similar and usually done at the same time. The subtle difference is that observation focuses on skill and learning whereas scanning focuses on safety and monitoring management. The teacher has to do both, thus observation will be covered next in this chapter.

Concepts Into Practice

Ryan is observing Mr. Lyon teach. Mr. Lyon changed positions. During the first few observations Ryan did not know why Mr. Lyon moved across the gym. By the fifth observation, Ryan was scanning and could see that Mr. Lyon was using a desist. That is, he moved across the gym because two students were not participating.

OBSERVATION FOR SKILL AND CONFIDENCE

Teachers should spend a significant amount of class time watching children. Consider the rubrics in chapter 4 for locomotor skills and manipulative skills. Those rubrics and similar rubrics can be used to guide instruction and practice, help teachers conduct formative evaluation, provide corrective and reinforcing feedback, and evaluate at the end of a unit. Observation is a learned skill, so practice improves two dimensions of observation. First, it improves *what* we see. Watching for specific movements or behaviors starts with knowing what to look for. What a teacher is looking for depends on the situation. For example, the goal of a game may be passing the ball to many team members; thus, the teacher is looking for many passes. Another activity may focus on accuracy or distance of passes, so the teacher is watching for those characteristics. Sometimes teachers observe for behavior because a student, class, or activity demands that listening, following instructions, and cooperating are the most critical educational objectives.

When the lesson objective is problem solving or cooperation, the teacher should be observing for groups who are not functional. You might see one student standing apart from the others or two subgroups working rather than one. Rubrics developed for each activity help you focus on the target skills. You can glance at the rubric and be reminded of what you are hoping or expecting to observe.

Student confidence can also be observed by teachers. Students who are eager for a turn or who avoid turns show the range of confidence! Teachers should observe for confidence, behavior, and skill; unfortunately, teachers tend to focus on behavior rather than skill or confidence. Children who lack confidence may avoid physical activity. Teachers should identify children who lack confidence and work with them to increase confidence. How? First, identify the child's actual skill level and compare that to the perceived skill level. Children may lack confidence because they think they are "below average." Second, help the child recognize that skill improves when we practice and it is normal to have practice. Third, assist the child in understanding that each person is different and a variety of skill levels is normal. Finally, recognize improvement and help the child focus on improving. All of this begins with observing for confidence.

The second dimension of observation that improves with practice is remembering. With practice, teachers can recall information about performances and remember it and in greater detail. Often, you will not have time to take notes about performance during class, so you will sometimes need to remember information about a student's skill until the next time you see the student. Remembering can be incidental (things you recall without trying) or central (things you remember because you try). The importance of remembering children's performance suggests you should try to remember; make this central to your observation! Watch and remember what children are doing. Typically, this will be easier to do for the best and worst performers and most difficult for the average students. We suggest focusing to remember several of the average students; you are likely to remember the best and worst incidentally!

STRATEGIES FOR IMPROVEMENT

Practice, goal setting, and obtaining feedback can help teachers improve observational skills. Experience teaching allows the teacher to focus on observation because management is automatic and lesson content is mastered and no longer demands the teacher's full attention. In addition, more experienced teachers know what to look for, which makes observation more effective. Student teachers frequently report seeing much more during an observation of another teacher's lesson after student teaching than before student teaching.

To develop observational skills, first select the objective of the observation. Begin with one very specific target of the observation—for instance, the same foot leading in galloping. Second, observe several students doing the activity, then close you eyes and try to recall the performance of three students. Third, watch those three again and see if you were correct in your recollection. As you master observing and remembering three students, challenge yourself with five or seven students. Gradually shift to remembering only those who did not succeed on the task; in other words, you will begin to see those who are "outliers." You may want to mentally group students: those succeeding, those needing work on specific things, and those needing practice on every aspect of the skill. With practice, a teacher can observe and remember which students did not master the skill objective, who demonstrated unacceptable behavior, and trouble spots in the lesson (e.g., safety or management issues). The key to expert observation is knowing what you are looking for before the observation.

Videotaped teaching allows the teacher to observe the lesson and see what actually happened. This can provide feedback and guide improvement. A peer or mentor can also provide feedback that can help improve observational skills. This occurs frequently during field experience and student teaching when your supervisor will ask, "What did you notice about the two girls in the front row during the warm-up?" or will point to a child who needs special help during practice. They are guiding you to observe what they observe. Practice with challenging goals and feedback will result in better observation. For example, your cooperating teacher during student teaching may say, "Next time you teach, I want you to say something to the students—so I know you see them—every time one steps outside the boundaries." Seeing more allows you to provide more information to students, so they learn more.

Directions and Demonstrations

Directions, or instructions to the students, are one way to communicate what you want them to do. Instructions should be limited to three or fewer actions (Gallagher, French, Thomas, and Thomas 2002; Rink 1996). For example, "First person in each line, move across the gym, pick up a ball, and return to your place." Another example is "Step, then hop; do this on each foot." With the age and skill of the students, instructions can be more detailed and sometimes be increased in number. Try to associate instructions with cues that serve as reminders of bigger ideas. The cue for the previous example is "step hop," and as skill increases, "skip." Instructions often include examples or stories; these metaphors help students to get the big idea. After giving an example, review the steps or instructions again: "Remember three important things: (1) Move under control. (2) Change levels. (3) On the signal, change directions." Follow with the cues "control," "levels," and "directions."

Demonstrations, or the use of models, have been the focus of motor learning research. Several important guidelines have resulted from that research on who should be the model, how often to use a model, and when to use the model; these include the following (Thomas 1994):

► Correct demonstrations are important.
► Demonstrations help students to understand what to do the first time they try something new, so models presented before practice help the most.
► Limit demonstrations to three; then allow practice.
► Once skill has stabilized, additional demonstrations may help older children.
► Help the learner know what to look for (e.g., watch her feet).
► Peer models are effective for learning and motivation when the demonstration is correct.
► Expert models may not be helpful because the student can be intimidated by advanced skill.

Demonstrations allow teachers to model proper form in performing skills.

Reinforcement and Feedback

Reinforcement, or encouragement, is important to students in three ways. First, it lets them know you are watching. Second, it lets the students know that you care about their learning and effort. Third, encouragement suggests to the student that you believe he is capable of learning the task. The best situation for reinforcement is to use the sandwich technique, which combines reinforcement with feedback. Feedback is information that specifically identifies errors in skill execution or correct aspects of skill. The sandwich technique provides positive reinforcement with corrective feedback, followed by reinforcement. For example, "Good try; now take a bigger step. I know you can do it!"

Feedback is one of the two most important learning variables (practice is the other) and is one of the most difficult for teachers to master. Children associate feedback with skill development, which is important to them. Therefore, even though correcting errors is difficult for teachers—probably because it feels negative—this is an important part of teaching. Teachers generally find it easier to correct misbehaviors than errors in skill (Rink 1996; Thomas 1994; Gallagher et al. 2002). The implication is that skill errors are not under the

child's control, whereas behavior is. Consider this another way. Children who receive corrective feedback gain control over their skill; without feedback, children clearly do not have control. Feedback is empowering. Using the sandwich technique makes feedback a positive experience.

Since feedback and practice are important teacher issues and help students learn, you may want to examine these more carefully. You can observe a teacher and record her practice, feedback, and reinforcement behaviors or you may ask someone to watch your teaching using the recording sheet in table 14.3. The object is to provide each student with many practice trials and to provide feedback as often as possible to each student.

EFFECTIVE AND EXPERT TEACHERS

Expert teachers are opportunistic, which means they take advantage of unplanned situations. This is often called the **teachable moment.** Leadership, sportsmanship, and behavior are often best learned during teachable moments. Sport strategies can also be conveyed through unplanned events. Clearly, teachers must plan for teaching content but should also use unplanned opportu-

Table 14.3   Feedback and Practice

An observer should record the practice and feedback you provide during a lesson. Record the number of trials for each student, corrective feedback, and reinforcing feedback in the appropriate box.

Name	Number of trials	Corrections	Reinforcements

nities to enhance student learning. Experienced teachers see and utilize these opportunities more frequently than do beginning teachers. Reflection is one way to develop these skills: At the end of the class or of the day, you may realize you missed a teachable moment. That is okay, as long as you use this to prime yourself for the next time a similar teachable moment occurs. More information about using reflection to improve your teaching will be presented in chapter 16.

Concepts Into Practice

In his first kindergarten class of the morning, Ben introduced the concept of energy balance (e.g., calories in versus calories out) by relating snacks to activities. He asked the children what snacks they ate after school and what physical activities they enjoyed at home. The children did not name a snack until he specified, "What do you eat when you get home from school?" Then children mentioned cookies, juice, and chips. Several children offered activities such as gymnastics, soccer, and bike riding; then one boy said Monopoly. Ben then told the class that each time they moved—played sports or exercised—they used energy from the foods they eat, so eating was important for being able to play. After class, Ben realized he had missed a teachable moment, so he revised his lesson for the second class and was ready if another opportunity presented itself. In the second class, Ben said, "After school I am hungry and I usually eat a few of those baby carrots as a snack. Do any of you eat snacks after school?" Many children responded—several said, "Carrots." Then Ben asked about sports and activities. When a girl answered, "Playing Barbie," Ben was ready. He said, "I am sure playing with dolls is fun, but it is not very active. I bet you ride a bike or play tag—those are active!" He gave the girl a chance to respond and praised her for understanding the concept. Ben reflected, corrected, and used the teachable moment.

ABOUT EXPERT TEACHERS

"Each has an effortless, fluid, largely unconscious quality to their work that results from a certain automaticity and comfort level seldom reached by most of their peers."

—Dodds (1994)

The effectiveness of physical education teachers has been examined in many ways (Housner and Griffey 1985; Ennis 1994). However, the key characteristic of expert teachers is automaticity. Expert teachers use, monitor, and revise routines for management, practice, and instruction quickly and effectively, often while multitasking. Because the routines are efficient and demand so little cognitive attention, these behaviors are described as automatic. Teaching expertise develops with practice and hard work over several years (Graham 1992). Practice (experience) helps make the behaviors automatic. Although the behaviors mentioned in the previous section are important, teaching expertise is more than a series of discrete behaviors. Expert teachers automate those behaviors into routines that can be adapted quickly and accurately as needed. Thus, teaching begins as a set of skills, similar to those presented in the previous section (e.g., scanning, feedback). In addition, these teaching skills are combined with knowledge of the content (e.g., knowledge about physical activities). So we see that teachers progress from declarative knowledge to procedural knowledge; that is, they know what to do first and, after practice, develop if-then-do routines. Ten characteristics of experts are listed in figure 14.2.

Characteristics of Experts

1. Novices tend to hold literal views of objects and events, whereas experts make inferences about these objects and events. Experts are better able to make predictions than novices are.

2. Experts categorize problems to be solved at a higher level, whereas novices categorize problems by the surface characteristics of the problem.

3. Experts have extraordinarily fast and accurate pattern recognitions.

4. Experts may be slower than novices in the initial stages of problem solving.

5. Experts are sensitive to the task demands and social structure of the job situation.

6. Experts have been shown to be opportunistic planners.

7. Experts show self-regulatory or metacognitive capabilities that are not present in less experienced learners.

8. Expertise develops over long periods.

9. An expert's knowledge shows up in relation to the goal structure of the problem.

10. Expert sport participants possess a higher level of sport-specific motor skills than novices do.

Figure 14.2 Ten characteristics of expert teachers.

Expert teachers typically begin class with a review. For example, in an algebra class the teacher might review the assigned and completed homework before going on to the next topic. The purpose is to determine whether the students understand and are ready for more difficult information. If students are not ready based on the review, additional instruction or practice is provided before moving on. At other times, when students indicate readiness, the review is used to set the stage for the new information. Expert teachers often end class with a "teaser" by using homework or today's content to introduce what will happen in the next class and to pique student interest.

Expert teachers are proactive and take more time to make decisions than novices. For example, at the beginning of the year, expert teachers may devote several class periods to student routines, whereas novice teachers tend to start with content immediately. Novices often have control problems, which interfere with student learning. The time expert teachers spend establishing routines allows more learning in the long term. Expert teachers take more time to make decisions but take less time to implement the action plan based on the decision, when compared with novices. Experts may reflect on a problem longer than novices; this is most likely related to two other characteristics of experts. First, novices tend to make judgments based on surface characteristics—the way something looks. So, the novice may see several children standing in a group and assume the group is off task. The expert may see that the groups are actually working strategically or trying to solve a problem. Second, experts tend to categorize problems at a higher level and make accurate predictions. In order to do so, they probably need more time. Novice teachers have less experience on which to make decisions and less knowledge; therefore, they can make more rapid decisions—but often poor decisions. Expert teachers deliberately spend time trying to improve their

Novice . . . deliberate

Advanced beginner . . . insightful

Competent performer . . . rational

Proficient performer . . . intuitive

Expert . . . arational

Figure 14.3   Berliner's five-stage model.

teaching (instruction, planning, and evaluation). Expert teachers are opportunistic, taking advantage of the teachable moment and planning for maximal learning. Expert teachers want to see the instructional setting and plan around those constraints (along with others such as equipment and time). Experts recognize the impact of those factors on instruction (figure 14.3).

Berliner (1994) presents a five-stage model for teacher expertise. Novices are student teachers and new teachers (stage 1). Novice teachers are taught definitions and context-free rules. Context-free rules are generalized in order to fit almost any situation; in other words, one size fits all. Experience is more important to novices than verbal information. The list of seven considerations for demonstrations and the guidelines on where to stand during class that were presented earlier in this chapter are examples of context-free rules. This is essential for novice teachers, although not sufficient for expertise. Advanced beginner teachers are in stage 2, which occurs in years two and three. At this stage, teachers are able to combine experience with verbal knowledge, and they continue to gather experience. These teachers are often found without solutions for problem situations. After two or three exposures to these situations, the advanced beginner has a solution and is learning when to follow and break those context-free rules. In stages 1 and 2, teachers do not accept full responsibility for their actions, and they are not fully directing instruction. Stage 3 is the competent teacher, achieved by most fourth-year teachers. Two things distinguish competent teachers. First, they make good choices about what to do and how to achieve goals. Second, they can distinguish between what is important and what is not important. This stage is characterized by emotional responses to success and failure and full acceptance of responsibility. A few teachers become proficient performers (stage 4) at about year five. Intuition, procedures, and pattern recognition are new characteristics of this stage; decision making is still deliberate. The expert level (stage 5) is primarily distinguished from the proficient level by the fluid performance of the expert. The expert is not deliberate, but automatic. The expert seems to operate on intuition because decisions are rapid and accurate. Experts tend to monitor or reflect on problems but not on successes. For example, expert physical education teachers break the rules by moving into the center of the gym; they evaluate more frequently and are better prepared to complete complex teaching scenarios such as cooperative learning and peer tutoring. Thus, the expert teacher is arational—he does not follow the rules established as a "safety net" for less experienced teachers.

Four categories of pedagogical knowledge have been identified by Grossman (1990):

1. The teacher understands how to accommodate instruction to the developmental level of the student (e.g., cognitive, emotional, social, and physical development).

2. The teacher understands what the student knows about the skill—correct and incorrect information—and the context in which the skill will be used.

3. The teacher can select and apply curricular knowledge of a skill so students practice the skill.

4. Teachers must have multiple strategies for teaching content such as sports, dance, fitness, fundamental movements, and knowledge.

These four categories of knowledge apply to all teachers and work well with the Interstate New Teacher Assessment and Support Consortium (INTASC) standards presented in chapter 1. Teachers must have and be able to apply knowledge of their field and of child development. Further, teachers must have and apply specific pedagogical knowledge of management, instruction, curriculum, and evaluation. "Apply" means to use during instruction when students are present. So, although the chapters in this book may be discrete areas of information, each is designed to work with the other chapters to provide the knowledge you will need to be a proficient or expert teacher. Two things should be evident at this point. First, it is possible to learn to become an expert teacher. Second, moving through the stages of teaching will take time and effort. Therefore, you should set challenging but realistic goals for your teaching. The following are examples of instructional goals for a class:

▶ To provide concise instructions so most students (that is, a maximum of one or two who do not follow) follow the instructions the first time

▶ To provide one to three correct demonstrations per skill

▶ To provide a cue for each skill

▶ To provide specific feedback about skill to at least two different students using the sandwich technique

▶ To provide at least 10 practice trials for each student (for most skill activities)

▶ To name, touch, or make eye contact with every student in the class (not including taking attendance)

▶ To stand where all students can see and be seen

▶ To scan the class during practice every six seconds

▶ To evaluate student learning for each skill (the percentage of the students who were able to do the skill effectively)

SUMMARY

Teaching depends on planning and comprises personality and instruction. Instructional variables include directions (instructions), cues, demonstrations (modeling), feedback, evaluation, teacher position, and observation. Personality variables include voice, body language, eye contact, and facial expression. Each of these variables is important and will contribute in varying degrees to a teacher's success. For example, one teacher is an expert in planning lessons for maximal learning but is rather boring, whereas another teacher is entertaining and is able to adjust instruction during the lesson, which is necessary because her planning is relatively weak. Optimally, a teacher will be strong in all areas. Practically speaking, teachers must take advantage of their strengths and minimize their weaknesses. Further, teachers at all levels from novice to expert must plan, work, and reflect to continue improving. Teachers must integrate what they know about children, the content, and teaching to be effective. Effectiveness increases with practice when teachers reflect and select goals for improvement.

MASTERY LEARNING ACTIVITIES

1. Create a paired adjective list with characteristics of teachers. On the left will be descriptors of ineffective teachers, on the right of effective teachers. Here is an example:

   Unprepared   Prepared

2. Make a list of as many ways as possible that a teacher can interact with students to demonstrate that the teacher likes the student(s).

3. List as many different ways as possible to say each of the following:

good effort   good work

good citizenship   good behavior

4. Write a series of specific objectives for yourself, directed at developing teaching skills. The objectives should show progression (become increasingly demanding) and be focused on one of the teaching behaviors.

5. Describe your personality. Which characteristics are strengths or weaknesses as a teacher? What can you do to make the most of your strengths?

6. Observe a physical education class. From memory, try to recall skill details for five students. Alternatively, after teaching a physical education lesson, identify one student each with high, average, and low skill.

7. Observe a physical education teacher. How many of the characteristics of expert teachers did you see?

REFERENCES

Berliner, D.C. 1994. Expertise, the wonder of exemplary performance. In *Creating powerful thinking in teachers and students,* edited by J.N. Mangieri and C.C. Block, 161–86. Fort Worth, TX: Holt, Rinehart and Winston.

Dodds, P. 1994. Cognitive and behavioral components of expertise in teaching physical education. *Quest* 46: 153–63.

Ennis, C.D. 1994. Knowledge and beliefs underlying curricular expertise. *Quest* 46: 164–75.

Gallagher, J.D., K.E. French, K.T. Thomas, and J.R. Thomas. 2002. Expertise in sport: Relations between skill and knowledge. In *Children and youth in sport,* 2d ed., edited by F.L. Smoll and R.E. Smith, 475–500. Dubuque, IA: Kendall/Hunt.

Graham, G. 1992. *Teaching children physical education: Becoming a master teacher.* Champaign, Ill.: Human Kinetics.

Grossman, P.L. 1990. *The making of a teacher: Teacher knowledge and teacher education.* New York: Teachers College Press.

Housner, L.D., and Griffey, D.C. 1985. Teacher cognition: Differences in planning and interactive decision making between experienced and inexperienced teachers. *Research Quarterly for Exercise and Sport* 56: 44–53.

Passer, M.W., and B.J. Wilson. 2002. At what age are children ready to compete? In *Children and youth in sport: A biopsychosocial perspective,* edited by F.L. Smoll and R.E. Smith, 83–103. Dubuque, IA: Kendall/Hunt.

Rink, J. 1996. Effective instruction in physical education. In *Student learning in physical education: Applying research to enhance instruction,* edited by S.J. Silverman and C.D. Ennis, 171–98. Champaign, Ill.: Human Kinetics.

Thomas, K.T. 1994. The development of expertise: From Leeds to Legend. *Quest* 46: 199–210.

RESOURCES

Berliner, D. 1986. In search of the expert pedagogue. *The Educational Researcher* 15: 5–13.

LESSON PLANS

The following lesson plans represent the use of instructions, demonstration, and cues. In the grades K and 1 gymnastics lesson, notice how instructions and demonstration are used to give the students the idea of each skill. This is followed by practice, which uses cues or instructions. The skills are generally practiced using the whole method. For safety, a few students do each skill while the teacher provides guidance and keeps control. At the end of the lesson, the children are challenged to practice the skill that was most difficult—in other words, the skill that needs the most practice. For the gymnastics lesson for grades 2 and 3, the instruction is similar in format, but you will notice the skill expectations are higher. At the end of the lesson, children are asked to practice a variety of skills rather than focus on the most difficult. Two lessons for grades 4 and 5 are presented. Notice how new skills are presented similarly to how they were presented in the previous grades. At the end of the lesson, students are asked questions about the important parts of skill and are asked to assist peers with skill analysis and combining skills. Responsibility and freedom in older, more experienced students are encouraged.

The rhythmic lesson for grades K and 1 allows you to observe children. You can observe for following instructions, for skill (e.g., keeping the beat), for creativity (e.g., walking and creating movements to the beat), or for remembering (sequence of four movements to a beat). For grades 2 and 3 the lesson affords similar opportunities to observe children. In grades 4 and 5 the lesson focuses on learning and using a simple dance step, the Schottische. If you are well organized and give good instruction (directions, cues, and demonstrations), you will see students succeed. If students have trouble with this lesson, reflect on your teaching. At the end of the lesson, you can observe students for understanding and creativity.

LESSON **14.1**

Pretumbling and Animal Walks

Student Objectives

- Take turns practicing.
- Follow the safety rule of waiting for a turn.
- Perform one additional animal walk and one new balance activity.
- State the cues for the forward roll.

Equipment and Materials

- 1 mat (4 ft × 8 ft) per group
- 1 jump rope per mat
- Background music (optional)

Safety Tip

- During practice time, stop the music as a signal to sit and get organized.

Warm-Up Activities (7 minutes)

Use grades K–1 warm-up routine from lesson 8.1, page 180.

Skill-Development Activities (18 minutes)

Bear Walk

Arrange small groups, each at a mat. Remind the children that there should be only one child practicing at a time on each mat.

1. Describe and demonstrate the stunt: *With your hands on the floor and arms and legs straight, move one hand, then the foot on that side, then the other hand, then the foot on that side, rolling your body and "lumbering" while walking.*

2. Have the children practice the bear walk.

Puppy Run

Keep the same setup.

1. Describe and demonstrate the skill:

   Bend your knees, crouching down on all fours.

   Let your hands support some of your body weight, look forward, and run.

   Now try sitting and lying on the floor like a dog.

2. Have the children practice the puppy run.

Animal Walk Game

Have groups of four to six line up.

1. Describe and demonstrate the game:

   The first child in each line begins to walk like an animal. The rest of the children in the group follow.

   The leader changes to another animal walk, and each child in that line follows.

   I will surprise you and (at random times) *call out the name of the animal walk a group is doing. When a group's animal walk is called out, the first child in that line goes to the end of the line, and the second child becomes the leader.*

2. Have the children play the Animal Walk Game.

3. Variations: *Does a cat move the same way as a dog?* Cue the ideas of stretching, moving quietly, dragging the feet a bit pigeon-toed. Have the children move like cats. Then have half of the children be cats, the other half dogs. *How do cats and dogs play together? How does an injured dog move?* Sometimes they run on three legs or limp on one of the four. Have the children move like an injured dog.

Rocker, One-Leg Balance, Log Roll

Rocker

Arrange small groups, each at a mat. The children will have to take turns practicing, so line up the children to emphasize that only one child goes at a time.

1. Describe and demonstrate the skill:

   Beginning in a tight tuck while sitting with hands and arms tightly holding knees, chin on chest, and forehead against knees, roll backward onto your back.

   While your body weight is on your shoulders, change the direction of the roll and rock back toward your feet until your bottom and feet are the only parts touching the ground. Continue rocking from your bottom and feet to your shoulders, and then reverse.

2. Have the children practice the rocker. Cue the children: *As you rock, try to get your shoulders off the mat, then your legs and hips off the mat.*

One-Leg Balance

Continue with the same setup.

1. Describe and demonstrate the skill:

   Standing with your hands on your hips or waist, lift your left foot and place it against your right knee.

   Stand in this position for as long as possible.

   Then repeat, touching your right foot to your left knee.

2. Have the children practice the one-leg balance. Give the children this tip: *Try looking at a place on the wall to maintain your balance.*

Log Roll

Continue with the same setup, reminding the children to take turns practicing one at a time.

1. Describe and demonstrate the stunt:

   Lying on one side with your arms and legs together and stretched out (extended), roll onto your tummy and quickly over onto your other side, continuing rolling over until you reach the other end of the mat.

   You start the rolling motion by turning your head and shoulders, then your trunk and legs. Your hands and feet should not push to turn your body.

2. Have the children practice the log roll with their heads all in the same direction.

3. Have the children repeat, rolling the opposite direction. Cue the children: *Keep your arms and legs straight.*

Forehead Touch

Continue with the same setup.

1. Describe and demonstrate the stunt: *Kneeling with hands joined behind your back, slowly lower your head and chest until your forehead touches the mat. Keep your hands behind your back. Keep your knees and feet together throughout the whole movement.*

2. Have the children practice the forehead touch.

3. If children are having trouble with this, especially overbalancing to avoid hitting their heads, allow them to practice a few times with one hand behind their backs and the other in front of them on the mat—but allow them to support their weight with one finger only!

4. Remind the children: *Be sure that your knees and feet are together throughout. Be sure to keep your hands behind you. Go slowly!*

Tightrope

Keep the same setup, but place one jump rope at each mat.

1. Describe and demonstrate the skill, relating it to the circus tightrope walking, which some children may be familiar with: *Walk on the jump rope as though it were above the ground, trying not to step off.* Ask the children: *What helps us balance?* Demonstrate balancing by using arms, looking at a spot, and watching the rope about 18 in. in front of your feet.

2. Have the children practice walking on a "tightrope." Remind students to use their arms to balance.

3. Variation: You can expand the activity making the rope curved, wiggly, and other shapes.

Forward Roll

Keep the same setup.

1. Describe and have a child demonstrate the skill:

   Begin in a squat with your hands on the mat shoulder-width apart, chin on chest, looking at your tummy.

   Bend your arms to bring your shoulders closer to the mat, overbalance, roll onto your shoulders, and continue to roll with your legs tucked.

   Keep your heels close to your bottom and your knees close to your chest, until your feet touch the ground and you are squatting again. (Variations will be presented later for the take-off, roll, and landing phases.)

2. Have the children practice the forward roll. Cue each child in line: *Bend, hands on mat. Look at tummy. Straighten legs and roll onto your back. Stand up.* Or: *Hands on mat, chin on chest, bend arms, and straighten legs. Roll.*

3. Remind the children: *Land on your back.*

4. Don't worry if the children do not get all the way around to their feet. Stress the shoulder landing and keeping their heads out of the way.

Concluding Activities (5 minutes)

Regroup the children on mats according to what they need to practice (e.g., put those practicing the tightrope on one mat, the log roll on another, and the rocker on another).

Use this time to observe skills and offer individual instruction.

From *Physical Education Methods for Elementary Teachers, Second Edition,* by Katherine T. Thomas, Amelia M. Lee, and Jerry R. Thomas, 2003, Champaign, IL: Human Kinetics. Adapted from *Physical Education for Children: Daily Lesson Plans for Elementary School, Second Edition,* by Katherine T. Thomas, Amelia M. Lee, and Jerry R. Thomas, 2000, Champaign, IL: Human Kinetics.

Rhythmic Activities

LESSON 14.2

Keeping Time to a Beat

Student Objectives

- Move body parts to a beat.
- Step in place to a beat.
- Tap rhythm sticks to a beat.

Equipment and Materials

- 1 drum
- Music: "Sunshine" from *Modern Tunes for Rhythm and Instruments*, Hap Palmer (AR 523)
- 2 rhythm sticks per child

Warm-Up Activities (5 minutes)

Fitness Circle

Arrange the children in a large circle.

1. Have the children move continuously in a large circle, counterclockwise, changing movements on a drum beat or other signal. Cue the children (for example: *Walk with big steps, walk with tiny steps, run, walk on all fours, jump, hop, run lifting knees high, skip, leap*).

2. Use a drumbeat to set the pace, once the children have the idea of keeping a beat.
3. You can speed up the movement by speeding up the drumbeat.
4. Stop the drum, stopping the movement to change movement patterns.

Skill-Development Activities (20 minutes)

Keeping Time to a Beat

Have the children sit down, still in a large circle.

1. Play a rhythmic pattern on the drum as follows, providing a continuous sound so that the underlying beat is evident and varying the tempo (speed):

   Clap your hands to keep the beat.

   Tap your hands on your thighs (your shoulders, the floor) to keep the beat.

   Tap your feet on the floor.

   Move your head (shoulders, elbows, fingers) to the beat.

   Make punching movements overhead (in front of your body, to the side of your body) with your arms to the beat.

2. Keep the rhythmic pattern going on the drum.
3. Keep encouraging the children to keep the beat.
4. Repeat all methods of keeping the beat to the song "Sunshine."

Extension Activities (5 to 10 minutes)

Keep the children in a large circle.

1. Tell the children: *Walk in a circle to the beat, creating body movements to the beat of the music.*

2. Ask the children to create other ways to keep time to the beat.

Concluding Activities (5 minutes)

Movement to a Beat

Arrange the children in a large circle.

1. Play "Sunshine" and have the children perform the following sequence:

    Eight steps in place.

    Eight claps.

    Four punch movements overhead.

    Four punch movements forward.

2. Repeat four punches overhead and four punches forward.

3. Repeat the entire sequence.

From *Physical Education Methods for Elementary Teachers, Second Edition,* by Katherine T. Thomas, Amelia M. Lee, and Jerry R. Thomas, 2003, Champaign, IL: Human Kinetics. Adapted from *Physical Education for Children: Daily Lesson Plans for Elementary School, Second Edition,* by Katherine T. Thomas, Amelia M. Lee, and Jerry R. Thomas, 2000, Champaign, IL: Human Kinetics.

Gymnastics

LESSON  **14.3**

Locomotor and Tumbling Skills

Student Objectives

- Complete a forehead touch, a forward roll, or a donkey kick.
- Maintain a balance position after executing a locomotor pattern.
- State the reason for the head position when doing the forward roll.

Equipment and Materials

- 1 or more mats (4 ft × 8 ft) per group
- Background music (optional)

Safety Tip

- Review the safety rules.

Warm-Up Activities (5 to 7 minutes)

Listen and Move

1. Give the following instructions as quickly as the children can complete the tasks:

    Run 20 steps to the right.

    Make 10 big arm circles.

    Run 20 steps to the left.

    Touch your toes (bend knees slightly), *reach for the sky. (Repeat 5 times.)*

    Slide 10 steps to the right.

    Skip 10 skips forward.

    Jump as high as you can, 10 times.

    Hop backward 20 hops on your right foot, then your left foot.

    Twist your torso right, then left. (Repeat 5 times.)

2. Repeat the entire sequence at least once.

Warm-Up Routine

Stretches

Arrange the children in a long line on one side of the mat.

Head Stretches

Slowly move your head while providing support with your hands (chin to chest and up, then ear to shoul-der and up, ear to opposite shoulder and up, chin on chest). Repeat. Place your hands with palms above ears, fingers over top of skull.

Shoulder Circles

Roll your shoulders in circles forward, then backward (hands on hips).

Torso Stretch

With arms extended overhead, stretch to the side, rear, opposite side, front.

Hamstring Stretch

Bend to a squat position with hands on the floor in front of your body, then slowly straighten your legs upward until your knees are only slightly bent.

Ankle Rotations

Sitting on the floor, with legs extended in a "V" position in front, move your ankles so your feet and toes make circles.

Back Arch

Rolling over onto your tummy, with legs stretched out (extended) and together behind, arms extended in front, look up to the ceiling, lift legs and feet as high as possible. Keep your tummy on the floor and your legs straight and together.

Crunches

Do as many crunches as possible, up to 20. Bend your knees, place your fingers near your ears, with your hips at 90 degrees (making a corner of a square) and feet over hips or abdomen.

Push-Ups
Do as many push-ups as possible, up to 10. Keep your body straight, with your arms bending at the elbows to raise and lower your body.

Locomotor
Arrange the children in a large circle.

Skip Clockwise
Skip 24 steps clockwise (point), then go the other way and do 24 skips counterclockwise (point).

Vertical Jumps
Jump straight up, 5 to 10 in high (show height clearly).

Jog or Run
Try to jog or run in the circle for one minute without stopping.

Grades 2–3 Warm-Up Routine

Arrange the children in a line along one side of the mat.

1. Teach all parts of the warm-up as a routine.

2. Have the children perform the following sequence of steps:

Head circle right, head circle left,

Shoulder circle forward (3), shoulder circle backward (3).

Torso stretch (side, back, side, front); repeat 3 times.

Hamstring stretch (squat to straighten); repeat 5 times.

Ankle rotations inward (3), ankle rotations outward (3).

Back arches (5).

Crunches (20).

Push-ups (10).

(Move the children into a circle formation.)

Skip 24 skips clockwise, 24 counterclockwise, 10 vertical jumps.

Run one minute continuously around the circle.

Safety Tips

Review the class rules and the following safety rules:

- *Rule 1: Take turns. Only one child on a mat at a time. Try once, then allow the next child to have a turn.*
- *Rule 2: Do all tumbling on a mat.*
- *Rule 3: Stay at your mat until your teacher tells you to move.*
- *Rule 4: Keep your hands to yourself.*
- *Rule 5: Perform only those activities that are assigned to the mat.*
- *Rule 6: Be a good spotter.*

Skill-Development Activities (18 to 20 minutes)

Review the safety rules before introducing the new skills.

Forehead Touch

Arrange small groups at the mats. If there is no danger of children bumping into each other or falling off the mats, allow two or three children on a mat at once for this stunt only.

1. Describe and demonstrate the stunt:

   Kneel with your feet and knees tightly together and your hands clasped behind your back.

   Slowly lower your head until your forehead touches the mat.

   To finish, rise back to kneeling position without using your hands for balance or support.

2. Have the children practice the forehead touch.

Forward Roll

Arrange the children in small groups, each in a line at the side of the mat.

1. Describe and demonstrate the stunt:

Begin by squatting on the mat, with your hands placed just in front of and outside your feet and your arms outside your legs.

In one motion, straighten your legs (look at your tummy with your chin on your chest if possible), shifting about half your body weight onto your hands and arms.

Bend your arms to support more weight until you are using only your feet for balance.

Then move your hips above your shoulders and forward.

At some point your hips will overbalance, and your body will roll forward.

Land on your shoulder blades.

2. Have the children practice the forward roll. Tell the children: *Remember, keep your chin tucked close to your chest. The momentum will carry your body around in a circle, but your legs must stay tucked tightly. Keep your whole body curled into a ball to help you roll!*

3. Ask the children: *What is the correct head position for the forward roll?* (Chin tucked.)

4. Ask: *Why is this position important?* (To protect the head and neck, especially to keep the head from suffering impact during the roll.)

Donkey Kick

Continue with small groups, with only one child at a mat.

1. Describe and demonstrate the stunt:

   The object of this task is to get both feet off the mat at the same time and to support all your body weight with your hands.

   Begin by standing in the middle of the mat, facing the length of the mat. Place both hands on the mat, about shoulder-width apart.

   Keep your arms straight, but bend your legs slightly. Let your hands carry some of your body weight.

   As you kick your feet up and back, take all your weight on your hands. Keep your eyes focused on the mat, directly between your hands.

   Be careful not to kick very hard, because this may cause overbalancing, and you may flip over onto your back. The purpose is to get both feet off the ground and support your weight with your arms, not to get into a vertical position (90 degrees is safer).

2. Have the children practice the donkey kick.

Concluding Activities (5 minutes)

Pretumbling Skills

Review with the children the skills practiced earlier (basic leap, log roll, rocker, one-legged balance, and straddle scale).

1. Ask the first person in line at each mat to select and perform one of those stunts.

2. Then the next person has to perform a different stunt, and so on, until each child has had a turn.

3. If there is time, rotate to another first person in line and repeat. You may want to incorporate the tumbling from today's lesson as well.

From *Physical Education Methods for Elementary Teachers, Second Edition,* by Katherine T. Thomas, Amelia M. Lee, and Jerry R. Thomas, 2003, Champaign, IL: Human Kinetics. Adapted from *Physical Education for Children: Daily Lesson Plans for Elementary School, Second Edition,* by Katherine T. Thomas, Amelia M. Lee, and Jerry R. Thomas, 2000, Champaign, IL: Human Kinetics.

Gymnastics

LESSON **14.4**

GRADES **2-3**

Tumbling

Student Objectives

- Demonstrate balancing in different positions and on different body parts.
- Practice and refine the basic rolls.
- Observe and evaluate the technique of a partner.
- Create a movement sequence.

Equipment and Materials

- 1 or more mats (4 ft × 8 ft) per group

Warm-Up Activities (5 to 7 minutes)

Use Movement to Sounds from lesson 4.4, page 82.

Skill-Development Activities (18 to 20 minutes)

Create small groups, and assign each group to a mat for each activity.

1. Describe and demonstrate the two-knee balance, V-sit, 360-degree turn, and knee scale.
2. Have the children practice each stunt.

Two-Knee Balance

Kneeling with feet extended behind and hips straight, lift your feet off the mat and balance on your knees only.

V-Sit

Sit and lift your legs straight and together as high as possible, with your torso forming the other side of the V.

360-Degree Turn

Begin, standing still and straight. Bend your knees and rotate your arms and torso away from the direction you are planning to turn. Jump up and turn your head, torso, and arms as hard as possible in the direction of the turn. Land on both feet.

Skill Practice

Create partners within the small groups, and continue with each group at a mat.

1. Have the students practice the forward roll, straddle forward roll, backward roll, straddle backward roll, heel slap, run and takeoff, needle scale, and regular and straddle splits. Say to the students: *Observe your partner to see if he or she is using the correct technique.*
2. Ask the children: *Are there any pointers you can give your partner about technique? For example, you might say, "Your head was tucked on the roll, but you crossed your ankles."*

Concluding Activities (5 minutes)

Movement Challenges That Combine Skills

1. Challenge the children with the following movement combinations:

   A forward roll, immediately followed with a backward roll

   Backward roll from straddle to straddle, then a straddle forward roll

   A regular scale into a needle scale

2. Have the children create their own combinations.

From *Physical Education Methods for Elementary Teachers, Second Edition,* by Katherine T. Thomas, Amelia M. Lee, and Jerry R. Thomas, 2003, Champaign, IL: Human Kinetics. Adapted from *Physical Education for Children: Daily Lesson Plans for Elementary School, Second Edition,* by Katherine T. Thomas, Amelia M. Lee, and Jerry R. Thomas, 2000, Champaign, IL: Human Kinetics.

LESSON **14.5**

Body Shapes and Levels

Student Objectives

- Create movements at various levels.
- Create a short dance using body shapes and levels.

Equipment and Materials

- 1 drum

Warm-Up Activities (5 minutes)

Use Magic Movements from lesson 9.5, page 223.

Skill-Development Activities (20 minutes)

Levels and Collapse

Gather the children into an information formation.

1. Describe and demonstrate levels: *Movement can occur at different heights: high, medium, and low (e.g., on tiptoe, normal standing, and squatting).*
2. Describe and demonstrate collapse: *Drop to the floor, letting gravity pull you down in a way that looks as if you have no bones.*

Movement Challenges

Arrange the children in scatter formation.

1. Ask the children: *Stretch high and on the signal (drum beat) collapse to the floor.*
2. Repeat rapidly.
3. Repeat slowly.
4. Tell the children: *Pretend you are a puppet and the puppet master is pulling your strings to lift you tall and high. All of a sudden the strings begin to break. Collapse your wrists, your arms, your head, your shoulders, and your legs.*

5. Challenge the children with the following tasks:

   Make a different stretched shape and on the signal collapse into a low shape.

   Pretend you are a block of ice melting.

   Combine four walking steps, a high shape, and a low shape. Cue the children: *Walk, walk, walk, walk, high shape, low shape.* Repeat, having the children jump (hop, leap, skip).

   Make a medium-level shape.

   Each time you hear a drum beat, show me a different shape. Try wide, narrow, big, and small shapes. Beat the drum while the children practice making shapes.

   Combine four walking steps and then a high shape (a medium shape, a low shape). Repeat, having the children jump (hop, turn, leap).

Concluding Activities (5 minutes)

Have each child create a rhythmic activity, using walking, jumping, or hopping and a high, medium, and low shape.

From *Physical Education Methods for Elementary Teachers, Second Edition,* by Katherine T. Thomas, Amelia M. Lee, and Jerry R. Thomas, 2003, Champaign, IL: Human Kinetics. Adapted from *Physical Education for Children: Daily Lesson Plans for Elementary School, Second Edition,* by Katherine T. Thomas, Amelia M. Lee, and Jerry R. Thomas, 2000, Champaign, IL: Human Kinetics.

Tumbling

Student Objectives

- Change directions while skipping.
- Combine running and leaping and running and jumping.

Equipment and Materials

- 1 or more mats (4 ft × 8 ft) per group
- 1 yardstick or ruler
- Paper and pencil

Warm-Up Activities (5 to 7 minutes)

Use grades 4–5 warm-up routine from lesson 7.6, page 163.

Skill-Development Activities (18 to 20 minutes)

Skipping Backward

Keep the children in scatter formation.

1. Describe and demonstrate the skill: *Step back, hop, step back, hop.*
2. Have the children practice skipping backward.

Skipping Sideways

Make sure the children are still in scatter formation.

1. Describe and demonstrate the skill: *Step across the forward leg, hop, step, hop; step across the forward leg, hop.*
2. Have the children practice skipping sideways.
3. Have them practice skipping in each direction.

Change Directions

Make sure the children are still in scatter formation. Introduce changing directions while skipping.

1. Tell the children: *Without breaking rhythm, turn toward the open side of your body (the direction you can turn without moving your feet).*
2. Have the children practice skipping and changing directions.

Run and Jump

Make sure the children are still in scatter formation.

1. Describe and demonstrate the skill:

   You can jump for height or distance. Begin running, take off from one foot (a running step), and land on both feet.

   If the purpose is height, the angle of your take-off should be steeper, and your arms should move straight up and remain overhead on the follow-through.

   If the purpose is distance, the angle of your takeoff should be lower, and your arms should reach forward toward your intended landing area.

2. Have the children practice running and jumping.

Leap

Make sure the children are still in scatter formation.

1. Describe and demonstrate the skill:

   A leap is an exaggerated running step with a very long nonsupporting phase.

   Take off from one foot and land on the other foot, lifting high into the air and spreading your legs into a splitlike position. The arms can be held at shoulder height or to the side, or used to lift the body by working in opposition.

2. Have the children practice leaping.

Run and Leap

Create small groups, and assign each to a mat.

1. Describe and demonstrate the skill: *Take several small steps, then a long exaggerated one (leap), and continue with several steps, another leap, and so on.*

2. Have the children practice running and leaping.

Jump From Knees

Continue with the same setup.

1. Describe and demonstrate the stunt: *Kneeling on the mat, with your arms extended in front of your chest, swing your arms down and backward, then quickly upward as your legs straighten and push against the mat to lift your body to a standing position.*

2. Have the children practice the jump from knees.

Donkey Kick

Create small groups, and assign each to a mat.

1. Describe and demonstrate the stunt:

   The object of this task is to get both feet off of the mat at the same time and to support all of your body weight with your hands.

   Begin by standing in the middle of the mat, facing the length of the mat. Place both hands on the mat, about shoulder-width apart.

   Keep your arms straight, but bend your legs slightly. Let your hands carry some of your body weight.

   As you kick your feet up and back, take all your weight on your hands. Keep your eyes focused on the mat, directly between your hands.

   Be careful not to kick very hard, because this may cause overbalancing, and you may flip over onto your back. The purpose is to get both feet off the ground and support your weight with your arms, not to get into a vertical position (45 degrees is safer).

2. Have the children practice the donkey kick.

Skill Practice

Assign each child a partner within the groups at the mats.

Have the students practice the forward roll, straddle forward roll, backward roll, straddle back-

ward roll, heel slap, and regular and straddle split. Say to the students: *Observe your partner to see if she is using the correct technique.*

Forward Roll

Create small groups, and assign each to a mat.

1. Describe and demonstrate the stunt:

   Bend over and place your hands on the mat shoulder-width apart and, looking at your tummy and bending your arms, shift more and more body weight onto your hands as your legs provide less and less support.

   As your center of gravity moves forward, your body will overbalance and roll forward, hitting the mat on your shoulder blades. Continue to roll in a curved position.

   Bend your legs at the knees and accept weight on your legs as your shoulders leave the mat.

   Return to standing with your arms extended overhead.

2. Have the children practice the forward roll.

Straddle Forward Roll

Arrange partners on the mats.

1. Describe and demonstrate the stunt:

   This is actually two consecutive rolls. You start by doing a forward roll, then add the straddle part. Beginning in closed standing position with feet together and arms extended overhead, bend, placing your hands on the mat shoulder-width apart.

   Look at your tummy, bend your arms, and accept more and more of your body weight onto your hands as your legs decrease support.

   As your center of gravity moves forward, your body will overbalance and roll forward, hitting the mat on the shoulder blades. Continue to roll in a curved position.

   Now this stunt begins to differ from a regular forward roll. Keep your legs straight and spread apart in the straddle position so that you land on your legs for the first roll with your feet spread, body bent slightly forward, and arms extended forward.

   Begin the second roll immediately from the straddle position, with your head tucking under and your body moving forward to a shoulder-blade landing.

   Recover to standing with your feet closed, as in the regular forward roll.

Work with your partner—one partner stands in front of the roller after the roll phase to help him recover. Roller, reach out to your partner and try to shake hands as you come up. This will get your arms and weight forward by moving your center of gravity forward.

2. Have the children practice the straddle forward roll.

Backward Roll

Continue with the same setup, except partners are not necessary.

1. Describe and demonstrate the stunt:

   Begin standing, arms extended overhead (palms up) and your back toward the length of the mat and your chin moving to your chest. Lower your body to a tuck position by bending the knees. Overbalance your body backward to begin the roll, and remain in tuck position as your shoulders and hands contact the mat.

   Push with your hands to lift your body (hips, legs, and torso) over your head. Your head and neck should not support your weight and you should touch the mat as little as possible.

   As your feet touch the mat, straighten your arms until your feet are supporting your weight. Rise to standing with your arms extended overhead.

2. Have the children practice the backward roll.

Straddle Backward Roll

Continue with the same setup.

1. Describe and demonstrate the stunt:

   Begin standing in a straddle balance position, with your back toward the length of the mat.

   Move your hands between your legs as your torso moves forward to lower your body, with your hips moving back and down, until your seat touches the mat.

Move your hands to your shoulders as in the regular backward roll. Immediately roll your body backward, while your legs remain in the straddle position.

Recover to the straddle balance position.

2. Have the children practice the straddle backward roll.

3. Have the children extend the skill by beginning in closed standing position and rolling to a straddle balance, then rolling again from the straddle balance to a closed standing position (two rolls).

Heel Slap

Continue with the same setup.

1. Describe and demonstrate the stunt:

   The object is to touch your heels with your hands just under your seat, then land on both feet.

   Jump up from both feet, lifting both feet toward your seat while reaching back with your arms.

2. Have the children practice the heel slap.

Straddle Split

Begin in the straddle balance position and end with your legs extended as far apart as possible. If you are very flexible, recover into a regular split. Otherwise, lean forward, taking your weight on your arms and chest, then swinging both legs together to the rear to lie on your front.

Regular Split

Begin with your feet together in a "T" position, where one foot faces front and the other foot is perpendicular to and behind the front foot, with the feet meeting the heel of the front foot to the arch of the rear foot. Slowly slide one foot forward and the other backward, until your legs are fully extended.

Note: A child may also do regular splits with only one leg moving, while the other leg remains stationary. To recover, the child leans forward with the torso over the front leg and swings the back leg around to the side until it is touching the front leg.

Concluding Activities (5 minutes)

Movement Challenges That Combine Skills

Have the children create their own combinations.

Split Measurement

Measure the distance from the floor to the bottom of the leg at the hip for each child in either split position. Record. You can use this later to show improvement. Reassure the children that as they work on this skill, they will get better at it.

From *Physical Education Methods for Elementary Teachers, Second Edition,* by Katherine T. Thomas, Amelia M. Lee, and Jerry R. Thomas, 2003, Champaign, IL: Human Kinetics. Adapted from *Physical Education for Children: Daily Lesson Plans for Elementary School, Second Edition,* by Katherine T. Thomas, Amelia M. Lee, and Jerry R. Thomas, 2000, Champaign, IL: Human Kinetics.

Dance Steps

Student Objectives

- Perform a sequence of Schottische and step-hop steps to music.

Equipment and Materials

- Music: "Military Schottische" from *Basic Dance Tempos,* Honor Your Partner (LP 501A) (or other Schottische music)

Warm-Up Activities (5 minutes)

Schottische

Arrange the children in scatter formation.

1. Have the children listen to the Schottische music.

2. Using the Schottische step, have the children travel to the music.

3. Have them repeat, using both forward and backward Schottische steps.

Skill-Development Activities (20 minutes)

Schottische and Step-Hop Sequence

Arrange the children in a double circle, facing counterclockwise.

1. Have the children practice combining two Schottische steps and four step-hops. Cue the children: *Walk, walk, walk, hop; walk, walk, walk, hop; step-hop, step-hop, step-hop, step-hop.*

2. Have them practice in place, repeating several times.

3. Variations:

   Perform two Schottische steps moving forward (begin on the right foot), then four step-hops in place.

   Replace the four step-hops with rock steps: forward left, back right, forward left, back right.

   Perform the Schottische steps diagonally to the right and the left.

   Perform step-hops while moving forward (or turning in a circle).

Concluding Activities (5 minutes)

Schottische Step-Hop Routines

Assign each child a partner. Ask each pair to create a routine using two Schottische steps and four step-hops.

From *Physical Education Methods for Elementary Teachers, Second Edition,* by Katherine T. Thomas, Amelia M. Lee, and Jerry R. Thomas, 2003, Champaign, IL: Human Kinetics. Adapted from *Physical Education for Children: Daily Lesson Plans for Elementary School, Second Edition,* by Katherine T. Thomas, Amelia M. Lee, and Jerry R. Thomas, 2000, Champaign, IL: Human Kinetics.

chapter 15

Evaluating Students

Karishma, age 7

Evaluation, or making a judgment, is an important part of the teaching and learning process; it guides planning and instruction and is the basis for feedback and grading in physical education.

Learner Outcomes

The teacher will do the following:

- Define evaluation and describe the relationship among evaluation, instruction, objectives, and planning.
- Use evaluation appropriately for feedback, screening, assigning grades, adjusting objectives, and continual improvement of student learning.

- Identify a variety of assessment tools, including checklists, rating scales, rubrics, and tests
- Compare and contrast norm- and criterion-referenced measurement.
- Define and give examples of validity, reliability, and objectivity.

Glossary Terms

evaluation

validity

reliability

objectivity

norm-referenced testing

criterion-referenced testing

authentic assessment

grading

rubric

checklist

rating scale

The terms "grading" and "evaluation" are often used synonymously. However, grading is one of many applications of evaluation. Consider evaluation in the context of Bloom's taxonomy (see chapter 5). **Evaluation** is the highest level of cognition and is defined as making a judgment. Evaluation in the informal sense is used for feedback; in the formal sense it is used to evaluate performance. This chapter is near the end of the book not because evaluation is an afterthought but because evaluation must be firmly based on knowledge, comprehension, application, analysis, and synthesis. Evaluation is an integral part of the teaching and learning process. NASPE has provided broad guidelines for evaluation, which are presented in figure 15.1. Teachers develop objectives, plan, instruct (practice and feedback), and evaluate. Although NASPE advocates the use of

evaluation in program planning, assessment, and teacher improvement, the focus of this chapter is on evaluating students. However, understand that we use student evaluation to guide curriculum and instruction decisions and to evaluate our teaching. You can see this relationship in figure 1.2 (page 11), which is the foundation for the teaching and learning described in this book.

Teachers use evaluation for feedback and grading (figure 15.2). In addition, teachers may be asked to monitor health and other behaviors, such as height and weight, or do scoliosis screening by checking for curvature of the spine. Young children or developmentally delayed children should have their motor skills evaluated. Generally, screening tests are used for referral to healthcare professionals (e.g., school nurse), not interventions by the teacher. However, these are first steps

WE BELIEVE THAT

Based on our experiences and knowledge, we believe that the planning, implementation, and assessment of elementary physical education should be a continuous process. Assessment serves two functions: It evaluates the process of students in achieving program and individual goals, and it guides lesson planning and instruction. Thus assessment is essential to:

- guide diagnostic and prescription processes during teaching and learning;
- guide and motivate children toward established goals;
- evaluate the learner's response to the learning experience; and
- inform parents, learners, the school, and the community of the program's values and outcomes.

Many evaluative techniques should be used to better understand children in the program, including knowledge testing, anecdotal records, motor skills assessments, decision making in games and practice, health-related fitness testing, and teacher's observations of performance, attitudes, and feelings. *The single most important aspect of assessment is to review children's progress rather than rank children or compare them to norms.*

Finally, the physical education program is accountable to the children, school, and community for quality teaching and learning. Periodic assessment of the program is essential to the development of students' potential and this assessment should include guiding philosophy, student achievement, facilities and equipment, allocation and use of resources, and administrative and community support.

Figure 15.1 Statement of the authors' beliefs about evaluation developed from experience as well as use of NASPE documents.

Holt/Hale 1999 a, b; Mitchell & Oslin, 1999

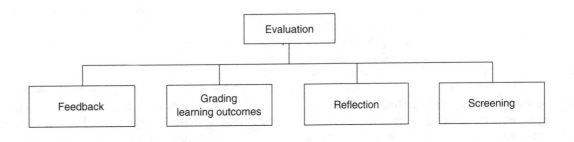

Figure 15.2 Purposes of evaluation in elementary physical education.

in the screening process. This chapter will cover performance evaluation of students and grading in physical education. The principles of evaluation apply to setting objectives, screening, reflecting, and giving feedback as well as grading and evaluating performance.

Teachers need to understand the principles of evaluation and grading for several reasons:

▶ So that appropriate measurements and assessments are selected per instructional objectives

▶ So that evaluation measurements are valid, reliable, and objective

▶ So that evaluation is used to improve student understanding and performance

▶ So that evaluation is used for continuous improvement of student learning

▶ So that grading practices are fair and represent important physical education objectives

The overall goal of elementary physical education is for children to be physically educated, or exposed to a physically active lifestyle based on participation in a variety of games or sports, dance, gymnastics, and fitness activities. Participation requires two areas of competency: knowledge and skill. Physically active lifestyles and physical fitness will flow naturally from development and practice of those competencies. Recall that evaluation of knowledge can be conceptualized as declarative (evaluating the facts and rules) or procedural (use of the knowledge). When an objective of physical education covers leadership or sportsmanship, those would also be part of the evaluation plan. Whatever domain is being evaluated (psychomotor, cognitive, or affective), the following principles of evaluation apply:

1. The evaluation focuses on an important educational objective.
2. Tests and measurements must be developmentally appropriate.
3. Validity, reliability, and objectivity are important considerations in evaluation.
4. Evaluation is used for continuous improvement.

VALIDITY IN EVALUATION

A valid test measures what it is supposed to measure and is both reliable and objective. **Validity** is the single most important concept in measurement and evaluation. A teacher must first determine whether the evaluation is valid—that is, does it represent the objective? **Reliability** means the result represents a typical performance—we will get the same answer each time. **Objectivity** means that the test or measurement is without bias. In other words, the test does not unfairly discriminate against a student. Thus, a student from a different cultural background will have an equal opportunity to perform well. Teachers are often afraid to make judgments because of the issue of objectivity. This means that objectivity has become more important in their practice than validity. Since evaluation is a judgment, teachers must use their knowledge and experience to make fair judgments. Avoiding making judgments is as poor a practice as being biased! Multiple-choice and true–false tests are called objective tests. It is easy to see why teachers often give multiple-choice and true–false tests. The question is whether these are valid measures of the objective. The trade-off between validity and objectivity will be discussed in greater detail later in this chapter. Physical edu-

cation presents the same challenges. It is safer—more objective—to evaluate using a knowledge test, factors like attendance or proper attire, and quantitative skills analysis (e.g., how fast one runs or the number of times one hits the target). However, these may not be valid when compared with objectives such as "play basketball, demonstrate teamwork, adopt a physically active lifestyle."

A frequent problem in testing arises when students are sick or have a personal problem at the time of the test. On one hand, the teacher needs to have a test score that is representative of the student's typical performance. On the other hand, the teacher must be unbiased in dealing with students. Some teachers place more emphasis on "fair to all"; consequently, everyone takes the test at the same time, regardless of individual circumstances. Validity, reliability, and objectivity are viewed as a hierarchy, with validity as the most important and the others subordinate and embedded. An evaluation should be valid, reliable, *and* objective. The teacher should make a "judgment" and allow the individual student to take the test at a different time. The unbiased teacher would do this for any student with a circumstance that would produce potentially unrepresentative scores. Ideally, an evaluation is perfectly valid, reliable, and objective. Unfortunately, in the real world, compromise is often necessary.

Validity is most important partly because it includes reliability and objectivity. However, validity is most important independent of reliability and objectivity (Morrow, Jackson, Disch, and Mood 2000). Likewise, reliability issues are more "important" than objectivity issues. So, in the example of a cultural problem interfering with obtaining a representative score, reliability could be viewed to have priority over objectivity.

This same concept must be applied to the type of test or measurement selected for the evaluation. If a multiple-choice test is a valid measure of the objective, using a multiple choice test is good. However, if the objective is about playing a game or using knowledge in a game, a multiple-choice test may not be a sound educational choice. Once again, we can see a trade-off between validity and reliability or objectivity. The more valid, or real world, the test is, the less reliable and objective the test may be. This problem applies to all tests, measurements, and evaluations. Sometimes objectives seem to contradict each other when measured; this further complicates the issue. For example, children need to demonstrate motor skills during game play, and working as a group is important. A student may demonstrate being a good team member by passing the ball to a teammate; however, this means the student will neither practice nor demonstrate the skill of shooting a goal. Thus, the less valid way of measuring shooting skill is better. Classrooms face the same challenge. For example, a teacher wants to encourage the development of vocabulary but realizes that penalizing spelling errors often reduces experimenting with new words. The conflict is between two equally important and opposing objectives. These examples demonstrate why validity is an important consideration. Teachers can reduce student and parent concern over these issues in several ways:

- By explaining the purpose of the test to the students
- By describing how the test results will be used
- By allowing students appropriate practice or experience with the test material before the test
- By following acceptable and consistent testing procedures

Children are evaluated for a variety of reasons in physical education, including improvement of student learning.

KNOWING: TRADITIONAL ASSESSMENT

Two general categories of traditional assessment are norm-referenced and criterion-referenced testing; these categories apply to evaluating knowledge, motor skills, and fitness. **Norm-referenced testing** expects a range of performance; in fact, the assumption is that the scores will fit the bell-shaped curve. This means that most students have similar scores in the middle of the distribution and fewer students are spread among the higher and lower scores. The vertical axis is number of people and the horizontal axis is the scores (figure 15.3). **Criterion-referenced tests** are based on mastery learning and place students into two categories: master (successful) and nonmaster (unsuccessful). The criterion can be established in three ways: based on norms from a norm-referenced test, based on an arbitrary standard, and by contrasting two groups. An example of an arbitrary standard is the height one has to be to ride certain rides at the amusement park. Contrasting groups is done by comparing two known groups on the test (e.g., beginners and experts) using the cut-off as the point where the curves for the two groups cross (figure 15.4). In the example, the score (average) where the curves overlap would be used to separate the two groups. A teacher could use this to group students for play so that students of more equal skill play with and against each other. Similar groupings are used to determine students who are ready for more advanced skills and students who should continue practicing basic skills. Many prepared tests presented in books or journals are created using either norm-referenced or criterion-referenced methods. This is one characteristic teachers should consider when selecting published tests. Most often, teachers construct their own tests; sometimes they use one of these techniques to provide feedback to students. In case of norm-referenced tests teachers often report the percentile for a student (e.g., 50th percentile equals the middle) or the rank of a student on the test (e.g., in the top 10). In the case of criterion-referenced tests, the teacher may report a successful or unsuccessful performance, may say "you met the goal," or may place a student in a group based on the test score.

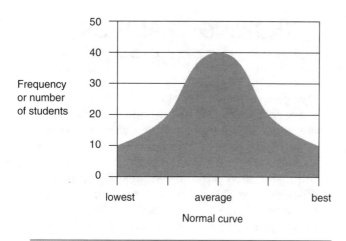

Figure 15.3   Normal curve.

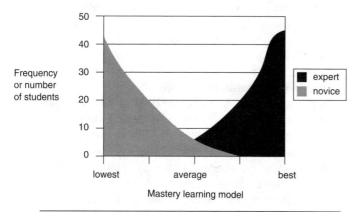

Figure 15.4   Using overlapping curves to determine masters and nonmasters.

One type of test (e.g., norm- or criterion-referenced) is not necessarily better or worse than another. The critical issue is selecting the appropriate type of test based on the objective and then interpreting the test results appropriately. The four frequently measured aspects of physical education are knowledge, skill, fitness, and game play. So, one way to decide how to evaluate is to consider the aspect being evaluated.

Declarative knowledge is necessary but not sufficient for success in games and sport. Children must know the rules, definitions, and basics of the movements before they can participate. Teachers who teach rules, definitions, and movement parameters should evaluate students' declarative knowledge. Traditional tests, such as multiple-choice tests, can provide information about student knowledge; comprehension; and even application of the rules, definitions, and basics of the movements.

Sport and motor skills tests often examine skills out of context and focus on product rather than

process. For example, one could examine free throw shooting skill as a skill test or use free throw shooting from actual games. Since performance in a game is probably the objective, the latter would probably be more valid. However, sometimes using actual play is not practical. In a game, players have different opportunities and are influenced by the play of others. It would be possible to play a game or several games and never shoot a free throw. Skills tests are often used to determine readiness to play a game. Game play, although valid, might not be the best way to determine readiness to begin game play or to evaluate skill. Students with experience playing would have an unfair advantage, and students do not have equal opportunities for performance in a game. Techniques for measuring sport skills and knowledge in context, as well as process evaluations, will be covered in the next section.

Higher-level thinking skills (analysis, synthesis, and evaluation) and procedural knowledge can sometimes be tested using traditional tests, such as essays. However, two limitations are evident with the traditional approach: First, the language, reading, and writing skills of the student influence the outcome. This is a particular problem for young children. Second, time is critical in many physical activity settings, and traditional tests take time. A related problem is the difference between knowing what to do and being able to actually do it. A fan may know what to do in a game, but the fan may not be able to execute the skill. This is typical in novices; they know what to do before they can actually perform the skill in the context of the game.

Careful construction and use of tests to measure knowledge are important for two reasons: First, this produces the most accurate information. Second, the evaluation is stronger and more defensible. Validity, reliability, and objectivity are part of careful test construction. Expert teachers use tests carefully in several ways:

▶ They include evaluation in the planning process so that as objectives are written and lessons are developed, they are considering how the objective will be evaluated.

▶ They spend time searching for tests, modifying those tests if necessary, and as a last resort construct their own tests.

▶ They know the answers to written tests before administering the test.

▶ They evaluate the test at two times—before administering the test and afterward. To do this, have a colleague look at the test before giving it, asking, "Is it developmentally appropriate? Is this a valid test of the objective?" After the test, look at the results. Did the best students do well? Did several students have the same problem? Is there a reasonable explanation for the problem?

▶ They make the test challenging but fair. Expert teachers do not try to make the test difficult. Teachers do not have to make tests difficult to obtain a range of scores, because some students will not prepare for the test and will be unsuccessful. Tests that are artificially difficult are not valid.

▶ They help students understand that testing and evaluation represent student work and performance. Evaluation guides students to improvement.

Some things we may want to test do not fit the norm-referenced model very well; these include activities in which only a few scores are possible, such as free throws made in 10 attempts. Further, criterion- and norm-referenced measurements focus on outcomes, which may be a limitation. For beginners, progress is slow and, as we learned in chapter 4, often observed in the way a skill looks (process) long before the outcome changes. This means that many outcome-based tests will not capture valid performance and change. Once again, using free throws a an example, a child might throw zero, then after practice, still throw zero. However, improvements in form could be observed and perhaps after practice the ball hit the basket's rim, indicating the shot was closer but was just not in the basket! There are times when traditional testing, either norm- or criterion-referenced, is appropriate. Alternatives will be presented later in this chapter. There are times when traditional testing provides the following important information:

▶ Tracking improvement to motivate the students

▶ Comparing to normative data for screening (health, fitness) or fun

▶ Determining readiness

▶ Grouping students

▶ Assessing your program

APPLYING AUTHENTIC ASSESSMENT

Authentic assessment is an alternative to traditional testing used to evaluate performance. Traditional tests, such as multiple choice, number of free throws made, and timed mile run, are sometimes criticized for poor validity—the tests did not represent the target skills or knowledge. Authentic assessment and performance evaluation have shifted the focus to learning outcomes rather than test scores. The U.S. Congress (1992) defined performance assessment as "testing methods that require students to create an answer or product that demonstrates knowledge or skills." The shift in assessment philosophy is parallel to a shift in instructional style from teacher centered (lecture) to student centered (engagement). There are three characteristics of authentic assessments:

1. They represent higher-order cognitive skills.
2. They simulate real-world tasks.
3. They shift responsibility to the student for documenting learning.

Examples of authentic assessments are observations, portfolios, checklists and rating scales, performances, and projects. Authentic assessment is consistent with both a constructivist approach and active learning and also with mastery learning and criterion-referenced measurement. One difference is that authentic assessments often use more than two categories of performance (successful and unsuccessful). Norm-referenced testing would be at the opposite end of an assessment continuum from authentic assessment.

The emergence of authentic assessment and the learner-centered approach is part of the standards and benchmarks approach favored by many school districts (Morrow, Jackson, Disch, and Mood 2000; Lambert 1999; Mitchell and Oslin 1999). Samples of benchmarks for grades K, 2, and 4, and assessments for those representing the National Content Standards are presented in table 15.1. Validity is generally less of a problem with authentic assessments. However, students may have difficulty understanding what a written assignment has to do with physical education. One reason validity is not such an issue with authentic assessment is that students are given the assessment criteria at the beginning of instruction. Often, students do not know how they will be evaluated in norm-referenced testing situations until the time for evaluation. When using a norm- or criterion-referenced test, inform students early in learning about the test and how it will be used and allow students to practice the test. Reliability and objectivity are still challenges for the teacher in authentic assessment. To improve reliability and objectivity, teachers can do several things:

▶ Develop clear and specific criteria for the assessment.
▶ Ensure that the person doing the assessment understands the criteria.
▶ Practice the assessment.

Rubrics can be developed for virtually any skill, knowledge, or behavior. One advantage of rubrics is that both the student and evaluator have the same information before the assessment. Rubrics have been presented in previous chapters (e.g., the locomotor and manipulative rubrics presented in chapter 4 and the teaching rubric presented in chapter14). Table 15.2 is a rubric for leadership, sportsmanship, and teamwork.

Table 15.1　Sample Benchmarks and Assessments Based on National Content Standards

Content standard	Grade	Benchmark	Assessment
Demonstrates competency in many movement forms and proficiency in a few movement forms	K	Runs, walks, hops (one foot), and gallops forward using mature form. Moves at fast and slow speed Moves at high, medium, and low levels	Teacher observation using rubric Teacher observation Teacher observation
	2	Runs, walks, hops (each foot), gallops (each foot), slides, and skips forward using mature form Combines locomotor patterns Throws, catches, kicks, or strikes using mature form Catches and strikes a tossed object	Teacher observation using rubric Teacher observation Teacher observation using rubric Checklist
	4	Throws, catches, kicks, and strikes using mature form Combines balancing and other nonlocomotor skills with loco-motor skills using smooth transitions Demonstrates a sequence of two or more gymnastics skills Performs movements to music with the beat and in proper sequence	Teacher observation using rubric Teacher observation Checklist Checklist
Applies movement concepts and principles to the learning and development of motor skills	K	Correctly names walk, run, gallop, hop, and jump	Teacher observation
	2	States the characteristics of a mature walk, run, gallop, hop, and jump	Written or oral report
	4	Detects and corrects errors in locomotor skills and manipulative skills	Written test

Table 15.1 *(continued)*

Content standard	Grade	Benchmark	Assessment
Exhibits a physically active lifestyle	K	Participates in vigorous activity during class	Teacher observation
	2	Participates in a variety of physical activities	Journal
	4	Describes the benefits of a physically active lifestyle	Written test
Achieves and maintains a health-enhancing level of physical fitness	K	Demonstrates moderate-to-vigorous activity for at least 10 min without stopping	Teacher observation
	2	Understands why heart rate goes up during vigorous exercise	Class discussion
	4	Completes activity necessary for a test of cardiovascular fitness	Mile run test
Demonstrates responsible personal and social behavior in physical activity settings	K	States class rules	Teacher observation
	2	Uses equipment safely and as intended	Teacher observation
	4	Accepts personal responsibility for following the rules	Teacher observation
Demonstrates responsible personal and social behavior in physical activity settings	K	Willingly plays with others	Teacher observation
	2	Cooperates and takes turns during activities	Teacher observation
	4	Participates willingly in activities that represent a variety of cultural views	Student project
	K	Works with a partner to solve a movement challenge	Teacher observation
Understands that physical activity provides opportunities for enjoyment, challenge, self-expression, and social interaction	2	On verbal request, moves in a way that expresses joy, sadness, or fatigue	Observation
	4	Writes about three physical activity experiences that have brought enjoyment, challenge, self-expression, or social interaction	Journal entries

Adapted from *Moving Into the Future: National Standards for Physical Education* (1995) with permission from the National Association for Sport and Physical Education (NASPE), 1900 Association Drive, Reston, VA 20191-1599.

Table 15.2   Leadership, Sportsmanship, and Teamwork Rubric

	Take some time to think before acting	Thumbs up	Double thumbs up
Leadership	Interferes with the learning of others, bullies or bosses others, has tantrums or pouts	Leads when asked, coaches when asked	Coaches classmates, knows when to lead and when to listen
Sportsmanship	Does not follow or understand rules, does not share or play well with others, does not try	Follows rules most of the time, shares with others, demonstrates efforts	Voluntarily follows rules all the time, gives maximum effort all the time
Teamwork	Refuses to work with others, fights or argues with others, makes negative comments to others, has difficulty understanding feelings of others	Willingly works in pairs or groups most of the time, does not say negative things to others, when prompted understands feelings of others	Supports all classmates with positive comments, works with any classmate all of the time, takes turns fairly, understands feelings of others

Use this rubric to assess student performance on these three skills. The information should be discussed with the student (and possibly the parents) so that the student can see how and where to improve.

FEEDBACK TO STUDENTS AND PARENTS

One goal of evaluation is continuous improvement. Therefore, students and their parents need to be informed of students' status. Feedback should occur during regular grading cycles and as information is available. Providing information only during regular grading periods limits continuous improvement because the information needed for the improvement is not available during the practice period. At the beginning of the school year, parents and students should be informed about the goals and objectives of the physical education program, the activities included in the program, and administrative policies (e.g., attendance, participation, dress code). Formal feedback is provided through the formal grading cycles. Informal feedback such as portfolio checks, rubric results, and journals should be provided as appropriate. For example, pretest information from a rubric would help parents provide practice at home and would identify for students the important aspects of a skill. Providing informal feedback to parents from evaluations allows parents to be partners in education. Further, the additional information can help parents understand the meaning of grades in physical education.

Concepts Into Practice

Ms. Corey used a rubric to evaluate students on three skills: jumping a self-turned rope, bouncing a playground ball, and skipping. She sent the rubric home with each child; the parent was asked to sign the rubric and send it back to school with the child. Ms. Corey left a place for parents to comment. A mother made the following comment: "I had no idea that Jason could not jump rope. We bought one on Friday and have practiced all weekend! The next time you give this test, he will be ready. P.S. It was fun to practice jumping rope together."

Continuous improvement also applies to teachers. Good teachers adjust instruction and practice after evaluating student learning. Informal evaluations for feedback, pretests, and other ongoing measurements provide information to teachers that should influence teacher behaviors, planning, and practice. Continuous improvement for the teacher is impossible without evaluation of students.

USING TESTS

Standardized tests, such as the FITNESSGRAM or President's Challenge, are often used for fitness. Other standardized tests are published in books and journals. Before using any test, read the explanation of the test. This usually includes information about validity, reliability, and objectivity; the purpose of the test; and the intended audience. Many tests come with manuals that explain how to administer the test, scoring methods, and other important information. Following the test instructions is important because the results are influenced by how the test is administered. The advantage to standardized tests is that the work of creating the test is done for you. However, you must still learn how to administer and interpret the test.

Fitness tests are often used to monitor physical activity in children. If children do well on the test, the assumption is that the child is physically active. Sometimes, teachers use the results to see if fitness improves. This is fine if fitness is trained during class or assigned as homework. Fitness scores may also be used in grading. The only case in which this is acceptable is when fitness is trained as part of the physical education program; even then it is risky because some components of fitness are difficult to influence. Evaluation of fitness can also be used as an educational tool to describe the components of fitness and typical activities that train those components. Using fitness test information as a tool for understanding is appropriate.

Motor performance tests are generally used for screening to assess developmental level in young children or to determine placement for adapted physical education. Although there is a place for these tests, it is not in elementary physical education.

Sport skills tests can support teaching and learning of sports. They are useful in several ways:

- They can be motivational.
- They may provide information about student competence to inform planning and instruction.
- They can be used as practice drills.
- They are often used as part of a grading system but should not be the only or primary form of evaluation.

Sport skills tests should be carefully selected based on the age and skill of the students and

should match the educational objectives. The NASPE checklist for assessment is a good guide for teachers to use when assessing students' work in physical education (figure 15.5).

The teacher in charge of the physical education program

- ❏ is competent in the observation and assessment of children.
- ❏ is capable of assessing and working with students with special needs.
- ❏ uses assessment as a continuous aspect of the program.
- ❏ assesses individual student progress toward achieving program objectives.
- ❏ uses assessment to improve teaching.
- ❏ uses assessment for describing the program to parents.
- ❏ uses assessment as a means of motivating students to self-improvement.
- ❏ uses assessment to assist students in goal setting rather than comparison to other students.
- ❏ objectively assesses students' movement and skill development.
- ❏ objectively assesses students' physical fitness.
- ❏ makes provisions for periodic evaluation of the total physical education program by other teachers, supervisors, and community.

Figure 15.5 NASPE checklist for assessment.

Reprinted from *Guidelines for Facilities, Equipment and Instructional Materials in Elementary School Physical Education* (2001) with permission from the National Association for Sport and Physical Education (NASPE), 1900 Association Drive, Reston, VA 20191-1599.

GRADING

Schools, districts, and states have a variety of policies on grading in physical education. Sometimes a grading system is mandated; for example, all subjects are graded "satisfactory," "needs improvement," or "unsatisfactory" or are graded with letter grades (passing grades usually include A, B, C, and D). At other times, the teacher is responsible for developing a grading system. The most important factor in any **grading** system is to convey important information about student performance. A grade of "C" or "needs improvement" does not outline for the student or parent what to do. Physical education report cards are helpful because more information can be presented to both the student and parent. Regardless of the type of grading system used, several guidelines apply to assigning grades:

1. For elementary school–aged children, grades should be based on as many components as possible. No single event (e.g., a test, game, or day) should contribute more than 10 percent of the final grade. This means there should be at least 10 things on which the grade is based.

2. Grades should represent distinct performances. This means that the students earning a specific grade are similar to each other and different than students earning other grades.

3. Grades should represent important physical education objectives. Therefore, grading on attendance, shoes, and other administrative criteria is not considered a "best practice." Grades should be based on motor performance and knowledge.

4. Grades should provide information to students and parents that facilitates improvement.

We recommend a physical education report card. If a single grade is required, the report card can be designed so that the card demonstrates how the final grade was determined. Although comments are not required on any report card, parents and students usually appreciate individualized comments that accompany it.

A physical education report card could be based on the national standards and benchmarks for each grade (table 15.3). Using the guidelines, the teacher would evaluate several benchmarks in each of the seven standards. The report could end there or be turned into a grade based on the individual components from each standard. This would inform parents and be consistent with the standards approach to assessment. Teachers must decide at the beginning of a year the value for each component of the grade. For example, one teacher might use each of the seven standards equally for a grade, whereas another teacher might place greater value on standards 1 (movement skill) and 3 (physically active lifestyle). The second teacher might combine scores from standards 2, 4, 5, 6, and 7 at 10 percent each; standard 1 at 30 percent; and standard 3 at 20 percent for a final grade. In either case, the individual benchmarks and standards must be converted to a component grade and then a final grade. Two ways to do this are subarea grading and assigning numeric values.

In subarea grading, letter grades (e.g., "A," or "satisfactory") are counted, and the most frequently occurring is the grade assigned. So, a student who had A, A, A, A, B, A, A for the seven standards would receive a final grade of A. When subarea grade is not obvious, the letter grades can be converted to numbers: A = 4, B = 3, C = 2, D = 1, and F = 0. The scores are summed and divided by the number of scores. The average number is then converted back to a letter grade. Thus, the grades of A, B, B, C, B, A, A would equal 4, 3, 3, 2, 3, 4, 4, for a total of 23; this divided by 7 is 3.29, for a B grade. If the subareas (in this case, standards) are weighted differently, so that standard 1 is 30 percent, standards 2 through 5 are 10 percent each, standard 6 is 20 percent, and standard 7 is 10 percent, then using the previous example, the scores would be AAA, B, B, C, B, AA, A, (4 + 4 + 4 + 3 + 3 + 2 + 3 + 4 + 4 + 4 = 35/10 = 3.5, or 6 of 10 grades of A) for a final grade of A.

Converting to mathematical scores works in a similar way. Each standard is assigned a point value. If the standards are equally valued, the points will be 100/7, or 14 points each. Various performances are assigned points, so a perfect performance would be 14, an average performance might be 11, and so forth. The points are summed to create total points of 100, which then can be converted to a letter grade using a grading scale (e.g., 90 to 100 = A; 80 to 89 = B). Standards can also be assigned different point values: Standards 1 and 3 can be assigned 30 and 20 points each, respectively, and the remaining standards can be assigned 10 points each.

Schools and teachers should give careful consideration to what the grade means in terms of the distribution of students. From the previous section, it should be clear that every child cannot be above average. In fact, the normal curve tells us that only half can be above average and two-thirds are about (or around) average. If a "C" represents average, then 4 to 6 of 10 students will be average ("satisfactory" or "C"), 1 to 3 will be above average, and 1 to 3 will be below average. Unfortunately, many parents and students feel that average is unacceptable. This notion is related to the issue of grade inflation, which means that grades are higher than would be predicted based on the normal curve. Anchor points are the performance a grade represents (e.g., "C" as average or "C" as satisfactory). "Average" implies that 40 to 66 percent of the students will perform in this range. "Satisfactory" may mean the minimum acceptable score, with more students electing to be above this point. You can see that satisfactory

Table 15.3 Sample Physical Education Report Card and Grade Based on National Content Standard

Content standard	Benchmark	Yes/No
Demonstrates competency in many movement forms and proficiency in a few movement forms	Mature form (see rubric) Locomotor skills: Walk Run Hop Gallop Slide Skip Jump Manipulative skills: Throw Catch Kick Strike	☐ ☐ ☐ ☐ ☐ ☐ ☐ ☐ ☐ ☐ ☐ ☐ ☐ ☐ ☐ ☐ ☐ ☐ ☐ ☐ ☐ ☐
Applies movement concepts and principles to the learning and development of motor skills	Names three locomotor skills Demonstrates fast and slow	☐ ☐ ☐ ☐
Exhibits a physically active lifestyle	Participates actively during class Reports being active out of class	☐ ☐ ☐ ☐
Achieves and maintains a health-enhancing level of physical fitness	Participates for 15–20 min without stopping Can hang by arms for 30 sec Can do 10 crunches	☐ ☐ ☐ ☐ ☐ ☐
Demonstrates responsible personal and social behavior in physical activity settings	Moves under control Does not interfere with others Helps others Treats equipment well	☐ ☐ ☐ ☐ ☐ ☐ ☐ ☐
Understands that physical activity provides opportunities for enjoyment, challenge, self-expression, and social interaction	Demonstrates enjoyment, sadness, and fatigue by moving Cooperates with a partner Demonstrates effort	☐ ☐ ☐ ☐ ☐ ☐
Demonstrates understanding and respect for differences among people in physical activity settings	Identifies a difficult skill Identifies an easy skill Works well with those of different skills	☐ ☐ ☐ ☐ ☐ ☐
Final grade	Needs improvement Meets standards	☐ ☐ ☐ ☐

Adapted from *Moving Into the Future: National Standards for Physical Education* (1995) with permission from the National Association for Sport and Physical Education (NASPE), 1900 Association Drive, Reston, VA 20191-1599.

and average can represent two very different messages, although both are represented by "C." In schools or classrooms where criterion-referenced measurement and mastery learning are the philosophical orientation, grades are most likely to be successful or unsuccessful. Schools, school districts, and teachers should consider carefully how grades are conceptualized—that is, criterion- or norm-referenced—and determine the anchor points for grades. This is the same issue faced in the classroom. The two differences are content and information conveyed by the grade. In the classroom, parents and students are likely to see many grades representing performance before a report card. In physical education, the only representation of performance may be the grade on the report card. Neither classroom teachers who teach physical education nor physical education specialists are likely to send home daily, weekly, or monthly reports about a student's progress in physical education. Classroom teachers do send home students' written work, representing spelling, math, reading, and other subjects, on a regular basis.

These methods apply to any system for evaluating benchmarks and standards. To be valid, the weighting of an objective, standard, or benchmark should represent three concepts:

1. Time spent
2. Emphasis
3. Importance

So, one way to consider weighting of objectives or standards is based on time spent; this should also be representative of what is most important and what was emphasized. Sometimes, less time is spent, but a concept is very important and is emphasized so that it is weighted heavily when compared to the time spent. Ultimately, grades should be valid, reliable, and objective. Remember, regardless of the method you use to calculate grades, you need to consider three important issues:

1. Grades inform parents and students about performance (skill and knowledge).
2. Grades represent important educational objectives.
3. Students with the same grade are similar, and students with different grades are meaningfully different.

Informing parents and students at the beginning of the year of the grading method and the expected grade distribution is a good practice. After grades are assigned, reporting the actual grade distribution is also a good practice. Under no circumstance should individual students' grades be posted or reported; students and their families have the right to expect that grades and other performance information be confidential (chapter 12 provides more information on this issue). Teachers should respect students by restricting discussions of student grades and performances to professional conversations. Casual talk in the teachers' lounge is not a professional context.

SAMPLE INSTRUMENTS FOR EVALUATION

Rubrics, rating scales, and checklists are often used to evaluate skills in elementary school–aged children. **Rubrics** must define at least two levels of performance. The descriptions of the levels show the evolution of the skill from a lower to a higher level. Several rubrics have been presented in previous chapters. **Checklists** usually employ two categories—observed and not observed—whereas rating scales use multiple categories. The **rating scale** for creative rhythmic activities uses three categories (seldom, sometimes, and nearly always) and allows teachers to observe on three occasions. The checklist for basketball skills (grades 4 and 5) provides a yes–no response scale for the observation. These instruments focus on the way a skill is performed (process) rather than the outcome (product). Rubrics provide information about the steps along the way that are not provided in rating scales or checklists. All provide valuable information to the students and their parents about student learning and performance.

Table 15.4 shows how a rubric can be turned into a checklist or rating scale. For comparison, table 15.5 shows a rating scale, and table 15.6 shows a checklist. When the performances of students in a class are similar, a rating scale or checklist works well; however, these may not cover all levels of performance and may not provide necessary information for improvement. Rubrics show what came before and what comes after, whereas checklists extract information and often focus only on the most advanced skill level.

Table 15.4 Rubric for Hopping

Circle the best descriptor in each column or row.

	Most effective	Still improving	Improving	Needs improvement	Rudimentary
Leg swing	• Swing leg leads projection	• Swing leg pumps but is in front of body	• Swing leg inactive in front	• Swing leg high in front or to side	
Body position	• Weight transferred smoothly from foot to ball for take-off	• Projected take-off for several steps	• Body leans forward steps	• Momentary flight from pulling motion for 1–2	
Arm action	• Arm opposition	• Arms assist from front of body position • Arms in semi-opposition	• Arms reactive and winging	• Arms stationary	

Checklist for Hopping

Check yes or no for each skill:

Swing leg pumps but is in front of body	Yes ☐	No ☐
Projected take-off for several steps	Yes ☐	No ☐
Arms assist from front of body position or arms in semi-opposition	Yes ☐	No ☐

Rating Scale for Hopping

Check appropriate box:

	Always	Sometimes	Never
Swing leg pumps but is in front of body			
Projected take-off for several steps			
Arms assist from front of body position or arms in semi-opposition			

From *Physical Education Methods for Elementary Teachers, Second Edition,* by Katherine T. Thomas, Amelia M. Lee, and Jerry R. Thomas, 2003, Champaign, IL: Human Kinetics.

Table 15.5   Grades 2–3: Rating Scales for Rhythmic Activities

Name _____ Class _____

Date _____   Date _____   Date _____

Skill	First			Second			Third		
	3	2	1	3	2	1	3	2	1
Is able to vary the *rhythm* of locomotor skills: Walk Run									
Is able to vary the *speed* of locomotor skills: Walk Run									
Is able to demonstrate heavy movements light movements									
Is able to create a movement to a stimulus (word, feeling, rhyme)									
Can create a simple dance using locomotor skills and shapes									
Is able to produce the actions for singing games: Bingo Paw Paw Patch									

*3 = nearly always, 2 = sometimes, 1 = seldom

Reprinted, by permission, from K.T. Thomas, A.M. Lee, and J.R. Thomas, 2000, *Physical education for children: Daily lesson plans for elementary school*, 2nd ed. (Champaign, IL: Human Kinetics).

From *Physical Education Methods for Elementary Teachers, Second Edition,* by Katherine T. Thomas, Amelia M. Lee, and Jerry R. Thomas, 2003, Champaign, IL: Human Kinetics.

Table 15.6   Checklist for Basketball Skills

Name _____   Class _____

Observation date _____

	Yes	No
Chest pass		
Ball is held with fingers.		
Elbows are bent and close to body.		
Feet are in stride position at release.		
Wrists are snapped at release.		
Arms follow through toward receiver.		
Dribbling		
Ball is controlled with fingers.		
Knees are slightly bent.		
Body is flexed over ball.		
Head is up with eyes looking forward.		
One-hand push shot		
Ball is held with shooting hand behind and under ball.		
Ball is supported by nonshooting hand.		
Knees are flexed in preparation.		
Legs and arms are straightened as ball is released.		
Shooting hand follows through toward target.		

Reprinted, by permission, from K.T Thomas, A.M. Lee, and J.R. Thomas, 2000, *Physical education for children: Daily lesson plans for elementary school*, 2nd ed. (Champaign, IL: Human Kinetics).

From *Physical Education Methods for Elementary Teachers, Second Edition*, by Katherine T. Thomas, Amelia M. Lee, and Jerry R. Thomas, 2003, Champaign, IL: Human Kinetics.

PORTFOLIOS AND JOURNALS

Portfolios have become an important part of authentic assessment in education because portfolios can document what teachers are doing and provide evidence of student learning.

Teachers must decide several issues when considering to use portfolios:

- ▶ What will be placed in a student portfolio?
- ▶ Who will enter the material?
- ▶ Why is this information included?
- ▶ How will the information be used?

Traditionally, teachers have recorded student work by class or groups of students (e.g., squads, grades). Portfolios shift the focus to organizing by individual students. Each student has a folder, and both students and teachers place materials in the folder. The teacher can use the portfolio to monitor her students' work and to evaluate their progress. Students assume responsibility for many of the items placed in the portfolio; this can reduce the teacher's workload. For example, students may complete a journal, which is placed in the portfolio each week; or they may have homework, which is completed and filed in the portfolio. Parents may see the entire portfolio during a parent–teacher conference, or portions of the portfolio may be sent home for parents to review. Student portfolios may follow students from grade to grade, where the progression of a student's learning is most obvious.

Consider Including These Items in Student Portfolios:

- ▶ Fitness assessment data
- ▶ Self-assessment of skills
- ▶ Student journals
- ▶ Skills rubrics
- ▶ Student drawing of PE activities
- ▶ Quizzes and other written work
- ▶ Charts recording growth

Two types of information or "artifacts" are included in student portfolios: those that are required by the teacher and those that are optional. Teachers must consider carefully what to require and how it will be used as well as what optional material may be included and how that will be used. For example, teachers may organize artifacts around the seven National Association for Sport and Physical Education (NASPE) content standards (see chapter 1), around other themes (e.g., skill, knowledge, fitness and activity, cooperation), or around the grading criteria. Regardless of the organizing themes and content, a summary sheet or checklist of the required items and a log for the users (e.g., student, teacher, and parent) are helpful.

At this point most teachers think, *How am I going to organize information for all my students?* For a physical education specialist, this could be from 3 to 400 students! There are several ways to handle portfolios; the most common is to use file folders—one for each child. One class or grade can be placed in a crate or other similar container to store and transport the portfolios. This container is available to students during specific times (e.g., during class or before school). Generally, teachers should keep the portfolios because artifacts and entire portfolios can be lost or damaged when students have them. With the electronic age, portfolios can be electronic; that is, teachers, students, and parents can access portfolios via a Web page or CD or in a computer laboratory. Teachers can set up a physical education Web site, make folders for each student (older students can create their own folders), and make the information secure so only a specific parent or child can read or enter information.

Student journals are also popular. For classroom teachers, journaling about physical education or physical activity may seem a natural way to assess physical education and provide writing practice. This may seem less obvious for the physical education specialist. Clearly, journaling is an integrated activity. More important, though, is the information gained from reading student journals. Student understanding is evident in journals and can be assessed for grading purposes or to inform teaching and learning.

SUMMARY

Evaluation is the final link in the teaching and learning circle. Evaluation informs teaching and is a major factor in learning. Evaluation must be planned during the curriculum and lesson planning process. As the teacher selects objectives, she will need to consider how the objectives are to be evaluated. Validity, reliability, and objectivity provide meaning and substance to the evaluation process; therefore, these sometimes influence the objectives of instruction. Objectives should focus on important educational outcomes. Evaluation will then be on educational outcomes, as will grades. Evaluation has many purposes, including screening, grouping, and grading. Grading must follow the principles of evaluation and must provide information to students and parents about learning as well as specific information to facilitate improvement. Many types of assessment should be used, such as norm-referenced, criterion-referenced, and authentic assessments as well as a variety of measurements, including cognitive tests, rubrics, portfolios, and journals.

MASTERY LEARNING ACTIVITIES

1. Find a physical education test for elementary school–aged children. If the test does not have a stated objective, write one. Critique the test based on validity, reliability, and objectivity.

2. Select one National Content Standard and write a benchmark for each grade (K–5), using the same skill or a variation of the skill. The benchmarks should clearly demonstrate progression from grade to grade.

3. Select one skill and develop a norm-referenced, criterion-referenced, and authentic assessment for that skill.

4. Write a one-page description for parents of a physical education grading system for grades 2 and 3.

REFERENCES

Holt/Hale, S.A. 1999a. *Assessing motor skills in elementary physical education.* Reston, Va.: NASPE Publications.

Holt/Hale, S.A. 1999b. *Assessing and improving fitness in elementary physical education.* Reston, Va: NASPE.

Lambert, L.T. 1999. *Standards-based assessment of student learning: A comprehensive approach.* Reston, Va.: NASPE Publications.

Mitchell, S.A., and J.L. Oslin. 1999. *Assessment in games teaching.* Reston, Va.: NASPE Publications.

Morrow, J.R., A.W. Jackson, J.G. Disch, and D.P. Mood. 2000. *Measurement and evaluation in human performance.* 2d ed. Champaign, Ill.: Human Kinetics.

U.S. Congress, Office of Technology Assessment. 1992. *Testing in American schools: Asking the right questions.* OTA-SET-519 February. Washington, D.C.: Government Printing Office.

RESOURCES

Schiemer, S. 2000. *Assessment strategies for elementary physical education.* Champaign, Ill.: Human Kinetics.

Thomas, J.R., and K.T. Thomas. 1983. Strange kids and strange numbers: Assessing children's motor development. *Journal of Physical Education, Recreation and Dance* 54: 19–20.

LESSON PLANS

Three lessons plans using different types of assessment are presented. [A checklist is used to assess gymnastics at the end of a unit. Students' names go at the top of the column. The lesson suggests that you place children in the same order that they are listed on the checklist to do the tasks; this saves time because you do not have to search the list for a name.] A health lesson on fitness and activity uses a crossword puzzle to check for understanding in second and third graders. Finally, a lesson actually conducting the test from lesson plan 15.3 is presented for grades 4 and 5.

Gymnastics

LESSON **15.1**

Tumbling Checklist

Student Objectives

- Evaluate one's own performances of the various skills.

Equipment and Materials

- 1 mat (4 ft × 8 ft) per group
- Background music (optional)
- 1 copy of the Grades K–1: Checklist for Tumbling per group (see appendix)

Teacher Objectives

- The teacher will observe and evaluate the children's performance, using either the checklist or informal observation.

Warm-Up Activities (5 minutes)

Use grades K–1 warm-up routine from lesson 8.1, page 180.

Skill-Development Activities (20 minutes)

Skills Checklist

Arrange the children at the mats in small groups corresponding to the order on your checklist. See Checklist for Tumbling on the following pages.

Repeat one at a time the following skills: log roll, rocker, two-knee balance, forward roll, backward roll, one-leg balance, forehead touch, donkey kick, tripod, and elbow-knee balance.

Extension Activities

Set up the mats as described for the checklist. Invite another teacher, your principal, or other "honored" guest to observe the children.

1. Have the children run through the tumbling activities. You could also review the animal walks and locomotor skills.
2. Have each group of children select a stunt per member of their group and decide the order in which their group will present the stunts.
3. Allow each group to demonstrate for the rest of the class.

Concluding Activities (5 minutes)

Keep the children with their groups at their mats. Tell the students: *Show your group the one skill you did the very best today!*

From *Physical Education Methods for Elementary Teachers, Second Edition,* by Katherine T. Thomas, Amelia M. Lee, and Jerry R. Thomas, 2003, Champaign, IL: Human Kinetics. Adapted from *Physical Education for Children: Daily Lesson Plans for Elementary School, Second Edition,* by Katherine T. Thomas, Amelia M. Lee, and Jerry R. Thomas, 2000, Champaign, IL: Human Kinetics.

Checklist for Tumbling

(Kindergarten competencies are noted with #.)
(First grade should do all skills competently.)

Name											
Forward roll#											
Begins squatting on mat, hands placed on mat in front of and outside feet.											
Has arms outside of legs.											
In one motion, straightens legs while looking at tummy.											
Begins to support body weight with arms; keeps hips above shoulders and moving forward.											
Lands on shoulder blades.											
Keeps legs tucked.											
Lands on feet (first).											
Does not use hands to push under hips.											
Backward roll#											
Begins in squat position with back to length of mat.											
Place hands on shoulders, palms up.											
Presses chin close to chest.											
Begins motion with rocking movement.											
Touches mat with bottom, back, shoulders-hands, head-hands, in sequence.											
When hands touch, child pushes by extending arms.											
Recovers (lands) on feet (first).											

Checklist for Tumbling

(Kindergarten competencies are noted with #.)
(First grade should do all skills competently.)

Name											
Log roll#											
Begins lying crosswise on mat with arms and legs extended.											
Initiates rolling motion by turning head and shoulders.											
Keeps body straight and doesn't use hands or feet to make motion.											
Makes three complete turns, or moves length of mat.											
Rocker#											
Begins lying on back with hands grasping knees.											
Initiates motion by thrusting head forward and "pumping" body.											
Achieves 90-degree range of motion without releasing grasp of hands and knees.											
Does three consecutive repetitions.											
Two-knee balance#											
Begins kneeling (with hips extended so buttocks do not touch legs), arms extended to each side.											
Lifts feet from mat so that only knees are supporting body weight.											
Keeps both feet off of floor while maintaining balance. Balances for five seconds.											

Name											
One-leg balance											
Begins standing with hands on hips.											
Keeps one leg raised until foot clears floor, stopping near knee of support leg.											
Maintains balance for 10 seconds.											
Forehead touch											
Begins in kneeling-squat position (knees, legs, and feet on floor; buttocks on calf of leg), hands joined behind back.											
Bends slowly forward until forehead touches mat.											
Raises to kneeling position without using hands											
Donkey kick											
Begins standing.											
Bends at waist, hands placed shoulder-width apart on mat.											
Kicks feet and legs out and up behind while supporting body weight with arms.											
Moves feet up and down together.											
Tripod											
Begins in squat with hands and arms on mat outside knees and legs.											
Bends forward until forehead touches mat.											
Bends arms and touches knees to elbows.											
Supports body weight with arms.											
Maintains balance for five seconds.											
Elbow-knee balance											
Begins in squat with hands on mat outside legs.											
Touches elbows to knees.											
Holds up head.											
Shifts weight from feet to hands.											
Maintains balance for five seconds.											

From *Physical Education Methods for Elementary Teachers, Second Edition,* by Katherine T. Thomas, Amelia M. Lee, and Jerry R. Thomas, 2003, Champaign, IL: Human Kinetics. Adapted from *Physical Education for Children: Daily Lesson Plans for Elementary School, Second Edition,* by Katherine T. Thomas, Amelia M. Lee, and Jerry R. Thomas, 2000, Champaign, IL: Human Kinetics.

LESSON

Physical Activity and Fitness

Student Objectives

- Distinguish between physical fitness and physical activity.
- Name one benefit of physical activity.

Equipment and Materials

- 1 copy of crossword per child
- 1 pencil per child

Health Concept (30 minutes)

Gather the children into an information formation for the entire discussion.

Physical Fitness and Physical Activity

1. Introduce the concept: *Physical fitness and physical activity are part of good health and help us to grow. Physical fitness is being able to meet some standards for muscle strength and endurance, flexibility, and cardiovascular (aerobic) endurance. Having a healthy amount of body fat is also part of fitness.*

2. Tell the children: *Physical activity means a person does things that require large muscles, and such a person does not spend all day sitting down. If we take a walk, use the stairs, clean house, or work in the garden, we are being physically active. Being physically fit or active reduces the risk of certain diseases (e.g., diabetes, heart disease) and encourages our bones to grow stronger, helps us make bigger muscles, and keeps our bodies from storing too much fat.*

3. Do the crossword on the next page individually. Down are words associated with health-related fitness; across, with physical activity.

CROSSWORD

Across

1. Don't ride, _____!
2. Making flowers and good health
3. _____ to work instead of driving to work

Down

1. Muscular _____
2. Over and over again
3. Heart fitness
4. Bending and stretching
5. Not too much or too little, but just right

From *Physical Education Methods for Elementary Teachers, Second Edition,* by Katherine T. Thomas, Amelia M. Lee, and Jerry R. Thomas, 2003, Champaign, IL: Human Kinetics. Adapted from *Physical Education for Children: Daily Lesson Plans for Elementary School, Second Edition,* by Katherine T. Thomas, Amelia M. Lee, and Jerry R. Thomas, 2000, Champaign, IL: Human Kinetics.

Fitness

LESSON **15.3** *Testing Aerobic Fitness*

Student Objectives

- Perform the one-mile run.
- Work cooperatively with a partner.

Equipment and Materials

- Stopwatch
- Cones to mark testing area
- Recording forms
- Music

Warm-Up Activities (5 minutes)

Individual Stretching Exercises

Arrange the children in scatter formation.

1. Briefly discuss the importance of good flexibility and how stretching can improve flexibility.
2. Describe and demonstrate the individual stretching exercises. Emphasize safety guidelines:

   Move slowly into each stretch, stopping when you feel a slight tug. It should not hurt!

   No bouncing!
3. Have the children complete the individual stretching exercises.

Sitting Toe Touch

Sitting with legs straight and feet together, reach your fingers toward your toes, bringing your face toward your knees, and hold for five seconds. Relax. Repeat several times.

Trunk Twister

Sitting with feet shoulder-width apart and hands clasped in front of your chest, keep your arms horizontal (demonstrate). *Rotate slowly to the right and left, holding each position for five seconds. Repeat several times.*

Forward Lunge

Standing with feet together and hands on your hips, lunge forward with your right leg, keeping your left leg straight. Your right knee should form a right angle (corner of a square). Hold the lunge position for five seconds and return to starting position. Then lunge with your left leg forward. Repeat several times, alternating right and left legs.

Skill-Development Activities (25 minutes)

One-Mile Run Test

Create partners in two groups, one partner from each pair in each group.

1. Tell the children:

   One child from each pair will run the mile first. The other will count the number of laps.

   I will call out each child's time as he crosses the finish line for each child's partner to record.

   Then we'll switch and let the other group run.
2. Give the children a short break and the opportunity to get water after running.

From *Physical Education Methods for Elementary Teachers, Second Edition,* by Katherine T. Thomas, Amelia M. Lee, and Jerry R. Thomas, 2003, Champaign, IL: Human Kinetics. Adapted from *Physical Education for Children: Daily Lesson Plans for Elementary School, Second Edition,* by Katherine T. Thomas, Amelia M. Lee, and Jerry R. Thomas, 2000, Champaign, IL: Human Kinetics.

chapter 16

Growing As a Teacher

Nina, age 7

J ust as an education is more than a collection of courses, becoming a teacher is more than completing a program of study. Teaching is a daily and long-term learning opportunity. Reflection and self-evaluation contribute to teacher growth and are possibly the most powerful forces in creating positive change. Other sources of information include external reviews of your work, continued learning, professional activities, and extending the mission of your school and your work to a wider audience.

Learner Outcomes

The teacher will do the following:

- ▸ Explain reflection and the benefits from being a reflective teacher.
- ▸ Describe portfolios and how working, professional, and employment portfolios are used.
- ▸ Understand why lifelong learning is important.

- ▸ Describe collaboration and list several of its benefits.
- ▸ Identify several ways teachers can extend learning beyond the walls of the school.
- ▸ Present one or more ways to develop as a professional.

Glossary Terms

reflection
working portfolio
teaching philosophy statement
vita

professional portfolio
employment portfolio
service

As you observe experienced teachers—particularly expert teachers—you may think, *Teaching looks easy*. Most students will agree, however, that student teaching, although very rewarding, is also the most difficult semester of their college careers. Good teachers just make it *look* easy—in part because of all the unobserved hard work they do. Another factor is experience. Practice does make it better—but not easy. During student teaching, you are probably going to wonder how your cooperating teacher does so much and for so many years! Unfortunately, the dropout rate for new teachers is high. One reason for this is that teaching is hard work and often offers a low salary. New teachers feel inadequate and isolated; they feel disappointed in their performance and sometimes in the profession. The dropout rate has become a crisis in education for three reasons: First, the costs associated with preparing and inducting new teachers is high—so a teacher dropping out is expensive to the system. Second, most teachers improve during the first five years, so dropping out early means the efficiency of the system is reduced—the optimal situation would be for all the teachers to have at least five years of experience. This also explains why it may be difficult to get your first job and easier to get your second job! Third, children perform better with more experienced teachers. Student test scores improve each year for the first five to seven years of a teacher's experience (Berliner 1994).

The information in this chapter is important for teachers for several reasons:

- ▶ Teachers want to improve their teaching.
- ▶ Teachers must be able to document teaching performance.
- ▶ Teachers may need assistance in obtaining a job.
- ▶ Teachers need to transition from student in teacher education to professional teacher.
- ▶ Teachers do not want to drop out of teaching.
- ▶ Teachers will often seek new challenges.

Thus, this chapter will cover reflection as a technique to improve teaching; portfolios as learning, professional, and employment tools; collaboration; service; and professionalism.

REFLECTION

Reflection is a necessary tool in the process of becoming an expert teacher. Recall that expertise can begin after 10,000 hours of practice—but practice is not a guarantee of expertise. The practice must be deliberate—with feedback and corrections (Ericsson, Krampe, and Tesch-Römer 1993). **Reflection** on the teaching learning process—thinking, feedback, and correction—is critical when improvement is the goal.

Thus, teachers should evaluate their own teaching and may evaluate the teaching of others. For example, students observe experienced teachers, student teachers observe cooperating teachers, and teachers observe peers. Teaching and learning are complex and should be examined together because one influences the other. Teachers plan, manage, instruct, demonstrate, provide feedback, and evaluate, generally in that order. Each of those categories includes many behaviors that provide information about the teacher's success (Lee 1991).

"In the domains in which they are acquiring their abilities, developing experts learn more from experience than do the rest of us. It is highly motivated learning in which they are engaged, whether it is the acquisition of baseball knowledge, chess moves, or computer programming. Their learning probably is also reflected upon more than is the learning in which others engage."

—David Berliner (1986)

Many teacher education programs require students to keep a journal during field experience because this forces students to reflect on their teaching. Supervisors can read the journal and provide feedback—to improve the reflection or to solve teaching problems. The critical ingredient is not the writing but the thinking; however, writing does tend to clarify thinking. The phenomenon has been called communicating to learn. Most of our communication education was focused on learning to communicate. The reverse process is now the accepted educational procedure—communicating to learn. Whether written, oral, or cerebral, reflection about teaching is critical to improvement.

Teachers can use videotaping to watch their teaching and then reflect and plan for change. Teachers can also ask a colleague to observe and provide feedback (table 16.1). They can use student performance and learning to inform their teaching. In fact, teachers should use each of these sources of feedback. Some reflection will be spontaneous—you realize that something is not working and you think, *How can I change this so it will work?* Other reflection is more deliberate and covers longer time periods. Both types of reflection are important.

Reflection and self-evaluation allow teachers to make positive changes in their occupation and ultimately benefit the students with whom they come into contact.

Table 16.1　Lesson Evaluation Form

Name of teacher:　　　　　　Date:　　　　　　Name of observer:

Objective	Activity	Formation (draw this)	Cues	Number of trials or time	Feedback/evaluation

PORTFOLIOS

Portfolios have been used in many fields as the primary documentation of work; for example, in art or advertising, portfolios are used during training and while searching for employment. Recently, portfolios have become an important part of authentic assessment in education, because portfolios can document what teachers are doing (Melograno 1999). Portfolios communicate this information in several ways. First, teachers think about and refine what they believe and what they do to enhance student learning. As teachers write about their teaching and student learning, the written communication becomes a learning experience—this is what is called communicating to learn. Second, portfolios demonstrate a teacher's communication skills as well as his planning, philosophy, and teaching activities.

Portfolios help teachers grow, address licensing and certification issues (e.g., INTASC standards), and assist schools and universities during reviews. They may also enhance teachers' employment opportunities. Three types of portfolio are discussed here: a working portfolio in which to store information about your teaching, a professional or presentation portfolio that highlights your best or most recent work, and an employment portfolio that extends the presentation portfolio to include information required in the job market.

Working Portfolios

Working portfolios can be viewed as a storage system for activities, ideas, and other support materials. A working portfolio is more than a filing system, but it certainly includes a filing system. Pre-service teachers should begin saving and systematically filing samples of their work. No unit plan, bulletin board, or philosophy statement should be considered the final product, at least not until you retire from teaching! Systems for filing can be organized around themes (or learning centers) and by age group.

Items to Include in a Working Portfolio

- ▶ Teaching statement
- ▶ Short- and long-term goals
- ▶ Resume or vita (updated regularly)
- ▶ Unit plans
- ▶ Lesson plans
- ▶ Sample bulletin boards
- ▶ Evaluation instruments
- ▶ Teaching evaluations
- ▶ Journals
- ▶ Reflections
- ▶ Photos
- ▶ Videos

Beginning with broad themes (e.g., locomotor skills and manipulative skills) or team sports works well. As you collect more information, you will want to add more specific categories, such as softball, soccer, and basketball. Organizing by the class in which the work was completed works, especially early in your college career. As you collect materials, be certain you document the source. For example, one lesson might be downloaded from a Web site, another might be a class handout, and a third given to you by a friend. Recording this information is important for two reasons. First, you may need to give credit to the source at a later time, and as your portfolio grows you won't be able to remember every source. Second, you may want to go back and get additional information from that source later. Materials from your working portfolio may be used in your professional portfolio or may become resources for you as you plan and teach. Working portfolios document to you and others the progress you are making as a teacher.

Working portfolios include many types of materials, including computer disks storing copies of important work (always keep a paper copy of important information); videotapes of teaching and other performances; papers; critiques; class written work; evaluations by employers, supervisors, and teachers; samples of creations; and virtually anything else. Generally, it will take filing boxes to handle the volume of materials in a working portfolio. Hints: Use dividers and labels and color code materials. A working portfolio is a source of infor-

mation—information that you may need to access very quickly. Keeping information in electronic files is helpful. For example, update your resume or vita on a regular basis, review your teaching philosophy statement before each school year, and add awards and performance evaluations at the end of each school year.

A **teaching philosophy statement** should be based on your values and be specific in how those values will affect your curriculum decisions and instructional strategies. You should describe a typical class, overview your curriculum and evaluation procedures, and present your point of view on diversity issues such as gender and disabilities (Seldin 1997). A philosophy statement is usually five to seven pages, double spaced, but can be presented in a one-page abstract form. The key to a good philosophy statement is to avoid generalities, such as "I want to cure all the problems in the world by being a teacher" or "I will be the best teacher ever," and to focus on specific activities, behaviors, and beliefs. For example, "By shifting responsibility to students for _____, _____, and _____, I will help them learn to be independent thinkers and better team members" is a specific action that is tied to a personal value. The teaching philosophy statement should reveal a great deal about you as a person and teacher.

The resume or **vita** is a record of what you have accomplished. Individuals have different beliefs about the amount of personal information included in a vita. You may feel comfortable including your age, gender, family status, and other descriptive information; however, you do not have to reveal this in your resume or during an interview. Your vita should include certain information. Figure 16.1 provides a suggested format; however, there are many possible formats. Two critical aspects of a resume or vita are that all information must be accurate (i.e., truthful) and the document should be neat and error free (i.e., no typographical or spelling errors).

Presentation or Professional Portfolios

The purpose of a presentation or **professional portfolio** is to highlight your best work. The portfolio is often used in performance evaluation of teachers for career ladder programs, merit pay, master teacher programs, and recognition award programs. In creating the professional or presentation portfolio, select materials from the

Bjorn T. Teach

Physical Education Specialist

Work address: Home address:

B. Pettifor Elementary School   123 School Street
1507 Market Street   Urbana, IL 61822
Champaign, IL 61825
Phone: 555-555-1212   555-555-2121
e-mail: borntoteach@champaign.edu.k-12

Education

Institution	Degree	Year
Iowa State University	BS in Health and Human Performance	2001
Podunk Center High School	High school diploma with honors	1995

Licenses, endorsements, certifications, and authorizations

Agency	Title	Date
Iowa Department of Education	Initial beginning teacher	2001
Iowa Department of Education	Coaching authorization	2001
Illinois Department of Education	Professional teacher	2001
American Red Cross	First responder	1999-2002

Teaching experience

School name and address	Position	Dates
Bonnie Pettifor Elementary School 1507 Market Street Champaign, IL 61825	Physical Education Specialist	2001-
Kate Thomas Elementary School 3345 Jewell Drive Ames, IA 50010	Student teacher	2000

Other work experience

Employer	Job duties	Dates
ISU Clone Kids	Gymnastics instructor	Summer 98, 99, 00
Ames Public Schools	Substitute educational assistant	99–00
Kids Care	Child care provider	98–99

Awards and other recognitions

ISU College of Education Dean's List (6 times)	98–00	
College of Education Outstanding Student Teacher	2000	
Harry Schmidt Outstanding Male Senior Award	2000	
Phi Kappa Phi National Honorary		1999

Figure 16.1   Sample of a resume or vita.

working portfolio depending on the use of the portfolio. For most professional uses, the philosophy statement or at least part of it should be included. Photos and other visual material are helpful. Often, only portions of units or lessons are included; this helps reduce the reading and increase the visual impact. Dividers and color coding are helpful in guiding the reader through the portfolio. Presentation portfolios can be used during parent conferences to share information about you and your program with parents. Once again, an electronic version rich in visual elements may be more practical. CDs, Web pages, and videos capture the imagination of the audience and present your best work. Another alternative, depending on the use, is a large presentation board that uses photos and other visual materials to demonstrate your best work.

Employment Portfolios

Once again, **employment portfolios** display your best work. However, employment portfolios should be targeted at the specific employer. Doing your homework about the school or school district is critical. A section (which should also be included in your letter of application) that matches your goals and skills to the characteristics of the school (e.g., mission statement, school improvement plan, demographics, and organization) demonstrates two things. First, it shows that you have a genuine desire to work in this setting. Second, it shows that you understand their needs and that you match those needs perfectly. You will want to select work samples that target the unique aspects of the school (or district), so the artifacts may vary depending on the job for which you are applying. Remember that each district and school is different; at different schools within a district, each person who will interview you or look at your credentials may place greater value on one aspect of your materials over another. This means that each part of your application package—or employment portfolio—should be the best you can produce and should represent you as well as possible. What will people say when they look at your materials? Samples of positive comments are presented in the text box titled "Concepts Into Practice."

Components to Include in an Employment Portfolio

1. Letter of application (a copy of the one you mailed with your application), which describes why you want to teach and why this school is perfect for you and highlights your credentials as they relate to this job

2. A copy of the district application

3. Your resume or vita

4. A list of references and your relationship to them (highlight how and what they know about your teaching); obtain prior permission to use them as references

5. A statement of your short- and long-term goals

6. Your teaching philosophy statement

7. Sample unit and lesson plans including evaluation instruments and bulletin board photos or sketches

8. Evaluations of your teaching by supervisors and peers; other related evaluations

9. Other materials (videos, awards, samples of written work, copy of teaching license)

Concepts Into Practice

Chris is applying for a job in the Newcastle School District. His employment portfolio has been reviewed by several people in the district. When they meet to discuss each candidate, they say the following about Chris:

Director of human resources: "The application is complete and has no errors. I like his letter of application because it demonstrates his ability to communicate."

Curriculum director: "His unit plans are clear and creative and he includes many support materials, like the bulletin boards and handouts. He included evaluation materials for each lesson and unit."

Principal: "Two things were important to me—First, I can see from his philosophy statement that he will care about the kids and work hard to help them learn. Second, his letters of recommendation from his supervising and cooperating teachers say he is a team player—I need that in my school."

Teacher: "He doesn't have any years of experience, but he has a number of service learning and related work experiences on his vita. That shows he will probably be ahead of a new teacher and he has worked hard to learn about teaching before his first job."

Parent: "As a parent and school board member, I am impressed with his computer and technology skills. His CD has video clips of his teaching! I think he can help us in that area, too."

Assistant principal: "Everything looks great. I am impressed with the letter from his methods professor. I could almost see him teach just from reading her letter and evaluation."

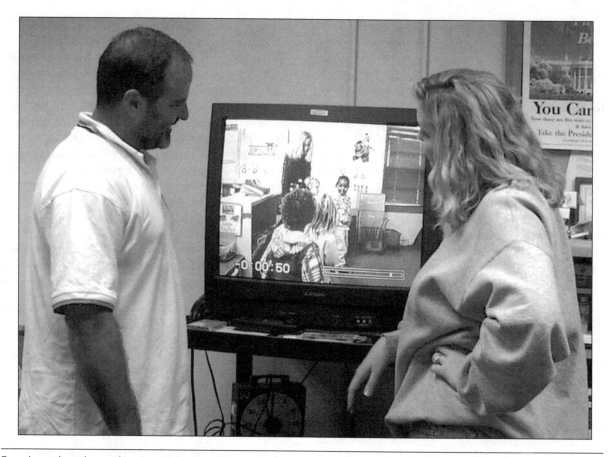

Experienced teacher and novice teacher working together.

LIFELONG LEARNING

Educators value learning. Educators want their students to value learning and to continue to learn—during vacations and after graduation. Teachers usually model this behavior as demonstrated by reading, traveling, and searching the Internet for new information. We provide those tools to our students and have them ourselves. Our learning as teachers continues in the informal sense of reflection, in the formal sense of evaluation by supervisors, and in other ways as well.

Professional learning may occur in workshops and advanced university courses and by securing additional endorsements or certificates. School districts and professional associations provide opportunities for teachers to learn—some voluntary and others mandatory. Some of these experiences are to help teachers meet the mission of the school; others are more content specific. In addition, teachers have the opportunity to select meaningful experiences from a variety of professional organizations. Attending a conference is one way to meet other professionals, to learn from them, to share with them, and to learn from experts. Schools often provide the opportunity for teachers to take professional leave days to attend conferences. We encourage you to try this!

Personal lifelong learning is also important. Your life is more than just teaching, and your teaching will be enhanced by having a variety of interests. Reserve some time for yourself, and try something new each year. You may better understand your students' likes and dislikes if you try new activities, because you will like some better than others. Classroom teachers are accustomed to reading the popular books their students are reading. Physical education specialists benefit from this activity as well, for two reasons: First, it opens new areas of communication with their colleagues and students. Second, it opens opportunities for integration of physical eduction and classroom subjects.

*S*elect a popular book elementary students are reading, such as *Harry Potter.* Create a game or physical activity based on the book.

COLLABORATION

Working with others is inherent in the teacher's job description. You will need to work with administrators, parents, other teachers, and, of course, your students. In addition to those job-related collaborations, we encourage you to seek community support for your teaching. This may not be something you do your first year of teaching; but as you have time and feel comfortable, look for those in the community who may be able to help you. For example, if you are doing a unit on India or Australia, you may find a person or group who plays cricket—a popular game in those countries. If you are near a university, you can contact the international student group for that community contact. This collaboration could lead to a demonstration or instruction in a new activity, learning about language and customs—a perfect integration and collaboration. Other sources of collaboration are the local health clinic or medical society, the public health department, the recreation department, and local businesses and service groups. Service clubs (e.g., Rotary, Lions, fraternities) are capable and often willing to support your school projects. Several schools we work with have intergenerational projects, in which elderly community members work with teachers and students. These take a variety of forms, from reading to young people to intergenerational meals. Each was arranged because a teacher collaborated, went into the community to build a relationship, and followed through to bring the community into the classroom. Collaboration with the state department of education or the nearest university faculty is also a possibility. Sharing ideas and sharing workload are two benefits of collaboration.

OUTREACH

Earlier in the book we discussed the expectations for teachers and the idea that expectations for teachers are higher than for other people. Part of those expectations are that teachers do **service** beyond the teaching job. Sometimes service is completed by working with the food drive or advising the yearbook committee. At other times, service uses your skill, interests, and expertise in other ways. Perhaps you serve on the advisory committee for the parks and recreation department or YMCA or you are a member of a service group (e.g., Lions, Rotary). Teachers have written grants to bring preschool programs or nutrition education to their schools. Each of these is a service beyond the job.

PROFESSIONALISM

In chapter 12, we presented information on professional ethics and behavior. Professionalism is also demonstrated by belonging to and participating in professional educators' associations, mentoring, continuing formal education, and extending professional horizons.

Organizations are available at the national, state, and often local or regional levels for a variety of specializations. Two groups you should know about are the National Education Association (NEA) and the American Alliance for Health, Physical Education, Recreation and Dance (AAHPERD). NEA is a politically powerful organization open to all teachers (www.nea.org). AAHPERD is the primary organization for health, physical education, and dance teachers. AAHPERD (www.aahperd.org) provides membership benefits, such as publications, low-cost insurance, and advocacy. You can learn more by going to the respective Web sites. We are mentioning only two of the oldest and largest teacher organizations; you can investigate other organizations yourself. The point is that joining and participating by reading the association literature, attending meetings, and perhaps becoming an officer or presenter are ways to demonstrate your professional loyalty.

Mentoring is another professional act. Teachers work hard and are busy. They provide advice and opportunities to pre-service or new teachers as part of their professional service. This allows teachers to leave a professional legacy and is often a rewarding and invigorating experience. Being a good mentor requires time, effort, and knowledge. Thus, mentoring is recognized as a valuable part of a teacher's work.

Master teacher and national board certification programs are designed for teachers to extend themselves. These programs recognize excellent teaching and are usually highly selective. Generally, teachers must have several years of experience before entering the program, and completion of the program will take two or more years. Why would a teacher want to do this? Challenge, recognition, and learning are all factors in a teacher's decision to enter one of these programs. Moving into administration has been the traditional way for excellent teachers to achieve increased status and salary. This was counterproductive to education—the best teachers were forced to leave teaching to gain recognition. These programs are an answer to that dilemma—teachers are recognized and rewarded for *teaching*.

Graduate education is another venue for growing as a teacher. Many options are available for teachers, from online and commercial degrees to traditional full-time graduate programs. AAHPERD produces a list of graduate programs, which is helpful in making a decision. For teachers interested in a graduate program to increase pay (usually called steps), the type of program does not make much difference. If you want to learn more about teaching or about the fields in which you are teaching, the program does matter. Degreed teachers can pursue three categories of graduate degrees: master of science (MS), master of education (MEd), and master of arts (MA). The MS and MA degrees usually require a thesis and prepare students for a variety of professional experiences. For example, some students will continue in a doctoral program, others may teach at a community college, and others will remain in their present teaching position. The MEd is usually a degree tailored to teachers and is considered the terminal degree. Usually it does not involve a thesis, but it often involves a final project or internship or both. Graduate education is expensive in terms of tuition and the time invested, so careful consideration is a must. Check into the school, consult with the faculty, and ask your principal and other mentors what they think before you decide what to do and where to go.

SUMMARY

The teaching profession presents several challenges to new teachers:

- ▶ Continuing to learn
- ▶ Meeting the expectations of parents, students, and administrators
- ▶ Transitioning from student to teacher
- ▶ Dealing with the frustrations of a challenging new career
- ▶ Developing partnerships and collaborations
- ▶ Maintaining your personal identity

Supports are available to help teachers deal with these challenges. The primary challenge is to improve as a teacher. Professional associations and

continuing education are sources of additional information that can help you increase your effectiveness. The most important and effective method is reflection and self-evaluation. Portfolios and journals are helpful reflection and self-evaluation tools. Teachers participate in service activities within their schools and outside the school in the community. These activities are important to your professional development. Your personal life is also important because it influences your teaching directly and indirectly.

Teachers need to collaborate and, with experience, will go beyond the required collaborations. Teachers can seek collaborations in the community or through outside professional connections. Each collaboration has the potential to be a learning experience for you and your students. Formal learning, in the form of workshops and graduate education, also contributes to growing as a teacher.

MASTERY LEARNING ACTIVITIES

1. Create a vita or resume for yourself.
2. Begin a working portfolio. Develop an organizational system to store materials.
3. Develop five activities to include in a student portfolio that are based on the NASPE standards.
4. Find the national board certification standards for physical education teachers and make a list of what should be in the portfolio.
5. Identify the strengths and weaknesses of various types of presentation portfolios (e.g., electronic, video, paper, and presentation board).
6. Design or make a Web page, CD, or video portfolio.
7. Compare the graduate programs at two universities on the following characteristics:
   a. The goal of the program
   b. The ranking of the program (or the university graduate program if the program is not ranked)
   c. The course work and other expectations (do they require you to attend full time?)
   d. The time and cost of a master's degree
8. Investigate a professional organization. Find out the cost and benefit of membership. When does the group meet and where? What is the mission of the organization?

REFERENCES

Berliner, D.C. 1986. In search of the expert pedagogue. *The Educational Researcher* 15: 5–13.

Berliner, D.C. 1994. Expertise, the wonder of exemplary performance. In *Creating powerful thinking in teachers and students,* edited by J.N. Mangieri and C.C. Block, 161-86. Fort Worth, TX: Holt, Rinehart and Winston.

Ericsson, K.A., R.T. Krampe, and C. Tesch-Römer. 1993. The role of deliberate practice in the acquisition of expert performance. *Psychological Review* 100 (3): 363–406.

Lee, A. 1991. Research on teaching in physical education: Questions and comments. *Research Quarterly for Exercise and Sport* 62: 374–79.

Melograno, V.J. 1999. Preservice professional portfolio system. In *Assessment series physical education teacher preparation,* edited by D. Tannehill. Reston, Va.: NASPE Publications.

Seldin, P. 1997. *The teaching portfolio: A practical guide to improved performance and promotional/tenure decisions.* 2d ed. Boston: Anker Publishing.

RESOURCES

Dodds, P. 1994. Cognitive and behavioral components of expertise in teaching physical education. *Quest* 46: 153–63.

Ennis, C.D. 1994. Knowledge and beliefs underlying curricular expertise. *Quest* 46: 164–75.

Graham, G. 1992. *Teaching children physical education: Becoming a master teacher.* Champaign, Ill.: Human Kinetics.

Grossman, P.L. 1990. *The making of a teacher: Teacher knowledge and teacher education.* New York: Teachers College Press.

Hebert, E., A.M. Lee, and L. Williamson. 1998. Teachers' and teacher education students' sense of efficacy: Quantitative and qualitative comparisons. *Journal of Research and Development in Education* 31: 214–25.

Housner, L.D., and D.C. Griffey. 1985. Teacher cognition: Differences in planning and interactive decision making between experienced and inexperienced teachers. *Research Quarterly for Exercise and Sport* 56: 44–53.

Glossary

academic learning time—Time on tasks associated with improved outcomes for some sectors of the population.

active supervision—Has three characteristics: proximity, scanning, and positioning.

aerobic training—Designed to improve cardiovascular fitness. You must exercise (swim, jog, cycle) 3 days per week, for 20 minutes at your training heart rate ($[220 - \text{your age}] \times .70$).

allocated time—The time spent in school for instruction and practice.

anaerobic threshold—The point at which the body can no longer keep up with the oxygen demands or the waste build-up in the muscles.

anxiety—The negative extreme of arousal.

attention—Cognitive capacity or space in short-term memory, vigilance, or focus.

authentic assessment—A form of evaluation as close to the real-world setting as possible and that places responsibility on the student and demands higher-level thinking or critical thinking.

best practice—A way to do something that maximizes the opportunities to gain from the experience.

blocked practice—Practice order for several skills: practices all of one, then moves on to another skill, practicing all of that skill.

body composition—Dividing body mass into components of lean and fat tissue.

body language—Nonverbal messages sent by your positions and movements.

breach of contract—Breaking a promise (usually a written contract).

Buckley Amendment—Educational information must be confidential; only students and their parents are to be aware of most information about student progress.

capacity—The size of memory.

chain of command—A specific order in which to do something (e.g., report an accident).

checklist—An assessment instrument that has a list of criteria evaluated as performed or not performed.

class rules—Have two purposes: to keep students safe and to allow learning.

class signal—Most are indicators for students to stop, look, listen, and be quiet as quickly as possible.

closure—Summarizes the day's learning and allows you to do a quick check for understanding.

cognition—Thinking.

competence—The skill or capability to do a task.

competition—Playing against an opponent (e.g., two tennis players compete, two baseball teams compete).

constant practice—Repeating one skill over and over.

control processes—Specific cognitive actions that facilitate memory.

cooperative learning—A teaching approach designed to encourage students to take responsibility for their own learning and to work cooperatively with a group to accomplish a goal.

criterion-referenced tests—Test is based on mastery learning and places students into two categories: master (successful) and nonmaster (unsuccessful).

decision making—When something unusual is observed, then the teacher must take appropriate action.

declarative knowledge—Factual information stored in memory.

demonstrations—Using a model (teacher or child) to show how to do a skill.

desist—Use of teacher proximity to control misbehavior.

development—A combination of growth, maturation, and experience.

developmentally appropriate—Programs that meet the needs of children based on their age, maturation, and interests.

diastolic pressure—The minimum pressure just before a heart beat.

direct instruction—Emphasis is on class control with little opportunity for students to choose between alternatives and make decisions about their own learning.

directions—Communications to students (e.g., where to go, what to do).

duration—Same as time; the amount of training in minutes or repetitions.

dynamic balance—The ability to maintain a balanced position while moving through space.

educational outcome—Learning in content areas is often defined in educational outcomes or learning outcomes.

effect sizes—Calculated by dividing the difference between two means (e.g., boys' running speed minus girls' running speed) by the standard deviation of the means; if the answer is zero or close to zero, the effect size suggests the two groups are not different; an effect size of .5 is moderate and .8 is large.

ego orientation—Undertaking a task because doing so brings status.

employment portfolio—A sample of a professional's best work used to demonstrate competence during the employment search.

evaluation—The highest level of cognition (in Bloom's taxonomy) and is defined as making a judgment.

experience—External or environmental; includes factors such as nutrition, education, and home life.

expertise—The knowledge possessed by a high-level performer; in sport often an athlete "ranked" by some standard (top 10 golfers in the world).

exploration—An open-ended, divergent, problem-solving process.

extrinsic feedback—Information about performance that cannot be obtained by the performer.

extrinsic motivation—Doing something because of an inducement (parents' desire, trophy).

facial expression—Nonverbal messages sent by the face (e.g., happy, sad).

FIT principle—Acronym for training involving frequency, intensity, and time.

flexibility—Range of motion for a joint.

flow—The amount of control present in a movement; ranges from free to bound. A bound movement is under complete control of the performer and can be stopped at any moment.

force—The amount of energy expended for a movement; can range from light to heavy.

formations—Include shapes, groups, and spacing typically used to organize students.

frequency—The number of training sessions per week.

fundamental movement patterns—General movement patterns such as throwing, catching, running, and jumping.

fundamental skills—General patterns of skills that emerge and are refined during early childhood.

general space—Space in which the group is participating.

grading—Assigning values to performance (grading a paper).

growth—Change in body size that results from more and bigger body cells and more intercellular material.

guided discovery—An indirect approach used when the teacher wants the students to discover a solution through a series of questions.

indirect instruction—Provides opportunities for student involvement, with teachers establishing a learning environment to help students discover solutions on their own.

individual differences—Variability among people on a given task.

individualized education program—Instructional plan for a child with one or more disabilities.

information processing—A model to examine problem solving and memory, a part of cognition; it includes perception, working memory, and long-term memory.

initial and concluding activity—Events used to begin and end each class (not the same as warm-up and concluding activities).

instruction—Includes directions, demonstration, feedback, cues, and evaluation as behaviors teachers complete to influence student learning.

INTASC standards—10 learning outcomes to teacher education programs that apply to all teachers, including those teaching physical education.

intensity—The percent of maximum for the training.

intrinsic feedback—Information about a performance gained from sensory information.

intrinsic motivation—Doing something because the child wants to.

learning contracts—A written agreement of what the student is to accomplish in a specified time period.

learning—Four definitive characteristics: Learning results from practice, learning is permanent, learning is dependent on feedback, and learning is demonstrated by retention and transfer.

liability—Cases that attempt to prove the responsible person did not meet the standard of care and that there was damage resulting from the injury.

location—Where you stand during teaching.

locomotor skills—Movements that take us from one place to another, including running, jumping, and hopping.

management—A set of techniques used to control students and create a safe environment; these include routines and rules.

manipulative skills—Movements used to interact with an object, such as object projection (kicking, striking, throwing) and object interception (catching).

maturation—Rate of progress toward a mature state, which is controlled genetically by the child's chronometer (biological time clock).

memory—Comprising two parts: working (short-term) memory, which is limited in capacity; and long-term memory, which is unlimited and where knowledge is stored.

mission—Elementary schools help children become contributing members of our society; the schools serve children, their parents, and the wider community or society.

motor milestones—Rudimentary movements (e.g., sitting, rolling over) that can be observed during the first year of life (infancy).

muscle endurance—Repeated muscle contractions at less than maximum effort.

muscle strength—The maximum amount of force a muscle can produce at one time.

negligence—When you are responsible for an injury (i.e., you did not act in a reasonable and prudent way based on the situation to prevent the injury).

nonlocomotor skills—Skills that do not move one from place to place (e.g., balancing, stretching, bending).

norm-referenced tests—Test expectation is for a range of performance (in fact, the assumption is that scores will fit the bell-shaped curve).

objectives—Should be stated in terms of observable student behavior.

objectivity—Is the measurement without bias (i.e., fair to all children)?

ontogenetic skills—Learned skills that vary by cultural and peer group (e.g., roller-skating, skiing).

opposition—In motor skills, refers to the arms working in tandem with the legs (i.e., when the right arm goes forward, the left leg goes forward).

overinclusive stage—The inability to select the critical element to solve a task.

overexclusive stage—To focus attention on one aspect of the stimulus array and ignore all others.

pace—Rate of talking.

personal space—Space surrounding each child.

phylogenetic skills—Movements observed in all individuals in a group (e.g., walking).

physical activity—Sport, exercise, physical education, and play that make an important contribution to child development.

physical education—A planned sequential K through 12 curriculum that provides cognitive content and learning experiences in a variety of activity areas such as basic movement skills; physical fitness; rhythms and dance; games; team, dual, and individual sports; tumbling and gymnastics; and aquatics.

physical fitness—Three components to physical fitness: cardiovascular endurance, body composition, and musculoskeletal health (flexibility, muscle strength, and endurance).

physically active—Describes a person who engages in a minimum of 60 minutes per day of movement, 30 minutes of which is moderate to vigorous.

physique—Description of the way a body looks, an example being somatotyping.

practice—Repetition and a critical ingredient in learning.

procedural knowledge—Information about how to do something and is a result of learning.

professional ethics—Often a code of conduct established by some group. Here, the teachers' code of conduct.

professional portfolio—Used to highlight your best work.

proficiency barrier—An explanation for children's not mastering the fundamental skills; usually a result of too little practice or ineffective instruction.

progression—Moving from inefficient and ineffective skill performance to an efficient and effective level; improvement or mastery of increasingly difficult tasks.

proximity—The distance between the supervisor and the object of supervision.

puberty—When the genital organs mature, the secondary sex characteristics (facial and body hair and a deeper voice) develop, and we become sexually mature (able to reproduce).

random practice—Practice order for several skills: same skill cannot be practiced two times in a row.

rating scales—An assessment instrument that uses numbers to denote levels of performance.

readiness—Capability of a child to do a task (e.g., reading readiness means the child has all the skills prerequisite to reading).

reflection—Studying the teaching and learning process—thinking, feedback, and correction—is critical when improvement is the goal.

reinforcement and general encouragement—General positive statements, such as "good job," "nice try," and "keep it up."

relative age effect—In sports with an age "cut-off," the oldest athletes are identified as the best.

reliability—Is the measurement consistent? Does it represent a typical performance?

role taking—Putting yourself in someone else's place.

rubrics—A form of authentic assessment with at least two levels of verbal description of the levels of performance.

scanning—Sweeping the area with the eyes to observe.

scope—The content of the program in terms of its breadth or range throughout the academic year.

sedentary—A person who is inactive (e.g., a person who sits at work and during leisure time).

selective attention—Appropriate information is used and all other information is ignored.

self-concept—The way a person views himself.

self-efficacy—The confidence an individual has in accomplishing a specific task.

sequence—The order for teaching the progression of curriculum from year to year, reflecting the timing and depth of the program.

service—Working with groups inside (e.g., school yearbook staff) and outside (community food drive) the school.

skill—Competence to perform a task, specifically a physical movement task such as catching a ball.

social comparison—When children evaluate themselves against others.

speed—Rate of movement; can range from slow to fast.

speed-accuracy trade-off—Effects of movement speed on movement accuracy and vice versa.

standard of care—What a reasonable and prudent person would do under the circumstances.

static balance—The ability to maintain a stationary position for a specified period of time.

station teaching—Equipment, tasks, and types of practice are located at various places; but students can practice different tasks and can progress at individual rates.

stature—Height.

statutes—Established by the government and guide operations of many entities (e.g., Title IX).

strategic knowledge—An understanding of control processes and how to use them.

structured physical activity—Physical education as a sequential instructional program that focuses on skill acquisition.

supervision—State of a responsible adult being present, mentally and physically, to assure reasonable safety for students.

systolic pressure—The maximum pressure immediately after a heart beat.

task orientation—Undertaking a task for personal satisfaction.

task sheets—Used to communicate to individual students the activities to be accomplished.

teachable moment—Unplanned opportunity for learning.

teaching philosophy—Should be based on your values and be specific in how those values will affect your curriculum decisions and instructional strategies.

time-out—Isolating a student, physically and in terms of instruction.

tone—Emotion of your voice (e.g., angry, happy).

tort—Civil legal action, often when parents of a student sue the school (and possibly the teacher).

transition—Physical transition moves students from one location, or formation, to another; cognitive or activity transition changes "gears"; students may stay in one place but be expected to do something very different.

unstructured activity time—Recess; when children have a chance to be physically active and relieve stress.

validity—Does the test measure what it is suppose to measure? Does it represent the objective?

variability—Differences within or between people (e.g., a single child may perform the same task in different ways; likewise, two children may perform very differently).

variable practice—When one dimension of the task changes (e.g., distance to the target).

vigilance—Length of time that one can allocate attention to a particular task.

visual angle—The range or percentage of the area one can see from a particular location.

vita—A record of what you have accomplished.

volume—Loudness of your voice.

warm-up—A 3- to 5-minute vigorous activity at the beginning of the lesson.

working portfolio—Viewed as a storage system for activities, ideas, and other support materials.

Index

About the Authors

Katherine T. Thomas, **PhD**, is an associate professor of health and human performance at Iowa State University, where she teaches a variety of teacher education and motor development courses. Dr. Thomas also has taught at Arizona State University, Southeastern Louisiana University, and Southern University at Baton Rouge. Her research and numerous publications focus on skill acquisition in sport and exercise and the relation of physical activity to health. She has external grant funding in excess of $800,000 to study physical activity and is the physical activity consultant for the USDA's Team Nutrition. However, Dr. Thomas says that the most relevant experiences to the writing of this book were her early positions as a graduate assistant and as an instructor in elementary schools and a college teaching laboratory. These experiences enabled her to find out firsthand what does and doesn't work in a physical education class.

Dr. Thomas is a member of the American Alliance for Health, Physical Education, Recreation and Dance (AAHPERD) and the North American Society for the Psychology of Sport and Physical Activity (NASPSPA). She received her doctorate in physical education from Louisiana State University in 1981.

Amelia M. Lee, **PhD**, is a professor and chair of the department of kinesiology at Louisiana State University. In addition to her 25 years as a teacher educator, Dr. Lee has 10 years of experience as a physical educator at elementary schools in Louisiana and Texas. She has published many articles on children's learning and motivation in physical education and has served as a physical education consultant to more than 20 school districts. Dr. Lee is a member of the American Educational Research Association (AERA), and she has received the Scholar Lecture Award from the AERA's Special Interest Group on Learning and Instruction in Physical Education. She is a member of AAHPERD and has received an Honor Award from AAHPERD's Curriculum and Instruction Academy. Dr. Lee earned her doctorate in physical education from Texas Woman's University in 1972.

Jerry R. Thomas, **EdD**, has taught elementary physical education methods and children's motor development for more than 30 years. He is a professor and chair of the department of health and human performance at Iowa State University. Dr. Thomas also has been a professor at Florida State, Louisiana State, and Arizona State Universities. He has written more than 200 published papers, books, and chapters including many on children's motor skills. Dr. Thomas is former president of the American Academy of Kinesiology and Physical Education and NASPSPA. In addition, his scholarly work in physical activity has earned him the titles of C.H. McCloy Lecturer for children's control, learning, and performance of motor skills; Alliance Scholar for AAHPERD; and Southern District AHPERD Scholar.

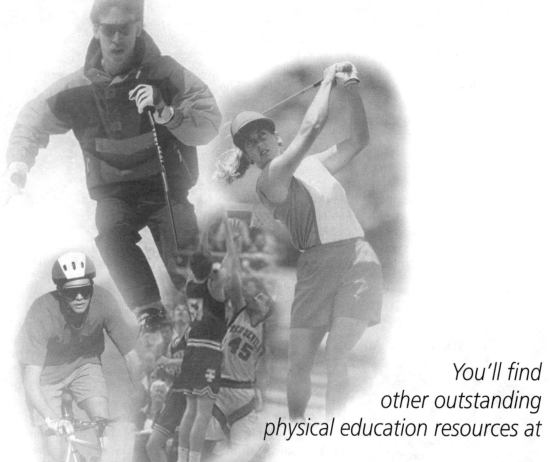

*You'll find
other outstanding
physical education resources at*

www.HumanKinetics.com

In the U.S. call

800-747-4457

Australia 08 8277 1555
Canada 800-465-7301
Europe .... +44 (0) 113 255 5665
New Zealand 09-523-3462

 HUMAN KINETICS
The Information Leader in Physical Activity
P.O. Box 5076 • Champaign, IL 61825-5076 USA